D0164561

ENCYCLOPEDIA OF SPORTS IN AMERICA

ENCYCLOPEDIA OF SPORTS IN AMERICA

A History from Foot Races to Extreme Sports

VOLUME ONE

Colonial Years to 1939

EDITED BY
MURRY R. NELSON

GREENWOOD PRESS
Westport, Connecticut • London

Library of Congress Cataloging-in-Publication Data

Encyclopedia of sports in America, two volumes : a history from foot
races to extreme sports / edited by Murry R. Nelson.

    p. cm.

  Includes bibliographical references and index.

  ISBN 978-0-313-34790-0 ((set) : alk. paper) — ISBN 978-0-313-34792-4
((vol.1) : alk. paper) — ISBN 978-0-313-34794-8 ((vol.2) : alk. paper)

  1. Sports—United States—History. 2. Sports—Social aspects—
United States—History. I. Nelson, Murry R.

  GV583.E64   2009

  796.0973—dc22   2008034749

British Library Cataloguing in Publication Data is available.

Library of Congress Catalog Card Number: 2008034749
ISBN: 978-0-313-34790-0 (set)
     978-0-313-34792-4 (Vol. 1)
     978-0-313-34794-8 (Vol. 2)

First published in 2009

Greenwood Press, 88 Post Road West, Westport, CT 06881
An imprint of Greenwood Publishing Group, Inc.
www.greenwood.com

Printed in the United States of America

The paper used in this book complies with the
Permanent Paper Standard issued by the National
Information Standards Organization (Z39.48–1984).

10 9 8 7 6 5 4 3 2 1

CONTENTS

Volume One, Colonial Years to 1939

Volume Two, 1940 to Present

ACKNOWLEDGMENTS

This book was supported, from its conception, by my Greenwood editor, Kristi Ward. She responded favorably to the idea of these volumes, sold the publisher on the idea, and encouraged me in each step of the writing and editing process. I thank her and all of the staff and editors at Greenwood and its affiliates who worked on the production of this book. The North American Society for Sport History is the professional nexus for many of the authors. That organization has provided inspiration, friendship, and intellectual growth for me over the past fifteen years. During the 2007–2008 academic year I held a Fulbright Senior Chair at the University of Debrecen, Hungary, which allowed me the time and freedom to edit this book. I express my thanks to both the Fulbright Program (sponsored by the U.S. Department of State) and the University of Debrecen Institute of English and American Studies for their support. My students at the institute read and responded to a number of the chapters, and I thank them for their comments and questions.

INTRODUCTION

Sports are pervasive in the United States. Every day images appear on television, through the Internet, on billboards, on the radio, and elsewhere, indicating the impact of sports on the lives of Americans. Sports stars are emulated, revered, and sometimes reviled, but they are always recognized and discussed. This basic pattern of sport and its involvement with Americans has been apparent for at least the past eighty-five years, since the end of World War I and the creation of a more "leisure-time" culture.

This two-volume work provides insights, information, and perspectives on the role of sports in American history, as well as reflects on historical events of the various eras that in turn affected sports in the culture. Though the book is not meant as a tribute to sports, it shows instances where sports have provided contributions of admirable character, and also where sports have exemplified the crass and hypocritical aspects of American society. The volumes thus show how sports have reflected the qualities of American society through the decades and allows for a better understanding of both sport and society.

ABOUT THIS WORK

The purpose of *Sports in America: A History from Foot Races to Extreme Sports* is to provide a resource that is easily accessible as a reference, yet is more than just a list of names and dates. There are a number of excellent scholarly works that examine the history of sports in American life. Most are aimed at the scholar or are developed as textbooks in history, American studies, American culture, or foundations of sport courses. Those volumes are very good at serving those purposes. There are also reference works that provide lists of data regarding sports records and achievements. These, too, are numerous and successfully fill a niche. *Sports in America* sets a goal of doing a bit of both. The authors provide a scholarly foundation, but in a style meant for the general reader. There are ample data within each chapter, but these data are contextualized and discussed within the larger fields of sport and American history.

The book is arranged chronologically, with thirteen chapters, most discussing American sports a decade at a time. The book begins with the settlement of American colonists and their interests in sport (chapter 1) and continues in the next chapter through the Civil War to 1890. From that point forward, the chapters cover decades of American history. Each chapter is meant to focus on the same general themes and concepts as much as possible. The first two chapters examine an America much different from that in the 1890s. This earlier America was far more rural and less developed, and people had less real leisure time. The preference for more individual recreation activities faded away toward the end of the nineteenth century as team-oriented sports began to characterize the American sports landscape. Today, the sports of football, basketball, at both the amateur and professional levels, and professional baseball dominate the sports headlines with individual sports like professional golf and tennis also receiving a lot of coverage. Beyond this a number of sports have large followings, depending on the region of the country. These include professional and college hockey, auto racing, and track and field.

The book is aimed at the general reader who is seeking information on a particular era, sport, concept, or individual from the nation's sports history. The chapters are meant to be stimulating and complete on their own, but the volumes can also be read in sequence.

About the Chapters

Each chapter begins with a general overview of the historical era, continuing with a focus on sports within that era. The most popular of the team sports—baseball, football, basketball, and hockey—are examined in each chapter, with the exception of the first two chapters. The amount of attention paid to each sport is meant to reflect the amount of attention that each sport received societally within the era covered in the chapter. After the team sports sections, sports for individual competitors, such as boxing, golf, tennis, and others, are discussed. The final chapter includes "xtreme sports" and computer games.

The chapters' authors were selected on the basis of their research and scholarship within the period examined, the sports examined, or their general knowledge and writing for a broad-based audience. Nancy Struna, the author of chapter 1, which traces sport from the settlement of the American colonies until the Civil War, is an expert on colonial history and the games and recreations that were engaged in at that time. She weds the colonial experience and the creation of a new citizen, an American, with the creation of new sports and games for Americans, which were built on the foundations of England. Gerald Gems, the author of chapter 2, picks up the "story" at the Civil War and carries it through 1889, a period of about thirty years. During this time the first professional teams and leagues were formed in the United States, and sports began to take a new and different path in American life. Professor Gems has written widely on this era, mostly within the urban landscape, and this chapter draws on his great expertise in the academic area.

Chapter 3 begins the decade approach that characterizes the remainder of the book. The 1890s are examined by Matthew Llewellyn, who has won awards for his research into this era in sport. In the 1890s more American sports were being refined and even invented, such as basketball and volleyball. The 1900s was a decade of reform, reflective of the changes that were sweeping American society as a result of progressivism and the concept of "muscular Christianity." James Nendel draws on his research in this era to present the decade and its reform movements in both sports and society in chapter 4.

The 1910s, the topic of chapter 5, encompassed some of the highs and lows of American sport and society, as a result of the great devastation of World War I. Sarah Bair has done research and writing on this era, and that work is reflected in her presentation of that decade in American sport The 1920s have been called a "golden age" in American sport and that chapter, written by Murry Nelson, a respected researcher and writer on this period, presents the heroes and events of this period against the backdrop of a postwar boom.

Mark Dyreson, who has written widely about the Olympics in the twentieth century, with the assistance of some of his best doctoral students, covers American sports in the 1930s in chapter 7. The period of economic retraction in American society had both its counterparts and counterpoints in sport of that decade. Sports were a source of hope and escape. In the 1940s that escape was modified as the world went to war once again. American sports suffered from shortages of able-bodied athletes, as did American society in general. Ronald Briley, a historian of many sports of this era, brings the period and the sports to life with his chapter 8 examination. A period of postwar boom, as followed World War I, also followed World War II, and chapter 9 on the 1950s has many parallels to the 1920s. The big change, however, is the growth of opportunities for African Americans in sports and, to a significantly lesser degree, across society. Murry Nelson is the author of this chapter.

The 1960s chapter (10) is by Maureen Smith, who has written widely on the era with an emphasis on African Americans in sport of this time. In this decade African Americans made their first significant and broad-based impact on professional and college sports. Chapter 11, on the 1970s, was written by John Wong, whose work on professional hockey has been widely praised. Wong closely examines the 1970s and the impact of gender equity as a major force of the period. That focus on gender equity is carried forward into chapter 12 where Sarah Fields looks at the 1980s from her perspective as scholar and lawyer. The final chapter, on 1991 to the present, is a bit different because it covers a slightly longer period of time and has the additional goal of speculating on sport in the American landscape of the near future. Jaime Schultz, from the University of Maryland, has enlisted some of her top doctoral students to augment her great expertise in this era.

All of these authors have had the latitude to cover issues and concerns of their periods in their own ways, but within a broad chapter structure. Thus, these chapters are personal as well as informative, but other scholars might choose different points of emphasis, were they to examine the same eras. There are real analyses and evaluations of the periods, rather than just simple accounts of events and persons, giving a depth to the work.

Sports in America: A History from Foot Races to Extreme Sports can be used in a variety of ways, depending on the goal of each user. For the general reader, there may be interest in a particular sport, such as basketball, and its changing status within American society over the past hundred years. Because there is a separate section on basketball in each of the chapters, beginning with the 1890s, a reader can limit him- or herself to that topic, and get some notion of the sport over the years as well as some of the key players and events in each era. This type of pursuit could work with any of the major sports examined in each chapter.

Another reader may be interested in one particular time period, such as between the world wars. Thus, the chapters on the 1920s, 1930s, and 1940s could give an overview of both societal events and the impact of sports during those decades. The index also provides numerous opportunities to pursue specific people noted in sports throughout American history.

These notions can be modified and reshaped for school work on the part of high school or college students. *Sports in America* is a great initial source to research a topic and has the benefit of offering other recommended resources, including books, articles, Web sites, and films to provide more information on American sports.

Introduction

Since the American colonies were settled, Americans have played games, which have become more and more developed and organized over each ensuing period of American history. American sports represent much of what is associated with Americans themselves. American athletic competition is fierce, and many Americans seem to be aggressive in their business and professional dealings as well. Success in sport comes from a willingness to practice for long hours to perfect both techniques and basics. So, too, do we see such practices pervade American culture in general. Americans, for better or worse, work far more hours per week than their European counterparts. Americans also seem to play harder. There's an intensity to American culture and sport that permeates all areas of the country, a negative ramification of which is that many Americans simply don't know how to relax. This may carry over into American sport participation and fan behavior.

The study of American sports and sport history is a relatively young field and has had to fight for recognition as a legitimate field of study. There is little argument over the interest that sport holds for most Americans, but many academicians see a scholarly interest in such activities and behaviors as less "legitimate." Of course, many fields within social sciences, as well as history, held various canons of scholarly behavior and study that only began to be questioned and revised within the past fifty years. In some instances, such as in sport history, those canons were only really broadened and accepted within the past twenty-five years.

Americans have been reading about sports figures and contests for nearly one hundred years. Sports pages became pervasive in major American daily newspapers in the 1920s, and their popularity certainly led to the publication of sport biographies and other sports stories. Many renowned authors started within sports and later moved into more "respected" writing, including Ring Lardner, Paul Gallico, Westbrook Pegler, and more recently, Mitch Albom.

Major sport historians in the United States were inspired by the work of John Betts, and general sport histories by luminaries like John Lucas, Ben Rader, and Ron Smith have laid a solid foundation for further work in sport history in general, as well as histories of various American sports specifically. Some journalists-turned-historians have penned useful histories, such as the work of Robert Peterson, who wrote very readable volumes on African Americans in baseball, early football, and a history of professional basketball. All major sports have histories that trace their origins and impacts within the United States, with baseball dominating this field by far. Harold Seymour and David Voigt, in particular, have written ground-breaking volumes, and their work has been often cited and acknowledged. So, too, must we acknowledge all of these excellent writers and research by earlier sport historians. *Sports in America* draws on this prior research as well as popular history and popular writing about sports, and provides a comprehensive hybrid work about sports and the American Republic written by academicians with sport as a scholarly interest. The writing style is easy and unstudied, but the content is not. It reflects deep understanding and interest in basic questions about sport. Such issues include:

- How African Americans were accepted in various sports and how they responded to the lack of acceptance in various venues;
- The role of the news media in creating sports rivalries and larger fan interest in sports, particularly in the earlier parts of the twentieth century;
- The opportunities for women in sports and how they were able to engage in various sporting enterprises;
- The effect of various wars on the growth, development, or stagnation of various American sports and the role sports played during these conflicts;
- How America and Americans performed in the Olympic Games, once they were revived in 1896;
- Economic impacts that sports had on American society and how economic cycles affected the way sports were perceived and carried out;
- How an American "sporting culture" developed amid the larger notion of American culture;
- The role of government in the development of the American sporting culture;
- How the development of American professional sports reflected the changing demographics of America generally;
- How American sports heroes became among the most recognized persons in American culture, beginning in the 1920s; and
- The participation of various ethnic groups in American sports and the development of parallel sports leagues.

Though not all of these issues are discussed in every chapter, they provide an impetus for much of a chapter's content. We hope you learn more about our cherished American tradition of sports throughout United States history and are inspired to research more.

TIMELINE

Christmas 1621	Governor William Bradford forbids "play" on Christmas Day (the first notion of "Blue Laws").
1740s	A "Physical Club" is established in Boston.
1823–45	"Great Races," pitting a top northern and top southern horse, held.
1840s	Knickerbocker Base Ball Club of New York established.
1844	New York Yacht Club founded in Newport, Rhode Island.
1845	New York Rules of Base Ball codified by Alexander Cartwright.
1852	First intercollegiate rowing race, Harvard versus Yale, takes place on Lake Winnipesaukee, New Hampshire.
1858	National Association of Base Ball Players established.
1869	National Trotting Association established in Rhode Island.
	Cincinnati Red Stocking established as first professional base-ball team. First intercollegiate football game played (Princeton vs. Rutgers) in New Brunswick, New Jersey.
1871	National Association of Professional Base Ball Players organized.
1875	Kentucky Derby established at Churchill Downs in Louisville, Kentucky.
	Intercollegiate Association of Amateur Athletics of America (IC4A) formed for track competition.
	Ice hockey invented at Victoria Arena, Montreal, Canada.
1876	National League formed with teams in Chicago, Cincinnati, Boston, Philadelphia, Brooklyn, Louisville, Hartford, and St. Louis.
1881	U.S. National Lawn Tennis Association (USLTA) established.
1885	Cuban Giants black baseball team formed in New York.
1886	*The Sporting News* is first published.

1887	Buffalo Bill's Wild West Show, featuring the shooting of Annie Oakley and Lillian Smith, travels abroad.
1889	Walter Camp and Caspar Whitney select first collegiate football All Americans.
	Moses Fleetwood Walker is last African American to be on a major-league roster until 1947.
1890	Players' League (also called Union League or Brotherhood League) is established.
	John Owen of Detroit becomes first to break 10 seconds (9.8) in 100-yard dash.
1891	Basketball invented by James A. Naismith in Springfield, Massachusetts.
1892	Senda Berenson introduces basketball to the female student population of Smith College, Northampton, Massachusetts.
	First heavyweight boxing champion, John L. Sullivan, recognized under the Marquis of Queensbury rules.
	Sullivan is defeated by James Corbett for heavyweight championship.
1893	First eighteen-hole golf course created in United States, at the Chicago Golf Club.
1895	Volleyball invented by William G. Morgan in Springfield, Massachusetts.
1896	Under the leadership of Baron Pierre de Coubertin the modern Olympic Games are revived and staged in Athens, Greece.
1900	Western League renamed as American League and emerges as major league under leadership of league president Ban Johnson. First franchises are located in Chicago, Baltimore, Boston, Philadelphia, Washington, DC, Cleveland, Detroit, and Milwaukee.
1900	Second Olympiad held in Paris, France.
1902	First Rose Bowl Game played as Michigan defeats Stanford 49-0.
1903	First World Series of major-league baseball is played between Pittsburgh Pirates of the National League and the Boston Americans. Boston wins.
1904	Jack Chesboro of the New York Highlanders (later the Yankees) wins forty-one games, still a record.
	Buffalo Germans win all of their games at the Olympics in St. Louis and become known as first great basketball team.
1906	Chicago Cubs win 116 games (of 154 played), still a record.
1908	Fred Merkle fails to touch second base at the end of the game and the Giants lose, necessitating a playoff with the Chicago Cubs for the National League title, lost by the Giants. The inaction is known as "Merkle's Boner."
	Olympics held in London.

Jack Johnson defeats Tommy Burns in Australia to become first black heavyweight champion.

1909 Cork-center ball introduced into major-league baseball, increasing offensive production and power hitting.

1910 Jack Johnson defeats Jim Jeffries in "The Battle of the Century" and retains his heavyweight title.

1911 First Indianapolis 500 automobile race held is won by Ray Harroun in a Marmon Wasp.

1912 Jim Thorpe wins decathlon at Olympics in Stockholm, Sweden, and is declared the world's greatest athlete by King Gustav V.

1913 Notre Dame University finishes the football season undefeated for the second year in a row, led by quarterback Gus Dorais and receiver Knute Rockne and their use of the forward pass.

Francis Ouimet becomes first amateur to win U.S. Open golf tournament.

1914 World War I begins in Europe.

Federal League forms and begins play as third major league, siphoning players from the other two leagues.

1916 Professional Golfers Association (PGA) formed in New York City.

1917 United States enters World War I.

National Hockey League formed with three founding teams—the Montreal Canadiens, Montreal Wanderers, and the Ottawa Senators.

1918 New York Celtics reorganized as Original New York Celtics by James Furey.

1918 Eight Chicago White Sox players are offered bribes to throw the World Series, though some do nothing but fail to report the bribe offer.

1919 Sir Barton becomes first horse to win racing's Triple Crown by winning the Kentucky Derby, the Preakness, and the Belmont Stakes.

1920 Potential club owners meet in automobile showroom in Canton, Ohio, to form what will become the National Football League (NFL), called the American Professional Football Association.

National Negro Baseball League is founded by Rube Foster.

Man o' War is retired after winning twenty of twenty-one races in which he was entered.

1921 U.S. Supreme Court declares that baseball is not an illegal monopoly.

Paul Robeson joins Fritz Pollard as the first two African Americans in the American Professional Football Association (APFA).

1922 APFA changes its name to the National Football League.

1923	Bob Douglass forms the Harlem Renaissance professional basketball team.
1924	Harold "Red" Grange of the University of Illinois scores five touchdowns and passes for a sixth as the Illini rout the University of Michigan and the Grange legend is born.
	First modern-era Winter Olympics held in Chamonix, France.
1925	Grange debuts as a professional player with the Chicago Bears and the game is the first to be broadcast nationally.
1926	Bobby Jones is first American golfer to win both British and U.S. Open in the same year.
	Gertrude Ederle becomes first woman to swim the English Channel and sets a record time.
1927	Babe Ruth hits sixty home runs to break his 1921 record of fifty-nine homers in one season.
	Gene Tunney defeats Jack Dempsey in the famous "long count" fight to retain the heavyweight championship won from Dempsey the year before.
1928	Johnny Weissmuller retires from swimming, not having lost a free-style contest in eight years, and after winning five gold medals and setting sixty-seven world records.
1929	Philadelphia Athletics score ten runs in the seventh inning of game 4 of the World Series to defeat the Chicago Cubs, 10-8. The A's win the series in five games.
	Stock market crash begins the Great Depression worldwide.
1930	Bobby Jones retires from golf after winning thirteen major championships in the 1920s.
	First World Cup soccer tournament held in Uruguay. Uruguay defeats Argentina, 4–2, in finals.
1931	Notre Dame coach Knute Rockne dies in airplane crash in Kansas.
1932	Winter Olympics held in Lake Placid, New York, and Summer Olympics held in Los Angeles.
	Mildred "Babe" Didrikson wins two gold and one silver medal at Olympics.
	Franklin Delano Roosevelt becomes president and initiates his New Deal programs.
	Major-league baseball holds its first All-Star game in Comiskey Park, Chicago.
1934	Carl Hubbell strikes out five American Leaguers in a row in All-Star game.
1935	Babe Ruth retires.
1936	Baseball Hall of Fame founded in Cooperstown, New York.
	New York Yankees win first of four straight championships.

Olympic Games held in Berlin, Germany, where Jesse Owens wins gold medals in the long jump, 100-meter dash, 200-meter dash, and the 400-meter relay. He also is named Associated Press Athlete of the Year.

1937   National Basketball League (NBL) begins play.

Joe Louis wins heavyweight boxing championship.

Brooklyn Dodgers and Cincinnati Reds play first televised baseball game.

1938   National Invitational Tournament (NIT) begins play in New York with Temple University the first champion.

Helen Wills wins her fifth Wimbledon tennis title of the decade.

1939   The first National Collegiate Athletic Association (NCAA) postseason tournament is played with the finals in Evanston, IL. The University of Oregon is the first champion.

World Tournament of Professional Basketball is inaugurated in Chicago with the New York Renaissance the initial winners. It will continue until 1949.

World War II begins in Europe.

Little League Baseball begun in Williamsport, Pennsylvania.

Lou Gehrig removes himself from New York Yankee lineup after 2130 consecutive games, a record. He dies in 1941 from ALS, popularly called "Lou Gehrig's disease" after that.

New York Yankees win fourth straight world championship.

1940   Alice Marble wins her fourth U.S. Open tennis tournament in five years.

Chicago Bears defeat Washington Redskins 73-0 in the NFL title game, the most lopsided defeat in history.

1941   Whirlaway wins horse racing's Triple Crown.

Joe DiMaggio of the New York Yankees hits in fifty-six straight games.

Ted Williams becomes last hitter to exceed .400 batting average in a season (.406).

1942   Chicago Studebakers and Toledo Jim Whites integrate the NBL by signing African American players.

1944   All American Football Conference formed as second pro league.

1945   Branch Rickey of the Brooklyn Dodgers signs Jackie Robinson to a contract, the first African American to be signed by major-league baseball in the twentieth century. Robinson debuts at Montreal in 1946 and enters the majors in 1947 with the Dodgers.

George Mikan, the greatest basketball player of the first half of the twentieth century, leads DePaul University to the NIT basketball title.

Byron Nelson wins eighteen consecutive professional golf tournaments.

World War II ends.

1946   Basketball Association of America (BAA) begins play as a professional basketball league.

Glenn Davis ("Mr. Outside") of the U.S. Military Academy (Army) wins the Heisman trophy, following the 1945 triumph of his running back teammate, Felix "Doc" Blanchard ("Mr. Inside"), who won in 1945.

1948   Citation wins Triple Crown of horse racing and later becomes first horse to win $1 million in prize money.

First postwar Olympics are held in St. Moritz (Winter) and London (Summer).

1949   National Basketball League and Basketball Association of America merge to form the National Basketball Association (NBA).

1950   The All American Football Conference merges with the National Football League

Civil War breaks out in Korea, leading to the Korean War.

City College of New York (CCNY) wins both the NIT and NCAA basketball championships, first and only time that this has been done.

1951   New York Giants come back from 13½ games back in August to win National League pennant.

College basketball betting scandals are exposed, involving many of the nation's top teams.

1952   Summer Olympics held in Helsinki, Finland, and Winter Games in Oslo, Norway.

1953   Boston Braves relocate to Milwaukee and set off a chain of franchise shifts during the 1950s that mirror the population shifts of the country.

The New York Yankees win their fifth world championship in a row.

Don Carter named Bowler of the Year for first of six times in the next ten years.

1954   The U.S. Supreme Court declares school segregation by race illegal in the case of Brown v. Board of Education of Topeka, Kansas.

Minneapolis Lakers, led by George Mikan, win four NBA titles in the first five years of the league.

1955   Brooklyn Dodgers win their first and only world championship.

1956   First Olympics held in Southern Hemisphere (Melbourne Australia).

Rocky Marciano retires as heavyweight champion, undefeated in his career.

	Don Larsen pitches first, and only, perfect game in the World Series.
	Babe Didrikson, greatest female athlete of the half-century, dies of cancer.
1957	Notre Dame ends Oklahoma's forty-seven-game win streak, the longest in college football.
	New York Giants and Brooklyn Dodgers announce that they will move to San Francisco and Los Angeles, respectively, beginning with the 1958 season.
1958	Baltimore Colts defeat the New York Giants in overtime, 23-17, to win the NFL championship in a game dubbed "the greatest ever played."
	Althea Gibson wins second consecutive U.S. Open singles and double tennis titles, as well as Associated Press Female Athlete of the Year.
1959	The Chicago White Sox win their first pennant in forty years and end the Yankee string of pennants at four.
1960	Winter Olympics in Squaw Valley, California. Summer Games in Rome.
	American Football League begins play with teams in Boston, Buffalo, New York, Houston, Denver, Los Angeles, Oakland, and Dallas.
1961	Washington Senators move to Minnesota and become the Twins. New franchises are awarded to Washington, DC, and Los Angeles as major-league baseball expands for the first time in the century.
	Roger Maris hits sixty-one home runs to break the record of Babe Ruth set in 1927.
1962	New baseball franchises are awarded to New York (Mets) and Houston (Colt 45s).
	Wilt Chamberlain of the Philadelphia Warriors scores 100 points in a game.
	A week after fighting Emile Griffith for the welterweight title, Benny "Kid" Paret dies from injuries he sustained in the fight.
1963	Beatles begin the first of the "British band invasion."
	President John F. Kennedy is assassinated.
1964	The Olympics are held in Asia for the first time when Tokyo hosts the Summer Games.
	Cassius Clay defeats Sonny Liston for heavyweight title. Clay changes name to Muhammad Ali to reflect his Muslim faith.
1966	Texas Western University becomes the first NCAA champion to start five African Americans as they beat Kentucky for the title.
1967	American Basketball Association begins play with eleven franchises: Anaheim, Dallas, Denver, Houston, Indiana, Kentucky, Minnesota, New Jersey, New Orleans, Oakland, and San Diego.

National Hockey League expands from six to twelve teams, adding Oakland, Los Angeles, Minnesota, Philadelphia, Pittsburgh, and St. Louis.

Green Bay Packers defeat the Kansas City Chiefs, 35-10, in the AFL-NFL World Championship Game, later renamed the Super Bowl.

1968   Mexico City hosts first Olympics held in Latin America. Bob Beamon jumps twenty-nine feet, two inches in the long jump and Dick Fosbury wins high jump with the "Fosbury Flop," which revolutionizes the event. Tommie Smith and John Carlos stand in a "black power" salute during the playing of the American national anthem.

Arnold Palmer becomes first golfer ever to have $1 million in lifetime winnings.

Open era in tennis begins, allowing professionals to play in all major tournaments.

1969   Bill Russell retires after leading the Boston Celtics to eleven championships in thirteen NBA seasons.

"Miracle Mets" win World Series of baseball.

1971   World Hockey Association with twelve franchises, though number and franchise locations change by 1972 when league begins play.

1972   Education Amendments Act signed by President Nixon. Contained therein is Title IX, which will change women's sports forever.

Killing of members of the Israeli Olympic team puts pall over Munich Olympic Games.

Major-league baseball players go on strike for first time.

1973   UCLA wins seventh consecutive NCAA men's basketball championship.

Miami Dolphins win Super Bowl VII, completing the only undefeated season in the modern NFL.

1974   Hank Aaron hits home-run 756, breaking Babe Ruth's lifetime mark.

Muhammad Ali knocks out George Foreman in the "Rumble in the Jungle" heavyweight title bout in Zaire.

1975   Ali beats Joe Frazier in heavyweight title bout, "The Thrilla in Manila" (Philippines).

1976   Four American Basketball Association teams (Denver, Indiana, San Antonio, New York Nets) join the NBA and the ABA ceases to exist.

1979   World Hockey Association ceases to exist with four franchises (Edmonton, Hartford, Quebec, Winnipeg) entering the NHL.

1980	Moscow hosts Summer Olympics, but United States and other countries boycott the Games over Soviet invasion of Afghanistan.
	Bjorn Borg wins fifth consecutive Wimbledon tennis title.
	Entertainment and Sports Programming Network (ESPN) begins broadcasting
1981	Major-league baseball players strike for fifty-one days.
1984	Michael Jordan is drafted by Chicago Bulls and signs $2.5-million endorsement contract with Nike.
	The NFL Colts abandon Baltimore for Indianapolis in the middle of the night.
	Los Angeles hosts the Summer Olympics, boycotted by most countries of the Soviet bloc.
1986	Len Bias, number 1 draft pick in the NBA draft dies of cocaine overdose, days after the draft.
	NCAA gives Southern Methodist University (SMU) the "death penalty," forbidding them from playing football in 1987, as a result of recruiting violations.
1988	At Summer Olympics in Seoul, South Korea, Ben Johnson, 100-meter champion, is disqualified for steroid use, the first track and field athlete to be found guilty of such practices.
1989	The Loma Prieta earthquake in the Bay Area disrupts the World Series between the Oakland Athletics and the San Francisco Giants for ten days before the A's complete a four-game sweep.
1990	Wayne Gretzky named Male Athlete of the Decade by Associated Press.
	Edmonton Oilers win their fifth Stanley Cup hockey title in seven years.
1993	Don Shula wins 325th game as NFL coach, surpassing the record set by George Halas of the Chicago Bears.
1994	Winter Olympics held in Lillehammer, Norway, the first Winter Games on a new four-year cycle.
1995	Cal Ripken breaks Lou Gehrig's streak of 2130 consecutive games and goes on to play in 2632 consecutive games.
1996	Summer Olympics are held in Atlanta.
1997	Women's National Basketball Association (WNBA) begins play.
	Carl Lewis retires after winning nine Olympic gold medals in track in four Olympics.
	Tiger Woods wins his first Masters golf tournament by twelve strokes.
1998	Mark McGwire and Sammy Sosa battle to break Roger Maris's record sixty-one home runs in a season and both do. Sosa ends up with sixty-six, McGwire with seventy.
	The Chicago Bulls, led by Michael Jordan, win their sixth NBA championship in eight years.

1999   United States wins Women's World Cup in soccer.

            Serena Williams becomes first African American since Althea Gibson to win U.S. Open Tennis tournament.

2000   Tiger Woods wins U.S. Open golf tournament by fifteen strokes.

2001   Barry Bonds hits 73 home runs to break the record of seventy set only three years before.

2002   Winter Olympics held in Salt Lake City, Utah.

            Pete Sampras retires from tennis with fourteen Grand Slam titles and is later named Outstanding Tennis Player of the period 1965–2005.

2004   NHL lockout goes 310 days, a record for a North American pro sports league.

            Boston Red Sox break "The Curse of Babe Ruth" and win first World Series title since 1918.

2005   Between 1995 and 2005, the University of Tennessee (3) and the University of Connecticut (5) win eight NCAA Women's Basketball championships.

            Lance Armstrong wins seventh consecutive Tour de France cycling race.

CHAPTER 1

AMERICAN SPORTS, 1607–1860

Nancy L. Struna

OVERVIEW

Few citizens of the United States today would recognize many of the sporting practices known to their predecessors before 1860. Some of the names assigned to the activities were the same, of course: hunting, fishing, racing, and cockfighting, for example. Even the word *sport* had different meanings, as its etymology suggests. The word itself may have derived from the Middle English *disport*, which in turn derived from the French *desporter*, meaning "to carry away from." In ordinary language from at least the fifteenth into the nineteenth centuries, people sometimes used *sport* as a noun to mean *diversion*, or *display*, or *amusement*. At other times, they also used it as a verb: to *divert*, to *display*, or to *amuse*. In the middle of the seventeenth century, the *Oxford English Dictionary* (2nd ed.) even identified "amorous dalliance and intercourse" as one definition for sport.

Between 1607 and 1860 sport gradually moved away from *disport* and began to acquire its contemporary attributes: rationalization, rule-bound, organization, specialization, and quantification (Guttmann 1978, 15–55). This process was part and parcel of the larger economic, political, demographic, and cultural transformation of the British colonies that had become an independent nation, the United States. Originally a land shared by native Americans and European colonizers, by the middle of the nineteenth century it had become an independent, industrializing country to which people from many of the world's countries had migrated and which was about to be torn apart by civil war. These two stories are deeply entwined and are the subject of this chapter.

Until 1783 the Atlantic coast, populated by thousands of English men and women, remained under British control, the Declaration of Independence (1776) notwithstanding. Thus, it is not coincidental that colonial sports often resembled British forms and drew on British (including English, Irish, Scottish, and Welsh) conventions, rules, and formats, even as they were being adapted to fit local North American conditions and interests. It is also not coincidental that many early national and antebellum (before the American Civil War) sports continued to reveal linkages to Britain. On the eve of the Civil War, and beyond in some cases, the specter of Britain and especially England weighed heavily on sports in the United States in many ways.

This is not to suggest, however, that early American sports were simply mirror images of British sports. They were not. Throughout the roughly 250 years this chapter covers, distinctive demographic, geographic, and economic conditions also affected the shape of sports and the emerging nation. Native Americans inhabited what became the United States long before the British appeared. Africans arrived by 1618, and thousands upon thousands of them were forcibly shipped from their homelands late into the eighteenth century. Other European ethnic groups also migrated to the New World, and all of these peoples and their traditions affected the forms and forums of early American sports. Then, too, until the Civil War the gender ratio was rarely equal, and in the early years, especially in the South, there were six men for every woman. To this day, the consequences of this uneven gender ratio and the gendering of sport and society are not fully known, but what is clear is that the male definition and domination of modern American sports took root in these early years.

The geography and economy of the British colonies that became states also affected and were affected by early American sporting life. Compared to Britain, and the rest of Europe for that matter, North America was vast and had many more mountains, lakes, and rivers, all of which could be obstacles or avenues for sporting contests. Land was always a lure, and its availability continued to seem vast even after the Civil War, with colonial and early national Americans using the land for sports in distinctive ways—for expansive race courses, for base-ball diamonds, for long-distance running and race-walking. Although equality of access for all social and economic classes was never achieved in the United States, the land underlay a predominantly agricultural economy, as well as sports that drew from rural and agricultural lives and lifestyles, through the 1860s. Sports figured prominently at festivals and fairs through the middle of the nineteenth century, and until then as well, horse races, fistfights, and field sports were the dominant forms, in contrast to our contemporary dominant trilogy of football, basketball, and base-ball. The seeds for these forms only gradually rooted after the transition to capitalism and the gradual urbanization it both spurred and was fueled by had begun.

SPORTS AMONG NATIVE AMERICANS

On the eve of the seventeenth century, the "New World" was new only to Europeans active in overseas exploration, trade, and, gradually, colonization. For thousands of years, people had inhabited North America—roaming the plains, plying the rivers and lakes, seeking harmony with nature, warring with each other. As did people on other continents, they lived in clans, tribes, and, eventually, nations. Different groups of Native Americans had also developed extensive patterns of exchange, of trade, both among themselves and with others. Some nations produced agricultural products that Europeans would envy, like tobacco and maize, and for most, religion figured prominently in ordinary life. They also had specialized roles for particular individuals, such as chiefs and shamans, in what were hierarchically organized societies. Indeed, Amerindian societies were as complex as were those of Europe.

Much of our information about Native Americans was filtered through the cultural lenses of Europeans. Consequently, what they said they saw among the indigenous people may tell us more about the observers than the observed. Moreover, the English adventurers apparently recorded what they recognized, including cultural relations and practices that resembled their own. One pattern, for example, revealed different tasks performed by men and women. In 1610 William Strachey, the secretary for the London Company at its outpost in Jamestown, recorded that Amerindian men "fish, hunt, fowle, goe to the warrs, ... and such like manly exercises," while the women "sow their Corne ..., dresse the meat brought home, and ... beare all kyndes of burthens, and such like" (Strachey 1612, 114). Twenty years later, Edward Winslow, a member of the Plymouth plantation in Massachusetts, recorded a similar observation. The men "employ themselves wholly in hunting, ... except at some times they take some pains in fishing." The women, in contrast, "carry all their burdens" and "have all household care lying upon them" ("Winslow's Relations," in Young 1844, 363).

White observers also commented on specific Native American recreations, which they recognized and occasionally approved. The indigenous people approached hunting and fishing very seriously, John Smith concluded, and "they esteeme it a pleasure and [are] very proud to be expert therein" (Smith 1986, 2:118, 1:164). Numerous European travelers identified gambling as a practice common to Native Americans, both men and women, and saw that recreations and sports were central features of rituals and community celebrations. In Native spiritual ceremonies, for example, women and men danced for hours at a time, while harvest festivals and victory celebrations included foot races, lacrosse, dancing, and singing—all "much like ours heare in England." Football was another game included in Native rituals and festivals that Capt. Henry Spelman, who lived in Virginia for a decade and a half, recognized. He also noted, however, that the

Sioux Indians racing horses, near Fort Pierre. (Courtesy of the Library of Congress)

La Crosse. (Bodmer, pinx. ad. nat.; engraved by Rawdon, Wright & Hatch. Courtesy of the Library of Congress)

football players were women and young boys, who scored goals just as did players at home but who "never fight nor pull one another doune" (Smith 1986, 1:cxiv). Strachey also recognized a ball game similar to English bandy, a wooden ball and curved bat contest that eventually influenced the development of cricket.

An old-time buffalo hunt. (Courtesy of the Library of Congress)

Until about 1630, sports were a kind of common ground between Native Americans and some Europeans, a fact recognized by local leaders in the English outposts. The governors of Plymouth, for example, invited to marriages and harvest festivals "many of the Indians ... whom for three days we entertained and feasted." When colonists went to Native villages to trade, they participated in celebratory feasts and an occasional contest. In 1623 Edward Winslow and his companions even challenged the tribesmen of King Massasoit "to shoot for skins." The Indians refused, proposing instead that "one of us shoot at a mark." The event ended, Winslow concluded, with the Native Americans left in a state of wonderment "to see the mark so full of holes" (Young 1844, 231, 210–11).

The significance of contests and matches and displays of physical prowess among Amerindians, as well as between Native Americans and Europeans, during the early seventeenth century seems clear. Physical feats were important to both peoples; they formed the core of work and play, reputation and ritual, and survival. As was the case among the English migrants, the cultural styles of the original nations in America were largely defined in and by physical acts, and it is probably not an overstatement to say that Native American popular culture was largely a physical culture. Not too many years down the road, however, this physical culture would also open them to domination by Europeans. Diseases would wrack their bodies, battles would decimate their ranks, skin color would key their subordinate status. And once the Amerindians were too weak to resist, European Americans incorporated Indian sports within their own repertoires.

SPORTS AMONG THE ENGLISH COLONISTS

Among Europeans, the British were not the only colonizers of the New World in the late sixteenth and early seventeenth centuries. Spain and Portugal had extensive claims in South and Central America. Spain also claimed much of what became Florida, the land along the Gulf Coast, and from what became Texas westward through California. Holland sent Henry Hudson to explore what became eastern Canada, and his successors constructed estates and trading posts in New Netherlands, or New York. Eventually as well, Swedes sent colonists to the region surrounding the Delaware River, where they struggled in what became the colony of Delaware.

British colonists were the dominant group on the east coast of North America, however. After 1607 English trading companies sent thousands of working men and, eventually, some women, to secure outposts or establish what they hoped would be permanent plantations along the Atlantic. The early colonists transferred some British sports, just as other Britons did to places like India and Africa in subsequent centuries. Field sports were relatively common endeavors, partly because some colonists carried muskets and carbines, had string to use as fishing lines, and could make poles from saplings. The need for food also encouraged hunting and fishing, as did exchanges with the native inhabitants.

As was the case in other nonindustrial societies, including those of Native Americans, ordinary English people constructed few boundaries between work and play. From the beginning, the men commissioned to govern the colonies discovered that the transfer of Old World sporting practices conflicted with the goals of the trading companies that financed the settlements. At Jamestown, Virginia, the

Seventeenth-century English hunter with crossbow. (© Eon Images)

first permanent outpost established by these companies, some of the migrants who had been sent to build shelters and plant food rejected such tasks in favor of hunting gold, bowling in the streets, gambling at other games, or escaping to live idly among the Natives. In 1608, when John Smith arrived to take command of the small and barely surviving village, he divided all the men, gentlemen included, into teams that spent "4 hours each day" in work. The rest of the time, Smith admitted, they devoted to "pastimes and merry exercise." He could get no more from them, he later explained, because the laborers "were for the most part footmen" and the "adventurers brought to attend them … never did know what a dayes worke was" (Smith 1986, 1:258–59, 2:225).

What the colonists had brought to the shores of Virginia was the traditional English leisure preference, and the pattern was not limited to Jamestown. In 1615, when Capt. Samuel Argall traveled to a nearby village, he concluded that only about half of 400 inhabitants were "fit for husbandry and tillage." The others continued "to wait and play than worke" (Smith 1986, 1:262). Even in the early plantations in Massachusetts, also established by trading companies, the preference for recreations was visible in the 1620s. At both Cape Ann, a fishing post, and Plymouth, the colonists who were company employees played games and enjoyed customary revels and alehouses and did not work regularly enough to produce a profit for the companies.

Two of the most famous incidents from this phase of English colonization also show the preference for play over productive work among the colonists whom the companies had sent to labor. One occurred in Plymouth, which was a plantation jointly funded and populated by the London Company and some dissenting Protestants, the "Separatists" led by William Bradford. In 1621 on Christmas Day, which the Separatists did not celebrate, Bradford and his followers were about to go to the fields to work. They expected the company's servants to accompany them, but the men, who were not co-religionists, claimed that it was "against their conscience" to work on Christmas day. So Bradford permitted them to stay behind. When he returned, however, he found the laborers "in the street at play openly; some pitching the bar, and some at stool-ball and such like sports." Bradford immediately ended their recreations and turned their argument on its head: it was "against his conscience that they should play and others work" (Bradford 1952, 97).

The other incident occurred a few years later, near the end of the period of trading company control. Not far from Plymouth in eastern Massachusetts was a private fur-trading post known as Mount Wollaston, where Thomas Morton, a well-off English trader, held sway. Morton was an avid hawker and had found five kinds of hawks in the wilds of New England, which he "reclaimed, trained, and made flying in [a] fortnight." He also eagerly celebrated traditional English festivals, including May Day. So he and his men brewed a "barrell of excellent beare" and erected an eighty-foot-high may pole that was a focal point for traditional festive practices "with the help of Salvages" (Morton 1632, 49, 89–90; Bradford 1952, 204–5). Around it, Morton, his men, and their Native allies danced and drank, and, according to their critics, engaged in "great licentiousness." They continued to do so long past May Day—until the Naumkeag planters cut down the pole. Eventually, Puritan authorities at Boston arrested Morton and shipped him back across the Atlantic.

The removal of Thomas Morton marked a turning point for the history of English sports in New England. Had Morton lived in Virginia, both he and the freewheeling ways he relished might have met the same fate. By the late 1620s and through the 1630s, more people who either opposed or were ambivalent about traditional English labor-leisure patterns and sporting practices migrated to both regions. They did not eliminate all traditional sports and recreations, but they did abandon some forms and adapt others. In both the North and the South, the one-time outposts became permanent colonies, inhabited by more planters, people who moved their families, servants, and stock to North America. The wealthiest planters also signed single people, both female and male, to indentures, or contracts that had the servants working a set number of years (four to seven) for the employer in exchange for freedom, a suit of clothes, and land—should the servant manage to survive. Land was plentiful, but labor was scarce, and one consequence for many was hard physical labor, as the words of an indentured servant suggest. Since she had arrived in Virginia from England, she began, "the axe and the hoe have wrought my overthrow." For five years she had known only "sorrow, grief and woe." Each dawn brought a common routine: "so soon as it is day, to work I must away," and what play she had was only "at Plow and Cart." In all, her record ended, "in misery I spend my time that hath no end" (Cott 1972, 31–33).

As did this servant, other colonists generally were less able—some were even unwilling—to reproduce the rich sporting traditions they had known in Britain in the middle decades of the seventeenth century, a pattern explainable by two sets of factors. First, much that had supported Britain's rich sporting canvas was absent. There were few nobles and landed gentlemen to serve as patrons of popular sports. Except for carbines, muskets, and an occasional sword as well, little of the equipment that the colonists might have used in English-style games, contests, and festivals existed. A similar statement was true for animals; horses were few, and bulls were far too valuable as breeding stock to be used in baits.

Second, whether for survival or to establish a freehold, the colonists had to make accommodations—with the climate and environment, with each other, and with superiors in what remained a master-servant, or governor-governed, social structure. Masters expected servants and wage laborers to work, as the servant's words above make clear. Those who chose not to work or make other accommodations deemed necessary by superiors faced a spate of laws, such as those seen in Puritan New England and in other reformed Protestant-influenced civil societies along the Atlantic coast.

The Puritans—or, at least, the ruling Puritans—have taken an unfair and inaccurate rap from some sport and social historians, and the mythology that they rooted out most sports persists. In reality, Puritan leaders specifically and colonial authorities more generally opposed only some practices, especially ones that wasted time and money or encouraged social disorder and what they considered immorality. They forbade gambling and blood sports. They also legislated against some contests in some contexts, such as horse racing in towns—not because racing was inherently bad but because such events occasionally injured passersby. Further, they disapproved of sports on the Sabbath, which stretched from sundown on Saturday to the same time on Sunday, in part because authorities wanted people to rest so that they could work when the week began anew. Through much of the seventeenth century, New England colonists upheld a strict Sabbath, as did officials in other North American colonies, including the Dutch settlements in New York. The relatively strict Sabbath was one of the legacies of the colonists to later generations of Americans, and it persisted into the twentieth century.

Another legacy was the association of particular practices with utility, usefulness, and positive outcomes. Sports that could be productive, as well as those that benefited workers, were not only permitted but also gradually became more widespread. In New England, the Puritan-influenced legislature and local town governments—as well as assemblies in other English colonies—defined such practices as "lawful" sports. These forms included hunting, fishing, horse races away from towns, and almost any matches, contests, or displays of prowess that produced a physical training or relaxation effect. In Massachusetts, the ball games favored by youths were not unlawful as long as they did not endanger nonplayers, and at midcentury among the responsibilities assigned to freshmen at the recently established Harvard College was that of providing upperclassmen with balls. Then, too, by the 1660s merchants and ministers from Boston, the largest town in the English mainland colonies, had begun to take trips to nearby hot springs where they not only bathed in the warm waters but also walked for exercise. Puritans knew well the rejuvenating and relaxing effects of physical exercise.

Field sports also benefited from the Puritans', and more generally, Protestants', emphasis on utility and gain. By the middle of the seventeenth century, legal hunting was probably more widespread than it was in Britain. Expanded land ownership was partly responsible for this fact, but the reality that hunting supplemented tables and incomes also mattered. So Chesapeake servants had muskets, and especially on holidays and in the winter they could "hunt the Deer, or Bear, or recreate themselves in Fowling" (Beverley 1705, 308–10). In Massachusetts Bay small farmers incorporated field sports—fishing, fowling, and hunting—within their daily regimens. Here, too, law guaranteed hunting and fishing rights, even on public lands, as early as 1641. Eventually as well, legislatures and some town officials in all the colonies offered bounties for the hides and heads of vermin, those destructive or dangerous animals such as wolves, squirrels, and deer. In time, the bounty system encouraged commercial hunting.

This process of adapting sports to the New World context quickened as the seventeenth century lengthened, and one result was that sporting practices proliferated. Men who were engaged in the cloth-making industry in the coastal town of Rowley, Massachusetts, for example, played a version of English football (soccer) on a beach in their bare feet against their rivals from a nearby town. Colonists of Dutch and Swedish ancestry in the middle colonies—New York, Delaware, and Pennsylvania—pursued skating and sleigh races. Large landowners in Virginia, in the fashion of British gentlemen, organized cricket games, occasional foot races, and a particular form of horse racing, quarter-mile racing, that owed both to the spread of native horses and the fact that they were still relatively small. Their common planter neighbors borrowed from Native Americans a field sport known as fire hunting in which they herded deer into a thicket, set the bushes on fire, and then shot the animals as they tried to flee the flames and smoke. Enslaved Africans brought from Africa or the Caribbean to work the rice fields in South Carolina produced a distinctive combination of swimming and hunting. According to one observer, they "swim and dive well ... go naked into the Water, with a knife in their hand, and fight the Shark, and very commonly kill him" (Lawson 1709, 158). Throughout the colonies as well, community gatherings and celebrations proliferated after 1680, in part because a critical mass of women emerged. Raisings in New England villages, harvest festivals in the plantation society of the Chesapeake, and fairs in many festivals owed much to the presence of women, who assumed their traditional roles as providers of food and drink and for whom these affairs provided opportunities for contacts with neighbors and relatives. In small towns such as Annapolis and Williamsburg, as well as larger ones such as Charleston, New York, and Boston, women also triggered changes in the content of public celebrations for military victories and royal anniversaries.

These and other sporting practices resulted from a number of changes in colonial life in the final decades of the seventeenth century and the early years of the eighteenth century. The demographic transformation was particularly critical and dramatic: people were living longer and there were more people, primarily from natural increase. The British and Anglo-American population alone expanded from approximately 35,000 in 1640 to more than a quarter of a million by 1700, a figure that included greater numbers of women and colonists from Africa and other countries in Europe. Coupled with broader transatlantic economic forces, the population growth and diversification stimulated geographic expansion, as well as an increase in trade and commercial activity.

Simultaneously, trade and commercial activity also expanded, and the consequences for sports were evident in a number of places. More tavernkeepers sold food and drink for customers in more places, and they frequently provided sports such as animal baits in back lots and bowling alleys or greens. Merchants, who not only were aware of what was happening in Britain but also wanted to expand their inventories and their customer base, imported more goods for recreations not seen before, such as cricket, lawn bowling, and billiards. Especially in the largest towns and cities, local government officials and entrepreneurs responded to the demands of their citizens and patrons for commercial entertainment options. People could now fish from public docks in New York City and hunt ducks in a public marsh near Boston.

EIGHTEENTH-CENTURY SPORTING STYLES

Sports proliferated in the eighteenth century, but not all sports were for all people. More visibly than had been the case earlier, sports were badges of rank, among the gentry, merchants, and large landowners, and the increasingly vast and diverse ordinary folk. We can make sense of practices and patterns of both groups by focusing on two styles. Gentlemen and women produced a sporting style in which particular sports, the equipment required, and the times and sites for sports resembled the style of the European and especially the British upper rank. The sporting style of ordinary people was less cohesive, in part because of the variability and diversity of the people, but it did present some similar behaviors and expectations.

Sports for the Upper Ranks: Horse Racing, Billiards, and Fishing

The dominant Anglo-American upper-rank sporting style resembled that of the British upper rank. Sports had long been requisite practice among the British upper rank, which many of the colonial gentry aspired to be like. A British gentleman was literate, witty, and relatively well-mannered, at least in public, and he was a man of grace, power, and agility. His female counterpart, though physically different from and considered inferior to men, was to be healthy, gracefully mobile, and conversant in the rules and conventions of the arts of physical improvement and refinement. To be cultivated, men and women needed to acquire skill in and knowledge about sports such as fishing, sailing, dancing, cards, and races. Both sets of expectations made their way across the Atlantic.

Colonial gentlemen and women pursued sports and recreations throughout the year. Winter was the time for balls and dances, indoor card games, ice skating, and club dinners—at least once every two weeks. Early spring, when rains swelled the rivers, marked the beginning of the fishing season, which lasted until early fall. Cockfights, ball games, and horse races began about the same time and peaked between April and June. By the 1770s one could attend a race virtually every week in a different town in Virginia and Maryland, and a calendar of sorts ensured that races did not occur in two areas at the same time. July and August were for cricket games in the South, swimming, and the beginning of the hunting seasons that, with different animals and fowl in turn, lasted through early winter. By September the fall races began, and when they ended in November, they overlapped with hunts and the beginning of the dancing season.

Little if any of this activity occurred by chance. Another distinguishing characteristic of gentry life was organization, and organizations known as clubs emerged. Some clubs built from existing local networks of gentlemen, as was the case with the Schuylkill Fishing Company, which formed outside Philadelphia by 1732 and whose members constructed rules and regulations for fishing. About the same time, jockey clubs in Maryland and South Carolina organized and then reorganized in these colonies and elsewhere at mid-century. In the 1740s merchants and lawyers established a "Physical Club" in Boston to "strengthen and render active their Bodies," while merchants and rice planters around Charleston organized two hunting clubs (Hamilton 1948, 116).

Club members, as well as other upper-rank colonials, also ordered sport-specific equipment, either from abroad or from colonial artisans. From Europe they imported a range of goods, including battledores for an indoor version of badminton, stopwatches to time races, ivory billiard balls, and quail and dog calls. Provincial craftspeople supplied other equipment, especially card and billiard tables, swords and foils, sleds and carriages, and an assortment of leather goods. These specialized goods and animals in turn came to be used and housed on distinctive

Depiction of a tennis match from Johann Commenius' *Obis Sensua-lium Pictus*, 1658, one of the earliest known illustrations of a form of the modern game of tennis. (© Eon Images)

Colonial dancing pavilion, Put-in-Bay, Ohio. (Courtesy of the Library of Congress)

sporting facilities. On the grounds of plantations and estates, for example, stables housed the thoroughbred race horses that improved one's stock, earned stud fees, and transported the owner quickly and gracefully from place to place. Bowling greens, which were sites for entertainment and parts of the symmetrical pattern of the outdoors, spread across expanses of grass between estate entrances and great houses. Game preserves stocked with deer covered hundreds of acres of meadows and woods and served as experiments in land conservation and arenas for the chase.

A particularly visible and socially significant sport formalized by the colonial gentry was thoroughbred racing, which drew from but did not replicate racing in the homeland. The British form was a distance contest on a straightaway, and it probably emerged first among civil servants, military officers, and large landowners in New York. But as was so often the case, colonists eventually adapted the British format, by running on a round or oval course, in part so that other colonists could see the races and so that the genteel race men could be well seen.

The particular history of oval racing possibly began in the Chesapeake. In the 1730s, once some men had acquired large amounts of land, from 10,000 to 300,000 acres, they also needed larger, stronger horses to ride. So they began to import full-blooded stock from England to improve their small native stock, and by the 1740s these bigger horses required a different kind of sporting test, one of endurance rather than short bursts of speed. Thoroughbred races consisted of several heats, each of two, three, or four miles, depending on the age and gender of the steed. The most important races, however, were usually twelve-mile contests, or three heats of four miles apiece.

By the 1760s thoroughbred races were vibrant public affairs from New York to Georgia. Occasionally the races matched an owner-breeder from one colony against his peers from another. Even New Englanders knew enough about the sport to attend contests in towns in other regions and to praise or criticize a victorious rider. Significant as well, the races were so important that few people left anything to chance. Some planters kept meticulous breeding and foaling records, as well as accounts of stud fees, club dues, prizes won, and wagers won and lost. Newspapers announced race meetings, as well as the formula by which pairings for match events (between two horses) and the entries for both subscriptions (races to which all entrants contributed) and sweepstakes (winner-take-all contests) were determined. The two variables in this formula were the "bloodedness" of the horse and the weight of the jockey. Full-blooded horses had to carry the heaviest weights, while one-eighth-blooded horses carried less. The basis for modern handicapping, these predetermined equivalencies were important to setting up fair races.

More than any other sport perhaps, thoroughbred racing expressed much of what gentlemen and -women wanted to believe about themselves and to have others believe about them. It was an adapted and complex British sport with written rules and specific procedures. Race men and women—and women did race, though not as frequently "in public"—displayed physical prowess as well as the cultivation and refinement that bound the colonial upper rank to the contemporary British gentry. Racing among themselves, too, they distinguished or set themselves apart from ordinary colonists—without excluding the small farmers, servants, and slaves who remained so important in and to the gentry style of life.

Sports for the Lower Ranks: Fishing, Hunting, Fighting, and Other Pastimes

For their part, ordinary colonists, who were the large majority of early Americans, also had access to many sports. They represented many ethnic and racial groups from Europe and Africa, and many occupational groups, including artisans and small farmers, slaves and seamen, housekeepers and shopkeepers, and more. Some people lived in towns or cities, while others spent their entire lives on family farms, small plantations, or isolated cabins in the backcountry. None was rich, and more than a few were poor, surviving on the economic margins. Specialized equipment was rare, and even the horses and boats used for racing doubled for travel and transport. Fields, forests, lanes, rivers, docks, taverns, and houses remained common sites for sports, and the practices themselves often drew from and occurred within the tasks and rhythms of farming, fishing, trapping, trading, and domestic chores. Matches, or events that pitted one person against another, were common, as were small group and communal events.

Numerous sports were similar in form and format to those earlier generations of colonists participated in. This was particularly true of field sports such as hunting and fishing. There was also a broad array of centuries-old gatherings in which sports and recreations often figured prominently—weddings, fairs, frolics, holiday celebrations, and evening gatherings. Dances were traditional practices at weddings, although the precise forms varied from group to group. Africans favored jigs and individual rhythmic performances to the accompaniment of fiddles, while New Englanders of British stock performed variants of reels known as country dances. Fairs in Pennsylvania and Maryland featured races, both on foot by white and black runners and on horseback. Frolics begot relatively simple games, drinking and eating, and sexual license—the practices of carnival.

Ball games also reappeared with some regularity, albeit for a short time, in community festivities in Georgia, the final British-claimed colony on the mainland of North America, established in 1732. Georgia's migrants initially consisted of a few English men and women of means, Austrian religious dissenters, and tenants and laborers from north of London. This latter group brought with them games they had known in England—cricket, football, and quoits—and which they participated in on holidays, royal anniversaries, and other days of remembrance.

Yet ball games had no staying power in Georgia or anywhere else, among Anglo-American and African American adults. By the 1760s and 1770s cricket play was rare, limited primarily to British soldiers, officers, and merchants, while boys engaged in football. Several factors may help to account for the short life of ball games. First, many of the gatherings of ordinary people included both men and women, and sports that were meaningful in these settings often appealed to and incorporated both genders—as the traditions of ball games did not. Second, during the middle decades of the century, the number of traditional holy days continued to diminish in the wake of the Great Awakening. Finally, and especially in the South, the skills and the structure involved in ball games simply had no fit in the experiences of southern males. The physical skills of throwing, catching, and batting were not the actions one took to obtain food, to settle a dispute, or to gain renown. Ball games also involved men participating in groups, if not teams, and such groups and gangs, though not unknown, were not the norm, except in the

Deep South among enslaved African and African American field hands. White male Southerners worked in pairs or small groups—a father and son and a slave or servant or two, for example—or they worked alone.

There was, however, one sport that flourished among southern small farmers and working men: fistfighting. "Rough and tumbling," as it was known locally, regularized and acquired distinct conventions primarily among farmers, laborers, and itinerant trappers and traders who lived near the Appalachian Mountains during the second half of the eighteenth century and were both literally and figuratively on the margins of society. Theirs was a predominantly male, oral, face-to-face culture, and fistfighting appealed. As Elliott Gorn has so aptly written, rough and tumbling contests were affairs of honor among intensely competitive individuals (Gorn 1985, 1986). Contestants used any and all of their skills—kicking, slugging, wrestling, and gouging—until an opponent could no longer continue.

Other sports, too, were primarily meaningful to and practiced by distinct groups of people. In Philadelphia, for example, one of the characteristic recreations of laborers was bull baiting. Either near taverns or just outside the city limits, butchers provided the bulls and staged the baits in the evenings when dockworkers, servants, and apprentices could steal some time for themselves. There were also spinning contests of some New England townswomen in the 1760s. Spinning was a traditional female skill, and competitive spinning was a female equivalent to male contests with ordinary skills such as riding (racing) and shooting (hunting). It seems likely, too, that contemporary politics shaped the events. Participants in the pre-Revolutionary boycott movement, the women refused to continue to import cloth and clothing from Britain and so they resurrected spinning. Dividing themselves either by neighborhood or by skill level, they raced to see which group could produce more yarn.

The boycott to which the Massachusetts spinners contributed was a harbinger of things to come in the British colonies. A decade later, legislative leaders in all thirteen colonies cited multiple British injustices and, urged on by their own provincial assemblies and some citizens, declared independence from Britain. Their Declaration of Independence (1776) was followed by what subsequent generations dubbed the Revolutionary War (1776–81). Unlike most subsequent wars in which Americans fought, this War for Independence did not substantially alter the course of sporting life, although it was bitterly contested and brutal for the combatants. Indeed, the war itself directly affected the daily affairs of only about 10 percent of the colonial population, according to historians' estimate. Both the Continental Congress and some state legislatures railed against waste and, thus, gambling. Areas subject to battles or British and Continental army intrusions suffered substantial property damage, including the thoroughbred stock in the South especially. But observable changes in Americans' sporting experiences were relatively few and gradual through the end of the eighteenth century and owed less to either the war or the immediate political consequences of American independence than they did to ongoing demographic, economic, geographic, and cultural changes.

SPORTS IN THE EARLY NATIONAL AND ANTEBELLUM YEARS

Natural increase and immigration expanded the population of the United States markedly after 1800, from 5.3 million to 33.4 million in 1860. Much of this increase concentrated in urbanizing areas: one of twelve people lived in urban areas by mid-century, compared to only one in 100 in 1800. For other people, cities were simply places where individuals and families outfitted themselves for the westward journey. Via newly completed canals and railroads, by foot and horseback, or in wagon trains, thousands of people made their way through the land acquired from France through the Louisiana Purchase (1803), the annexation of Texas (1845), the Mexican Cession (including California, 1848), and the Oregon country (1848). Before the Civil War, in short, the United States stretched from the Atlantic to the Pacific.

The economic and commercial picture was more complex, as were the patterns of peoples' lives and livelihoods. On the one hand, after 1780 the United States rapidly industrialized, fueled by an increasingly complex capitalist economy. Some people acquired substantial wealth from this process, while unskilled urban laborers, both men and women, struggled to make ends meet much as had their laboring predecessors. Agriculture, which markets had always shaped, generated different produce, expanded markets, and persisting inequality. Many small farmers worked their fields and, depending on the vagaries of the weather and the environment, either managed or failed to eke out marginal livings. Southern planters, as well as some Northerners, retained slaves, and slaves in turn tried to maintain some degree of control over their lives via families and religion. Not coincidentally, too, there was considerable resistance both to forces of control and to the changes that were beyond individuals' control. Slave rebellions occurred, urban laborers sought refuge from the rigors of work in taverns, and native-born citizens mobilized against immigrants. Eventually, of course, the most striking incidence of resistance resulted in the War Between the States, or the Civil War.

Not surprisingly or coincidentally, after 1780 American sporting life resembled a quilt with multiple and often starkly contrasting patterns. Some scenes revealed the persisting social power of traditional sports. In both the North and the South, for example, thoroughbred races revived in the second decade of the nineteenth century and became significant, mostly urban-centered commercial spectacles, some of which had crowds of 70,000 or more. Racing drew some energy from its ties to agricultural "improvement" and from the developing sectional controversy. In industrializing urban centers, fistfighting retained its appeal among laboring men, and ethnic tensions provided a new source of social fuel for the fights. On southern plantations slaves and slave owners maintained many of the sports, as well as the fit of sports in the rhythms of ordinary life and work, that were common to their forebears. Migrants to the Midwest and beyond—across the Mississippi River and then the Rocky Mountains—transported and then adapted practices that their ancestors had known. So did Latinos who continued to populate Texas and other Mexican-controlled territory, including California. Their ancestors had introduced matches and displays derived from their work with cattle and horses, many of which remained vibrant in the nineteenth century and by mid-century began to shape the sport of rodeo.

But the early- and mid-nineteenth-century sporting quilt captured another set of scenes as well, especially in urban centers. The ongoing capitalization and commercialization of sports propelled the nascent sporting goods industry well beyond its base in the work of individual crafts people, and by the 1830s and 1840s one could purchase many kinds of goods and equipment in stores and from mail-order houses in eastern cities. Newspapers covered events as never before, especially those that featured violence, and new migrants expanded the period's sporting repertoire with practices such as gymnastics and track and field. Class competitions emerged in the still small and elite private and church-run colleges, while educators, medical doctors, and popular magazines encouraged some sports and physical exercise as methods of improving or maintaining health. They also encouraged middle-class women to participate in exercises and "amusements," even as middle-class men took to "athletics." By the 1850s entrepreneurs were renting facilities and grounds to sport-specific clubs, and urban spectators were willing to pay fifty cents to see base-ball "all-star" games. In the next decade, first the telegraph and then the transatlantic cable made possible once unimagined possibilities for communicating the results of sporting events. The timing was propitious: competition between American clubs and teams and their counterparts in other nations was already underway.

This other style contained behaviors and meanings that Americans today will recognize as emergent modern ones. Many of the physical skills incorporated in games and other contests had little to do with the tasks of ordinary life in its ordinary settings; they were skills like throwing and catching balls on diamonds, lifting dumbbells in gymnasia, and running around a track with a cinder surface. Written rules often governed what one could and could not do with these skills, although some degree of training and invented strategies could enable one to, if not circumvent the rules, use them to one's advantage—to win. In short, and in contrast to traditional sports, modern ones were consciously rationalized and specialized. They were also about winning and leisure and any beneficial end that players could conjure up for them. In time as well, they would be structured and promoted via complex bureaucracies and sold as reflectors of the dominant culture's conception of what was American.

Traditional Sports before the Civil War

Traditional sports such as fistfighting flourished throughout the United States and territories that would become states before 1860. Indeed, a traveler could have seen events that resembled eighteenth-century practices almost anywhere in what was an increasingly broad canvas. Between the Appalachian Mountains and the Mississippi River, many villages and towns had courses on which horses ran, and for the express purposed of improving the breed. In Ohio and Indiana farmers hunted "vermin," especially bats and deer, in the fall after the harvest was complete and before the snows came, much as had their ancestors in Maryland and Virginia. Women from the Deep South who migrated with their families to Texas continued to spin and quilt in groups and occasionally competitively, both for enjoyment and to produce needed goods, as had New Englanders nearly a century earlier. Fur trappers played cards, gambled, and drank at their rendezvous and during the long winter nights in their cabins in the Rocky Mountains. On the northern Great Plains, Native Americans persisted in tests of individual physical skills, games and gambling, and hunts, all of which maintained traditional linkages between religious rituals and sports and between work and play.

Two sets of experiences enable us to view in some depth the forms and the fit of traditional sports in rural, agrarian America before the Civil War. One set derived from below the Mason-Dixon line and as far west as Texas. Here hundreds of thousands of African Americans endured the rigors of the "peculiar institution," slavery. Some of them worked in the fields and houses of wealthy planters who raised

Extra, Extra!! The Fight That Almost Wasn't! Hyer defeats Sullivan in 16 rounds in a field, after narrowly escaping authorities. Hyer wins $10,000; Sullivan grievously injured.

Mythical newspaper headlines? A script for a slapstick comedy? Today perhaps, but not in the mid-nineteenth century. The "fight that almost wasn't" really did occur—in Kent County on Maryland's Eastern Shore on February 7, 1849. Six months of planning preceded this match, which was to take place on Poole's Island in the Chesapeake Bay. The principals, New York butcher Tom Hyer and James "Yankee" Sullivan, an immigrant from Ireland by way of Australia, were already there. Hundreds of spectators were also departing from Baltimore by steamer when local law enforcement authorities learned about the event. As was the case in other eastern states, prizefighting was illegal in Maryland, and officials intended to stop this one. So a local militia seized a privately owned boat and set off across the Bay toward Poole's Island, where they hoped to capture the fighters. Once they arrived, they did arrest two men, who turned out to be stand-ins for Hyer and Sullivan. Embarrassed and frustrated, the militia returned to their boat and restarted the chase—only to run aground. Meanwhile, the fight party had moved east to the mainland of Kent County. Here on a snow-covered field they hastily erected the required twenty-four-square foot ring out of locally cut pine, ropes, and halyards from their steamers. The match proceeded without any more hitches, and within eighteen minutes it was all over. Hyer knocked Sullivan out and left with the $10,000 purse. Sullivan, unconscious and injured, was taken to a hospital. Hyer retired two years later, and Sullivan, now thoroughly recovered, proclaimed himself the new champion of fistfighting.

cotton, rice, or indigo for markets at home and abroad. Many more labored on the farms or as artisans for small landowners, shopkeepers, and merchants. All, however, shared a common legal status; they were considered the property of their owners. They also commonly experienced the vicissitudes of hard work and poverty and the struggles to construct families and communities.

In this largely agrarian region, the rhythms and traditions of agricultural life and the traditions of the people affected the content and opportunities for sports and other recreations among the slaves. As did many whites, for instance, African Americans continued to order tasks concurrently rather than sequentially in time, to link necessary and recreational tasks. When they hunted or fished, for example, slaves were both acquiring necessary food and enjoying themselves. Then, too, tasks and demanding taskmasters and mistresses, rather than clocks, drove time. Consequently, although slaves might steal a few minutes for recreations between tasks, they often obtained substantial blocks of time between the seasons, at night, on Saturday and Sunday afternoons, or during holidays. Traditional activities, in turn, filled these minutes and hours. A cockfight on a Saturday afternoon, a foot race on a path back to the cabin, a horse race when two slaves met on a road—all were common.

Rodeos in the Southwest

Another set of traditional experiences flourished farther west among people who lived and worked in what would become the states of Texas, New Mexico,

Arizona, and southern California. Originally inhabited by Native Americans, much of this great land mass had been claimed and colonized by Spain and then Mexico. Especially during the seventeenth and eighteenth centuries, people of Hispanic descent had migrated north and established ranches and villages. They also transported displays of prowess and contests derived from their work with cattle and horses. Eventually many of these skilled physical performances would be collected in the sport of rodeo.

Before rodeo, however, there was *charreria*. Charreria incorporated activities invented by the Spanish conquistadors who brought horses and cattle from Europe to the New World. As early as the sixteenth century, roping, riding, and taming wild horses and bulls were important tasks among ranch owners and hands in New Spain. Thereafter, as ranching spread, these tasks retained their economic significance, and men especially practiced and refined their roping and equestrian skills. In time, as a hierarchically structured society emerged in New Spain, these skills also acquired considerable social significance. For the *charros*, the ranch hands, small farmers, and others among the native-born Mexicans who comprised a middle rank, skilled performances with ropes, in races, and against wild bulls and horses enabled them to display their prowess and compete with one another for prestige and place in emerging communities. These displays and contests in turn became badges of rank and dimensions of the traditions that simultaneously expressed what it meant to be a charro and distinguished the charros from both the wealthy Europeans who stood at the top of Mexican society and the Native Americans who had been reduced to the bottom.

During the final decades of Mexican rule in the Southwest, the displays and contests of the charros persisted. The seasons of cattle ranching and the Roman Catholic calendar produced numerous festivals, holidays, and Sundays, all of which were enlivened by charro events. Fancy roping, bull riding, and wrestling were common, as were many forms of racing, including the traditional chicken race, the goal of which was for a rider to pull a chicken suspended from a tree or half-buried in the ground as he was galloping at full speed. Even more dangerous, and thus a more telling test of one's skill and courage, were the *paso de muerte*, or pass of death, and the *colear*, a residual work skill, both of which had become a sport. In the former event, riders galloped alongside wild horses, leaped onto their backs, and then rode them until they calmed down. In the latter, a group of charros took turns riding into a corralled herd of bulls; then each rider grabbed a bull's tail, pulled it under his leg, and literally twisted it until the bull fell to the ground. (These events are still performed today in Mexican American rodeos.)

The Anglos who first witnessed these affairs watched in awe; there were no precedents for most of these Latino practices in their own histories. Between 1835 and 1848, however, a series of military and political confrontations between Mexicans and the ever more numerous Americans resulted in the eclipse of colonial rule and charro hegemony. Yet neither the charros nor charreria passed from the southwestern sporting scene. Anglo ranchers and hands, a few African American cowboys, and martial groups such as the Texas Rangers adopted charro practices and invented additional events. By mid-century the amalgam of customary practices that would comprise rodeo was in the making.

Traditional sports also persisted in the burgeoning urbanizing areas in the United States before the Civil War. From Boston to Savannah on the eastern seaboard to as far west as Chicago and St. Louis, towns and cities were bustling places capable of sustaining a variety of practices. People were continually coming and going and invariably available as consumers and producers of both prearranged and impromptu displays of prowess, races, and games. Owing to both the natural and built environments, there was also a good deal of space available for sports. The rivers and streams around which many towns had built up made fishing possible, either with homemade or manufactured gear. Roads, large parcels of undeveloped land, and taverns were the sites for both impromptu and prearranged animal baits, ball games, shooting contests, and foot and horse races, while bustling ports provided access to lakes or the ocean for swimming, rowing races, and yachting. About the only specialized venues for sports were bowling greens and race courses, and both served multiple sports.

The demography and economic activity of many towns and cities also were conducive to traditional practices, especially traditional male practices. Women were less visible outside the home or in dark and dingy factories than they had once been, displaced by the economy, law, and male immigrants. Men thus continued to control many sporting sites and opportunities, although they occasionally welcomed women as spectators or as partners in the sexual escapades associated with taverns. Then, too, these men either saw themselves or were seen as members of the traditional ranks, even though a nontraditional segment, a middle class, was emerging. Substantial wealth from land, commerce, shipping, and industry placed one in the upper rank and afforded one time, money, and incentives to invest in horse racing, yachting, gambling, club formation, and, on occasion, to reprise their roles as patrons. There were also laborers aplenty who worked in the factories, or served as seamen, carters, and street cleaners, or toiled in the shops and crafts that fed the market economies and role specialization of capitalizing, urbanizing areas. Although their work was regularizing, many laborers still had slack times when the mills stood idle, or the ships were out, or machines were down for cleaning. There were also patriotic holidays such as Independence Day, Saturday afternoons, and evenings. As well, taverns and saloon visits provided leisure time for meals, drink, and camaraderie.

The context of antebellum urban settings thus ensured that sports traditionally popular among men, such as horse racing, fistfights, animal contests, and a variety of tavern games, not only survived but also thrived. With entrepreneurs willing and able to capitalize on the new industry of public entertainment, particular events became commercial spectacles that drew several hundred or many thousands of people, especially from the ranks of the landed and mercantile elite and the laboring classes. Whether they gathered together or separately—at a club or tavern, on a track or road, respectively—both wealthy and poor reveled in the displays of prowess that traditional sports provided, as well as the excitement and wagers they inevitably generated.

Two sports in particular captured the imaginations and reinforced the traditions of these segments of the antebellum urban male population. One was horse racing, especially the thoroughbred form, which was probably the most visible organized public sport in towns and cities, at least once it revived early in the nineteenth century. The Revolutionary War had destroyed many horses, and for some years races had diminished in frequency. Gradually, however, jockey clubs and track owners in the South arranged more races in towns and cities, the traditional sites

The Great Foot Race

Gambling accompanied virtually every sporting practice before the Civil War especially the one in 1836 that contemporaries billed "The Great Foot Race." In January of that year, a possibly bored John Cox Stevens, eldest son in a New York family known for its agricultural and engineering prowess, bet his friend Samuel L. Gouverneur that a man could run ten miles in under an hour. Gouverneur took the bet, and Stevens organized and advertised the race. Set for after the thoroughbred race season on Long Island's Union Course, this "great trial of human capabilities" drew nine contestants, all farmers, artisans, and laborers. A tenth man, Francis Stevens, tried to enter, but the judges ruled that he hadn't registered in time. That Stevens was the only athlete of African descent likely did not escape the judges' scrutiny.

The promise of $1000 to the winner, along with the possibility of an extra $300 if only one person met the challenge, likely enticed some of the contestants. Some runners either had completed races before or had trained, more or less systematically, for the event. For example, John Mallard (5′6½″, 130 pounds), a thirty-five-year-old farmer from Otsego County, New York, had a personal best of sixteen miles in one hour and forty-nine minutes. This time, however, he "was not sober" when he started, and he fell in the fifth mile. The local favorite was Isaac Downes, a twenty-seven-year-old basketmaker from Suffolk County, Long Island, who "had been well trained under his father." At 5′5″ and 150 pounds, Downes wore blue and white colors, but no shoes and stockings, and he "gave in" in the next-to-last mile. Before the race, George Glauer, a Prussian-born rope-maker (5′6½″, 150 pounds), had run from New York to Haarlem and back (24 miles total), and backed his belief in his own ability to win with a $300 bet.

Spectators lined the roads and the ferries from 9:00 A.M. onward for the early afternoon race. The day was windy; the crowd large (estimates offered a range of 16,000–20,000 people), well lubricated, and eager to bet not only on who would win but who would finish, in what order a contestant would finish, whether someone would finish, and so on. In the end, Henry Stannard, a twenty-four-year-old Connecticut-born farmer, finished the distance sixteen seconds short of an hour. He, too, had trained before the race, and he might have completed the ten miles in two minutes fewer had the wind not been so strong. Stannard had a tag-a-long patron, however, John Cox Stevens himself, who rode beside the runner, keeping him apprised of his and others' times at each mile mark and cheering him on. In keeping with sporting customs of the elite, Stevens also accompanied Stannard to the host Jockey Club dinner and fete. The "Great Foot Race" ended as it had begun, a traditional performance of patrons and athletes and white, male privilege on display ("The Great Foot Race" 1835).

---

for organized thoroughbred racing. A similar movement in the North proceeded more slowly, in part because moral societies opposed to gambling succeeded in having state legislatures illegalize the sport. The laws remained in effect until just before 1820 when propertied men, including many who lived in towns and cities, formed agricultural societies to promote agrarian production and interests, including racing. Their members appropriated the old colonial rationale for racing, improving the breed, and offered it now as a national interest. Once they successfully lobbied legislators to repeal antiracing laws, they resumed subscription and match events that blended old and new. The traditional format of multiple heats each two to four miles in length prevailed, but they often took place on mile-long tracks built in or on the outskirts of urban areas by entrepreneurs who wanted to cash in on this "national interest."

The quarter century after 1820 was something of a golden age for traditional thoroughbred racing. Many towns and cities east of the Mississippi River had tracks on which spring and fall racing occurred, much as had been the case in the eighteenth century. In many places agricultural interests were certainly apparent; people came to watch, wager, and arrange for winning animals to stand at stud on their farms. Yet, the popularity of thoroughbred racing was not simply the result of powerful rural interests. The sport also appealed to urbanites, rich and poor alike, and in cities such as New York and New Orleans, they transformed races into significant public celebrations, akin to modern Super Bowls. Wealthy men and women purchased the best seats where they were comfortable and easily seen by the crowd. For laborers, the races were an excuse to miss work for a day or more, to meet and drink with friends, and to wager. Newspapers sent reporters to the tracks, local politicians made appearances, and owners of transport companies and tavern owners both eyed the crowd expectantly, awaiting the dollars they stood to make.

The Great Races

But it was neither rural, agricultural needs nor urban commercial interests that helped to account for the emergence of a racing series that lived up to the sport's billing as a sport of national importance. Sectional politics did; they fueled a series that began as a personal challenge by a Northern breeder to any counterpart in the South and quickly became the partisan "Great Races." Run between 1823 and 1845, these contests matched the "best" horse of the North and its counterpart from the South, usually on Long Island's Union Course. The first race featured one of the most famous horses in American history, Eclipse, who defeated a southern steed financed by a syndicate in the best of three four-mile heats. Thereafter, the races occurred irregularly but with a vengeance, as first Southerners and then Northerners tried to redeem the honor of their region. Through 1836 the matches also focused on two men, John Cox Stevens, from a wealthy industrial family in New Jersey, and William R. Johnson, a planter from Virginia. Each man consistently selected his region's horses and organized the syndicates that funded the training and the wagers, usually $10,000 aside, which comprised the purse. By 1836 as well, it was also clear that the outcome of a given match hinged not only on a syndicate's ability to find the best horse in a region but also on the training of the horse and the strategy employed by the jockey.

By any standards, the Great Races had no parallel in the contemporary American sporting scene. Throughout the South hundreds of people traveled to see a given year's chosen horse, as the train that transported it to New York stopped for fuel or for another rally. At the Union Course estimates of the crowds ranged from 60,000 to 100,000 through 1845, although the latter figure was probably high: 100,000 people was about one-third of the population of New York City in 1840. The matches also drew visible state and national political leaders from both regions, and on occasion Congress adjourned so that senators and representatives could journey to Long Island. Finally, no sporting event—and few other

John Cox Stevens: Sporting Patron, Promoter, Owner, Athlete

Twentieth- and twenty-first-century sports fans around the world are used to seeing (a) wealthy men operating as owners of sport teams and clubs and (b) usually clear boundaries between players and owners, promoters, and so on. Athletes today can, of course, acquire considerable wealth during their careers, and some use the money and their renown to become coaches, owners, organizers, and promoters. A brief look at the career of one man, John Cox Stevens, makes clear both the similarities and the differences between his time and our own.

John Cox Stevens (1785–1857) came of age in the early national period when a dominant ideology among eastern elites focused on internal improvements. Three prior generations of Stevenses had accumulated substantial capital from agriculture, land sales, and shipping and trade ventures in the southern New York–northern New Jersey area. John and his brothers committed their wealth to promoting "improvements"—in horse breeding, steamship engineering, and railroad construction. His sporting endeavors thus were neither accidental nor coincidental. Early national and antebellum thoroughbred, yacht, and foot racing were about "improvement"—of the breed, the fleet, and the man—at least among those who could afford this line of thought.

Stevens was what one might call a working sportsman; he was not one of the much-maligned (and later in the nineteenth century) "leisure class." At his estate in Hoboken, Stevens studied bloodlines, the "science" of equine and human physical training, and, eventually, what could be called the aerodynamics of shipbuilding. He sought investors and arranged syndicates to support thoroughbred and yacht racing, and he served as president of the New York Jockey Club and first commodore of the New York Yacht Club. A staunch supporter of national interests, Stevens was the northern driver of the Great Races, which pitted not just northern steeds against southern ones but also native speed against English speed. Steven's national commitment persisted and, perhaps, strengthened over time. He commissioned and captained the sloop *America* in what became the first America's Cup yacht race, and he rented out a portion of his Hoboken estate known as Elysian Fields to clubs that were adapting ball games into "America's game."

contemporary events—received the newspaper attention or the partisan rhetorical flourishes that the races did. Long before the Civil War, these dramatic contests pitted the North against the South, and contemporaries knew it.

Despite its popularity and significance, however, the series ended abruptly in 1845. There is little evidence to suggest that contemporaries were aware that the match between the northern horse, Fashion, and her southern opponent, Peytona, which the latter won in two heats, was the final event. Several factors combined to forestall other races and, in fact, to undercut thoroughbred racing in the East. First, a series of economic recessions left various members of the thoroughbred industry—breeders, track owners, and jockey clubs—in serious financial trouble. Those who could afford to also had begun to invest in other commercial ventures, including entertainments, a movement that provided more options for one-time consumers of racing. Indeed, by the 1850s urban race courses such as Long Island's Union Course would offer mule races and ball games rather than thoroughbred affairs, which now centered in Kentucky, Tennessee, and farther west. Finally, the sectional politics that had once encouraged the races had become more divisive. Nationally visible debates over the extension of slavery, industrial versus agricultural policies, and states' rights in the face of union might were the consequences of widening material and ideological differences between Northerners and Southerners. They were also too significant for the proponents of racing to overcome. Except for isolated pockets in the South, the sport and its traditions did not survive the turmoil of the 1850s.

A similar fate eventually befell another antebellum urban sport, fistfighting. By the 1850s, it, too, was waning as a popular practice. In its heyday, however, fistfighting was probably as common and popular among its supporters and the keepers of its traditions as was thoroughbred racing. The difference, of course, was that the supporters of fistfighting were a smaller segment of the population. They were urban working men, tavern owners, and a few members of the wealthy elite.

As a historical practice, fistfighting had no single point of origin and no linear development. We are quite certain that it had occurred since humans began contesting with one another for place, prestige, or property. On both sides of the Atlantic across the centuries, several versions formalized. One became customary among upper-rank men who believed that they needed to defend themselves; they produced the stand-up, almost sparring "art" of self-defense. By the second half of the eighteenth century, men in the colonial backcountry engaged in "rough and tumbling," described earlier. Simultaneously, in Britain supporters of the art of self-defense and practitioners of the occasionally unrestrained fisticuffs entered into a patron-client relationship, which resulted in the regularizing and commercializing of fistfights. Upper-rank patrons thus supported strong young men, including some from the working class, in local bouts for monetary prizes. Newspapers announced the bouts, and a code of conduct that described what one could and could not do governed fighters' behaviors after 1743. This was Broughton's code, so named for its author, Jack Broughton. The code negated hits below the belt and when a fighter was down, and it provided for thirty seconds between rounds, "seconds" for both contestants, and referees. It also constructed boundaries for rounds and bouts. A round began with each fighter toeing the scratch line in the center of the ring and ended when one of the competitors went down. A bout concluded when either contestant could not return to the scratch line to start another round.

In the early nineteenth-century United States, these multiple forms of fist fighting persisted. "Rough and tumbling" remained popular in the backcountries, the ever-moving western areas of states and territories. The "manly art of self-defense," also called "scientific pugilism," appealed to urban and plantation gentry alike, and instructors provided classes in their rooms or the homes of the wealthy. Finally, urban working men and some young gentlemen, also known as the "fancy," favored the version governed by Broughton's code. They were one-half of a transatlantic fighting fraternity, at the core of which lay common practices and values. Newspaper accounts of fights, the production of training manuals, journeys by American fighters to Britain, and the migration of Britons to the United States sustained the fraternity through the mid-nineteenth century.

These human exchanges energized the fights and the fighting fraternity in another way as well. In 1811 Tom Molineaux, an ex-slave who may have acquired his freedom because of his fighting prowess, traveled to England to challenge the English champion, Tom Cribb. Upper-rank Britons who patronized the fights there, including the man on whose estate Cribb had trained, both feared and were awed by Molineaux, as apparently were the working men with whom Molineaux had spent much time in local taverns. National chauvinism and a race bias were both evident, and on the day of the fight, the betting reflected their unease. Round by round, the odds shifted from one fighter to other until the outcome became predictable. Molineaux had not been able to train thoroughly, and Cribb defeated him in eleven rounds.

Throughout the first half of the nineteenth century, dynamic ethnic and race relations fueled prizefighting in the United States, much as they had the Molineaux-Cribb match. Any fraternity is a relatively closed and tight-knit group, and its members are often willing to defend their customs and prerogatives. Certainly this was the case with the urban American fight fraternity of the 1830s and 1840s. Many of its working-class members were of English descent, and their personal economies were marginal at best. Well-paying jobs were scarce, and they feared the competition for those jobs that free African Americans, women, and increasing numbers of Irish immigrants provided. Not surprisingly, then, the fight fraternity constructed an early color line, and it either held women in low esteem or exploited them in sexual, work, and household relations. For English Americans, the Irish were a special challenge; not only did they have to fight them but also they had to beat them, to a pulp if possible. This ethnic antagonism was evident in Tom Hyer's defeat of James Sullivan in Maryland in 1849.

English-Irish tension, which owed much to historical relations of the two groups in Britain, stoked many antebellum fights, especially in New York, the center of organized prizefighting. A case in point was a contest between Christopher Lilly and Thomas McCoy at Hastings on the Hudson River, which had resulted from a quarrel at a tavern in 1842. As was the case in horse racing, the "purse" was actually the product of the two men's wagers on their own prowess, $200 aside. Unlike horse racing, however, the number of heats, or rounds in fight parlance, was unlimited. Broughton's code governed the fight, and both men had a distinctive style of fighting, a strategy for besting the opponent. Lilly intended to throw punches at McCoy's neck and head, while McCoy planned to launch a whole-body attack. Through the first fifteen rounds, neither man gained the advantage. By round 30, however, Lilly's punches were finding their mark; forty rounds later, McCoy was "a most unseemly object." His forehead and eyes were black and blue; his left eye swollen and nearly closed. Still the bout continued—until the 118th round. Even then as he lay drowning in his blood, McCoy cried out, "Nurse me and I'll whip him yet" (Gorn 1986, 76). Another round never occurred. McCoy died on the spot, and the fight ended.

Except for its length, the McCoy-Lilly fight was not unusual in the 1830s and 1840s. Many fights concluded after one of the opponents was either too injured to continue or dead, a fact that opponents of prizefighting did not miss. The largely unrestrained physical behavior, as well as the excessive drinking and frequent misbehaviors of supporters, helps to account for the numerous states' laws passed to outlaw the sport. In the face of its widening illegal status, some supporters did try to justify the fights, the fighters, and the violence. One proponent was Frank Queen, who owned the New York Clipper, which both covered and staged prizefights. Queen argued that fistfighting was a "manly" sport that developed physical prowess, bravery, and heroic qualities. Few of the opponents of fighting, however, believed his arguments, even though some of them would eventually offer similar justifications for other sports.

Queen's defense of fistfighting did resonate with the antebellum urban fight fraternity. For many of these men, fighting remained meaningful, which is why they pursued it—even to their deaths. Fistfights were displays of prowess and affairs of honor; they were practices in which contestants achieved fame and status, as well as some income on occasion. Fight "heroes" were honored and so too was the camaraderie of the fraternity. Important as well, much of what the fights involved and were about stood in marked contrast to the values and practices of the increasingly evident and dominant "civilized" classes of urban America, especially the emerging middle class. Working men valued raw physicality, face-to-face confrontations, drinking and gambling, the community of men who lived and died by their rules rather than somebody else's, and the rhythms of task discipline (and the fight was a task) rather than those artificially imposed by the clock or the workplace supervisor. Prizefighting thus was about freedom and traditions, which insured both continuity with past generations of working men and a place in their history—the history of Anglo-American working men. As such, prizefighting was also a means of resisting, even opposing, an emerging but encroaching cultural style that valued change, looked toward the future, and wrote a very different history.

ANTEBELLUM HEALTH REFORM

Opposition to traditional sports such as fistfighting mounted in the decades immediately before the Civil War, especially in urban centers. Civil authorities repressed the practice with laws and, when those failed, they interrupted events or, as the 1849 affair in Maryland indicated, ran the principals out of town. Citizens who exerted considerable local authority—by virtue of their occupations, education, wealth, or even family—also spoke and wrote against fights, races, and baits. They railed against what they saw as brutality in the ring and pit, and they just as vehemently opposed the accompanying drinking and gambling that wasted money and dulled the senses of participants and spectators alike.

A loose but discernible collection of these citizen critics of blood sports constituted a group that historians have called health reformers. They were ministers, educators, private citizens, and members of both the orthodox (MDs) and the "irregular" (e.g., homeopathic) branches of the emerging medical profession. They saw first-hand what conditions were like for other citizens in the urbanizing, industrializing urban centers of the East. As the population rapidly expanded, houses proliferated along narrow streets and alleys; demands outstripped supplies of clean water; horse manure and human wastes piled up on thoroughfares. Population density and poor sanitation, in turn, increased the risks of disease, especially epidemic diseases such as smallpox, while contemporary medical practices, including the use of leeches to bleed ill patients, did not always insure recuperation. Poverty, the lack of refrigeration for food, the seasonal availability of vegetables and fruits, and the rapid construction of shops and factories without adequate lighting and ventilation made matters worse.

Antebellum health reformers also shared in the ideological legacy of the Enlightenment, a strong belief in the primacy of the physical world and humans' ability to think rationally about and effect change in it. Fleshed out over time, this newer belief system attributed agency to human beings and made possible the construction of individual rights and responsibilities that the Declaration of Independence and the Constitution embraced. It also underlay the faith in human perfectibility manifest in often-related arenas of "improvement": agricultural innovation, the building of canals and railroads, religious revivals, and expanding public education.

The people who constructed and promoted health reform conceived of health as a complex state in which two relationships were paramount. One involved an individual's moral, mental, and physical conditions and attitudes, which not only had to be "proper" but also compatible. In other words, a desirable and appropriate physical condition could emerge only if desirable and appropriate moral and mental conditions also existed. The second relationship was that between an individual and his or her environment. A person's physical, moral, and mental well-being depended on one's ability to live in a state of harmony with nature and society. The critical requirement for achieving health thus was living a balanced life, a life of harmony and interdependence.

Despite these shared beliefs, health reformers touted a variety of prescriptions and regimens. One early spokesperson for health reform, Sylvester Graham (1794–1851), embraced a contemporary physiological principle known as vitalism. a theory that tried to explain how and to what effect stimulation occurred. Organs and organisms, this theory maintained, possessed vital forces, which were conceived almost as internal pressure points. Stimulation of an organ's vital force was critical to its functioning and, hence, the process to which it was central—the stomach for digestion, for example, or the lungs for respiration. Many things could induce stimulation, but not all of them produced beneficial action on the part of an organ. The "wrong" kind or amount of food, for example, stimulated the stomach to reject the food by vomiting rather than to begin the process of digestion.

Graham's embrace of vitalism led him to champion a number of causes, including vegetarianism. He maintained that vegetables, fruits, and a bland diet prevented the stomach from being mis-stimulated and thus less prone to generating gastrointestinal distress. Not coincidentally, of course, vegetarians' arguments about diet fueled some of the mounting opposition to traditional blood sports—and their red-meat produce. Graham also talked long and loudly about the need to improve people's diets in other ways. He even promoted a homemade, wheat-grain bread as an alternative to bakery bread, whose makers occasionally used plaster of paris to stretch and reduce the cost of flour. A later generation recognized Graham's efforts on behalf of improved diets by naming the graham cracker after him.

Another significant figure in the antebellum health-reform movement was Catharine Beecher (1800–1878), who took a different approach. Beecher came from a well-known and locally esteemed New England family whose members were famous—or infamous, depending on one's views—for their support of social "improvement" causes, including abolition. In the late 1850s Harriet Beecher Stowe, Catharine's sister, became something of a cause célèbre among people who favored the abolition of slavery when she published *Uncle Tom's Cabin*. Catharine never quite achieved the national acclaim that Harriet did, but she was a prolific author. She published numerous articles and books, including *Treatise on Domestic Economy* (1841), *Letters to the People on Health and Happiness* (1855), and *Physiology and Calisthenics for Schools and Families* (1856).

In contrast to Graham, Beecher's prescriptions stressed moderation as the key to improving health. A healthy diet, for example, was a "simple" diet rather than a strict vegetarian one. A person did, of course, need to abstain from liquor but not from other "strong" beverages such as tea and coffee. Indeed, Beecher suggested, abstinence from food that one enjoyed, as well as other "luxuries" and pleasures, would actually do more harm than good to one's health in the long run.

Beecher's emphasis on moderate behavioral changes and remedies may have been a function of the portions of the antebellum population about whom and for whom she wrote: women and, to a lesser extent, children. Few, if any, health reformers believed that women could develop the physical strength or mental discipline and astuteness of men, and Beecher was no exception. In the curricula of the female seminaries she organized in Connecticut and Ohio, she incorporated "domestic" exercises, such as sweeping, which were to produce the physical skills necessary for keeping healthy households, as well as moderate walking and riding (never racing) in the open air, simple "amusements" (read nonstrenuous games), and rhythmic gymnastics. She expected women and girls to exercise their muscles, but not because she anticipated strength gains. Exercise was to stimulate internal organs and processes, prevent the holder's "naturally" weak muscles from atrophying, and decrease the risks of debilitating physical and nervous illnesses to which women were naturally susceptible.

Other reformers championed Beecher's use of exercise and other organized physical activities to improve health in the 1850s. In fact, systems of exercise proliferated, either as training regimens for athletes or as gymnastics, which was also encouraged by the post-1848 migration of Germans who brought their Turnvereins (gymnastic societies) to the United States. Toward the end of the decade, Diocletian Lewis developed a system of lighter gymnastics, which included adaptations of some of Beecher's exercises, and became a prominent spokesperson for physical training and a promoter of gymnastics in schools.

Few antebellum health reformers actively championed the alternative sporting style that was emerging among some of their contemporaries. They did, however, provide one of the enduring justifications for emergent modern sports, health. Before the Civil War, as well, some supporters of what historians have come to call athletic sports, one of the dominant types of modern sports, incorporated both the rhetoric of improvement popularized by health reformers and their linkage of physical health, mental health, and moral health—the body, mind, and spirit trilogy. One such man was Thomas Wentworth Higginson, a Massachusetts minister and soon-to-be colonel of a Northern regiment in the Civil War. In 1858 he wrote an essay entitled "Saints and Their Bodies" for a popular magazine. He began the piece by lamenting the lack of attention that Christian religious leaders over the centuries had paid to the human body and physical health. Fortunately, in Higginson's judgment, the current generation of "saints" was beginning to recognize the importance of their bodies and the benefits, including enjoyment, that they derived from active, outdoor sports. He was pleased that both the clergy and their congregations had begun to value the "athletic virtue" on which the ancient Greeks had placed such a premium.

Higginson was an early American proponent of the English-defined ideology known as "muscular Christianity," a set of beliefs that linked one's moral condition with one's physical conditioning. The social power of muscular Christianity lay

Diocletian Lewis and Gymnastics

Diocletian Lewis (1823–88) developed an American system of gymnastics, which included adaptations of some of Catharine Beecher's exercises, and became a prominent spokesperson for physical training and a promoter of gymnastics in schools. A late antebellum reformer, Lewis had a career that is also telling about how receptive to physical training and improvement some middle-class urbanites had become. Not coincidentally, his work contributed to and benefited from the broadening interest in active, athletic sports—the kind about which Thomas Higginson spoke so favorably.

Unlike Graham and Beecher, Lewis was not a native New Englander; instead, he was born and reared in New York state and studied homeopathic medicine in Ohio. At one time or another, he advocated temperance, sexual hygiene, improved nutrition, the homeopathic practice of using small doses of drugs to cure diseases, and phrenology, the pseudo-science that maintained that bumps on the skull revealed the conditions of one's mental faculties. In part because of the illnesses of his wife and other family members, however, he eventually decided to focus on preventing ill health, rather than curing diseases. Gymnastics became his answer.

By the 1850s gymnastics had only a short history in the United States, but between 1825 and the 1840s German émigrés had introduced to the United States a system of gymnastics that incorporated large pieces of apparatus and had been devised in their country earlier in the century. This system of the German American "Turners" remains the basis for Olympic gymnastics today. Subsequently constructed, both here and abroad, were other "systems" of gymnastics that invariably concentrated on natural movements of the body—running, jumping, twisting, lifting, and so on. Beecher's "system" of calisthenics and movements to music—her rhythmic gymnastics—was one; Per Henrik Ling's Swedish gymnastics, also a rhythmic, "natural" system, was another. Lewis's system incorporated elements from both of these approaches, and he promoted it as an alternative to the German system, which he considered to be too demanding, and thus inappropriate, for women, children, and older or sickly men.

The Lewis system of gymnastics provided a series of small apparatus exercises, dancing, and marching. Numerous exercises employed beanbags, which he invented; for example, partners tossed a bag between themselves or one person simply threw it up in the air and caught it with one hand. He also used rings, which were wooden circles about six inches in diameters, in about fifty exercises. These were not suspended rings but hand-held ones used for pulling, either individually or in pairs, and twisting, usually to music. Other exercises used Indian clubs, which resembled bowling pins, and wands. They, too, were accompanied by music, which Lewis believed encouraged enjoyment and provided a rhythmic discipline for the rhythmic movements. He also recommended that all movements take place in a well-lit, ventilated room with plenty of space—a healthy room.

Lewis also outlined his system in various articles and books, including what was essentially a how-to manual, *The New Gymnastics for Men, Women, and Children*. In 1861 he began a school, the Normal Institute for Physical Education, to educate future teachers of gymnastics and physical training; although it operated for only seven years, the institute's graduates, both men and women, found jobs awaiting them. As had Beecher before him, Lewis also started a school for girls, of whom he required two and one-half hours of gymnasium work daily.

some years in the future, once it became a cornerstone of YMCA programs of physical training and athletic sports, and it would bear on the rhetorical, even mythological distinction between the amateur athlete and the professional athlete. But its introduction in the late 1850s is telling both about the beliefs and attitudes of people such as Higginson and about the sports they valued, "athletic" sports. These were the sports Higginson admired—sports such as base ball, skating, rowing, and many others eventually. They were also predominantly middle-class practices that employed the body as an instrument and promised physical training, health, and human improvement.

THE BEGINNINGS OF MODERN SPORTS

As the previous sections have suggested, an alternative sporting style emerged after 1820, what we recognize as the "modern" sporting style. Like the influential health-reform movement, this style was the product of a distinctive segment of the antebellum population. For the most part, these people were neither the very rich nor the very poor; they were "middling" citizens who lived and worked in urbanizing areas and whose gradually emerging awareness of their shared interests and experiences underlay a class consciousness. They were men and women who saw traditional relations, roles, and identities unsettled by the physical and social experiences of urban life and work. Most had some education or training, and they desired to improve themselves and their stations in life. They knew competition; they counted successes and failures; they made rules to live by and expected others to carry out their special responsibilities to enforce laws and discipline. They also rejected traditional sports as brutal, wasteful, and even destructive.

The sporting style they constructed differed from the traditional one in a number of ways. Believing that time rather than tasks determined the rhythms of their lives, they both distinguished leisure from work time and assigned many sports and exercises to leisure. They also moved to impose time limits on some sports, either by directly linking the "end" of a performance to some span of time or by limiting and making more predictable the time an event might consume. At mid-century innings in base ball served this purpose, and after 1870 clocks defined the boundaries of many modern sports. Simultaneously, the tasks of work transferred to modern sports less frequently than was the case with traditional practices. Especially in games and other athletic contests, no one claimed that the central physical acts— batting, throwing, running distances, or jumping hurdles—drew from people's work. Indeed, middling urbanites came to view leisure sports as practices that compensated for experiences that they did not have at work and redressed conditions from which work and urban living more generally detracted. The makers of the modern sporting style also tended to form clubs and other associations with people whose interests and values were similar, and they intended these virtual communities to take the place of older, more organic communities.

At the core of these emerging subcommunities and the modern sporting style were distinctive practices that we today would recognize as "sports." They were, and are, practices such as harness racing, baseball, track and field, and many others, which share a number of characteristics. In contrast to traditional sports, modern forms are geographically widespread, and they have standard, formal rules that both convene and end contests and define the behaviors in which players can and cannot engage. On-field participants invariably have specialized roles, as do coaches, managers, and owners, and individuals and teams compete in or on sport-specific facilities such as diamonds and gymnasia, where they employ preplanned strategies for winning. Athletes' performances are often described numerically, which facilitates recordkeeping, and both the press and the institutions that claim individuals and teams as their representatives revel in the breaking of records and attribute symbolic significance to athletes' performances. Finally, complex organizations govern the sports and the performers, and as do fans, bureaucrats often rationalize and justify ordinarily irrational behaviors.

Harness Racing

It is probably not coincidental that what one historian has called the first modern sport, harness racing (or trotting), was a horse sport. Equine contests, including those involving horses harnessed to carts, had long been visible and meaningful as popular culture forms in the eastern United States, and they remained so even in urbanizing areas after 1820. Many people continued to rely on horses for personal and business use; in fact, the post-1820 expansion of people and of markets and marketable goods probably underlay interests in and opportunities for harness racing. The horses used in such races, which were initially impromptu, were also relatively inexpensive and of mixed breeds. All a race took were willing competitors and a street or lane, of which eastern urban areas had plenty.

At least in the one city where historians have reconstructed its history, New York City, early nineteenth-century harness racing owed much to the traditions and the traditionalness of another horse sport, thoroughbred racing. By 1806 harness racers were contesting on a thoroughbred track in Harlem, and twelve years later some aspects of a prearranged event resembled things that had occurred in thoroughbred racing for decades. The event was structured as a match race (between two horses), and the purse was really the wager. Slightly less than two decades later, the first known club, the New York Trotting Club, reproduced the local, traditional structures of thoroughbred racing. Its members even acted on behalf of their sport as jockey club members had for nearly a century. They regularized harness races on a biannual basis. They built a special harness track on Long Island. They promoted their sport on customary thoroughbred grounds, arguing that racing improved the breed.

During the 1830s and 1840s, however, the proponents of harness racing moved to modernize the sport in ways thoroughbred supporters never had. Subsequently, the histories of the two sports diverged in many ways. Eastern thoroughbred racing remained in the hands of relatively wealthy men, and its public visibility peaked in the mid-1840s. Harness racing, on the other hand, began and remained a sport of and for ordinary people, at least through the 1860s. The horses remained relatively inexpensive, fifty to one hundred dollars apiece compared to several thousands or more for thoroughbreds, and many working people were able to acquire and train horses for harness races. Moreover, harness racing benefited from both the acts on behalf of and the rhetoric of "democracy," which was the byword of Jacksonian America. Improvements to roads, for example, encouraged more people to travel by wagons, carts, and stages rather than individually on horseback; these travelers became spectators at, if not participants in, harness races. Urban newspapers and magazines supported and encouraged the races, as did the owners of racetracks, who fairly quickly saw harness races as more than fillers or substitute events for thoroughbred races.

By the late 1830s and early 1840s these conditions enabled, and probably encouraged, horse and track owners, spectators, and the press to hasten the modernizing and commercializing of harness racing. The format change to standard, mile-long heats was pivotal; shorter races, even ones with multiple heats, meant not only more events on a given schedule but also the potential for more races by and longer careers for horses. Buoyed by a willing, spectating public, track owners began to offer frequent, even weekly, trotting contests. Relatively small purses ($10–$250) characterized most of these races, but they did not deter horse owners from entering in part because they were running relatively inexpensive horses and running them more often. Some of these owners were also emerging as professional drivers, recognized for their skills, their commitments to racing, and their interests in winning. Budding capitalists, track and horse owners alike operated on small but sustainable profit margins—and the sport benefited.

By mid-century harness racing had eclipsed thoroughbred racing as a spectator sport in the New York area. There were simply many more races, betting fans, and press coverage of races locally and in other places across the nation. However, controversies were brewing. Charges of fixed races proliferated, and race fans occasionally took the side of either the accuser or the accused drivers. Of particular concern to some race people was the practice of "hippodroming," or the arranging and running of a race so that the principals could divide the gate receipts between them. Hippodroming may have affected the competitiveness in given contests, but it apparently did not unduly complicate betting or diminish spectator interest. Indeed, it probably insured that horses and drives renowned for their skills and capable of drawing crowds could find willing competitors, since the gate rather than a purse became the financial goal.

Race fixing persisted beyond mid-century and became more problematic after the Civil War, when harness races expanded numerically and geographically. Absent any other means of resolving the issue, the Narragansett Trotting Association in Rhode Island organized a meeting of track people in 1869. The result was the creation of a national governing body for harness racing, the National Trotting Association (NTA), whose members claimed responsibilities not only for writing rules to regulate the sport and horse and track owners but also for punishing people who broke the rules. It also functioned, and probably more effectively so, as a coordinating body and clearinghouse for local trotting associations.

The National Trotting Association was a significant step in the emergence of modern harness racing, particularly insofar as it claimed some power over and provided some services to local groups. It clearly stood as a third level of organization, above the clubs and the regional racing associations, and thus extended the practice of hierarchical governance, which traditional sports had never had. But the NTA was not the only thing that signified the modernness of harness racing in the 1860s and 1870s. The breeding of racehorses had become a rationalized, quasi-scientific process, and specialized breeding farms had emerged as more and more men of wealth entered the game. Their presence also ensured a modern division of labor, since they were increasingly less likely to drive their own rigs. The owners hired professional jockeys, and the jockeys trained for their craft and their tasks and received salaries. The transformation of harness racing was nearly complete.

Base Ball to Baseball

The making of another modern sport occurred in the antebellum period: baseball. Like harness racing, it was the product of urban middling people, and it owed much to traditional English and American ball games. Its critical structures were clubs, whose members made the rules, arranged games with other clubs, and even served as umpires. They also rapidly transformed the game from being a means to the ends of socializing and exercising to being an end in itself and, eventually, a business enterprise. And all of this and more occurred in about a quarter century, or the span of a single generation.

The precise origins of baseball remain shrouded in mystery. The only thing that is clear is that the man of the great myth, Abner Doubleday, did not devise the game. Baseball was likely an adaptation of traditional games played with bases, balls, and bats. Youths had played "base," "old-cat" games, stoolball, and rounders since the days of the Stuarts in England and during the eighteenth century in the United States. Of these games, historians generally agree that English rounders most directly bore on American baseball. Its name probably derived from the practice of "rounding" the bases (four of them) after a "striker" (batter) hit a ball thrown (or "bowled" underarm as in cricket) by the "feeder" (pitcher). Strikers were "out" when they swung and missed three feeds, hit a ball to the field that was caught before it bounced twice, or were hit by a ball while they ran the bases.

In the East during the 1820s and 1830s, young men and boys played locally specific versions of base ball, including one known as "town ball." New England villagers, Philadelphians, and New Yorkers had distinctive contests that they played irregularly, with various numbers of participants and varying numbers of bases arrayed in squares, diamonds, or even haphazardly. The collections of players were known as "fraternities," whose members had shared experiences, values, and expectations for years. Ball playing had been and remained one of those shared, binding experiences.

The making of modern baseball began in New York City at some point between 1842 and 1845 as one of these base-ball fraternities organized itself more formally as a club. In doing so, its members again drew on tradition, for clubs had existed in the region for more than a century. They were organizations of like-minded men, especially upper-rank men who shared economic, political, and social interests, including sports. However, the members of this base-ball club, the Knickerbocker Base Ball Club of New York, were professionals, managers, merchants, and other middling citizens. Consequently, to account for the precise timing of the Knickerbockers' appearance, we need to look beyond the traditions of ball games and fraternities to what was happening in contemporary New York. The city was undergoing dynamic changes that clearly affected the base-ball fraternity and probably encouraged the emergence of the Knickerbockers. The population was growing rapidly, many men worked away from their homes and neighborhoods, and both factors disrupted traditional relationships and ways of life. Club membership could redress some of the unsettlement people experienced because it afforded them opportunities for face-to-face relationships and experiences once common in traditional communities. Clubs were small communities, or subcommunities, of like-minded men who shared interests. Not coincidentally as well, clubs also separated their members from other urbanites, some of whom were also forming clubs of one kind or another. In the context of the larger picture, then, the Knickerbocker Base Ball Club simultaneously united its members and divided them from others. It thus figured in the reorganization of social relations and society in mid-century New York City.

The subcommunity that was the Knickerbocker Club resembled a medieval guild in both structure and function. A written constitution governed the affairs of the club, outsiders could only become members through election, and penalties awaited Knickerbockers who violated club rules. Members also provided themselves with a range of entertainments, including dinners and dances, and they undoubtedly had many opportunities to talk about business and politics. They were committed, as well, to playing base ball, and they constructed the version that first became known as the New York game and then as American baseball.

By 1845 the Knickerbockers had formalized and codified their preferred rules, in keeping with their interest in improvement and their faith in the value of regulated activity. Apparently written by Alexander Cartwright, who was then a clerk but later a partner in a book and stationary shop, the Knickerbocker code of rules combined elements from the British game of rounders with practices generated by members. From the British game, they borrowed the shape of the field: four bases arrayed in a diamond surrounded by open space. The areas that lay behind the lines from home to third and home to first they designated as foul territory, which was a departure from the rounders' field plan. They also defined the distances between bases (90 feet) and between the pitcher's area and home (45 feet) with a mathematical precision possibly drawn from their workplaces; businesses were increasingly dependent on quantifiable measures. To play, the club members probably either divided themselves into two groups or chose sides, with one to bat and the other to take the field. The pitcher had to throw underarm, and a batter's turn lasted until he hit a ball or swung and missed three pitches. "Outs" also occurred when a fielder tagged a runner between bases, received a ball and stepped on a base before a runner arrived there, or caught a hit ball on the fly or before it bounced twice (as in rounders). In another departure from rounders' practices, the Knickerbockers ended one unit's turn at bat after three outs and a contest after one side had scored twenty-one runs, or "aces" (from cricket). Both sets of limits likely made the length of a game more predictable or at least short enough to fit within the time the men could take from their work.

There is little evidence to suggest that the Knickerbockers intended to promote their game or to seek competitors before 1850. In fact, they played primarily among themselves, first on a lot in Manhattan and then on a section of the Elysian Fields rented from John Cox Stevens. Apparently only once did they compete against another club, the short-lived New York Club. However, as the Knickerbockers played, other base-ball fraternities likely observed them, and some of these fraternities organized their own clubs and adopted Knickerbocker rules after 1851. Written as it was, the Knickerbocker base-ball code was accessible and made possible a standard way of playing, which traditional sporting conventions transmitted by word of mouth rarely had. By 1855 base-ball clubs and interclub play existed throughout the city and in northern New Jersey, and the Knickerbocker game had become the New York game.

It also moved some distance toward becoming an American game, even though other versions of base ball persisted in some areas. Owing to newspaper accounts and travels by people such as Cartwright, New York base ball made its way to

The Knickerbocker Rules for Early Baseball

The only known original of the Knickerbocker Rules exists in the Baseball Hall of Fame in Cooperstown, New York. Below are the twenty rules written out by Alexander Cartwright:

1st. Members must strictly observe the time agreed upon for exercise, and be punctual in their attendance.

2nd. When assembled for exercise, the President, of in his absence, the Vice-President, shall appoint an Umpire, who shall keep the game in a book provided for that purpose, and note all violations of the By-Laws and Rules during the time of exercise.

3rd. The presiding officer shall designate two members as Captains, who shall retire and make the match to be played, observing at the same time that the player's opposite to each other should be as nearly equal as possible, the choice of sides to be then tossed for, and the first in hand to be decided in like manner.

4th. The bases shall be from "home" to second base, forty-two paces; from first to third base, forty-two paces, equidistant.

5th. No stump match shall be played on a regular day of exercise.

6th. If there should not be a sufficient number of members of the Club present at the time agreed upon to commence exercise, gentlemen not members may be chosen in to make up the match, which shall not be broken up to take in members that may afterwards appear; but in all cases, members shall have the preference, when present, at the making of the match.

7th. If members appear after the game is commenced, they may be chosen in if mutually agreed upon.

8th. The game to consist of twenty-one counts, or aces; but at the conclusion an equal number of hands must be played.

9th. The ball must be pitched, not thrown, for the bat.

10th. A ball knocked out of the field, or outside the range of the first and third base, is foul.

11th. Three balls being struck at and missed and the last one caught, is a hand-out; if not caught is considered fair, and the striker bound to run.

12th. If a ball be struck, or tipped, and caught, either flying or on the first bound, it is a hand out.

13th. A player running the bases shall be out, if the ball is in the hands of an adversary on the base, or the runner is touched with it before he makes his base; it being understood, however, that in no instance is a ball to be thrown at him.

14th. A player running who shall prevent an adversary from catching or getting the ball before making his base, is a hand out.

15th. Three hands out, all out.

16th. Players must take their strike in regular turn.

17th. All disputes and differences relative to the game, to be decided by the Umpire, from which there is no appeal.

18th. No ace or base can be made on a foul strike.

19th. A runner cannot be put out in making one base, when a balk is made on the pitcher.

20th. But one base allowed when a ball bounds out of the field when struck.

Baltimore, Cleveland, St. Louis, and San Francisco and even to army posts on the Great Plains in the latter half of the 1850s. Base ball also gained acclaim outside the baseball fraternity. Its proponents included people such as Thomas Wentworth Higginson who wrote for popular magazines and were concerned about the ill effects of urban life and living. The New York game, they maintained, was relatively inexpensive and thus available for many people, and it provided the kind of healthy, outdoor exercise that Higginson and his contemporaries in the health-reform movement had been urging urbanites to pursue. In subsequent years, both of these claims—for baseball's democratic and health-rendering potentials—would become key elements in its modern ideology.

Significantly as well, New York base ball gained the interest and support of the press, especially the newspapers. Reporters covered games between clubs and described the action on the field, as well as the social affairs that followed. A few journalists also actively courted base-ball clubs, shaped public perceptions of the game, and contributed to the making of the modern sport. On the New York scene the most influential of these journalists was Henry Chadwick, an English-born reporter who came to be known as the "father" of baseball. Chadwick, who wrote for the *Brooklyn Eagle* and the *New York Clipper*, authored many early guidebooks to the sport and devised box scores to report performance results. Box scores enabled the reading public to follow games more easily, and they encouraged the modern practice of keeping and breaking records. So did another of Chadwick's innovations: the batting average.

From early on, then, the press and baseball clubs forged an alliance that served both parties well over time. The clubs gained visibility; their sport, popular recognition; the papers, a subject that interested readers. Actually, "intrigued" readers might be a more apt term, especially after 1855 in the New York area where much was happening. Clubs proliferated, and games expanded both numerically and geographically. Some of the contests were also exciting. There were high-scoring affairs—42-37 and 51-6, for example—and rivalries developing between clubs. Discussions and debates about rules emerged, as did highly skilled players, position specialization, and even an "all star" series between the best players from New York City and their counterparts from Brooklyn (then an independent city) in 1858. Spectators, including gamblers, turned out in droves for the games and paid the hefty sum of fifty cents admission.

A kind of creative tension characterized base ball in the New York City area in the latter half of the 1850s. In part this owed to the appearance of new clubs, only some of which pursued the game as the fraternity had in the 1840s, as a means to the end of socializing. Other clubs emerged from distinct neighborhoods and workplaces. The Eckfords, for example, organized at the Eckford shipyards in Brooklyn, and the New York Mutuals from among the firemen of the Mutual Hook and Ladder Company No. 1. The members of these clubs continued to value the entertainments and conviviality that the base-ball fraternity had long held dear, but they also stressed competition—and winning. As Warren Goldstein (1989) has made clear, players from the ranks of clerks, craftsmen, and skilled laborers brought to the field of play practices and expectations meaningful in their work; they emphasized individual skill, unit cooperation, and "craft excellence." Even as they enjoyed themselves, members of the occupation-based clubs intended to improve themselves and to gain an edge over the competition. To gain that edge, some individuals and clubs practiced, albeit in scrimmages rather than with scientific training regimens, before work, at noon, and after work. Practice improved players' physical skills and, when combined with another carryover from work, specialization, enabled an individual to become quite good at playing a position and the game. Practice also showed on the field in victories over rivals. A few clubs even began to seek out skilled players to join them, and recruiting emerged.

Recruiting was apparently not widespread, let alone universal, but it was controversial. It subverted customary methods of club organization and membership, and the clubs had no system for addressing the practice. Thus recruiting was one of the issues that encouraged the Knickerbockers to call representatives from some New York clubs to a series of meetings in 1857 and 1858. The representatives discussed other issues as well: the length of games, what umpires could do about batters who refused to swing at good pitches, the Knickerbockers' own "fly rule," and the rights of junior clubs, or those whose members were under twenty-one. All five practices revealed and contributed to the tension between the social clubs and their more competitively inclined contemporaries. The latter two issues also implicated a question of considerable importance to the base-ball fraternity because it bore on the social identities of the game and its players. Was base ball to remain associated with children and child's play, or was it to be appropriate for adults and conducive to the development of "manly" qualities?

Resolutions to these issues emerged between 1858 and 1863, once the club representatives who attended the Knickerbocker-convened meetings formalized their relationship as a confederation and assumed power over rules and clubs. As was the case in harness racing, the confederation claimed to be a national association, the National Association of Base Ball Players (NABBP), although clubs outside of New York did not join until 1859. Like the NTA as well, the NABBP claimed to represent and to regulate the clubs; it thus introduced hierarchical governance to base ball. It remained on top—writing rules, devising and imposing penalties upon offenders, and promoting the game—until 1871, when yet another set of tensions divided the base-ball world.

The NABBP did resolve the issues it had initially faced, although perhaps only the advocates of competition judged the resolutions as adequate solutions. Club representatives decided that players had to remain bona fide club members, although they also had to be members for only a month before any given contest. Subsequently, they forbade clubs from paying players and enrolling paid players. The NABBP also determined that a game should conclude at the end of nine innings, rather than after a squad had scored twenty-one aces. The change virtually ensured that games would have ends, as competitors desired but had not always realized with the twenty-one-ace format. Moreover, closure would come before nightfall, which likely pleased spectators and players alike. The NABBP then solved the problem of batters not swinging at good pitches with a nontraditional construction: the "called" strike, which became the responsibility of umpires. It also begrudgingly accorded junior clubs the right to join the association but denied them voting rights. Apparently men who wished to distance their game from the pastimes of children did not realize that some people under twenty-one could play the game nearly as well as, and occasionally better than, those who were older.

The longest running debate within the ranks of the NABBP involved the fly rule, which addressed how a fielder put out a batter who had hit a ball. Proponents of the fly rule, beginning with the Knickerbockers, argued that catching a hit ball "on the fly" required more skill than did the traditional method of catching it after it bounced. Such a practice was thus more "manly" and could further distance the game from child's play. Opponents, however, associated the proposed rule change with the emphasis on competition, which they were resisting. In their view, maintaining the traditional out-after-one-bounce rule helped to ensure that the social traditions of the clubs—and the game as a social affair rather than a serious contest—persisted. Not surprisingly, perhaps, the opponents generally came from the social clubs, while those who proposed to substitute the fly rule for the one-bounce rule belonged primarily to the newer neighborhood and occupationally based clubs. The Knickerbockers, of course, were an important exception to this pattern, but they had always had a distinctive history within the history of New York base ball.

The struggle over the fly rule within the NABBP lasted until 1863, when enough members voted to adopt the rule as a part of a larger movement to advantage offenses and make games more exciting. By then as well, other things had tipped the scales in favor of competitive clubs that worked as units of physically skilled, strategically astute men to win hotly contested matches rather than "playing at" some children's game. Grounded in the "improvement" aims of Republican ideology and in capitalist economic goals and relations, contesting with and gaining an edge over others were experiences that many Americans expected by the 1850s and 1860s. The competitive interests and relations that had come to dominate in base ball thus differed little, if at all, from what one saw in politics, business, and, of course, the most dramatic and traumatic event of the period—the War Between the States. Moreover, aided by improvements in transportation and communication, members of competitive ball clubs were able to present their approach to the game to many more people. Visibility, renown, and even a degree of commercial stability and viability resulted. The days of professional base ball were almost on the horizon.

SUMMARY

The 250 years covered in this chapter witnessed important transformations in the history of the United States. The land itself originally belonged to Native Americans, who were gradually displaced once British trading companies set up outposts in the Chesapeake and New England, and as other European nations sent their own migrants to other sections of the "New World." The British outposts became colonies, and after about 170 years, the colonies became states in a new nation, which expanded in virtually every conceivable way until 1860.

Recounting the sporting experiences of colonists-become-citizens helps us to flesh out this compacted account. When the British laborers arrived to establish outposts, they brought with them sports common and longstanding in Britain, intricately tied up in erratic work rhythms and traditional festivals. Hunting certainly served multiple purposes, and the many gambling games, including bowling in the streets, might produce a few shillings for one player and certainly status among people for whom the important relations were made face to face. The harshness of life in the "wilderness," however, along with the arrival of reformist Protestant-led bands of colonists seeking to establish freeholds gradually resulted in more adaptations and some limits, at least through the 1670s.

Thereafter, traditional but adapted sports re-emerged as central practices in a rank-divided and geographically and demographically expanded society. Among men and women of significant wealth, sports such as thoroughbred racing, water sports, and field sports, along with dancing and gambling games, served as badges of rank and status. Yet, few, if any of these practices lost their ties to things that were important in ordinary life. For many planters, agriculture remained the primary economic activity, and horses and field sports remained necessary to improving agricultural output, to travel, to food stocks. Though fancier and more formalized and fashionable, in short, gentry sports remained traditional at their core. Absent the fancy and fashion, the same statement applied to ordinary people, whose sports, though more numerous and varied in form, remained tied to the "stuff of life."

For the colonists, the 1780s was a crucial decade. A peace treaty (1783) secured the independence gained from the defeat of British forces in the Revolutionary War, and a new constitution defined a national government (1789). Yet, the course of ordinary life, including sports, did not change as dramatically for many citizens as it would after the 1820s. In fact, as some easterners moved westward, as Latinos from Mexico moved north, and as immigrants from abroad moved into eastern cities, they maintained popular traditional practices. This was particularly evident in places where agriculture remained the core economic pursuit, as well as where relatively poor laborers struggled against competitors and capitalists. Hence, both rural America and the urban America of laborers provided fertile ground for traditional practices as late as, and in some cases, well beyond the middle of the nineteenth century. Horse races, fistfights, charreria, and field sports persisted and, in some places, became spectacles.

A new sporting style had rooted, unseen, in the 1780s, however. Enlightenment thought that had informed Republican ideology and the subsequent practical ideology of "improvement," coupled with the transition to a capitalist economy, underlay an emergent modern sporting style, characterized by rationalization, specialization, and the separation of sport (and leisure) from work, among other things. After the 1820s especially, health reformers provided one of the rationales for modern athletic sports, health. Other contemporaries from the urban middle class defined new rules for competing, established organizations (clubs, and eventually associations of clubs), and produced specialized equipment and facilities and thus drew new, modern sports—harness racing and base ball—from older forms. After the Civil War, these forms would become the dominant forms in the United States, and subsequent alterations in other sports would reveal similar characteristics.

RECOMMENDED RESOURCES

Print Sources

Adelman, Melvin L. 1981. The first modern sport in America: Harness racing in New York City, 1825–1870. *Journal of Sport History* 8 (Spring): 5–32.

———. 1986. *A sporting time: New York City and the rise of modern athletics, 1820–1870.* Urbana: University of Illinois Press.

Beverley, Robert. 1705. *The history and present state of Virginia*. Ed. Louis B. Wright. Chapel Hill: University of North Carolina Press, 1947.

Bradford, William. 1952. *Of Plymouth Plantation 1620–1647*. Ed. Samuel E. Morison. New York: Knopf.

Cott, Nancy F., ed. 1972. *Root of bitterness: Documents of the social history of American women*. New York: Dutton.

Dizikes, John. 1981. *Sportsmen and gamesmen*. New York: Houghton Mifflin.

Eisenberg, John. 2006. *The Great Match Race: When North met South in America's first sports spectacle*. New York: Houghton Mifflin.

Fabian, Ann. 1990. *Card sharps, dream books, and bucket shops: Gambling in nineteenth-century America*. Ithaca, NY: Cornell University Press.

"The Great Foot Race." 1835. *American Turf Register and Sporting Magazine* 6 (June): 518–20.

Green, Harvey. 1986. *Fit for America: Health, fitness, sport and American society*. New York: Pantheon Books.

Goldstein, Warren. 1989. *Playing for keeps: A history of early baseball*. Ithaca, NY: Cornell University Press.

Gorn, Elliott J. 1985. "Gouge and bite, pull hair and scratch": The social significance of fighting in the southern backcountry. *American Historical Review* 90 (February): 18–43.

———. 1986. *The manly art: Bare-knuckle prize fighting in America*. Ithaca, NY: Cornell University Press.

Guttmann, Allen. 1978. *From ritual to record: The nature of modern sports*. New York: Columbia University Press.

Hamilton, Alexander. 1948. *Gentleman's progress: The itinerarium of Dr. Alexander Hamilton, 1744*. Ed. Carl Bridenbaugh. Chapel Hill: University of North Carolina Press.

Kirsch, George B. 1989. *The creation of American team sports: Baseball and cricket, 1838–72*. Urbana: University of Illinois Press.

Lawson, John. 1709. *A new voyage to Carolina*. Ed. Hugh T. Lefler. Chapel Hill: University of North Carolina Press, 1967.

Morton, Thomas. 1632. New English Canaan. In *Tracts and Other Papers Relating Principally to the Origin, Settlement, and Progress of the Colonies in North America*, ed. Peter Force. 4 vols. Reprint. Gloucester, MA: Peter Smith, 1963.

Porter, William T. "Fatal Prize Fight Between Lilly and McCoy for $200 a Side at Hastings, N.Y." *Spirit of the Times*, September 17, 1842.

Ritchie, Andrew. 1975. *King of the road*. London: Wildwood House.

Seymour, Harold. 1960. *Baseball: The early years*. New York: Oxford University Press.

Smith, John. 1986. *The Complete Works of Captain John Smith*. Ed. Philip L. Barbour. 3 vols. Chapel Hill: University of North Carolina Press.

Strachey, William. 1612. *The Historie of Travell into Virginia Britainia*. Ed. Louis B. Wright and Virginia Freund. Nendeln, Liechtenstein: Kraus Reprint, 1967.

Struna, Nancy L. 1996. *People of prowess: Sport, leisure, and labor in early Anglo-America*. Urbana: University of Illinois Press.

———. 1993. Sport and the awareness of leisure. In *Of consuming interests: The style of life in the eighteenth century*, ed. Ronald Hoffman, Cary Carson, and Peter Albert. Charlottesville: University Press of Virginia.

Todd, Jan. 1998. *Physical culture and body beautiful: Purposive exercise in the lives of American women*. Macon, GA: Mercer University Press.

Verbrugge, Martha . 1988. *Able-bodied womanhood: Personal health and social change in nineteenth-century Boston*. New York: Oxford University Press.

Young, Alexander, ed. 1844. *Chronicles of the Pilgrim Fathers of the Colony of Plymouth, from 1602 to 1625*. Boston: C. C. Little and J. Brown.

Museums and Libraries

Colonial Williamsburg
The Colonial Williamsburg Foundation
P.O. Box 1776
Williamsburg, VA 23187-1776
(757)229-1000
http://www.colonialwilliamsburg.com
Restored eighteenth-century town site, based on years as provincial capital, with walking tours and extensive research facilities.

Harness Racing Museum
P.O. Box 590
240 Main Street
Goshen, NY 10924
(845)294-6330
http://www.harnessmuseum.com
Extensive historical collections of fine art, photographs, material culture, and books and
    other print materials.

National Agricultural Library
Abraham Lincoln Building
10301 Baltimore Avenue
Beltsville, MD 20705
http://www.nal.usda.gov
More than 3.5 million items, including rare books, manuscripts, and photographs, about
    agriculture, from the 1500s to the present; includes agriculture-related sports.

The National Baseball Hall of Fame and Museum
25 Main Street
Cooperstown, NY 13326
(607)547-7200
http://web.baseballhall.org
Extensive book and manuscript collections and other print materials, photographs and films,
    newspapers and periodicals, material culture; recommend appointments prior to
    research.

The National Sporting Library
102 The Plains Road
P.O. Box 1335
Middleburg, VA 20118-1335
(540)687-6542
http://www.nsl.org/
Research library with more than 16,000 books, manuscript collections, scrapbooks, photo-
    graphs, and historical periodicals about horse and field sports.

Old Sturbridge Village
1 Old Sturbridge Village Road
Sturbridge, MA 01566
(508)347-3362
http://www.osv.org
Reproduction of a New England village, 1790-1840, with a focus on everyday life and
    extensive research collections.

Shelburne Museum
P.O. Box 10
Shelburne, VT 05482
(802)985-3346
http://www.shelburnemuseum.org
Over 150,000 works of art, artifacts, and Americana, seventeenth–twentieth centuries dis-
    played in a walking village setting.

CHAPTER 2

AMERICAN SPORTS, 1861–1889

Gerald R. Gems

OVERVIEW

The Civil War devastated American society. All previous wars had been fought against foreign nations, but the Civil War pitted American citizens against each other, ravaged the South, and cost more than 620,000 lives from 1861 to 1865. Regional differences between the North and the South were apparent long before hostilities erupted into open warfare. The North engaged in a commercial and industrial economy, while the South was largely agricultural, with large plantations dependent upon slave labor. As the United States expanded westward throughout the nineteenth century new states entered the union, upsetting the political balance between free and slave states. Abolitionist societies, in which many women took a prominent part, advocated an end to slavery as an inhuman and immoral institution. The new Republican Party pronounced its opposition to the spread of slavery and when its candidate, Abraham Lincoln, won the presidential election of 1860, the southern states seceded to form their own country. The Southerners felt that the individual states had the right to run their own affairs; while the federal government viewed the Southerners' actions as a rebellion. Both sides marshaled their forces to impose their will on their enemies.

New technologies introduced ironclad battleships, submarines, and machine guns to the conflict with a horrendous loss of life. In 1863 President Lincoln issued the Emancipation Proclamation, which legally freed the African Americans from bondage in the rebel states. A year later the overwhelming manpower and resources of the North finally forced the South into submission. Lincoln, however, did not live to repair the damaged nation. John Wilkes Booth, a southern sympathizer, assassinated the president with a gunshot to the head as he watched a play in Washington, D.C., on April 14, 1865.

The years following the Civil War were known as the Reconstruction era, aimed at rebuilding the South and the torn nation. Among the major political and social issues were the place of the newly freed slaves in the society and the punishments meted out to the southern political and military leaders. Vice President Andrew

Johnson succeeded Lincoln as president; but his inability to reach a consensus with the Congress resulted in an impeachment, which he survived by only one vote. The Fourteenth Amendment to the Constitution, ratified in 1868, provided the former slaves with citizenship, and the Fifteenth Amendment, which became law in 1870, gave them voting rights. Several African Americans soon assumed political offices at the state and federal levels. They were joined by opportunists known as scalawags (Southerners) and carpetbaggers (Northerners who took up residence in the South), who gained official positions because the former rebels were deemed to be disloyal and unfit for leadership.

Ulysses Grant, the general who had led the northern forces to victory, served as president from 1869 to 1877. Although he was not personally dishonest, his terms were wracked by corruption as politicians and their friends enriched themselves at public expense. At the local levels political bosses ruled over entire cities, freely employing patronage and gaining power. The most notable, the Tammany Hall group, controlled New York City and much of the state. In 1881, shortly after James A. Garfield assumed the presidency, he was assassinated by a disappointed office seeker.

The Democrats and Republicans had conspired to resolve the disputed presidential election of 1876. The Democratic candidate, Samuel Tilden, won the popular vote, but was one vote shy of the necessary Electoral College requirements. The Republicans negotiated with the southern Democrats to deliver enough votes to their candidate, Rutherford Hayes, to gain the presidency. In return the Republicans agreed to remove federal troops from the South and allow the whites to regain control of political offices. The Republicans' abandonment of the blacks resulted in a virtual return to subservient conditions. Whites disenfranchised black voters by introducing literacy tests and property requirements, and through coercion. The Ku Klux Klan, a clandestine white vigilante group organized in 1866, reinforced white dominance by threats, beatings, and lynchings. Legal prohibitions, later known as Jim Crow laws, reinforced the segregation of the races. White landowners introduced the sharecropping system, which provided a small plot of land to the freedmen in return for a percentage of their crops as rent. The black farmers barely subsisted and the white overlords no longer provided the food, clothing, and housing given to the slaves, assuring that the African Americans would remain mired in poverty and dependence.

In 1881 Booker T. Washington opened the Tuskegee Institute, a vocational school for blacks in Alabama. The education provided students with industrial skills, but an unequal role in the American society, as they were relegated to workers rather than owners. Washington's compliance with segregationist attitudes and his willingness to accept a diminished social status for blacks earned him favor with whites, who acknowledged him as the leader of his people.

The Gilded Age

While African Americans languished in the economy, white entrepreneurs enjoyed fabulous wealth. The two decades following the Civil War were known as the Gilded Age, due to the enormous fortunes accumulated by ruthless capitalists known as "robber barons." Capitalism ran rampant during the era and materialism prevailed, as commercial rivals sought to capture or destroy competitors. Rivalries extended to the cities as businessmen competed for trade. In Cincinnati business-men hired the first fully professional baseball team in 1869 for a national tour to generate publicity. Chicago followed with its own pro team a year later. Despite a severe economic depression in 1873, several bankers, financiers, and industrialists flourished. Albert Spalding became a millionaire by forging a sporting goods com-pany that offered diverse products, sponsorships, enticements to athletes, and mar-keting strategies. Jay Gould's stock-market schemes, the consolidation of shipping and railroad lines by Cornelius Vanderbilt, the monopolization of the oil industry by John D. Rockefeller, and Andrew Carnegie's control of the steel industry pro-duced immense affluence long before the Sixteenth Amendment imposed an income tax in 1913.

The continual westward expansion of the country provided opportunities, chal-lenges, and afflictions. The Homestead Act of 1862 granted 160 acres of land to anyone willing to establish a permanent home. The legislation aimed at settling the western frontier; but much of the acreage had been granted to the railroad companies who built tracks across the continent (40,000 miles between 1865 and 1875). The Union and Pacific railways met in Utah in 1869, effectively joining the east and west. The discovery of gold and silver in the western territories brought fortune seekers from around the world, and all of the newcomers encroached on the lands of the Native American indigenous tribes. Despite repeated promises and treaties, the federal government ultimately safeguarded the intruders with federal troops. Such confrontations led to an ignominious defeat at the Battle of Little Big Horn, when Gen. George Custer and 265 soldiers met their deaths in Montana. Thereafter the Native American tribes were systematically hunted down, forced to reservations, and subjected to assimilation.

In 1879 the federal government founded the Carlisle Indian School in Pennsyl-vania, the first of many residential boarding institutes that took Native American children from their families and taught them to absorb white standards, values, and styles of dress. Students were required to speak English, cut their long hair, and learn vocational skills for the industrial economy. Sports became a primary means to inculcate the desired values and Carlisle produced one of the top football teams in the country by the turn of the century, as well as its most famous athlete, Jim Thorpe, who played professional baseball, football, and won two gold medals in the 1912 Olympics.

In addition to the Native American presence, the nativists (white Anglo-Saxon Protestants who considered themselves the founders of the country) faced the per-ceived threat of millions of foreign immigrants who sought a better life in the United States. Nonwhites, such as the Chinese, were excluded from immigration in 1882. Many others, primarily Europeans, settled as farmers in the Midwest. Saddled by exorbitant railroad rates, the farmers banned together in cooperative organizations known as "granges" in an attempt to circumvent the railways, mer-chants, and bankers that limited their profit. Other immigrants (10 million between 1865 and 1890) flooded the American cities in search of jobs.

Often living squalid lives in slums and tenements, workers began to form unions to better their lives. This banding together allowed employees to take collective action against employers. By acting together to confront a boss it was less likely that all would be fired from their jobs. With no minimum wage, employees worked six days per week, ten to twelve hours per day, and had no benefits if they were sick or injured. Children worked alongside adults in the factories, and immigrant families counted on their offspring as contributors to family welfare. Workers formed the Knights of Labor in 1869 and began taking collective actions to gain better wages and working conditions. In 1877 workers organized a national railroad strike that erupted in violence and millions of dollars in property damage. Employers reacted to labor conflicts by locking out workers and hiring the unemployed ("scab" laborers) to replace them. Such confrontations led to the Haymarket Massacre in Chicago in 1886 when police marched on a crowd of workers. A dynamite bomb, thrown by an unknown person, killed a policeman. The police retaliated with indiscriminate gunfire that killed numerous others. The resultant trial accused eight labor leaders of inciting the riot. Despite an international clemency movement and a faulty trial, four were hung and one was found dead in his jail cell. The others went to prison.

Armed conflicts between employers and employees continued for another half century; but employers devised other means to control their laborers' lives. In 1882 George Pullman, manufacturer of railroad sleeping cars, built a company town outside Chicago complete with an array of athletic facilities to keep the workers busy during their leisure time. The company teams and athletic spectacles brought much publicity to the Pullman enterprise, but when the owner cut wages and maintained rents during a depression in 1893, the seemingly content employees initiated a strike that required federal intervention.

In the 1880s social reformers attempted to address the economic, social, and political problems confronting the American society. The economic flows of the capitalist system created periodic recessions, usually in twenty-year cycles, and the depression of 1873, the worst in the United States up to that time, created widespread unemployment and misery. By 1875 half a million workers had lost their jobs and many farmers went bankrupt. The unscrupulous actions of politicians and the "robber barons" contributed to the despair. By the 1880s groups of middle-class moral reformers, known as Progressives, sought to rectify the problems by bringing greater order and efficiency to city governments, supplanting the greed and corruption with charity, and acculturating the immigrants in order to produce better American citizens. Jane Addams and Ellen Gates Starr founded Hull House, a settlement house (a social service agency) within a teeming ethnic immigrant neighborhood in Chicago, thereby initiating a new role for women as social workers. In addition to teaching English and civics they, like the Indian schools, used sports as a means to Americanize the local residents. Sandlots provided safe play spaces for small children, while team sports like baseball, and later basketball, taught competition (the basis for the capitalist economic system) and deference to authority (arguing with the referee might end up in expulsion from the game). Players also learned time discipline, teamwork, and social skills, all necessary for success in the middle-class value system. Soon schools and playground supervisors taught the same lessons in physical education classes.

The popularity of sports grew decisively during the period after the Civil War. Colleges began taking anthropometric (body) measurements of their students in 1861 and professors prescribed corrective gymnastics for those deemed to be physically deficient. Moralists and clergymen also prescribed gymnastics and wholesome sports as a means to obtain "Muscular Christianity" by making the body a strong housing for the spiritual soul. Wholesome sport became an antidote for the wayward practices associated with saloons, gambling dens, and brothels.

Technology and the media further popularized sporting ventures. The type-writer, invented in 1867, and the telephone, in 1876, combined with the telegraph to produce instantaneous results of sporting contests. Thomas Edison invented the phonograph in 1877 and patented the electric light three years later, enabling indoor and evening recreations and athletic contests to take place. Night baseball games started as early as 1883. Newspapers carried sports results, and sportswriter Henry Chadwick, a British immigrant, invented the box score and batting average that generated greater interest in ball games. Richard Kyle Fox, an Irish immigrant, took over the *National Police Gazette*, and his sensationalized coverage of crime, scandals, sex, and sports found a multitude of readers. Fox promoted athletic spec-tacles to cover in his newspaper, especially boxing matches, and he initiated a sys-tem of weight classes and awarded bejeweled belts to the champions to generate interest in the sport. Such publicity spawned the first national sports hero in the United States, heavyweight champion John L. Sullivan, and propelled baseball to prominence as the national game.

TEAM SPORTS

Baseball

Baseball had expanded rapidly in the New York City–New Jersey area and in Massachusetts even before the Civil War. The onset of hostilities slowed that de-velopment as many players joined the army. Still, club rivalries persisted through-out the era and some teams even paid players for their abilities. They did so by constructing enclosed fields, which enabled them to charge admission fees to spec-tators. Both James Creighton, who pitched for the Brooklyn Excelsiors in 1860, and Al Reach, who played for the Philadelphia Athletics in 1865, became acknowledged professionals. In 1861 Brooklyn (which did not become a part of New York City until 1898) and New York fielded all-star teams in a match for re-gional pride. The following year two top New York teams, the Eckfords and the Atlantics, played a charity game with the proceeds donated to soldiers injured in the war. Philadelphia sent a team to compete against those of New York, Brooklyn, and Newark, New Jersey, in 1862 and drew 15,000 spectators. Brooklyn and New York sent all-star teams to Philadelphia later that summer. Such excursions became commonplace throughout the war, with some games designated as fundraisers for the sick and wounded. While such charitable affairs espoused a noble purpose, they also symbolized the growing urban rivalries that were played out in sport.

The war helped to spread baseball beyond the Northeast as soldiers engaged in the game during their leisure hours in camps. They introduced soldiers from other regions to the sport, which consisted of competing sets of rules. The Massachusetts version utilized an irregular rectangular field, with home plate located midway between the first and third bases. The New York rules, which had been codified by Alexander Cartwright, secretary of the Knickerbockers club (and considered the "father of baseball"), as early as 1845, designated play on a diamond-shaped infield with equidistant bases. The New York version gradually displaced the Massachu-setts system as the predominant choice. The original rules had allowed fielders to catch the ball on a fly or a bounce, or to hit a runner with a thrown ball (called "soaking") to achieve outs. By the 1860s pitchers had to deliver the ball underhanded from a designated box located only forty-five feet from the batter. Despite such restrictions the curve ball began to baffle batters, and hitters adopted the bunt. Fielders had to catch the batted ball on the fly, rather than a bounce to gain a put out. Fielders did not begin wearing gloves until the mid-1870s, and the earliest gloves had no padding, resulting in many errors each game. As catchers moved closer to the batter they developed more protective equipment, such as the chest protector and catcher's mask in 1875. The ball consisted of loosely wound yarn, which did not travel a great distance. Home runs were rare. In 1879 Charley Jones led the league with only nine home runs and sixty-two runs batted in. Batters could still designate if they wanted the ball pitched above or below the waist until 1887.

As soldiers returned to their homes they formed town teams, and local rivalries soon developed. Even women's teams appeared on college campuses by 1865. Baseball quickly became the national pastime, superseding the British game of cricket, as the eastern teams from New York and Philadelphia competed with teams as far away as Chicago and Cincinnati. Chicago featured forty-five local teams by 1867

Cincinnati Red Stockings

The first fully professional team started out as an amateur contingent in 1867 and claimed the Midwest championship the following year. But rivalries with other midwestern cities led Aaron Champion, a young Cincinnati lawyer and aspiring politician, to assemble a group of businessmen as financial backers to field a fully salaried team in 1869. They hired Harry Wright, a British-born (1835) former cricket player, as player-manager. Wright's father had been a professional cricket player and his eldest son assisted him as an instructor. Wright worked as a player and teacher at cricket clubs in New York, Philadelphia, and Cincinnati before finally concentrating on baseball.

The financiers raised enough money to fund a national tour and provide $9,300 for salaries. Harry Wright hired his younger brother, George, as the star shortstop for a salary of $1,400. A substitute player got only $600 (still twice the annual income of a typical worker), and only one of the newly hired professionals was from Cincinnati.

The tour first traveled east and proved phenomenally successful. They did not lose a game, but had to settle for a tie with the Troy, New York, team when the latter's financial backer, the gambler John Morrissey, started an argument with the umpire (probably to protect the wagers) and the game was terminated. The team returned to Cincinnati triumphant and then embarked on a western tour to California. Its combined record was 57-0-1. Continuing into the 1870 season the professionals won sixty-three consecutive games until losing 8-7 in eleven innings to the Brooklyn Athletics. The team's success led midwestern rival Chicago to form its own professional team.

Despite the success on the field, the national tour generated a profit of only $1.25 and the businessmen of Cincinnati jettisoned Champion. The Wright brothers and other players left for the Boston franchise in 1871. Cincinnati entered a new professional team in the initial National League of 1876, but they were expelled in 1880 for selling beer and playing games on Sunday. From 1882 to 1889 the Cincinnati team competed in the American Association, considered to be a second major league at the time, and in 1890 it returned to the National League.

and had more than fifty company teams in local leagues three years later. Henry Chadwick, an English-born sportswriter for New York newspapers, helped to generate interest for the game with his book, *Beadle's Dime Base Ball Player* (the dime referred to the cost of the book), which provided instruction for players from 1860 to 1881 when publication stopped. Chadwick also introduced the American public to baseball statistics, such as the box score, the batting average, and a scoring system that tabulated home runs, hits, and total bases.

The new cities of the Midwest not only competed with the East for athletic supremacy, but competed with each other for the frontier trade. Cincinnati, Chicago, St. Louis, and Milwaukee all desired to be the commercial center that supplied the farmers and townspeople of the Midwest. The merchants of Cincinnati decided to promote their city by creating a fully professional baseball team (the Red Stockings) in 1869 as a marketing strategy. Professional players earned salaries between $600 and $1,500 for their services. They sent the team on a national tour from the East Coast all the way to California, and the value of professional players became readily apparent, as the team went undefeated (57-0-1). Chicago businessmen quickly assembled their own professional team, known as the White Stockings (later to become the Cubs), in 1870. The White Stockings traveled down the Mississippi River Valley, defeating Memphis 157-1, and later beating archrival Cincinnati.

The expanding railroad network crossed the continent by 1869, which made long-distance travel possible and relatively fast. Baseball became more like a commercial business for some city teams as they built specialized sites and paid contracted players, just like employees. The differences between amateur and professional players caused the latter to split from the National Association of Base Ball Players, which had been organized in 1858. Professional teams posed an unfair competitive advantage over amateurs. Gamblers infiltrated the game, corrupting some players, and portraying a negative image. In the heated rivalries even fans of amateur teams bet heavily on their club and they needed assurance of a legitimate contest. In 1871 the paid players organized the National Association of Professional Base Ball Players (NAPBBP) to administer and regulate the game and their annual conventions brought greater standardization to the rules. A loosely organized league endeavored to determine the national champion. Franchise fees cost only ten dollars and numerous small cities (at least twenty-five between 1871 and 1875) joined the league. The NAPBBP players earned salaries between $1,300 and $1,600 (about four times greater than average workers), although the best players got as much as $2,500.

Several issues continued to confront the practitioners, however. With numerous teams soliciting the best players for their big games, athletes often reneged on their contracts by leaving their original clubs for better offers at any time during the season. Such players became known as "revolvers" because they continually moved from one team to another. The NAPBBP did resolve one issue, that of African American players, by refusing to accept black teams as members of the organization. Although individual African Americans played on some teams, the exclusion of black clubs forced them to organize their own circuits. Black workers at the Adirondack resorts in upper New York formed talented teams that put on exhibitions for their wealthy patrons; while other black teams competed against white town teams and amateur contingents. The Dolly Vardens, an African American team, organized as early as 1867 in Philadelphia. The Chicago Unions, another black team, became a dominant force among amateur clubs in that city by the mid-1880s.

The NAPBBP attempted to introduce baseball abroad on a tour to England in 1874. The champion Boston Red Stockings played exhibition games with the Philadelphia Athletics players and engaged in cricket matches with local British teams. The English were not impressed, referring to the American national pastime as a boys' game, similar to the rounders played by schoolchildren. The denigration hurt American pride, as the United States strived to establish its own national identity apart from British culture. Years later an American commission would falsely claim (the Doubleday myth) that baseball was an American invention, established in 1839 in Cooperstown, New York.

In 1876 William Hulbert, a Chicago coal merchant and owner of the White Stockings team, resolved to earn greater profits and solve the problems of the professional association by reorganizing the league. Teams had previously arranged their own schedules, and noncompetitive teams simply refused to play. In 1872

Moses Fleetwood Walker (1857–1924)

Moses Fleetwood Walker was born on October 7, 1857, to mulatto parents in Mt. Pleasant, Ohio. One of five children, he attended Oberlin College and the University of Michigan. He played on the baseball teams of both institutions. By 1881 he played semipro baseball for a company team in Cleveland. In 1882 he married an Oberlin classmate, Arabella Taylor. He joined Toledo of the Northwestern League as a catcher in 1883. The following year the Toledo team joined the American Association, at that time recognized as a major league. Walker's brother Weldy also played for Toledo that year. White players, most notably Adrian "Cap" Anson, captain of the Chicago team, refused to play against blacks and Walker was released after the 1884 season. He continued to play for minor-league teams through the 1889 season. In 1891 he patented a new type of artillery shell but never enjoyed any profits. He was soon arrested, but acquitted, in the stabbing death of a white man.

Walker's wife died in 1895, leaving him with two sons and a daughter. He married another acquaintance from Oberlin in 1898, Ednah Jane Mason, but later that year he was arrested and sent to prison on charges of mail robbery. When released after a year he moved to Steubenville, Ohio, and purchased a hotel. By 1902 he edited a newspaper dedicated to African Americans. He bought an opera house in Cadiz, Ohio, in 1904, where he promoted stage plays and motion pictures. Four years later he wrote a book entitled *Our Home Colony: A Treatise on the Past, Present, and Future of the Negro Race in America*. Increasingly agitated by the racism that he experienced in the United States, he advocated a return to Africa. Walker gained other patents that improved movie reel projectors in 1920, the same year his second wife died. He sold his business and retired to Cleveland, where he died of pneumonia in 1924.

Light-skinned African American players masqueraded briefly as Native Americans or Cubans in order to play professional baseball. But eventually they were exposed and banished from the major leagues. In 1920 Rube Foster, owner of the black Chicago American Giants, formed the Negro National League, a professional circuit that paralleled the white major leagues. It was not until the advent of Jackie Robinson with the Brooklyn Dodgers in 1947 that black players reentered the national pastime.

First Nine of the Cincinnati (Red Stockings) Base Ball Club. (Courtesy of the Library of Congress)

only six of the eleven teams finished the season. The Boston team, which had hired away manager Harry Wright and most of the Cincinnati team, added star pitcher Albert Spalding from the Rockford, Illinois, team and easily won four pennants from 1873 to 1876. Hulbert acquired Spalding as player-manager for his Chicago team and invited representatives from only the top franchises to form the National League in 1876. Only cities of greater than 75,000 in population were permitted as members in order to ensure an adequate fan base. The original members consisted of Chicago, Boston, Philadelphia, Cincinnati, Hartford, Brooklyn, St. Louis, and Louisville. The league office scheduled all games to ensure an equal number for all teams and paid official umpires five dollars per game for the contests. It banned gambling, alcohol sales, and Sunday games to gain greater respect and promote the league as wholesome middle-class entertainment. It recruited a former U.S. senator to act as league president to provide further credibility. In 1877 four Louisville players were banned for life for throwing games, and the Cincinnati team was expelled for selling beer and playing on Sunday. Such actions reinforced the league's moral image.

The owners wrested control of league affairs from the former players' operation and asserted their authority in 1879 with the adoption of the reserve clause in player contracts. The maneuver "reserved" players to the team that originally signed them to a contract unless that team offered to sell or trade them. The owners rationalized the strategy as a means to prohibit the richest teams from buying all the best players; but it also removed the players' options and restricted their salaries to whatever the team owners offered them. The reorganization of the league and team owners' control thus represented a model for all future professional sports leagues.

Hulbert died shortly after founding the National League and Spalding assumed the club presidency and league leadership in 1882. Disgruntled owners of teams

Albert Goodwill Spalding (1850–1915)

Spalding was born the eldest of three children on September 2, 1850, in Byron, Illinois. When his father died in 1858 Albert was sent to Rockford, Illinois to live with an aunt and there he took up baseball as the star pitcher for a local team. He gained fame in 1867 when he defeated the barnstorming Washington Nationals, perhaps the best team in the country. By 1871 he was pitching for the Boston Red Stockings in the professional league, winning four championships from 1872 to 1875. He married Sarah Keith in 1875, a union that produced one son.

The next year Spalding pitched and managed the Chicago White Stockings team and, along with his brother, opened a sporting goods company. As principal shareholder, he became president of the Chicago team in 1882 and the acknowledged leader of the National League owners. By that time his business produced "official" baseballs and a booklet touted as the "Official Base Ball Guide." Spalding expanded his product line to include football, basketball, golf, bicycles, hunting, boating, and skating equipment. He not only diversified his product lines, but he also consolidated the industry by buying up rivals. Although headquartered in Chicago, he maintained a branch office in New York, and stores in Denver and Philadelphia. By 1909 the Spalding Company boasted of thirty stores in America and another six in foreign countries.

Not all of Spalding's marketing strategies proved successful, however. Before players adopted numbers to distinguish them from one another, Spalding promoted different-color socks for each position, an innovation unappreciated by the fans. His world tour of 1888 failed to impress the British, and their denigration of baseball as a children's game eventually led to the formation of the Mills Commission (1905–7) that, heavily influenced by Spalding, perpetrated the Abner Doubleday myth as the originator of baseball.

When Spalding's wife died in 1899 he married Elizabeth Churchill. In 1900 he was appointed the U.S. Commissioner of the Olympic Games. He moved to California and unsuccessfully ran for that state's U.S. Senate seat in 1910. He died in California on September 9, 1915, and the National Baseball Hall of Fame inducted him as an original member upon its opening in 1939.

that had not been invited to join the National League formed their own circuits. The American Association, established in 1882, served as a second major league during the decade. The banished Cincinnati team and several others that were also owned by brewmasters formed the new league, and they agreed not to raid players from the established National League clubs. The agreement and the success of the American Association led to a postseason series in 1884, a forerunner to the World Series that started in 1903.

Baseball teams also introduced new marketing strategies in the 1880s that would become standard procedures in the twentieth century, such as doubleheaders, night games, and ladies' days, which allowed free admission for women. The latter tactic had a dual purpose, for owners believed that the presence of females would curtail the rowdy behavior of the ballplayers. While the early players were largely American-born urbanites, increasing numbers of German and Irish offspring began to appear on professional teams. The most popular player of the era, Mike "King" Kelly, played for the Chicago White Stockings. Kelly's swiftness on the basepaths engendered a popular song, "Slide, Kelly, Slide," but Kelly's success was not due to speed alone. Kelly was known to cut corners when rounding the bases as the lone umpire was distracted by other matters. On one occasion he allegedly took the shortest direct route from first base, across the pitcher's mound, sliding in to third while an umpire argued with a fan. In another game Kelly patrolled the outfield in a thick mist. When the ball was hit over his head, he ran and leaped into the fog with an outstretched glove, depositing the ball on the pitcher's mound for the umpire to see. Fans and teammates went wild over the miraculous catch, until Kelly informed the latter by stating "nothin' to it, boys. I always keep a spare ball in my back pocket." Kelly's nighttime sojourns, however, often left him unable to play. As he languished in a hungover state on the bench one day, a pop fly was hit down the line. Realizing that neither the catcher nor first baseman would get to it, he jumped up and announced, "Kelly now substituting for Chicago," and made the catch.

Despite such ingenuity Albert Spalding was dissatisfied with Kelly's lack of playing time and had a detective follow him on his nightly adventures. The detective reported that Kelly had kept the younger players out until the wee hours of the morning drinking lemonade. When Spalding confronted Kelly with the report, the guilty player offered only one amendment. "I was definitely not drinking lemonade," he stated. Kelly, like others of the working class, asserted his masculinity through physical prowess and he assured Spalding that he drank whiskey, not the more feminine lemonade. Spalding promptly sold Kelly to Boston for the astronomical sum of $10,000 in 1887.

While a host of ethnic immigrant groups found some social economic mobility and status through professional baseball, African Americans found only temporary acceptance. Moses Fleetwood Walker, a catcher for the Toledo team in the American Association in 1884, lost his future opportunities at the highest level when white team mangers refused to play against him. Rather than forfeit game receipts, the Toledo manager acquiesced. Walker was forced to play with lesser teams and in Canada thereafter. Such "gentlemen's agreements" would affect baseball until 1947 when Jackie Robinson finally broke the color line.

The baseball rule-makers continued to adapt the game to enhance its attraction to fans throughout the 1880s. Over the course of the decade the base on balls was gradually decreased, with nine balls required in 1879 to only four by 1889. The

Michael Joseph "King" Kelly (1857–1894)

Kelly was born on December 31, 1857, in Troy, New York, to Irish immigrant parents. Upon his father's death the family moved to Paterson, New Jersey, where he dropped out of school to take work in a textile factory; but by 1873 he returned to Troy as a member of the city baseball team. He turned professional with the Paterson team two years later. While playing for Columbus, Ohio, in 1878 he was recruited for the Cincinnati Red Stockings, and transferred to the Chicago White Stockings in 1880 where he blossomed into a star and fan favorite. Kelly spent seven years with the Chicago team, usually as a catcher or outfielder, during which they won five league championships. Kelly led the National League in batting and in runs scored in 1884 and in 1886.

Kelly's salary of $2,500 in 1886 was still well below the top stars. His unhappiness over his salary and disagreements with team president Albert Spalding and team captain Adrian Anson over his drinking habits led to his removal to Boston in 1887. Kelly stole eighty-four bases for Boston in his initial season with the team, including six in one game.

In 1890 Kelly joined the Players League as a player-manager and his team won the league championship. With the demise of the league he led a Cincinnati team for a year before returning to Boston in 1891. He played briefly for the New York Giants in 1893 and retired the following year. In retirement he ran a saloon in New York and took to the vaudeville stage in a baseball play. In November 1894 he contracted pneumonia and died on November 8 in Boston. More than 5,000 fans showed up to view his remains. The Baseball Hall of Fame inducted Kelly in 1945.

pitching distance was lengthened to fifty feet in 1881 and overhand pitching was permitted in 1884. Three years later the batter was no longer allowed to call for a high or low pitch. In 1887 more definite balk rules were established and a batter hit by a pitch was granted a base. In addition to the rule changes, *The Sporting News* first appeared in 1886. Known as the "Bible of Baseball," it offered in-depth coverage of the sport and became essential reading for fans. In 1888 Albert Spalding determined to spread the game and his equipment to a global market. He organized a world tour with his White Stockings and a group of all-stars that traveled across the North American continent to California, and then to Hawaii, Australia, Egypt, and Great Britain. Once again, the English rebuffed his efforts.

Chicagoans, however, did adapt the game of baseball in a way that had dramatic effects in the twentieth century. In 1887 some wealthy socialites gathered at the Farragut Boat Club to listen to the telegraphic results of a big football game in the East. During a lull in the action one listener tied up a boxing glove and threw it at one of his companions. His friend grabbed a nearby broom handle and swatted it, and they soon figured out that they could play baseball indoors. The game eventually became known as softball, and a specialized ball and electric lighting allowed for indoor games. By the 1890s numerous "indoor baseball" leagues flourished in the city. By the turn of the century playground supervisors adapted it to their restricted spaces in order to teach immigrant youth the American values inherent in the game.

Despite the growth of baseball, its labor relations mirrored the problems of the larger society. Baseball players, like factory employees, were dissatisfied with their

John Montgomery Ward (1860–1925)

Ward was the second of two sons, born on March 3, 1860, in Bellefonte, Pennsylvania. His father died in 1871 and his mother in 1872, leaving him an orphan by the age of fourteen. A precocious student, he entered Agricultural College of Pennsylvania (now Penn State University) in 1873. There he was a founding member of the baseball club as a pitcher. After he was dismissed from the school for stealing chickens in 1877, he spent the remainder of the year traveling and offering his services as a baseball player to numerous town teams. In July 1878 the Providence, Rhode Island, team hired him and he began his career in the National League. As a pitcher with an excellent curve ball he won forty-seven games and struck out 239 batters in 1879, leading his team to the championship. The next year he pitched a perfect game, retiring the entire Buffalo team in order.

Ward transferred to the New York Giants team in 1882, but by 1884 injuries ended his pitching career. He switched to shortstop and led the league in stolen bases with 111 in 1887. Ward earned a law degree from Columbia College while playing for the Giants in 1885. He increasingly became involved in the labor disputes between players and team owners thereafter. With Ward as a primary force, the players formed their own labor union, known as the Brotherhood, in 1885. In addition to an instructional book on baseball, he wrote several articles for popular magazines that expressed the players' point of view, in particular, their disfavor with the "reserve clause" in their contracts that prohibited their ability to seek a new team and a higher salary.

By 1889 Ward and his co-conspirators had found enough disgruntled financiers to establish their own league. The financial backers had sought, and been denied, franchises in the National League. They organized the Players League and began play in 1890 with players and owners sharing any profits over $10,000. There was no reserve clause and players were guaranteed their salaries. Two hundred players joined the new organization, while only thirty-eight remained loyal to the National League. Albert Spalding managed to bribe some players and the financial backers of the new league. The stockholders accepted Spalding's offer to merge with the National League, ending the short mutiny, and reasserting owners' control over the rebellious players. In 1892 the National League co-opted the American Association in a similar fashion, putting it out of business. Such consolidation left the players with few choices.

Ward returned to the National League as a player-manager in Brooklyn and New York; then retired after the 1894 season. He represented players in their disputes through his New York law practice and in 1912 he became owner of the Boston Braves. He relinquished that role and became the business manager of the Brooklyn franchise in the new Federal League, a third major league that lasted only two years. He died of pneumonia on March 4, 1925, in Augusta, Georgia.

minimal salaries and the conditions imposed by their employers. Baseball players referred to themselves as "wage slaves" and in 1885 the National League players formed their own labor union, known as the Brotherhood of Professional Base Ball Players. In 1889 they organized a full-scale revolt by forming their own league based on socialistic principles in which players and financial backers shared in the profits. The Players League, sometimes referred to as the Union League or Brotherhood League, opened play in 1890. The defection of American Association players to the new league eventually led to the demise of the American Association, but Spalding proved more successful in his opposition. He scheduled National League games at the same time as those of the Players League in cities where both had teams, forcing baseball fans to make a choice. He threatened to banish all players who defected to the new league but then bribed star players to return to the National League. He then coerced the financial backers of the more-successful Brotherhood teams to desert their confederates by offering franchises within the senior circuit. The National League, with money in its coffers, sustained the losses of head-to-head competition, but won the war. Spalding's tactics forced the players to succumb after only one season.

Some historians have theorized that baseball grew so rapidly to become the national pastime because it replicated American business values. Baseball taught and reinforced particular characteristics in its adherence to teamwork and specialization, similar to the assembly line process in factories. The game also allowed for individualism when each batter faced the opposition. But as the American society became more urban and more commercial throughout the nineteenth century, baseball, played in open air parks and unregulated by the clock, still retained a nostalgic rural sentiment for many Americans. It would retain that feeling throughout most of the following century until superseded by professional football in the 1960s.

Football

Football had already surpassed baseball as the favorite sport on college campuses by the 1890s. Like baseball, it went through a multitude of rule changes to evolve into a distinctly American game, espousing particular American values. Football appeared in the earliest American colonies as the transplanted European folk game in which two sides kicked a ball to the opponent's goal. Similar informal and annually staged games took place on college campuses between intramural factions. At times upperclassmen challenged the lower classmen, or two classes combined to form a team against two others. The games provided an excuse, much to the chagrin of school authorities, for rival students to pummel each other and establish bragging rights. Such affairs crossed intramural lines in November 1869 when Princeton traveled to Rutgers for the first intercollegiate match in the United States. Both sides used twenty-five players in a soccer-style game that allowed players to advance the ball by kicking or hitting it with their hands. Rutgers won the initial contest 6-4, but Princeton won the following game, 8-0, a week later. Columbia joined the competition with Rutgers a year later.

Like baseball, different versions of the rules proliferated. A New York convention in 1873 aimed at resolving the matter. Harvard declined to join the conference and Yale maintained that batting the ball would make the American game distinct from British soccer. In 1874 Harvard agreed to a series of matches with McGill University, a Canadian school in Montreal. Both sides agreed to use eleven players per side. McGill introduced Harvard to the rugby style of football, which allowed players to run with the ball. Harvard defeated Yale in a rugby match the next year as approximately 1,200 paid fifty cents each to witness the match, setting football on the same commercial path established by the baseball teams. Harvard, Columbia, and Princeton formed the first intercollegiate league in 1876 under the rugby rules; but disagreements over the number of players per side continued to mar relations between the colleges. Harvard disputed Yale's claim to the championship in 1876, and the rivalries between the elite schools that eventually came to be known as the Ivy League led the New York Polo Club to offer a national championship trophy for a New York game that year. Such sponsorship for an athletic spectacle in the nation's media center assumed a commercial bonanza and created a model for future contests to be played on Thanksgiving Day.

The championship game of 1880, played in the snow between Princeton and Yale, resulted in a tie, but the thousands of spectators adorned in team colors, yelling, cheering, singing school songs, waving pennants, and blasting horns throughout the game exhibited the rowdy behavior expected of modern football fans. Large bets were placed on the rival teams and police had to eject some onlookers from the premises. The danger was much greater on the field. As early as 1876 opponents complained about Yale's "win at all costs" attitude and accused the team of trying to cripple the best players of their foes. The rules allowed for throttling (choking) and slugging an opponent three times before being ejected from the game. Both Princeton and Harvard adopted canvas jackets in 1877 and Yale added canvas pants the next year. The canvas could be smeared with grease to make ball carriers harder to tackle. Frederic Remington, who later became a famous American artist, played on the Yale team in 1878; and he allegedly dipped his canvas jacket in slaughterhouse blood before the game with Harvard to make it more "businesslike."

In 1880 Walter Camp, captain of the Yale team and a member of the rules committee until his death in 1925, proposed an innovation to the rugby scrum that initiated every play in a free-for-all. Camp suggested the use of a line of scrimmage with each team maintaining the ball for a half. The introduction of a scrimmage line clearly distinguished the evolution of American football from British soccer, but the disadvantages of the new rule became apparent in 1881 when both Princeton and Yale played defensively in a boring championship game. Each team controlled the ball for a half, giving ground, but safeguarding the ball in a scoreless tie. Camp rectified that condition by requiring teams to gain five yards in three tries (downs) or relinquish the ball. Over the next two years the rules committee continued to deviate from soccer; but the emphasis remained on kicking, as field goals counted for five points and kicks after a touchdown earned four points.

The game, like baseball, spread quickly to the Midwest and the West Coast. In 1881, and again in 1883, the University of Michigan traveled east to confront the eastern powers, sparking an ongoing debate between the regions. By the turn of the century the midwestern teams favored a fast style of play that featured end runs and reverses; while the East maintained its conservative approach toward mass plays and brute power. By 1882 football had reached Minnesota, Illinois, Wisconsin, and even Colorado. College football teams appeared on campuses in Kentucky as early as 1880, and schools in Maryland, Virginia, and North Carolina adopted the sport before the end of the decade. A Chicago high school football league initiated interscholastic play in 1884. Like baseball, football players became more specialized in their roles. By the mid-1880s tackles, guards, a center, and backs were identified by their particular assignments.

The brutality of the game, the loss of school time for away games, and the recruitment of players greatly concerned faculty members at the colleges. There were no distinct eligibility rules and the team captain or football club officers

Walter Chauncey Camp (1859–1925)

Walter Camp, born in New Britain, Connecticut, on April 7, 1859, became known as the "father of American football." An only child, Camp attended Yale University and played for six years on its football team (1876–82) at a time when there were no limits on years of eligibility. (He played both as an undergraduate and then graduate student.) In 1883 he secured employment at the New Haven Clock Company and eventually became its president and chairman of the board. He married Alice Graham Sumner, the daughter of a famous Yale professor, in 1888; but gained his greatest renown in football. As Yale's team captain he proposed many of the rule changes at the annual conventions that transformed football from a sport akin to soccer to a distinctly different American game. Among the changes were the reduction of players from fifteen to eleven on a side, the introduction of a line of scrimmage, a system of downs and distance required to retain the ball, allowance for tackling below the waist, and the scoring system that eventually transformed football from a kicking game to a running game.

After his playing days Camp stayed engaged with the football team as an advisor, akin to a head coach. His later duties assumed those of an early athletic director. His systematic administration of the football club produced an excess of funds that were used to recruit players and provide benefits for the team, providing the model for modern football programs. Yale amassed a phenomenal record between 1876 and 1910 with Camp at the head of the program, winning 95 percent of its games. It lost only fourteen times during those years. Other schools clamored for former Yale players to be their coaches, resulting in a national network of Camp protégés. In 1914 the university constructed the Yale Bowl, the largest stadium in the United States at that time with 70,000 seats.

Camp remained on the football rules committee until 1925, but he also initiated the first All-American team, along with sportswriter Caspar Whitney in 1889. Camp published more than 200 newspaper articles and authored over thirty books promoting the sport of football. During World War I the U.S. government enlisted him to direct the navy physical training program, for which he developed the "daily dozen," a series of exercises. He died of a heart attack on March 14, 1925, while attending a meeting of the football rules committee in New York.

decided on the acceptability of players. Sometimes faculty members joined their students on the teams. The school administrators moved to take greater control of the athletic clubs that were organized and operated by students. Cornell president Andrew White refused to let the football club travel to Cleveland for a game with Michigan by stating, "I will not permit 30 men to travel 400 miles merely to agitate a bag of wind [the football]." Rule revisions for 1884 intended to decrease the brutality of the game. Still Harvard faculty formed an investigative committee that observed four games. They found slugging occurred in each and reported that in the Wesleyan–Pennsylvania game a man was unfairly thrown out of bounds by an opponent. "Then, as he was rising, but before he was on his feet, his antagonist turned, struck him in the face and knocked him down, and returned in triumph with the ball." The committee recommended a ban on football, causing Harvard to temporarily resign from the football association.

In the initial games, the team captains arbitrated disputes between contestants, sometimes causing prolonged interruptions in the game. They were replaced by alumni who acted as judges; but as alumni became more involved in the fortunes of their individual teams some became less neutral, with consequent charges of favoritism. The alums were replaced by a single referee in 1885. An umpire was added to the game in 1888 and hacking, throttling, and tripping were eliminated. A touchdown, however, required a player to literally touch the ball on the end zone ground and declare a score. If one or more opponents could wrestle the ball away before he did so (called a "maul in goal") the score did not count.

School rivalries and school spirit kept alumni involved in the progress and success of their schools. After playing six years (as an undergraduate and then graduate student) on the Yale team Walter Camp remained as the coach and unofficial athletic director. As the dominant team of the nineteenth century, Yale players were sought after as coaches at other schools, forming a vast network. They and other alums informed Camp of top football players throughout the country. With the large sums accumulated from gate receipts Yale could offer substantial inducements to football recruits. Perhaps the most grievous case involved James Hogan, an Irish-born athlete who captained the Yale team in 1904 and made the All-American team three times. Yale not only provided free room, board, and tuition; they gave him a Cuban vacation, as well as a commission on sales of baseball programs and cigarette sales in New Haven. Other teams followed the Yale model to pursue success and obtain the national publicity garnered by the powerful eastern teams in the newspapers. Some schools used faculty members, graduate students, or even nonstudents as players for big games, others used "special" students, who attended only part-time or enrolled only during football season. Such students might enroll for only one class; but still be eligible to play on the team. Tramp athletes traveled the country in search of the best offers, similar to the revolving professional baseball players. In 1889 Harvard introduced spring football practice to better prepare the team and gain an advantage versus its chief rival, Yale. Many teams employed professional coaches, who served only during the football season. The new University of Chicago tried to gain control over the student athletic enterprises in 1892 when it hired Amos Alonzo Stagg, a former Yale star, as a faculty member and coach. By granting him a year-round position and faculty status as a professor, the university effectively took control of the students' athletic clubs as well as the income that they generated. In 1905 college administrators formed a national governing body to control such events, which became the National Collegiate Athletic Association (NCAA).

The 1887 Thanksgiving Day game between Yale and Harvard at New York's Polo Grounds drew 17,000 spectators, further establishing the commercial possibilities of college football. The national media attention provided the two schools with invaluable publicity. The game of football and its individual players received further recognition in 1889 when Walter Camp combined with sportswriter Casper Whitney to select the first All-American team from players at Harvard, Princeton, and Yale. Such selections established an arbitrary standard of excellence, providing fans with further reason for discussion and debate. The choices also idealized athletic heroes and tied them to patriotism as "All-Americans." Such heroic figures populated novels and boys' literature over the next century as role models for youth.

Football thus presented contradictory messages that persist today. Detractors abhorred the game's violence, lack of sportsmanship, win-at-all-costs attitude, commercialization, and use of ineligible players. Supporters claimed that it built character and required courage, self-sacrifice, teamwork, and an aggressive, martial spirit. They deemed the latter qualities extremely important for several reasons. American males had not experienced the opportunity to test their mettle and prove their bravery since the Civil War ended in 1865. If the United States was to achieve its place among the international powers of Europe the warlike qualities promoted by the game would be a necessity. The United States was already challenging Great Britain in its economic output and many Americans felt it their duty to spread democracy, capitalism, and Christianity around the world. The USA embarked on such a mission in the Spanish-American War of 1898, which made it an imperial power equal to the Europeans.

Psychologists and social critics also decried the increasing feminization of the American culture. Young boys were coddled by their mothers, taught by female teachers in elementary schools, and generally under feminine influences for much of their early lives. Women increasingly called for greater roles in the American society, the right to vote, and the right to education. The Woman's Christian Temperance Union, established in 1873, sought to ban alcohol, a traditional male pleasure. Women also accounted for one-third of all college students by 1880, threatening males' traditional leadership roles. Perhaps more disturbing to some men was the females' incursion into the traditional male bastion of sports. By the 1880s women expanded their sporting interest beyond the recreational pastimes to include tennis, golf, archery, and cycling. The engagement of women in a sport devalued that activity as a marker of masculinity. Football, however, remained and still remains a refuge for men.

SPORTS FOR INDIVIDUAL COMPETITORS

Boxing

Boxing gained virtually no benefit from science or technology; yet it held great popular appeal until the 1890s, perhaps due to its primitive nature. Rounds were fought until one contestant fell or touched the mat with no limit set on the number of rounds. Wrestling holds allowed opponents to throw as well as hit each other. Boxers fought until one opponent could no longer come to scratch, a line at the center of the ring, to start the next round or until one admitted defeat.

Unlike the amateur associations that regulated other sports, boxing had no singular governing body to enforce standard rules. Individual promoters, often saloon owners, staged bouts for the pleasure of the bachelor subculture that frequented their establishments. Boxing became especially popular in the western mining towns with a preponderance of young men, as females were in short supply. Few women braved the hardships of the frontier and the rough mining towns, so young men were largely left to entertain themselves. In the industrial cities of the East and Midwest as well, men congregated in saloons, which became the poor man's athletic club. There they found recreation by drinking, gambling, and playing cards and billiards. Some saloons offered food and even showers or other amenities. The saloon became the social and political headquarters, where one might find a job or pick up mail.

Prior to the Civil War many boxers, particularly Irish Americans, emerged from the ranks of political parties. The Democrats, in particular, employed "sluggers" who stood at the polls on election days to convince voters to pick a particular candidate. In 1860 Irish American John Heenan traveled to England to take on the British champion, Tom Sayers. The fight engendered much interest and nationalism on both sides, but ended in a draw.

The Civil War interrupted professional boxing matches; but soldiers took up the sport during their leisure time in camp in order to amuse themselves and to gamble on the outcome. After the war the sport faced the moral concerns of reformers who objected to its brutality and the gambling that it inspired. The reformers succeeded in banning boxing, or prizefighting as it was called, which relegated boxers to clandestine bouts in secret locations to avoid arrest. The fighters earned most of their money from side bets rather than large purses offered by the promoters. In such cases the boxer and his supporters might wager against an opponent and his friends, or his financial backers might supply enough money to cover any debts if he lost, so that he would not incur financial ruin.

In 1867 the Marquis of Queensbury, a Scottish nobleman, promoted a new set of rules to make boxing more humane and more acceptable. The new rules required the boxers to fight with padded gloves for three-minute rounds. The new rules forbade wrestling holds and declared one the winner if his opponent could not continue the fight within ten seconds after being hit (a knockout). The new rules took some time to gain acceptance in the United States (the first heavyweight championship under the new rules didn't take place until 1892), but promoters found other ways to circumvent the boxing laws. In the 1880s they offered bouts as "exhibitions" for club members, who paid an admission fee at the front door to become a member. The exhibitions were not judged, so there was no official winner or loser. Many of the early boxers thus had records with numerous "no decisions," amounting to a draw.

In 1880 Paddy Ryan, an American, knocked out Joe Goss, an Englishman, in a bare-knuckle fight that lasted eighty-seven rounds to be acknowledged as the heavyweight champion of the world. The heavyweight championship symbolized the world's toughest man and held great value in the Social Darwinian belief of the survival of the fittest. The nationalistic promotion of the fight helped Richard Kyle Fox, the publisher of the *National Police Gazette*, sell 400,000 copies of his lurid newspaper. Fox's promotion of boxing resurrected the sport, and his running feud with John L. Sullivan raised the latter to celebrity status and increased sales throughout the 1880s.

Sullivan knocked out Paddy Ryan in a bare-knuckle fight that lasted only nine rounds in 1882. Sullivan held the title for ten years, during which time he became the first national sports hero in the United States. A working-class Irish American, Sullivan built his reputation on his physical prowess by walking into saloons and challenging anyone in the house to a fight. His backers wagered and won by betting on him. Sullivan even offered $1,000 to anyone who could last four rounds with him. Once he became the champion he fought few fights other than exhibitions, but joined the vaudeville circuit as a performer, earning $1 million. Newspapers covered Sullivan's exploits on a regular basis, elevating him to celebrity status, and creating a cult of personality. His picture hung in virtually every saloon and even the wealthy admired his strength and physicality in an age that feared the

John Lawrence Sullivan (1858–1918)

Born in Roxbury, Massachusetts, on October 15, 1858, John L. Sullivan became the greatest sports celebrity of the nineteenth century. His parents were born in Ireland, and his father worked as a laborer in the United States; nevertheless, Sullivan completed elementary school and even attended a business college. His physical prowess, however, outshone his mental faculties. A skilled baseball player, he allegedly turned down a professional contract in that sport. Known as "the Boston Strong Boy," Sullivan gained a reputation by his feats of strength and by challenging saloon patrons to fight with him. He barnstormed the country, defeating local brawlers and professional boxers in the process. His victory over the former British champion Joe Goss in 1880 brought him to national attention. In 1882 he knocked out Paddy Ryan, the American champion, at a clandestine site in Mississippi due to the illegality of boxing at the time.

After the Ryan fight Sullivan toured the United States, challenging anyone to earn $1,000 if they could last four rounds with him. Only one did. In 1883 Sullivan battered the British champion, Charlie Mitchell, until police stopped the encounter. Sullivan bought a saloon and led a dissolute lifestyle, but enjoyed the acclaim of boxing fans throughout the country. In 1888 Sullivan traveled to France for a rematch with Mitchell. Fought in the rain, the contest ended in a draw after thirty-nine rounds. The next year Sullivan engaged in the last of the bare-knuckle (without gloves) championships when he met Jake Kilrain. Richard Kyle Fox, publisher of the *Police Gazette* newspaper and Sullivan's nemesis, sponsored Kilrain for the bout in Richburg, Mississippi. After seventy-five rounds Kilrain could not continue.

After the Kilrain bout, Sullivan embarked on a vaudeville tour and a series of boxing exhibitions. He held the heavyweight title for ten years and was the first athlete to earn more than $1 million for his efforts; most of which he dissipated on alcohol and women. During that time he refused to fight any black fighters, retaining the championship for whites only. In 1892 Sullivan defended his championship against "Gentleman" Jim Corbett in a gloved bout under the Marquis of Queensbury rules in New Orleans. The younger, better-conditioned Corbett knocked out Sullivan in the twenty-first round.

Sullivan published an autobiography in 1892 and again turned to the stage after his defeat. His marriage ended in a formal divorce in 1908. After years as an alcoholic he attempted to reform his life by becoming a temperance lecturer. He eventually retired to a farm in Massachusetts and died of a heart attack on February 2, 1918.

feminization of culture. Sullivan insured that the title would rest with whites by proclaiming a color ban once he became the champion, thereby refusing to fight any black fighters.

Sullivan defeated Jake Kilrain in the last bare-knuckle championship bout, held in a clandestine location in Mississippi, in 1889. The fight lasted for seventy-five rounds in 100-degree heat, further establishing the toughness of the competitors. Kilrain had been a junior rowing champion under his real name of Joseph Killion. But when the National Rowing Association was informed of his professional boxing adventures, under an alias, it promptly revoked his championship title and his amateur standing. The interpretation of amateurism at that time dictated that once someone became a professional in any activity, he was tainted for all future

The John L. Sullivan–Jake Kilrain boxing match at Richburg, Mississippi.
(Courtesy of the Library of Congress)

contests. Such rulings carried specific connotations for relationships between social classes in a republic that claimed to be a classless society. The values of sport were dictated by middle-class standards of decorum and propriety, just as owners continue to enforce their own standards of dress and behavior on athletes (their employees) today.

Horse Racing

As noted in the previous chapter, horse racing had been one of the primary sports of the early European colonists. Even in Puritan New England racing horses was rationalized as a necessary and utilitarian activity for breeding better stock. The breeders of the northern colonies bred their horses for endurance, while those in the southern colonies favored speed. In the antebellum period before the Civil War the two regions met in a series of national contests to determine the American champion. The war, however, destroyed much of the South, and the most famous of the southern race tracks, the Metairie Course in New Orleans, was forced to close in 1872.

Another form of racing (harness racing) involved trotters and pacers, horses that ran with a particular gait and pulled a sulky (a small cart with a driver). The sport had developed well before the Civil War as farmers raced their wagons to market in the urban areas. The first one there enjoyed at least a brief monopoly on the sale of crops with no competition to force lower prices. Sport historians claim that harness racing developed into the first modern sport in America in the New York area by the 1820s. After the Civil War, however, harness racing faced a transition as it began to lose its working-class roots. Wealthy owners began to breed trotters as a commercial enterprise. They formed the National Trotting Association in 1870 to standardize rules and registered such horses a year later. Sulkies, small two-wheeled carriages, replaced wagons, and races were run over shorter distances instead of the best of three heats over distances as long as four miles. The innovations, as well as bigger purses, increased fan interest as the sport spread from its eastern origins to the Midwest.

Thoroughbred owners followed the same pattern as the trotters. In addition to shorter races and more prize money, a system of handicapping rated horses according to their age, gender, and ability. Superior horses were given greater weight to carry in order to equalize the chances for others. Such procedures enhanced interest and led to greater betting on the outcome. Professional gamblers recorded their bets at the track and became known as bookies. The bookies set the odds on each horse before the race and collected bets at their appointed locations. In the larger cities gambling houses, known as poolrooms, operated somewhat clandestinely (corrupt police were paid off not to close them down or arrest patrons). At such places bets could be placed without attending the racetrack and telegraphic results gave almost instantaneous results to winners and losers.

During and after the war thoroughbred racing made substantial gains. In 1863 a group of wealthy New Yorkers founded the Saratoga Springs Race Track under the leadership of John Morrissey. Born in Ireland, Morrissey gained fame in the United States as a boxer. He opened a casino at Saratoga, which made him wealthy, and he turned to politics, serving in the U.S. House of Representatives. His career promoted the belief in sport as a meritocracy and one that provided social mobility for the poor and uneducated.

Thoroughbred racing reached the West Coast with the founding of Bay View Park in San Francisco in 1863. The success of the Saratoga venture led the richest New Yorkers to establish the American Jockey Club in 1865. Two years later they built Jerome Park, limiting membership to 1,300 elites. The grand clubhouse offered a dining room and ballroom for social occasions. In 1867 Jerome Park initiated the Belmont Stakes, still one of the most prestigious horse races in the United States.

In 1870 the wealthy residents of Baltimore founded the Pimlico Race Track in Maryland. That same year they initiated another of the Triple Crown races, the Preakness Stakes, naming the race after the original winner in 1870. The third of the Triple Crown races was instituted in 1875 as the Kentucky Derby at Churchill Downs Race Track in Louisville. It drew 10,000 spectators. It also launched the career of Isaac Murphy, the first great black jockey. Murphy won the Kentucky Derby three times (1884, 1890, 1891) and earned substantial sums of money before he succumbed to the pressures of racism and alcoholism at the age of thirty-five in 1896. He was the first jockey inducted into the Hall of Fame in 1955.

Perhaps the most ostentatious of all racetracks was built in Chicago in 1884. Known as Washington Park, it hosted the American Derby, first run in 1884 and the premier event of the era. The luxurious, private clubhouse separated the wealthy members from the middle and working classes, who had to sit in the 10,000-seat grandstand. Box seats allowed for those with the means to distance themselves from the general public. On race days the social elites arrived in their finery in horse-drawn carriages attended by liverymen. They sat symbolically above the masses or paraded on the promenade that ran around the clubhouse. Their afflu-ence marked them as different, and presumably better than others. There they could be viewed in what sociologist Thorstein Veblen called an "ostentatious dis-play," a means to establish and showcase their status not only among the onlookers, but among their peers as well in a form of competition. In a country that proclaimed a classless society, the wealthy used sports like horse racing, polo, and yachting (and golf until the advent of public courses) to create social bounda-ries and prescribed ranks.

The glory of Washington Park was short-lived, however, as social reformers suc-ceeded in closing down many of the tracks in the United States. While New York legalized betting at its tracks in 1887, moralists in Chicago and other big cities who opposed gambling in general, and the corruption that accompanied the pool-rooms, found success. The gamblers at many tracks had bribed jockeys or drivers of the trotters, doped horses, and even murdered owners. Some outlaw tracks operated in suburban areas outside the jurisdiction of local authorities, resulting in the moral crusade that led to the laws that banned racing. In the 1890s the wealthy then turned their attention to the new game of golf, one that needed a large parcel of land. They constructed courses on their private estates or formed private country clubs, where they could gamble in a variety of ways without interference from the government.

Rowing

Like harness racing, rowing contests developed among the boatmen who unloaded goods from ships in a harbor and transported them to shore. By the 1840s college students formed rowing clubs with sleek vessels purely for exercise and competition. The first intercollegiate athletic contest occurred in 1852 when a rail-road company invited the clubs at Harvard and Yale to row against each other on Lake Winnipesaukee in New Hampshire. The railway had built a resort on the lake and wanted to draw attention to the location. They offered expenses and a $500 pair of silver oars as a prize in an early example of the use of sport as a marketing strategy.

The rivalry between the two schools led to systematic training and special diets for the rowers by 1859, and by 1864 Yale hired a professional coach in order to defeat Harvard. Harvard traveled to England to race the Oxford crew in 1869. Oxford won due to a Harvard blunder and Americans called for a rematch on American soil. The interest in rowing races led to a $4,000 prize in a five-mile race between James Hamill and Walter Brown for the American championship in 1869. The Empire City Rowing Club offered a two-mile race for women in 1871. Yale had introduced the sliding seat in 1870, a technological advancement that pro-vided further advantage. Yale later pioneered the use of an indoor practice tank for its rowers.

Professional oarsmen emanated from the working classes and the best gained fame and a measure of social mobility. Both the Ward brothers and the Biglin brothers distinguished themselves throughout the 1870s. The Biglins gained fame as national champions and were rewarded with more lucrative jobs. They won even greater prominence when Thomas Eakins, a famous American artist, portrayed them in a series of paintings known as the "Rowing Pictures" that depicted the changing nature of American society.

The popularity of rowing led to a series of international matches with greater cultural comparisons drawn between the participants and their countries. The spreading belief in Social Darwinism promoted the idea of the survival of the fittest and that some groups had more enduring qualities and strengths than others. In 1878 Canadian Ned Hanlan defeated American Charles Courtney for $2,500 per side in Canada. In such races each rower, or the rower's financial backers, provided the stakes by each contributing an equal share. Hanlan also defeated the British champion in England and claimed the world championship until his defeat by an Australian, William Beach, in Sydney in 1884. Rowing thus became one of the first globalized sports.

The amateur rowers of the college teams considered professionalism to be demeaning and in poor taste. They raced for exercise and the glory of their schools. The National Association of Amateur Oarsmen was established in 1872 and a national amateur championship occurred the following year. The rowers at Cornell began using rowing machines in their practice sessions during 1874–75 as sport fostered new advances in technology. The competitions, known as regattas (from the early gondola races in Venice, Italy), received a great deal of publicity in the newspapers. By the 1880s the regattas attracted 30,000–50,000 spectators and the female students at Wellesley College formed their own rowing club and began adapting specific athletic uniforms for more active lifestyles.

Like Harvard and the professionals, the Cornell rowers traveled to England and Europe in 1881, but lost all of their races. Undeterred, seven schools formed the Intercollegiate Rowing Association in 1883. By the late 1880s the Yale crew members trained as much as two to three hours per day and both Yale and Harvard used rowers and other athletes as subjects in their scientific schools, conducting experiments on nutrition to try to determine the best fuel for human bodies to produce the greatest performances. Rowing clubs persisted, especially in the colleges of the Northeast; but they lost their previous popularity with the ascendance of football on the campuses.

Shooting Sports

Early colonists found firearms a necessity for hunting and protection and colonial muster days were scheduled to have local men form militias and meet for military training. Such training included shooting practice. At frontier taverns men often engaged in shooting contests, and by the nineteenth century turkey shoots became common forms of entertainment. In such contests a live turkey was staked to the ground at a distance from 110 to 165 yards. The first shooter to kill the turkey won it as a prize. Competitive target shooting emerged in New York City as early as 1833, and the Swiss and German immigrants of mid-century brought their shooting interests from Europe. They especially formed clubs in the Midwest, where they engaged in target shooting at bull's eyes 200 yards away. Rifled guns allowed for greater distance and accuracy. During the war New York City hosted a shooting fest in 1863 and national competition, lasting ten days, ensued in 1868.

The shooting of live pigeons became popular after the Civil War, until continued protests by concerned citizens and the American Society for the Prevention of

Cruelty to Animals curtailed the activity. Trap shooting with clay targets eventually replaced the live birds. The National Rifle Association organized in 1871 and built a ninety-acre rifle range on Long Island in New York. It held its first of annual matches that same year. Its founding members consisted of wealthy socialites, but it developed into and remains one of the most powerful political lobbying groups for gun owners of all classes.

In 1874 a New York gun club met the challenge of an Irish shooting club that had won the British championship. On their home soil the Americans defeated the Irishmen, then traveled to Ireland in 1875 to win the return match. The international competition proved more than a contest between clubs or individuals as the Remington and Sharps companies, U.S. manufacturers, supplied the American competitors with their latest products and backed them with the $500 stakes fee. Such sponsorship was meant to challenge the British leadership, not only in sport, but in product quality. Over the remainder of the century the United States would surpass the British in economic output to assume world leadership.

The Philadelphia Centennial Exhibition of 1876 offered an opportunity to showcase American wares and American technology. The fair featured the Corliss engine, the world's largest steam engine, and it also hosted an international shooting competition. Australia, Canada, Ireland, Scotland, and the United States entered competitors for the Palma Trophy, with the Americans triumphant. United States' marksmen successfully defended their international title in 1877 and 1878.

The growth of rifle clubs elicited concern among nativists, however. Many of the immigrant groups were closely allied with the labor movement and sharpshooters greatly alarmed employers. In Chicago, the center of labor unrest during the period, the German Lehr und Wer Verein (education and defense society) amounted to a workingmen's militia. When the group held a shooting contest in 1885 the entire police force and two regiments of the National Guard were alerted in case of an uprising. A year later the U.S. Supreme Court declared paramilitary groups to be unconstitutional. The workers fixed bayonets to their guns and marched in armed protest. Chicago soon erupted in the Haymarket Massacre, leading to fears of anarchists and, ultimately, the establishment of Labor Day on May 1, throughout the world.

In a more peaceful manner, women had also taken up the sport. Some, like Annie Oakley, proved more proficient than men. She and other female trick-shot artists traveled around the country giving exhibitions of their skills by the 1880s. Annie Oakley and her rival, Lillian Smith, attracted national attention. As members of Buffalo Bill's Wild West Show they traveled throughout the country and became international celebrities when the tour began traveling abroad in 1887.

Track and Field

Intercollegiate track and field competition originated as a sideshow to the regattas of the crew teams. But, like rowing, it had precedents in the working-class sport of pedestrianism. Pedestrianism implied walking, but the rules allowed competitors to "go as you please," meaning they could run or walk as a matter of choice, depending on their endurance capabilities. In 1861 Edward Payson Weston drew national attention when he attempted to walk from Boston to Washington, D.C., in ten days. He failed in that venture, but did manage to cover the distance between Maine and Chicago in twenty-six days, six years later, to win a prize of $10,000. Such commercialized tests of human endurance began as early as 1835 when wealthy promoter John Cox Stevens offered $1,000 to anyone who could run ten miles in less than an hour. Henry Stannard, a farmer from Connecticut, covered the distance with about fifteen seconds to spare.

Track and field events evolved out of the Scottish Caledonian Games of the 1850s. Desirous of maintaining their ethnic culture the Scots met on prescribed dates to compete with one another in running races, hurdles, jumping, pole vaulting, shot putting, hammer and weight throwing, caber (pole) tossing, and a tug of war. They offered cash prizes and eventually opened their competitions to non-Scots. By 1870 the Caledonian Games drew 20,000 spectators. That same year a Native American who competed under the name of Deerfoot lost to a Canadian Indian in a three-mile race for $400. By that time Deerfoot was forty-five years old and past his prime. He had earned a good living as a professional pedestrian in the 1860s, competing in England and setting a record for the one-hour run of eleven miles and 790 yards in 1863. Such races inevitably made racial comparisons between the competitors with consequent stereotypes attributed to whole groups based upon the performance of an individual. For example, Deerfoot's accomplishments led whites to believe that all Native Americans possessed innate endurance.

Deerfoot and others considered to be of low birth were not welcome as members of the New York Athletic Club (NYAC), founded in 1868. The NYAC admitted only the socially elite and soon set the standards for track and field competition in the United States. It constructed the first cinder running track in the United States, introduced the innovative spiked running shoe, established and standardized rules for competition, and produced the first national championships not only in track and field, but swimming, boxing, and wrestling as well. The NYAC championships, however, were limited to amateurs and excluded any working-class competitors who were deemed to be professionals because they worked as manual laborers or competed for prizes of value (cash or goods) that might be pawned. The upper classes assumed that such competitors could be bribed by gamblers and that they would not succumb to such temptations because they did not need the money.

In 1873 James Gordon Bennett Jr., the publisher of the *New York Herald* newspaper, presented a trophy, rather than a cash prize, for the winner of a two-mile race at the college regatta that year. The contest promoted greater interest in intercollegiate competition and helped Bennett to sell more newspapers. The following year the competition expanded to include a 100-yard dash, 120-yard hurdles race, a one-mile and a three-mile run, and a seven-mile walking race. Eight colleges competed for the trophies, and even more events were added for 1875. The colleges formed the Intercollegiate Association of Amateur Athletes of America (IC4A) in December of that year and track and field competitions soon divorced from the regattas to organize their own contests at the New York Athletic Club. The organization provided a bureaucratic governing body with rules, regulations, and records for competition, and the NYAC hosted the first national track and field championship in 1876.

The sport now known as cross country developed during the same period when runners, known as hares (rabbits), got a head start. They then dropped pieces of paper along their route for the hunters, known as hounds, to follow in the game of chase. Today cross-country runners are still sometimes referred to as harriers. By the 1880s cross-country running had developed into a sport of its own.

The interest in human endurance had popular appeal and numerous distance races attracted large crowds, especially from 1876 to 1880. The professional pedestrians engaged in six-day endurance races, resting intermittently on cots, with the one covering the greatest distance (by running or walking) declared the winner. Sir John Astley, an English nobleman, offered a silver and gold belt for an international championship race to be held in London in 1878, which was won by a Chicagoan, Daniel O'Leary. O'Leary lost the title to a British walker the next year; but Edward Payson Weston soon reclaimed the prize for the United States. An 1879 match for the Astley belt, held at Madison Square Garden in New York City, featured an English competitor, an African American, and several white Americans. Bookies set up shop within the arena and spectators placed bets as if at a horse race. A scoreboard tallied the distance covered by each participant. The contest proved so close that fans even stayed overnight, as three athletes covered more than 500 miles. The pedestrian events made Madison Square Garden a center for sports events and promoters offered as much as $20,000 in prize money for such affairs.

Women, too, took part in the pedestrian contests held in New York, Chicago, and San Francisco. By 1879 more than 100 women competed in the tests of endurance. Mary Marshall even defeated male contestants in a best of three races held in New York. Others, like German immigrant Bertha von Hillern, became celebrities, preaching the values of exercise. Ada Anderson, from England, competing in Brooklyn, covered 675 miles in 675 hours. Her record was extended by Madame Exilde La Chapelle, who walked 750 miles in 750 hours in a Chicago race.

Amateurs, however, distanced themselves from such professional meetings. In 1879 the New York Athletic Club joined with six other athletic associations to form the National Association of Amateur Athletes of America. The new organization adopted the rules of the NYAC, which held jurisdiction over amateur contests in the United States until 1888, when factions of the New York clubs formed the Amateur Athletic Union (AAU), which wrested control of amateur competition throughout the United States. The AAU soon initiated national championships in track and field, swimming, boxing, fencing, and gymnastics and became the governing body for amateur sport for nearly a century.

The rivalries between the athletic clubs revolved around the issue of amateurism and prestige. The athletic clubs, with their restrictive memberships, were status symbols, much like the racetrack clubhouses were for the wealthy. The NYAC built a five-story clubhouse in downtown New York at a cost of $150,000 in 1885. It included sleeping and dining rooms for members, as well as a gymnasium, swimming pool, billiard tables, a bowling alley, and a wine cellar. By 1888 the club acquired land for a country club with a running track, boathouse, and tennis courts. Other clubs spent even more to project their social status. The Boston Athletic Association doubled the cost of the NYAC structure at $300,000.

The athletic clubs argued over the definition of an amateur because it not only affected status but competition. For example, the Manhattan Athletic Club, a rival of the NYAC, provided an "athletic" membership to Lawrence "Lon" Myers. An athletic membership was not a full membership (possibly due to Myers's Jewish

James Gordon Bennett Jr. (1841–1918)

James Gordon Bennett Jr. was born in New York City on May 10, 1841, the son of a Scottish-born immigrant who became editor of the *New York Herald* newspaper. His father's boldness in that venture and the possible repercussions led him to send his son to Europe, where he was largely educated in France. In 1857 Bennett Jr. joined the New York Yacht Club at the age of sixteen and eventually became its youngest commodore. He served briefly (1861–62) in the Union Navy during the Civil War but first gained fame in 1866 when he won a transatlantic yacht race, a victory that claimed six lives at sea.

The younger Bennett assumed control of the *New York Herald* thereafter and increased sales by a combination of salacious and outrageous coverage of events as well as the use of technology. He utilized railroads, the telegraph, the transatlantic cable, special assignments, and teams of reporters. He created the news as well as reported it. Among such ventures, he funded the successful 1869 expedition of Henry Morton Stanley to Africa in search of the presumably lost British missionary doctor David Livingstone. Another adventure attempted to reach the North Pole (twenty expedition members died) and the quest for a Northwest Passage to Asia. His sponsorship of sports events made him perhaps the greatest sports promoter of the era. They included the support of Daniel O'Leary's pedestrian feats, the first intercollegiate track and field meet, horse races, boxing matches, the establishment of the first polo club in the United States (1876), and the building of the Newport Casino (1880), which hosted the national tennis tournaments from 1881 to 1914. Bennett was also a member of the American Jockey Club and promoted fox hunting in Virginia.

Bennett's brash and vulgar behavior at his fiancée's party in 1877 caused him to be ostracized from elite society and he fled to Europe, where he established the *International Herald Tribune*. He was a founding member of the Associated Press and a cofounder of a cable company that challenged the transatlantic cable controlled by Jay Gould.

Bennett maintained his interest in sports and established an eponymous trophy for yacht races. With the advent of new technology he awarded similar trophies for balloon races and auto racing. His lavish lifestyle and seemingly constant presence made him an international celebrity. At the age of seventy-three he married Baroness de Reuter, the daughter of the founder of the European news agency. He died in France on May 14, 1918.

ancestry); but entitled one to use the club training facilities and compete in the name of the club. Myers, a frail man of 5'8", afflicted with tuberculosis, and only 115 pounds, nevertheless held all the American running records from fifty yards to one mile at one time or another. The Manhattan A.C. sent Myers to England to compete against British runners, starting in 1881. Myers's victories brought much publicity to him, the club, and the United States. The Manhattan A.C. provided Myers with full-time employment at the club and in 1885 members raised another $4,000 in a benefit for him. Myers pawned hundreds of the trophies and medals that he won, yet managed to retain his amateur standing. Myers finally declared himself an open professional in 1886 so that he could compete against (and defeat) Walter George, the British middle-distance champion, in a series of stakes races worth thousands of dollars.

Such machinations drew the ire of other clubs that held to a strict definition of amateurism. With the advent of the AAU, greater enforcement of such policies banned recalcitrant athletes. Anyone who competed in an open meet (amateurs and professionals) or accepted anything more than a nominal prize could be branded as a professional and banished from all further competition. The quest for records and victories, however, did not preclude the aid of experts, science, and technology. College students began hiring professional coaches in the 1880s and Charles Sherrill, a Yale sprinter, introduced the crouch start in 1888. Photographic studies helped athletes to refine and better their technique and by 1890 John Owen of Detroit finally broke the record of 10 seconds for 100 yards, which had stood since 1868, when he ran 9.8, verified by six timekeepers with stopwatches.

ISSUES IN WOMEN'S SPORTS

In the period following the Civil War women made great strides in sport, but not without confronting social, physical, psychological, and medical issues. The myriad controversies ensued as women began to escape the traditional roles of wife, mother, and homemaker that had been assigned to them. By the Civil War women assumed the additional roles of nurses and teachers, but such positions did not upset the nurturing responsibilities accorded to them. Women dissatisfied with their plight and desirous of equal rights (such as voting and the ability to own property) organized a national women's convention in New York as early as 1848. They became increasingly active in national affairs thereafter, including suffrage, temperance, and abolitionism.

The courting (dating) etiquette of the second half of the nineteenth century, known as the Victorian Age, required formal introductions, approval by family members, and chaperoned dates. Young women began to depart from such expectations in their recreational activities. During the winters young women had long skated openly in the presence of men on frozen ponds, but a croquet craze in the 1860s raised new concerns about relations between the sexes. The large lawns of middle-class homes allowed enough space for mixed groups of men and women to engage in games in public view, without the necessity of a chaperone. The dynamics of the game, however, questioned the traditional psychologies attributed to women. While men were expected to be competitive in their capitalistic business enterprises, such qualities were seen (by men) as undesirable in women. The female croquet players, however, often cheated to win by moving or hiding the balls with their hoop skirts. They also relished the occasions that allowed them to knock the males out of play.

Such competitive tendencies were apparent in the formation of women's baseball teams in the 1860s as well. Women desired to be educated, but male physicians assumed that their delicate brains could not handle the stress of complicated study. After Vassar College for women opened its doors in 1865 the students soon formed baseball teams. At other women's colleges in the Northeast women organized rowing clubs and engaged in intramural competitions. The competitive desires of women were further exemplified with the introduction of tennis to the United States. Mary Ewing Outerbridge traveled to Bermuda where she witnessed the game being played by British colonials. In 1874 she returned to the United States with some equipment and received permission to set up a court at the Staten

Annie Oakley (1860-1926)

The most famous female athlete of the nineteenth century was born Phoebe Ann Mozee (various spellings) to Quaker parents on an Ohio farm in 1860. One of seven children, she had no formal schooling and her father died in 1866. Her mother was widowed three times. At age six Annie began shooting small game for the family's sustenance; still her mother had to send her to a county poor farm. She was also indentured to a cruel farmer and his wife before running away. At age sixteen she traveled to Cincinnati for a shooting match, where she defeated and so impressed the male star, Frank Butler, that they eventually married. She assumed the stage name Oakley, and the couple joined Buffalo Bill's Wild West Show in 1885.

Oakley's expertise with pistols, rifles, and shotguns as well as her trick shots soon made her the star of the show. Buffalo Bill's entourage traveled throughout the country, drawing huge crowds as it tried to recreate the vanishing frontier of the American West for city dwellers. The show was a major attraction in the biggest cities and towns, and in 1887 the troupe began excursions to Europe. Among the stunts that Oakley used to thrill the crowds were shooting a succession of glass balls tossed in the air. She shattered 4,472 out of 5,000 on one occasion. She'd also shoot a lit cigarette out of her husband's mouth. When a crown prince of Germany asker her to shoot one out of his mouth she requested that he hold it in his hand rather than his mouth. She also shot targets backwards while looking through a mirror. Such skills won her international fame.

In 1901 she suffered a serious back injury in a train wreck, which limited her travel and resulted in retirement from the Buffalo Bill show. She and her husband continued their own exhibitions and at the age of sixty-two she still managed to hit all 100 clay targets from a distance of forty-eight feet. She died on November 3, 1926, in Greenville, Ohio, but remains an American icon.

Island Cricket Club managed by her brother. By 1881 the U.S. Lawn Tennis Association organized and established a national championship at Newport, Rhode Island. Richard D. Sears won and held the singles title throughout the 1880s. The Philadelphia Cricket Club sponsored a women's championship by the end of the decade, and a professional tournament began in 1889.

During the 1870s and 1880s a roller-skating fad replaced croquet as a recreational pastime. Conducted in indoor roller rinks, skating, like croquet, allowed young people to mingle in a public sphere without a chaperone. During the 1870s women also joined archery clubs, which developed specific physical skills. A National Archery Association formed in 1879 through the initiation of Albert Spalding and others and a national tournament and women's championship was held at White Stockings Park in Chicago that year. While working-class women experienced greater physicality in their lives, the skaters and archers were middle-class participants, indicating that such interests crossed class lines.

The accounts of female pedestrians have already been detailed, but in the late 1870s women also took up cycling. By 1882 Louise Armaindo claimed the distance riding championship of America, covering 843 miles in seventy-two hours. She competed against men and embarked on an international tour across the United States to Australia and England. Most women, however, were content to join local cycling clubs, hundreds of which formed in the decade. A national organization, the League of American Wheelmen, was established at Newport, Rhode Island in

Bird's-eye view of tennis courts on Ladies Day. Staten Island ladies' lawn tennis club. (Courtesy of the Library of Congress)

1880 and soon gained political influence. The large number of cyclists lobbied their representatives for paved roads, even before the advent of automobiles. Paved roads proved much safer for the high-wheeled cyclists, who might take a "header" and suffer serious injury if their big wheels hit a stone in the unpaved roads.

The middle-class cycling clubs engaged in long excursions, sometimes of 100 miles, called century runs. Bicycle rides enabled young couples to outdistance their assigned chaperones, perhaps occasionally stealing an illicit kiss. By the mid-1880s a new "safety" bicycle was developed, with two equal-sized tires, making the sport even more popular. Mass-produced cycles brought the cost down and even the working classes were able to afford used bikes. The new technologies enabled people to travel faster and cyclists were fascinated by speed. Both men and women racers became known as "scorchers," but their velocity raised bigger issues. Speeding disrupted regular traffic and scared the horses ridden by many others. Parading cyclists also disrupted church services on Sunday; but the biggest controversies ensued over women riders.

Women wore fashionable bustle skirts during the cycling craze, but the long fabrics easily caught in the bicycle spokes, causing damage to the dress and possible injuries to the rider. In lieu of the skirts women adopted bloomers or pants to ease their difficulties. Such costumes, however, raised the ire of conservative males who feared that women who usurped male clothing would soon want to usurp men's privileged roles in the society. Women were already clamoring for the right to vote. Political leaders denounced female cyclists and some communities even passed laws to ban them from the streets. Preachers claimed that female cyclists were possessed by the devil. Adding to the concern, physicians worried that the female cyclists would damage their reproductive organs by bouncing on the seats, while moralists saw the practice as sinful.

Men, and some women, became perplexed by female participation in sport, particularly speed or power sports that they saw as suitable only for men. In the 1890s basketball quickly spread throughout the women's colleges and in 1895 the Vassar College women initiated a field day that included track and field events. Such activities opened new vistas for women and educators, and physicians continued to debate the proper role of exercise and competition for females. In the ensuing decades female educators would develop the play day concept, bringing schools together but mixing the teams, to avoid the social and psychological stresses that they saw in men's competitive activities. That decision had repercussions throughout the twentieth century and beyond, as administrators, coaches, and athletes continue to wrestle with the ramifications of Title IX, the 1972 law that attempted to provide equal opportunities for all.

SUMMARY

The Civil War both disrupted and curtailed sports; yet it also promoted and expanded some. While many athletes went off to war, soldiers learned to box and play baseball during their leisure hours. During the Gilded Age sports in general became more organized with bureaucratic associations serving as governing bodies that standardized rules, kept records, set eligibility guidelines, and resolved disputes. The practice of sport became more specialized as athletes began to assume particular roles and fashion specific equipment. Technological advances aided performance and reporting of sports events. The best athletes became professionals, earning a salary for their physical skills. In order to pay such salaries the athletic clubs and their events became more commercialized. Sport became a business with contests taking place at enclosed sites where spectators had to pay admission fees. Such operations required a large fan base, resulting in the concentration of professional teams in the larger cities, and the relegation of smaller locales to minor-league status.

Both baseball and football began to assume modern forms. The National League achieved owner control over the players and became the model for succeeding professional sport franchises. Intercollegiate football even surpassed baseball in popularity on college campuses and initiated the team spirit and revelry that continues to mark student life. Boxing resisted, and continues to resist, organization in any one unified governing body. Through the efforts of Richard Kyle Fox, however, it did distinguish separate weight classes to equalize physical mismatches. The adoption of the Marquis of Queensbury rules brought a measure of acceptability, and boxing produced the first great American sports hero in John L. Sullivan. The gambling and corruption that accompanied both boxing and horseracing left both in disfavor by the end of the period. Rowing also declined, as popular interest swayed to baseball, which assumed the status of the national pastime. Track and field maintained its attraction and even increased in interest with the introduction of the modern Olympic Games in 1896. Track and field held particular attention for scientists because it allowed for the measurement of human potential.

Perhaps the greatest gains in sport were made by women, who found in its practice a liberating experience. Sport became a vehicle for transcending the prohibitions of the Victorian world. Recreational activities allowed women to challenge the formal courting rituals and patterns. Sport spawned dress reform. As women adapted and adopted new clothing to fit their particular needs and discarded the restrictive corsets, hoop skirts, and bustles that limited their movement. Sport allowed women to experience a new physicality, revel in their bodies and their abilities, and disprove the stereotypical notions of female debility. By the 1890s the newspapers acknowledged in cartoons and essays the "new woman," who was athletic, self-assured, confident, and desirous of change.

RECOMMENDED RESOURCES
Print Sources

Gems, Gerald R. 1996. *Sports organized, 1880–1900*. Vol. 5 of *Sports in North America: A documentary history*. Gulf Breeze, FL: Academic International Press.

Gems, Gerald R., Linda Borish, and Gertrud Pfister. 2008. *American sport: From colonization to globalization*. Champaign, IL: Human Kinetics.

Gilfoyle, Timothy J. 2006. *A pickpocket's tale: The underworld of nineteenth-century New York*. New York: W. W. Norton.

Gorn, Elliott. 1986. *The manly art: Bare-knuckle prize fighting in America*. Ithaca, NY: Cornell University Press.

Gorn, Elliott J., and Warren Goldstein. 1993. *A brief history of American sports*. New York: Hill and Wang.

Hardy, Stephen. 1982. *How Boston played: Sport, recreation, and community, 1865–1915*. Boston: Northeastern University Press.

Isenberg, Michael T. 1988. *John L. Sullivan and his America*. Urbana: University of Illinois Press.

Journal of the Gilded Age and Progressive Era. Currently published at Department of History, Illinois State University, Normal, IL.

Kirsch, George B. 1995. *Sports in war, revival, and expansion, 1860–1880*. Vol. 4 of *Sports in North America: A documentary history*. Gulf Breeze, FL: Academic International Press.

Levine, Peter. 1985. *A. G. Spalding and the rise of baseball: The promise of American sport*. New York: Oxford University Press.

Mrozek, Donald J. 1983. *Sport and American mentality, 1880–1910*. Knoxville: University of Tennessee Press.

Riess, Steven A. 1989. *City games: The evolution of American urban society and the rise of sports*. Urbana: University of Illinois Press.

———. 1995. *Sport in industrial America, 1850–1920*. Wheeling, IL: Harlan Davidson.

Sage, Henry J. 2005–6. Politics in the Gilded Age. Sage History. http://www.sagehistory. net/gildedage/GildedAPolitics.htm.

Web Sources

Andrew Carnegie. The Gilded Age. *The American Experience*. http://www.pbs.org/wgbh/ amex/carnegie/gildedage.html.

A Classification of American Wealth, pt. 2, America in the Gilded Age. http://www.raken. com/American_Wealth/Gilded_age_index.asp.

The Gilded Age (1878–1889). America's Story from America's Library. http://www. americaslibrary.gov/cgi-bin/page.cgi/jb/gilded.

Sage, Henry J. 2005–6. Politics in the Gilded Age. Sage History. http://www.sagehistory. net/gildedage/GildedAPolitics.htm.

CHAPTER 3

AMERICAN SPORTS, 1890–1899

Matthew Llewellyn

OVERVIEW

The 1890s proved to be a decade of remarkable change in American history. As the western frontier gradually closed following the conclusion of the Indian Wars, the industrial revolution transformed the United States into a world economic leader. American corporations dominated the global heavy industries such as iron and steel. Though American workers enjoyed some of the fruits of industrial prosperity labor unrest was widespread, while women entered the workforce in growing numbers. With an expanding economy, millions of new immigrants arrived onto American shores in search of a new life and prosperity. The newcomers were met by nativist hostility. American race relations also reached a new low. Through a series of discriminatory laws and practices, white society segregated African Americans, treating them as second-class citizens and often brutalizing them. Away from the domestic scene, the 1890s also witnessed the acquisition of American territories abroad following success in the Spanish-American War. Moreover, considerable advances were made in many areas of American life including science, technology, education, and medicine. In this era of rapid change and sweeping transformation, sport established itself as a popular American pastime.

In the last decade of the nineteenth century, the United States, blessed with booming population growth and abundant natural resources, emerged as the world leader in total manufacturing output and annual economic growth. In an age of giant corporations, pioneered by capitalists such as John Pierpont Morgan (1837–1913), Andrew Carnegie (1835–1919), and John D. Rockefeller (1839–1937), the United States became the top producer of iron and steel in the world. New companies emerged, including General Electric and Carnegie Steel (later U.S. Steel), and American goods flooded international markets. Nevertheless, American economic growth was temporarily halted. In 1893 a financial panic due to the decline of American gold reserves sagged into the worst economic crisis in the country's history. Lasting over four years, the "Panic of 1893" pushed unemployment rates to an unprecedented high. Hundreds of American businesses, including railroad companies and steel mills, failed. Turbulent workers' strikes gripped the country. In spite of the depression, late nineteenth-century economic advances contributed to the development and popularity of sports throughout the United States. Higher wages and more structured workdays offered many Americans both the free time and the money to attend or participate in a wide spectrum of sporting activities.

In the midst of the nation's economic growth and depression, an influx of new immigrants, mostly from southern and eastern Europeans nations, swarmed into major American cities. Agricultural depressions and peasant uprisings had forced many Europeans to abandon their old homelands in search of a new life and prosperity in the United States. In order to process the large numbers of Italians, Russians, Hungarians, Slavs, Greeks, Jews, and others entering the country, the U.S. government opened Ellis Island in New York harbor on January 1, 1892, as the main receiving station for immigrants. As 3.6 million people poured into the United States in the 1890s alone, New York City (and Boston, Chicago, and San Francisco) emerged as the melting pot of immigrants from around the world. The arrival of immigrants from various ethnic and religious backgrounds fueled an intense American nationalism throughout the decade. Considered a threat to both American institutions and native interests, epidemics of violence broke out repeatedly. In this period of high ethnic tensions, sport emerged as both a positive Americanizing force and an avenue for immigrants to fulfill the American dream of increased wealth and social mobility.

In the 1890s American race relations reached a new low. Born out of contemporary notions of black racial inferiority, and fueled by economic, political, and social frustrations, de jure and de facto segregation spread throughout the nation. Racism took its most extreme form in the South as demonstrated by the increased prevalence of lynchings of blacks. Supported by "Jim Crow" segregation and discriminatory statutes, African Americans were excluded from active citizenship and were segregated in almost every area of southern public life, including railways, hospitals, living areas, and sports. De facto segregation also permeated throughout the North, where African Americans were treated as second-class citizens, prohibited from entering white restaurants and hotels, and were forced into living in all-black urban ghettos. African American educational elites such as Booker T. Washington (1856–1915) and W. E. B. Du Bois (1868–1963), were strongly divided on the issue of black advancement in American society. Washington, a Southerner, believed that blacks should focus on improving their economic skills in order to win white acceptance, while Du Bois, a Northerner, issued a direct challenge to the legal, political, and ideological injustices suffered by blacks throughout the country. For African Americans, sport served as both a positive and negative force. Even though successful black athletes enjoyed some luxuries and freedoms not available to other members of their race, sport reinforced racial stereotypes and, in certain instances, established a color-barrier preventing black participation.

As the nation's economy continued to grow, the boundaries of traditional gender relations gradually began to shift at the end of the century. Women began entering the workforce in increasing numbers, working predominantly in the teaching and clerical professions. Supported by the political demands of women's rights advocates, American women enjoyed greater social freedom and challenged traditional definitions of femininity. Although the ratification of the Nineteenth Amendment would have to wait until 1920, women were granted suffrage in Colorado (1893), Utah

(1895), and Idaho (1896), following Wyoming (1869). The expansion of the female labor force, however, was met by vocal opposition throughout the country. Based upon Victorian notions of womanhood, opponents of the "new womanhood" argued that American women were abandoning their domestic responsibilities and jeopardizing their physical well-being. In this contested environment, women's sporting participation was frequently limited, as many sports were deemed too dangerous and unsuitable for women. Despite these gender restrictions, American women searched for avenues in which to participate in sport.

The conclusion of the nineteenth century also witnessed the expansion of American territories abroad. Signaling a move away from the nation's traditionally isolationist role in world affairs, the United States went to war with Spain in 1898 over her oppressive treatment of Cuba. Led by future U.S. president Theodore Roosevelt (1858–1919) and his gang of "Rough Riders," the military conflict proved to be short-lived. After only 109 days, the United States achieved resounding military victories. The Spanish-American War proved to be an overwhelming success for the United States in many ways. Under the terms of the Treaty of Peace signed in Paris on December 10, 1898, the Spanish renounced all of their rights to Cuba and granted the nation independence. Cuba quickly became a U.S. satellite. The treaty also witnessed the United States' emergence as an imperial power. Aligned with the formal annexation of Hawaii in July 1898, the United States acquired the former Spanish colonies of Puerto Rico, the Philippines, and Guam. Within these new territories, American colonizers introduced sports such as baseball, football, and boxing as a means of solidifying colonial relations and teaching their new subjects important American values.

Back on home soil, advances in science, technology, education, and health care gradually improved the lives of countless Americans at the turn of the century. Electric trolleys and mechanical bicycles steadily replaced horse-drawn carriages as the most popular modes of urban transportation. Railroads connected far-flung American cities into a national grid. Improvements in technologies such as the printing press and the telegram contributed to the growth of the mass-media. These developments in transportation and communication proved pivotal to the spread of sport throughout the United States.

The field of medicine slowly modernized as well, placing a renewed focus on caring for and improving the human body. A growing number of medical specialists advocated increased physical exercise, while pioneers such as John Harvey Kellogg (1852–1943) trumpeted the benefits of a strictly vegetarian diet, including his own whole-grain cereals. In the 1890s, education also became more available as the number of public high schools steadily increased. Physicians and other theoreticians who banded together in the newly formed American Physical Education Association (1886) pushed the expanded school system to include physical education and sporting activities. Higher education also experienced similar gains as more students sought advanced degrees. Sport flourished on campuses. A new environmental movement also rose to prominence during this period. Political and social thinkers believed that they could counteract the adverse effects of industrial and urban living, such as disease and pollution, through the preservation of national parks and the creation of urban green spaces. As a growing awareness focused on improving the lives and health of Americans, sport transformed into a positive force in the attainment of national well-being.

TEAM SPORTS

Baseball: A Decade of Conflict

In a decade in which America experienced dramatic transformations, one thing remained consistent—the nation's affinity for baseball. The 1890s proved to be an era of unprecedented change and dissension within professional major-league baseball. Following the dissolution of the separatist Players League (PL) in 1890, the National League (NL) faced a renewed threat from rival professional circuit, the American Association (AA). Tensions quickly developed after a national board was established to determine which teams owned the contracts to specific players before they "jumped ship" to the PL. In an effort to clear up this confusion, clubs in both leagues were asked to provide a list of the players for which they held contracts. For reasons unknown, the AA franchise from Philadelphia failed to submit their list to the national board, leaving their star players Harry Stover and Louis Bierbauer available as free agents. Acting quickly, the NL's Pittsburgh team swooped in to sign Bierbauer, much to the chagrin of the AA, who labeled the Pittsburgh team as "Pirates," a name that has stuck ever since. Despite an immediate appeal from the AA, the national board ruled in favor of Pittsburgh. Infuriated by the ruling and the NL's stranglehold over professional baseball, the AA sought revenge. Collectively, AA teams began raiding NL rosters, recruiting additional financial support, and planting franchises in rival cities including Boston, Philadelphia, and Cincinnati. In the coming months, as the two leagues wrestled for control, the "Second Association War" plunged professional baseball into a state of decline.

The rivalry between the two major-league circuits had an enervating affect on professional baseball. Already reeling from the financial losses incurred during the player revolt of 1890, both leagues faced an economic crisis as competition for the best ball players drove salaries up to a record high. As both leagues continued to struggle, a truce seemed the only plausible solution. Subsequently, the "National Agreement" of 1892 proposed the formation of a revised National League. Composed of the eight original NL teams plus four from the AA, the new-look National League saved professional baseball from a seemingly certain economic collapse. The rights to the five remaining AA teams were paid for at an estimated cost of $130,000.

With peace restored, the National League entered the 1892 season rejuvenated and financially solvent. More important, with the absorption of the American Association, the National League asserted a complete monopoly over the highest level of professional baseball in the United States. As in the previous decades, the players were the ones to suffer under the new system. The absence of a rival major league eliminated competition between teams and drove player salaries down to an uncomfortable level. Reports indicated that in some instances player salaries were slashed by a staggering 40 percent. In the next few years, player salaries continued to decline as NL owners imposed an "unofficial" $2,400 salary cap. Remarkably, to cut costs further, the league also reduced squads to twelve players as opposed to fifteen. Seemingly overnight, the National League had wrestled power from the players, putting down their insurgency and reasserting complete dominance over professional baseball.

Rule Changes

Beyond the battles taking place for control of baseball off the field, the sport underwent a series of dramatic changes on the field. The 1890s witnessed the introduction of a number of rule changes that revolutionized the way that baseball was played. Over the course of the previous three decades, a fine balance had existed between offense and defense. Teams frequently struggled to record high scores and home-run hitting proved to be a rarity. In 1893 this pattern of impotent hitting began to change, due in part to the introduction of new pitching rules. The National League extended the distance between the pitcher's mound and home plate to an astounding sixty feet, six inches, ten feet further than the previous distance. Further rule changes also required pitchers to deliver the ball with their back foot fixed to a rubber slab, eradicating the "softball" like skip-step delivery that had beleaguered NL offenses for the past few decades. Seemingly overnight, teams witnessed a remarkable upturn in offensive prowess. Home runs were witnessed in NL parks throughout the country, average team scores increased, and a new expansive style of the nation's favorite pastime had emerged. For instance, whereas in 1892 only seven players hit .300 or above, in 1893, following the rule changes, an unprecedented twenty-six players achieved this feat. In fact, over the course of the entire decade seven players hit a whooping .400 or better average.

In an effort to offset the prodigious hitting of NL offenses, managers throughout the country began to develop a new "scientific" or "inside" style of baseball. Managers placed a new emphasis on field positions, ensuring that their smartest players held the most crucial positions, such as shortstop. This new attention to detail also pushed coaches to continuously drill into their players the fundamentals of effective defense. Subsequently, over time, attributes such as throwing to the correct base and backing up the thrower became a regular feature of a team's defensive armory. Attempts to temper the dominance of NL offenses, however, were not taken lightly. In response, the number of sacrifice bunts rose dramatically, made easier thanks to the increased distance between the pitcher's mound and home plate. Hit-and-run and squeeze plays also rose in prominence, along with more aggressive base running. Led by the example of Boston Beaneaters' star William "Billy" Hamilton, who amassed a remarkable 987 stolen bases in the 1890s alone, base-stealing became a common tactic in professional baseball.

Baseball's Tarnished Image

As offenses and defenses battled to assert their dominance, NL baseball developed a rather unsavory reputation for the aggressiveness of its play. Throughout the country, players sharpened their spikes in an effort to inflict deep wounds against their opponents when sliding into bases. Infielders tripped or blocked base runners. Catchers threw their masks in front of runners to hinder their progress toward home plate. More alarmingly, the clearing of the dugout became a frequent occurrence as heated rivalries spilled over into full-blown fistfights. No other team captured this bellicose spirit better than the Baltimore Orioles, one of the National League's most successful franchises throughout the 1890s. Led by their pugnacious player-manager John McGraw (1873–1934), the Orioles used a variety of dirty tricks such as verbal abuse to intimidate opponents and umpires alike.

The ferociousness on the diamond also transferred to the stands as spectators added to the National League's increasingly tarnished reputation. Over the course of the decade, the National League relaxed its traditional ban on both Sunday baseball and the sale of alcohol on the grounds. These policy changes, combined with the reduction of general admission to only twenty-five cents, shifted the traditional demographics of baseball spectators. Gradually, the league's intended middle-class audience was overrun by ethnic and working-class men eager to enjoy a hot Sunday at the ballpark with a beer. Predictably, as the tension reached a fever pitch during the game, drunken fans threw beer bottles and rained foul language on opposing players and umpires. Reports of umpires and opposing players being forced to leave the stadium hastily at the end of the game in fear of physical attack from home fans were not uncommon. Furthermore, the growing presence of people from ethnic groups such as Irish Catholics and German Jews attending ball games contributed to a dangerous spike in ethnoreligious violence. For the nation's urbane elites and powerful middle classes, the prevalence of player and spectator violence reaffirmed their convictions that professional baseball was a disreputable American sporting pastime.

Attempting to regain its middle-class fan base and its reputation as a purveyor of respectability, the National League launched an initiative to curb the outbursts of player and spectator violence. In 1897 the league strengthened the rules against fielders using their bodies to block runners off the bases. The following year, the league produced a new set of guidelines under the title, "A Measure for the Suppression of Obscene, Indecent and Vulgar Language upon the Ball Field." This initiative, aimed predominately at eliminating the roughhouse tactics employed by the Baltimore Orioles, stated that any player caught addressing a fellow player or an umpire in a "filthy" manner would be subjected to a fine, or worse, a lifetime ban from the game. Despite the threat of hefty punishments, the league's crackdown on disorderly conduct proved completely ineffective as not one single player was found guilty of violating the new guidelines.

The Rise of the American League

As the decade progressed, the National League faced more serious problems than unruly player behavior. The economic depression of 1893 lowered disposable incomes for millions of Americans and drove attendances down to an unprofitable low. In the 1890s the average game attendance across the country plummeted to between only 2,000–3,000 spectators, 500–1,000 less than recorded in the 1880s. Baseball's economic woes aside, the 1890s also revealed more fundamental problems that undermined the stability of the National League. Most notably, a substantial disparity existed between the top and bottom teams in the league. In addition to the Boston Beaneaters, who claimed five pennants including three consecutive titles in 1891–93, only Baltimore and Brooklyn won NL titles in the 1890s. At the opposite end of the spectrum, the league's worst team, the Cleveland Spiders, amassed a dismal record of only 20 wins in 154 games during the course of the 1899 season. The absence of both quality teams in New York, Philadelphia, and Chicago—three of baseball's historically powerhouse cities (as well as largest in population)—and an adequate playoff system added to the growing litany of problems affecting the National League.

As the National League continued to flounder, a rival league emerged intent on challenging for baseball supremacy. In 1894 Byron Bancroft "Ban" Johnson (1864–1931), a former Cincinnati sportswriter, took over the reins as president of the Western League, a struggling minor-league circuit. Intent on turning around the league's fortunes and cleaning up baseball's tarnished image, Johnson implemented a policy of hard-line reform. First, he claimed full control of the league's scheduling, introduced stricter rules prohibiting unruly player and spectator behavior, and worked to ensure that the league's struggling franchises remained financially solvent. The indefatigable Johnson also moved to break up the National League's monopoly over professional baseball. At the forefront of Johnson's grievances with the major-league circuit was its ability to be able to draft players from the Western League and other minor-league systems for only $500 per player. In Johnson's estimations, this figure was far too low. He asserted that the National League's penny-pinching contributed enormously to the failure of a number of minor-league teams who lost many of their star players for limited financial reward. In 1896 Johnson directly confronted the National League, demanding that they pay a higher premium for minor-league players. The Western League president also insisted that players could only be drafted after they had played at least two full seasons in the minor leagues. Both suggestions were unanimously rejected by the National League.

Angered at the ruling, Johnson upped the stakes by issuing a direct challenge to the National League. In 1900 Johnson took advantage of the wave of patriotism sweeping the country following success in the Spanish-American War by renaming the Western League the "American League" in an attempt to give it more of a national character. Johnson's biggest move came, however, when he planted four new franchises in Washington, D.C., Baltimore, Chicago, and Cleveland, the four cities recently vacated by the National League in 1900. Johnson's actions laid the framework for a "Great Baseball War" between both the National and American League circuits, a conflict that would consume professional baseball over into the early years of the twentieth century.

Apart from the power struggles and rule changes, baseball in the 1890s is perhaps best remembered for the enactment of a "color ban" that barred black players from the nation's favorite pastime up until Jackie Robinson's much-publicized entrance into the major leagues in 1947. Unofficial bans had prevented blacks from playing in the National League since 1872. Yet as many as fifty-four African Americans played professional baseball on integrated teams from 1883 to 1898. Nonetheless, most professional baseball teams enforced a "Gentleman's Agreement," whereby they promised not to field any black players. As Jim Crow racial segregation swept across the country, situations for black players rapidly deteriorated, culminating in the complete exclusion of blacks from white professional teams just prior to the turn of the century. In response to their exclusion, black players formed professional teams and began touring throughout the country. The most famous of these all-black teams were the Cuban Giants. Formed in 1885 by waiters and porters at the Argyle Hotel in Babylon, New York, the Giants took on all comers, blending showmanship with remarkable feats of baseball prowess. By calling themselves the "Cubans" and talking gibberish on the field, black players attempted to mask their African American ethnicity. By 1900 five major black professional teams were competing throughout the United States, including the Cuban Giants, the Cuban X Giants, and the Columbia Giants.

Basketball: The Invention of an American Pastime

On a cold winter's morning in December, 1891, James Naismith (1861–1939) invented the game of basketball. He created the new sport in Springfield, Massachusetts, at the School for Christian Workers (later renamed the International Young Men's Christian Association Training School and still later renamed once again as Springfield College). In an attempt to combat the boredom encountered by students during the long, harsh New England winters, Naismith devised basketball as indoor game. Although primitive by today's standards, the game spread rapidly within Young Men's Christian Associations (YMCA), Young Women's Christian Associations (YWCA), colleges, schools, and settlement houses throughout the country. Embraced by both men and women, basketball would grow to become one of the most popular sports within the hotly contested American sporting landscape.

James Naismith and the YMCA

The game's inventor, Naismith, was a thirty-one-year-old Canadian immigrant working at the school as an instructor. Born in Almonte, Ontario, Naismith was a graduate of McGill University, where he studied for undergraduate and divinity degrees. Dr. Luther Halsey Gulick (1865–1918), director of the gymnasium in Springfield and president of the college, challenged his faculty to devise a suitable game for students to be played indoors during the winter months. Recognizing the competitive element so firmly entrenched in American industrial life, Naismith moved away from the YMCA's traditional gymnastic and calisthenics exercises in favor of team-based competition. After experimenting with a variety of games including tag, baseball, soccer, lacrosse, and football, Naismith created basketball by attaching peach baskets, found in a storeroom, onto the lower rail of a balcony at each end of the school's gymnasium.

To the delight of Gulick and the school's student body, the first game was played in Springfield's gymnasium on December 21, 1891, with Naismith and his colleague Amos Alonzo Stagg (1862–1965), a future College Hall of Fame football coach at the University of Chicago, captaining the two nine-man teams. Unlike the complex rules that govern the modern game, Naismith's basketball could be played by adhering to only thirteen simple rules. Players could throw the ball in from any direction, but they could not strike it with the fist, run with it, or hold it to their body. Shouldering, holding, pushing, tripping, or striking an opponent in any way was strongly prohibited. Naismith's original rules also stipulated that any violation of the last rule would result into a foul, with three team fouls between goals counting as a goal for the opposing team. Of further importance, Naismith also assigned an umpire to call fouls and disqualify players who violated the rules. A referee was also designated to arbitrate on matters of scoring, timekeeping, and out-of-bound balls. Divided into two fifteen-minute halves, with a five-minute rest period in between, the game ended with the side with the most points declared the winner.

Naismith's invention of basketball exceeded all expectations. Led by some of Naismith's earliest students and fellow instructors at Springfield, basketball diffused to university campuses and schools across the country. Naismith himself traveled widely promoting his recent invention in cities including Albany and Troy, New

York, and Newport and Providence, Rhode Island. Stagg introduced the game to students at the University of Chicago in 1893, only a year after his appointment as the school's head football coach. In response to the game's burgeoning popularity, intercollegiate contests soon emerged. In fact, on February 9, 1895, the Minnesota State School of Agriculture defeated Hamlin in the first recorded intercollegiate basketball clash. Over the course of the next few years, colleges formed intercollegiate leagues in different regions of the country such as the New England League, which was comprised of Amherst, Holy Cross, Williams, and Dartmouth.

Basketball's greatest advances took place within the gymnasiums of YMCAs. On January 15, 1892, the YMCA's leading campus magazine, *Triangle*, published a detailed description of Naismith's new game, recommending basketball to YMCA leaders throughout North America. Seemingly overnight, basketball spread like wildfire, with more than 200 YMCAs in the United States and Canada introducing the game to their members. Set predominately on college campuses, especially along the Pacific coast and in the Midwest, YMCA chapters and gym-

Dr. James Naismith, inventor of basketball. (Courtesy of the Library of Congress)

nasiums promoted a specific brand of Protestantism known as "muscular Christianity." Arriving onto American shores from England in the mid-1800s, muscular Christianity pushed for the development of muscular bodies and moral souls, an ideology that became the seedbed of the YMCA. Basketball emerged as a vehicle for the promotion of muscular Christian beliefs. YMCA leaders believed that supervised athletic competition such as basketball would draw immigrant groups and the working classes away from debased amusements, taverns and saloons, and into a safe, Christian environment. YMCA leaders also trumpeted basketball as a means by which to inculcate the nation's youth with highly desirable traits such as self-control, discipline, and leadership, all of which were fundamental to being successful in a competitive capitalist society.

Alongside the overwhelming success of the men's game, basketball also proved to be remarkably popular among American women. Contemporary notions of females held that they were fragile and physically inferior to men, and so they were restricted from participating in many popular sports during the last decade of the nineteenth century. Basketball, however, proved to be an exception. Women's basketball began at Smith College, an all-girls school in Northampton, located only fifteen miles from Naismith's Springfield gymnasium. In a move led by Senda Berenson (1868–1954), an athletic director at Smith, basketball was first introduced to the students in 1892. Berenson's version of the game, modified to suit women's assumed physical capabilities, spread throughout women's colleges, high schools, and settlement houses across the United States. Despite being dressed in bloomers and thick black stockings, female basketball players quickly developed a reputation for the intensity of their play, much to the chagrin of some early observers who believed that women

Western High School girls' basketball, Washington, D.C. (Courtesy of the Library of Congress)

belonged only in the domestic sphere. Playing on small indoor courts, away from the critical gaze of men, American women embraced basketball with remarkable zeal. During a period in which Victorian beliefs constrained American women, the sight of young women playing competitive basketball aroused widespread criticism from male and female observers alike. Yet within five years of basketball's invention the first women's intercollegiate game was played, on April 4, 1896, between Stanford and the University of California at Berkeley.

Teaching the World to Play Basketball

Extending beyond the borders of the United States, basketball quickly reached both Asia and Europe before the close of the nineteenth century. Basketball was taken abroad by Naismith's former students, who held positions as Christian missionaries in far-flung countries throughout the world. Most notably, led by Dr. David Willard Lyon (1870–1949), China's first YMCA was established at Tientsin in 1895. Serving as the organization's athletic director, Lyon quickly introduced basketball to the members of the chapter in an effort to promote muscular Christianity, including both physical strength and religious devotion, among the Chinese people. Future missionary efforts in countries such as the Philippines also promoted basketball as a tool for the advancement of the Christian faith. Nevertheless, despite basketball's positive reception in the Far East, most European nations, especially Great Britain and Germany, rejected Naismith's invention as a game more suitable for girls than for boys.

Senda Berenson: A Pioneer for Women's Basketball (1868–1954)

In 1892 the appointment of Lithuanian immigrant Senda Berenson to the position of athletic director at Smith College changed the nature of the women's game dramatically. Berenson, a graduate of the renowned Boston Normal School of Gymnastics—the nation's first physical education teacher training school—promoted an adapted form of Naismith's basketball to her all-female student body. Conforming to the prevailing medical, psychological, and social concepts of a woman's physical capabilities, Berenson introduced stricter regulations for women's play in an effort to shift the current focus on competition to teamwork and cooperation. Dividing the court into thirds (front, center and backcourt), Berenson confined the six players (forwards, centers, guards) to their respective section of the court so that no player had to dash breathlessly back and forth. Under Berenson's innovative rules, players were only allowed to dribble the ball one time (later three bounces), and physical contact such as the snatching or batting of the ball from the hands of an opposing player was strictly prohibited.

Remarkably, Berenson's rule changes failed to dampen the enthusiasm of American women. Across the country, students organized interclass basketball contests on a daily basis, events that became the focal point of college life. With class colors and banners, female student bodies cheered as freshman challenged sophomores, and juniors took on seniors. With the game's burgeoning popularity, Berenson hoped to establish a single set of rules based upon her modifications. In 1899 Berenson organized a National Women's Basketball Committee under the umbrella of the American Physical Education Association (APEA), a professional society for the promotion of physical education (later termed AAHPERD). Through the Spalding Brothers' sporting goods company, the nascent committee issued its first official rulebook for the women's game in 1901.

Throughout her lengthy and successful career, Berenson became editor of sport magnate A. G. Spalding's (1850–1915) *Women's Basketball Guide*, a publication that helped promote the women's game throughout the United States. She later served as chair of the U.S. Women's Basketball Committee for six years. In 1911, after a career spanning nineteen years, the champion of women's basketball resigned from her position as athletic director at Smith College. During her tenure at Smith, Berenson redefined Victorian notions of "true womanhood" by encouraging American women to engage in physical exercise and sporting competition in a safe and controlled environment. In 1985, as a fitting testimony to her impact on both women's basketball and sport in general, Berenson was inducted to the Basketball Hall of Fame.

As basketball continued to traverse the globe, in the United States the game underwent a series of dramatic changes. The peach baskets that served as the goals in Naismith's original design were replaced by bottomless cord nets in 1893. Heavy wire-screen backboards followed shortly after. Prior to this change, a ladder had been used to retrieve the ball from the peach baskets. The year 1893 also witnessed the introduction of the pivot. In 1894 free throws replaced goals as the standard punishment for rule violations, and a standardized basketball, slightly larger than a soccer ball, replaced the older, heavier ball. Although Naismith envisaged basketball as being a strictly shooting and passing game, the dribble was introduced in 1896 by players trying to obtain better shooting angles. During this period a further rule change mandated that teams would be limited to only five players as opposed to the original nine. These changes only served to heighten the nation's interest in basketball. The Amateur Athletic Union (AAU) soon sponsored regular basketball tournaments, while early professional leagues slowly emerged prior to the turn of the twentieth century. Most notably, barnstorming swept across the country led by premier professional teams such as the Buffalo Germans and the New York Wanderers.

Unlike the most popular major American sports such as football and baseball, which have obscure origins in European folk games and evolved for centuries from more primitive forms, Naismith's basketball had no historical roots. Additionally, basketball did not require a large outdoor space or expensive equipment. Rather, Naismith's game could be played both indoors and outdoors, in teams or individually, and with the only additional requirement of a ball. Subsequently, as the process of urbanization continued to draw millions of Americans into the nation's largest cities, limiting the space for play, basketball emerged during the last decade of the nineteenth century as a convenient and affordable sporting pastime.

As basketball flourished, one of Naismith's former students, William G. Morgan (1870–1942), followed his mentor's lead by inventing another popular ball game— volleyball. A graduate of Springfield College, Morgan took a position as director of physical education at the Holyoke, Massachusetts, YMCA. During the early months of 1895, Morgan invented his new game for his business-class members who found basketball too exhausting. Throughout the remainder of the decade, volleyball followed basketball's lead as it spread like wildfire across the country.

College Football: The "King" on Campus

In the last decade of the nineteenth century, football asserted itself as the king on college campuses throughout the United States. Led by elite eastern schools such as Harvard, Princeton, and Yale, football evolved from an informal, student-controlled pastime into a multimillion-dollar national spectacle. With the absence of a professional league (which was not created until 1920) football spread like wildfire across the country, forging regional styles of play and establishing important football traditions. Nevertheless, the growth of college football sparked renewed calls for its abolishment. Critics condemned the game's growing violence and brutality, and questioned its place in institutions of academic learning.

By the 1890s college football looked remarkably different from the rugby-style game that first emerged in the 1870s on the prestigious campuses of Harvard and Yale. With the exception of the forward pass, which had still not been introduced, radical new rule changes established football as a distinctly American pastime. Divided into two halves as opposed to four quarters, football lasted two hours and twenty minutes as measured by a continuous play clock. Teams consisted of eleven players on a side who often played both defense and offense. Substitutions were limited to such an extent that if a player left the game he could not return. Rather than the present-day four downs to make ten yards, the rules required players to make five yards in three downs. The field was 110 yards long, and end zones did not yet exist. Furthermore, touchdowns counted for only four points instead of six, the kick after counted for two rather than one, and successful field goals earned a team five points.

The Invention of Volleyball

During the early months of 1895, William G. Morgan (1870–1942), director of physical education at the Holyoke, Massachusetts, YMCA, invented the game of volleyball. Gaining inspiration from his former teacher, James Naismith, and his recent creation of basketball at the nearby Springfield YMCA College, Morgan set out to invent a lighter recreational activity that would cater to his center's older, business-class members who found basketball too exhausting. Blending elements of basketball, baseball, handball, and tennis, Morgan introduced his new, less physically demanding game at a YMCA sports conference at Springfield College. Volleyball, or minonette as it was originally called due to Morgan's use of a badminton net, received a favorable reception. Under Morgan's original rules, volleyball was played by two teams who each pushed an oversize ball back and forth over a six-foot, six-inch high net. Morgan also stipulated that each team would comprise nine players, an "out" would be called if the ball landed outside the perimeter of the court or hit the floor after more than one bounce, and the game would be played in nine "innings," with "three outs" allowed before a team lost a serve.

In 1896 Dr. Alfred Halstead of Springfield College suggested that Morgan drop the title "minonette" in favor of "volleyball," since, in Halstead's opinion, players seemed to be "volleying" the ball back and forth over the net. With its new name and an official set of published rules, volleyball swept throughout YMCAs, YWCAs, schools, and colleges across the United States. Incorporated in physical education programs, volleyball became a popular sport for both men and women. By 1900 the game's growing popularity signaled dramatic changes to Morgan's original rules. Through the Spalding Brothers' sporting goods company, a new, lighter-weight ball was introduced in an effort to speed up the game and allow for the introduction of more dynamic plays. Under the recommendation of the Physical Directors Society of the YMCA, the first-bounce rule and the use of innings were both eliminated. In its revised form, twenty-one points constituted a game and the net was raised to seven feet. Furthermore, balls landing on the side line of the court were deemed "in" and balls rebounding from the walls were considered out of play.

In light of the sport's early success, Christian missionaries employed volleyball as a vehicle for the promotion of their brand of muscular Christianity. Before the close of the nineteenth century, volleyball spread north across the border to Canada, and as far away as Asia and Latin America. During World War I American soldiers brought the game to Europe.

To some extent, these rule changes transformed college football into a national spectacle. Attracting huge crowds, often as big as 40,000 for games between the big-time eastern colleges, schools were forced into enclosing their playing fields, erecting permanent seating and selling entrance tickets. The reason for this enormous growth can be explained in part by the development of the sports media. Newspaper editors throughout the country viewed college football as a perfect way in which to fill the sports pages in the fall when horse racing and baseball were out of season. Subsequently, with the absence of a professional league, college football became national-headline news. Successful coaches were celebrated, star players were worshipped, and exciting plays were sensationalized. Attracting higher public visibility and widespread acceptance, college football was transformed overnight into an important part of the American sporting landscape.

As a result of the remarkable growth of the college gridiron, universities began establishing many important football traditions. Organized cheering sections and pep bands were formed, fight songs were composed, and school colors and mascots were chosen. Also during this period, the tradition of homecoming, which included parades, banquets, and dances, was established. The annual Thanksgiving Day football game also rose to prominence in the 1890s. Viewed as the most important date on the social calendar, the event quickly became a grand spectacle for students, alumni, and the local communities alike.

Violence and Brutality in Football

On the field, a radical new rule change heightened the violence and brutality of the college game. In 1888 Yale University's football czar, Walter Camp (1859–1925), introduced a new rule that made it permissible to tackle the ball carrier below the waist. As a result, colleges abandoned the more open running game in favor of a system of closed formations often referred to as "mass momentum plays." The heavy concentration of players attempting to move the ball the required five yards in three attempts often brought knees in contact with heads and heightened the prevalence of serious injuries. In 1892 Harvard University devised the most renowned mass-momentum play of the late nineteenth century, the "flying wedge," an offensive V-shaped formation that would protect the ball carrier and simultaneously deliver a severe blow to the players on the first line of defense. Even with abolition of the "flying wedge" and similar mass-momentum plays in 1894 following widespread public criticism, the game remained extremely dangerous. Concussions, broken limbs, bruised faces, and sprains became routine occurrences as players collided at full speed without the benefit of a helmet or padding. In some instances, the brutality of college football left some students dead or severely maimed. The violence and brutality on the field often transferred to the stands as students from opposing schools often clashed in bloody riots. In some instances, fistfights and the brandishing of weapons left fans severely injured or dead.

Alongside the growing violence, another major abuse in college football at the end of nineteenth century was the prevalence of the "tramp" athlete. As universities sought to enhance their prestige through success on the football field, they frequently relaxed their matriculation requirements to such an extent that talented players were able to enroll, star for the college team, and then depart either after a big game or at the end of a semester. During the 1894 season, for example, the University of Michigan fielded seven (out of the eleven starters) who had neither enrolled in school nor attended any classes. Lured by the financial incentives offered by boosters and alumni eager to see their alma mater succeed, tramp athletes emerged throughout the country.

Unsurprisingly, the frequency of player injuries, on-campus student violence, and the growing commercialism of the game attracted widespread criticism from reformers, moralists, and politicians throughout the country. Many university presidents aligned with their faculty members in strong opposition to the place of football on college campuses. Led most notably by Harvard University president Charles Elliot (1834–1926), opponents argued that college football jeopardized the health of the student body by glorifying violence and brutality, encouraged habitual violations of the rules, and diverted time from a student's studies and daily life.

Football U. of M. alumni team '99. (Courtesy of the Library of Congress)

By condemning the game's win-at-all cost commercial spirit and calling for moderation and reform, opponents argued that college football proved incompatible with the educational mission of American universities. Interestingly, in contemporary American society the same arguments continue to be lodged against college football and intercollegiate sports in general. In some instances, faculty took their opposition of the college gridiron to the extreme by abolishing football altogether. In the 1890s alone, schools such as Trinity (later Duke), Georgetown, Columbia, and Alabama abolished football for varying lengths of time. In 1893 even U.S. president Grover Cleveland was forced to abolish the year's Army-Navy annual football contest due to the game's escalating violence.

Nevertheless, in spite of the widespread opposition toward college football, few university presidents were willing to ban the game from their campuses. Fearing a student revolt, or simply recognizing the importance of the financial rewards and public prestige associated with the game, university presidents turned a blind eye to the evils of college football. More commonly, a growing body of advocates for college football, which included future U.S. president Theodore Roosevelt (1858–1919), defended the game on the grounds that it supposedly helped built the necessary character and strength needed for a new industrial and urban lifestyle. Based on a belief in Social Darwinism and its "survival of the fittest" ideology, many of the nation's leaders claimed that college football instilled the masculine and martial virtues needed for American men to govern themselves, their country, and the world.

Geographical Diffusion of Football

Despite the frequent clashes over the place of football on college campuses, the game continued to spread rapidly throughout the country during the 1890s. From its roots and early development in the prestigious Ivy League schools of the Northeast, college football spread to every region of the country. Throughout the Midwest and the South, college campuses caught football fever. In March 1892 a game between Stanford and California even signaled the arrival of football in the Far West. Colleges large and small took up the game in part due to the demands of the student body and in part as a means by which to emulate the powerful eastern institutions such as Harvard, Princeton, and Yale. University presidents established football on their campuses simply because they recognized the game's ability to build a national reputation for their schools, attract new students, and create alumni support.

The geographical diffusion of college football led to the development of regional styles of play. While established eastern schools relied heavily on their defense, budding western schools adopted an all-out attacking style. Similar regional differences were witnessed in the South, where schools developed their game around a quick, pass-oriented brand of attack. The growth of college football throughout the country also led to the establishment of regional conferences, the first of which was the Western Conference (predecessor to the Big Ten), established in 1896. As the game continued to grow, the nexus of power enjoyed by prestigious Eastern schools such as Yale was gradually being threatened, namely by the universities of Chicago, Minnesota, and Michigan.

Despite the rising democratization of the college game, football remained a predominately white institution in the 1890s. Even though African Americans were in the minority on both college campuses and the college gridiron, a handful of talented black athletes played on some of the leading college teams in the nation. Perhaps the most prominent was William Henry Lewis, a native-born Virginian and son of former slaves, who played for and captained both Harvard University and Amherst College in Massachusetts. In fact, Lewis proved so successful that in both 1892 and 1893 he was chosen to Walter Camp's prestigious "All-American" team. Football authorities later named him as the most dominating "center rush" of the entire decade. Other black football players rising to prominence during the decade included Lewis's teammate at Amherst, William Tecumseh Sherman Jackson, and University of Michigan star George Jewett. The last decade of the nineteenth century also witnessed the beginning of college football on black campuses as Livingston and Biddle College of North Carolina competed in the first official game in 1892.

Ice Hockey: The Diffusion of Canada's Favorite Pastime

Prior to basketball's invention, another popular team sport, ice hockey, was invented and popularized in Canada. Although primitive forms of ice hockey date back to sixteenth-century Europe, scholars have argued that the game was officially invented on March 3, 1875, when a handful of friends gathered at the Victoria Skating Rink in downtown Montreal to play the first recorded indoor hockey game. Following the game's foundation, ice hockey slowly headed south across the border into the northern United States. During the 1890s hockey developed into an important part of the hotly contested American sporting landscape at the amateur, intercollegiate, and eventually professional levels. A national affinity for team sports, a cold-weather climate, and new opportunities for sporting participation made the northern United States a perfect site for the development of ice hockey prior to the turn of the twentieth century.

The 1894–95 season marked the arrival of an ice hockey craze in the United States. Teams in Baltimore, Minneapolis and a handful of other U.S. cities were reported to be playing organized, competitive ice hockey on a regular basis. In fact, the city of Baltimore built the nation's first indoor arena with artificial ice. Marking the opening of this new facility on December 26, 1894, Johns Hopkins University challenged the Baltimore Athletic Club in an enthralling clash that ended in a 2–2 tie. Fourteen months later on February 1, 1896, Johns Hopkins, led by their captain, Canadian-born Sam Mitchell, took on Yale University in the first ever intercollegiate ice hockey game. The game also ended in a 2–2 tie.

An international contest took place in Minneapolis on February 18, 1895, between the University of Minnesota and the Winnipeg Victorias. International competitions between U.S. and Canadian teams continued to grow in regularity during this period. For instance, on January 23, 1896, a four-team international tournament was held in St. Paul, Minnesota. Comprised of teams from Winnipeg and the host city, St. Paul, the four-team event represented the first international tournament ever held in the United States.

The Intercollegiate Hockey League

Following Johns Hopkins and Yale's lead, intercollegiate ice hockey quickly germinated throughout the country during the 1890s. In fact, prior to the turn of the twentieth century, the University of Maryland, Cornell, Princeton, Brown, Columbia, and Harvard all began experimenting with Canada's newest sporting import. Typically, American students first learned the game by watching and receiving instruction from their more-experienced and better-skilled Canadian neighbors. As the game continued to grow in colleges throughout the United States, an Intercollegiate Hockey League was formed. Comprised of the powerful northeastern schools of Harvard, Yale, Brown, Princeton, and Columbia, the new league officially opened in the 1899–1900 season. This was the first official intercollegiate ice hockey league in the United States.

The Amateur Hockey League

Meanwhile, as the intercollegiate game continued to develop, Canadian expatriates living in New York City introduced ice hockey to the Empire State under the auspices of the New York Hockey Club. During the 1896–97 season, the New York Hockey Club played games against the Baltimore Athletic Club, the Montclair (NJ) Athletic Club, and two teams from Montreal. With the development of the game in New York City a local four-team Amateur Hockey League was established in November 1896. Kicking off the 1896–97 season, most of the teams played their games at the renowned St. Nicholas Arena in Manhattan, which officially opened its doors to the public on November 7, 1896. Operating as an exclusive ice hockey arena until 1906, upon which it began holding boxing contests, St. Nicholas served as the preeminent venue for both amateur and intercollegiate ice hockey games in the United States. Throughout the remainder of the decade, up to its eventual decline in 1917, the Amateur Hockey League flourished, eventually adding a number of teams from Boston. During the 1890s, records also indicate that a similar amateur league was in operation in Baltimore.

As ice hockey prospered, amateur teams began forming across the United States in cities such as Philadelphia, Boston, Pittsburgh, St. Louis, and within many small communities in Michigan and Minnesota. By the turn of the twentieth century the game spread to Cleveland, Chicago, Detroit, Buffalo, St. Paul, and as far west as San Francisco. In the coming years, however, ice hockey in the United States would shake off its amateur roots and instead thrive at the professional level. Beginning with the creation of the Western Pennsylvania Hockey League in the early 1900s, a small-scale, semiprofessional circuit, and later with the formation of the International Hockey League in 1904, professionalized ice hockey reigned supreme.

The Olympic Games Reborn

In 1896 the Olympic Games were revived. Baron Pierre de Coubertin (1863–1937), a French nobleman, led the movement to recreate the ancient Olympics (776 BCE–394 CE). Disheartened by his nation's defeat and surrender in the Franco-Prussian War of 1871, Coubertin sought to revitalize French society through sport. Based on the German excavations of Olympia, which began in 1875, Coubertin determined that an international sporting event would ignite national popularity for sport and improve the physical fitness of the average French youth. Looking longingly toward Great Britain, the creator of modern sports and the most powerful nation during the late nineteenth century, Coubertin theorized that if France adopted a British sporting culture, it would regain its status as the leading nation in the world. Furthermore, Coubertin also believed that an Olympic revival could help establish peace and understanding among the nations of the world. Coubertin idealistically envisioned a world of nations participating peacefully but competitively in Olympic competition rather than meeting violently on the battlefield. As Coubertin would later learn, however, the forces of nationalism and politics often served to exacerbate, rather than advance, international relations.

Coubertin's efforts to revive the Olympic Games were further inspired by a series of national Olympic competitions held throughout Europe since the seventeenth century. Most notably, the "Much Wenlock Olympian Games" held in Shropshire, England, annually since 1850, served as one of the earliest precursors to Coubertin's Olympic revival. Comprised of a mixture of athletic and traditional country sports such as quoits, football, and cricket, the Much Wenlock Games fired Coubertin's heart for creating an international athletic festival. Another important harbinger to the modern Olympic Games also took place decades later in Greece, the true home of athletic competition. Known as the "Zappas Olympic Games" (Greek Games), this event was held on four occasions in 1859, 1870, 1875, and 1889, and was comprised of mainly agro-industrial, cultural and athletic contests.

Reviving the Olympic Flame

In search of support for his plans to revive the Olympic Games, Coubertin headed to the United States in the winter months of 1889–90 where he found an ally in William Milligan Sloane (1850–1928). Sloane, a devout Quaker and professor of history and politics at Princeton University, shared Coubertin's passion for using modern Olympic competition as a tool for promoting international harmony and building moral character. Sloane ensured Coubertin that he could count on American assistance and set out to create the American Olympic Committee (AOC).

Buoyed by Sloane's pledge of support, Coubertin left the United States determined to bring his ideas of an Olympic revival to fruition. The first public discussion of Coubertin's proposal was held at a meeting of the Union des Sociétés Françaises de Sports Athlétiques (USFSA) on November 25, 1892. Unfortunately, Coubertin's audience proved less than receptive, widely denouncing the idea of reviving an ancient athletic festival. Undeterred, Coubertin traveled widely in an effort to drum up support, including trips to Great Britain and a return visit to the United States in the fall of 1893. Upon returning to his native France, Coubertin presented his proposal at an International Congressional meeting on June 16, 1894, held at the Sorbonne in Paris. After deliberating, the International Congress voted unanimously to revive the Olympic Games and to establish the International Olympic Committee (IOC). Coubertin's calls for the creation of an international sporting spectacle had finally been answered.

Based on the ancient Olympic system of staging competition on a quadrennial basis, Coubertin and the newly established IOC decided that in keeping with the classical Greeks, the modern Olympic Games would take place on a similar four-year rotation. Furthermore, due to a misunderstanding of the nature of the ancient games, Coubertin announced that the modern Olympics would only be available to amateur athletes. In reality, the athletes that participated in the ancient Olympics were full-time professionals who earned huge sums of money and received widespread recognition. With the Olympic movement restored, only one question remained: where would the first modern Olympic Games be held? After some deliberation, Coubertin made the suggestion that Athens should be awarded the right to host the Games, as a fitting testimony to the city's obvious historical connections to the Olympics. Following a unanimous vote, the IOC awarded the first modern Olympic Games to the Greek capital city.

The First American Olympics Team

Following the announcement of an Olympic revival, on March 2, 1896, a small contingent of American athletes boarded a steamship from Hoboken, New Jersey, and began the long transatlantic voyage to Athens, Greece. Supported by private financial donations, the American team, comprised mostly of Princeton students and members of the Boston Athletic Association (BAA), enjoyed first-class accommodation aboard the North German Lines' steamer *Fulder*. The team, determined to demonstrate to the rest of the world the strength of American athletics, engaged in rigorous physical training on the ship's deck.

On April 6, 1896, His Majesty King George I (1845–1913) officially opened the modern Olympic Games in Athens. After a gap of more than 1,500 years (the last Games were believed to have been held in 394 CE) the Olympic Games were reborn, with 241 athletes (all male) from fourteen nations competing over a nine-day period. Coubertin's quaint idea of an Olympic revival seized the world's imagination; 40,000 fans, including many European and American tourists vacationing in the Mediterranean, packed into the newly refurbished Panatheniac Stadion eager to witness Olympic competition for the first time.

In the track and field events, American athletes reigned supreme. Former Harvard undergraduate James B. Connolly (1865–1957) claimed first place in the triple jump. In doing so, Connolly hopped and jumped (he used a two-hops-and-a-jump

James B. Connolly: The First Olympic Champion (1865–1957)

On April 6, 1896, Irish American athlete James Brendan Connolly won the triple-jump gold medal at the first modern Olympic Games held in Athens, Greece. In winning the event, Connolly became the first Olympic champion in over 1500 years, since the conclusion of the ancient Games in 394 CE. Born on November 28, 1865, as one of twelve children to Irish-Catholic parents, John and Ann (O'Donnell) Connolly, in South Boston, Connolly enjoyed a remarkably successful career, first as an athlete, and then, in later life, as a novelist and journalist.

In his youth Connolly attended Harvard University and studied classics. In his determination to participate in the 1896 Olympic Games, Connolly quit his undergraduate studies. Ranking near the bottom of his class, Connolly was refused permission to compete for his country by the chairman of the university's "Committee on the Regulation of Athletic Sports." When his dean advised him against going to Athens because he might not be readmitted, Connolly declared, "I am not resigning and I am not making application to reenter. But I am going to the Olympic Games, so I am through with Harvard right now. Good day sir." Connolly's determination paid off. Representing Boston's Suffolk Athletic Club, the young Irish American claimed gold in the triple jump using an unorthodox style of two hops and a jump instead of the more commonly used hop, skip, and jump technique (this technique was legal in 1896). Connolly also achieved success in both the high- and long-jump competitions, placing second and third respectively.

At the 1900 Paris Olympics, Connolly tried to repeat the success that he had at the 1896 Athens Games. Despite a heroic attempt, the Irish American athlete had to settle for the silver medal, finishing behind his American colleague Meyer Prinstein (1878–1925). When his athletic career came to an end, Connolly focused his energies on cultivating his writing skills. Again Connolly's hard work paid off, as he went on to become America's foremost writer of maritime tales. Throughout a lengthy career, the former Olympian wrote twenty-five full-length works and more than 200 contributions to a variety of newspapers and journals, including, reports on the performances of American athletes at future Olympics. In recognition of his remarkable career, Harvard University, the school he briefly attended, awarded Connolly an honorary doctorate degree in 1949. Connolly, however, declined the honor. On January 21, 1957, James Brendan Connolly died in his hometown of South Boston.

---

technique) into the record books by becoming the first modern Olympic champion. Boston Athletic Association athlete Thomas Burke (1875–1929) won the 100- and 400-meter races, while his club colleague Thomas Curtis (1870–1944) triumphed in the 110-meter hurdles. Other notably American performances included Ellery Clark's (1874–1949) double-gold winning performances in both the high- and long-jump competitions, and Princeton's Robert Garrett (1875–1961), who won victories in the shot-put and discus events. With the exception of Australian Edwin Flack's (1873–1935) victories in the 800- and 1500-meter events, and Greece's Spyridon Louis's (1873–1940) climatic victory in the marathon, American athletes swept the track and field events. In total, the United States claimed eleven firsts, seven seconds, and two thirds (medals were not introduced until 1904), demonstrating to the rest of the world the dominance of American athletics.

Despite the relative success of the inaugural modern Olympic Games, the International Olympic Committee experienced considerable growing pains during its formative years. Most notably, Coubertin and the IOC faced widespread criticism from the Greeks who argued that the Olympic Games should be held on a permanent basis in their country. Supported by King George I, Greece attempted to seize the Olympics for themselves. Nevertheless, a defiant Coubertin persisted in his attempts to share the Games among the nations of the world. Ignoring Greek advances, Coubertin and the IOC awarded the 1900 Olympic Games to the city of Paris. Greece's disastrous entry into a war with Turkey in 1897 ended Greek efforts to keep the games on their soil.

Paris 1900 Olympics

As the second Olympic Games drew near, the United States began preparations for their defense of their self-proclaimed Olympic title. Led by the American Olympic Committee and their leader, James E. Sullivan (1862–1914), the U.S. team began to take shape as athletes from the University of Pennsylvania, Princeton, Georgetown, and several other universities and athletic clubs committed themselves to compete. Using his experience as secretary of the Amateur Athletic Union, Sullivan primed the American athletes for Olympic competition by scheduling the team to compete at the British Amateur Championships, held in London on July 7, 1900. Following an overwhelming display of athletic talent, the victorious American team headed to Paris for the Olympic Games.

In an effort to attract wider international recognition for his Olympic movement, Pierre de Coubertin decided to hold the Games in conjunction with the Exposition Universelle Internationale (the Paris World's Fair). Coubertin's decision appeared to pay off, as a remarkable 997 athletes from twenty-four nations competed. Unlike the first edition of the modern Olympic Games in Athens, the Paris Olympiad witnessed women compete for the first time (22 women). Nevertheless, by the time the track and field events began on July 14, 1900 (the Games officially opened on May 14), the Olympic Games had gotten lost in the midst of the World's Fair. Limiting Coubertin's role, the exposition organizers spread the athletic events over five months and deemphasized their Olympic status to such an extent that many athletes went to their graves without ever knowing that they had participated in the Olympics.

Despite the organizational problems, American athletes proved unbeatable once again, at least in track and field. Led by Ray Ewry's (1873–1937) three first-place finishes in the standing high-, standing broad-, and standing triple-jump competitions and Alvin Kraenzlein's (1876–1928) remarkable four winning performances in the 60-meter sprint, 110- and 200-meter hurdles, and the long jump, American Olympians won seventeen of twenty-two track and field events. When the Games finally concluded on October 28, 1900, the United States had retained its Olympic crown. More joy soon followed, as the IOC awarded the Games of the Third Olympiad to the United States, home of the Olympic champions.

SPORTS FOR INDIVIDUAL COMPETITORS
Boxing: The Birth of a New Era

As international athletic festivals such as the Olympics began to slowly emerge, at the domestic level the 1890s proved to be one of the most important decades in the history of boxing within the United States. When John L. Sullivan (1858–1918) defeated Jake Kilrain on July 8, 1889, for the world heavyweight championship crown, it signaled the end of an era in professional prizefighting. The Sullivan-Kilrain title bout proved to the last bare-knuckle fight in the sport's history. The introduction of the Marquis of Queensbury rules, a stricter set of guidelines that governed the sport and mandated the use of gloves, revolutionized boxing, helping to make it a more respectable American sporting pastime. Over the course of the decade, the days of surreptitious, illegal, bare-knuckle fights were gradually replaced by legitimate, highly commercialized bouts that pushed boxing from the periphery to the center of the nation's sporting interests.

Historically, critics of professional prizefighting opposed the sport on the grounds that the sight of two men inflicting physical harm on one another was extremely brutal, an expression of savagery unsuited to the progressive tempo of American industrial life. The high rate of participant injuries and deaths, the dominant presence of immigrants and working-class fighters, and the prevalence of gambling, alcohol, and vice, tarnished prizefighting in the eyes of the nation's urbane elites and powerful middle classes. Nevertheless, the new rules allegedly sanitized boxing, ushering in a new era of respectability. They prohibited wrestling, holding, gouging, and blows below the belt. Three-minute rounds and ten-second knockdowns also became standard features of professional prizefighting. The introduction of five-ounce padded gloves proved to be the most favorable innovation, as proponents of boxing argued that the gloves would soften blows and limit the risk of physical injury or, even worse, death. Ironically, late nineteenth-century observers failed to notice that padded gloves actual heightened the risk of injury as boxers were now able to throw considerably more punches to the head without damaging their hands.

John L. Sullivan: Heavyweight Champion of the World

In the 1890s, boxing's biggest superstar was the Irish American world heavyweight champion, John L. Sullivan. In fact, the "Boston Strong Boy," as Sullivan became known, was an American sporting celebrity, and perhaps during the 1890s the nation's most famous citizen. Following his defeat of Kilrain, the popular champion embarked on an acting career, appearing on stage in both the United States and Australia. He was deplored by critics, but loved by his fans, and his popularity grew. Unfortunately, the popular Irish American champion fell to drinking and this, combined with poor diet, saw Sullivan balloon to a remarkable 250 pounds, a figure considerably over his fighting weight. With mounting financial problems and deteriorating health, the thirty-four-year-old Sullivan planned a return to the ring.

On March 5, 1892, the Boston Strong Boy issued a direct challenge to anyone brave enough to try to take away his coveted world heavyweight crown. Looking for another big payday, Sullivan demanded that the fight purse be set at $25,000, with an additional $10,000 side bet. Nevertheless, Sullivan's offer was not open to just anyone. Maintaining a policy that he had held throughout his entire professional boxing career, Sullivan drew the color line and refused to fight Australia's black heavyweight champion, Peter "Black Prince" Jackson (1861–1901). Jackson, a native of the Virgin Islands, claimed the black heavyweight crown in 1888 following his defeat of Canadian champion George Godfrey. Sullivan's stance reflected the prevalence of racism within the United States as Jim Crow racial laws and de facto segregation became firmly embedded within the nation's institutions. Sullivan's racist beliefs aside, the world heavyweight champion avoided black fighters partly because he feared a backlash from his loyal supporters and also because he was unwilling to jeopardize his reputation by losing to a black fighter.

With the fight scheduled for September 7, 1892, at the Olympic Club in New Orleans, American boxer, James J. Corbett (1866–1933) emerged as the likely contender. Supported by bookmakers and sporting men, "Gentleman Jim," as he became known, managed to raise the necessary funds for the right to challenge Sullivan for the world heavyweight title. In contrast to his pugnacious Irish American opponent, Corbett proved to be somewhat of an enigma in professional boxing. Hailing from a respectable middle-class family in San Francisco, Corbett was a member of the city's prestigious Olympic Club. Unlike the scores of immigrant or working-class fighters that learned their trade on the streets of the nation's urban ghettos, Corbett learned how to box at a lavish sparring club in his home city. Moreover, the clean-cut, intelligent, and highly skilled Corbett held a respectable job as a bank clerk before transferring his skills to the ring, a world apart from the laboring jobs that previously sustained most fighters. Despite his comfortable upbringing, Corbett knew how to throw a punch. Over the course of his short career, "Gentleman Jim" had already scored knockout wins against respectable opponents such as Jake Kilrain and Jewish champion Joe Choynski. A grueling sixty-one-round draw against Australia's "black giant," Peter Jackson, further enhanced Corbett's budding reputation. The sight of Corbett competing in a heavyweight championship bout signaled the dawn of a new era in professional boxing, as the "manly art" no longer remained a preserve exclusively for the nation's immigrant and working classes.

The Modernization of Boxing

In the last decade of the nineteenth century, New Orleans emerged as the boxing capital of the United States, similar, perhaps, to Las Vegas in the contemporary era. As the venue for the upcoming Sullivan-Corbett world heavyweight championship bout, New Orleans held a rich boxing history, holding regular prizefights since the 1880s. On March 14, 1890, the New Orleans city council passed an edict that legalized boxing matches fought under Queensbury rules. The ruling was based upon the provisions that no liquor could be served, no fights could be staged on Sundays, and all promoters had to contribute at least fifty dollars to charity. The city's prestigious Olympic Club soon overcame the final legal hurdle by defeating the old antebellum antiprize-ring statutes in court, establishing the right to hold glove fights to the finish for a purse.

With the legal barriers in New Orleans eliminated, the stage was set for high-profile professional boxing matches. On January 14, 1891, Jack "the Nonpareil" Dempsey (1862–96), not to be confused with his more famous namesake, challenged British-born "Ruby" Robert Fitzsimmons for the middleweight crown. Held at the Olympic Club's new 3500-seat arena, Fitzsimmons easily overcame his haggard opponent to clinch the championship title plus an $11,000 cash purse. The lavish settings for the Dempsey-Fitzsimmons fight proved to be in stark contrast to the muddy fields and floating barges that set the stage for the illegal bare-knuckle bouts of years gone by.

Following the Olympic Club's success, a handful of the city's athletic clubs began promoting professional fights on a regular basis. Seemingly overnight, the competition between clubs to stage fights transformed professional boxing into a business enterprise. Recognizing the lucrative financial rewards, clubs began competing with one another to sign prominent contenders. In the hope of staging the most popular fights, clubs offered sizable purses in the hope that gate receipts would exceed total costs. New Orleans athletic clubs also helped regulate boxing on more a professional, business-like model. The old six weight classifications conceived by press mogul and sports promoter Richard Kyle Fox (1846–1922) became standardized. Unlike the old bare-knuckle era, referees became club employees and were empowered to award decisions if the fight went the distance and stop bouts if a fighter's life was in peril. Limited rounds were enforced, and the old challenge system, whereby boxers would call out opponents on the pages of the popular sporting newspapers, was eliminated. In stark contrast, club owners now arranged fights, rented or built indoor arenas, and hired agents to finalize contracts. In light of these changes, the demographics of boxing spectators changed dramatically. As boxing became a legitimate form of commercial entertainment, the respectable middle classes, such as doctors, lawyers, and police commissioners, openly announced their support, along with more affluent allies such as press baron Joseph Pulitzer (1847–1911).

Sullivan vs. Corbett

As boxing took a giant leap toward modernization, the stage was set for the showpiece event of the decade, Sullivan versus Corbett for the world heavyweight crown. In the buildup to the Corbett-Sullivan fight, the Olympic Club held a series of championship bouts including George "Little Chocolate" Dixon's (1870–1908) September 6, 1892, featherweight-title defense against American challenger Jack Skelly. The 5'3", 118-pound Canadian-born Dixon was the first black athlete to ever win a world title in any sport after he defeated Englishman Edwin "Nunc" Wallace in 1890 to claim the world bantamweight crown in sensational style. The following day, the prefight excitement reached a feverish pitch as over 10,000 spectators, including a small number of women, converged on the Olympic Club in New Orleans to witness Sullivan and Corbett battle. Weighing in at a hefty 212 pounds, Sullivan appeared overweight, a sharp contrast to his younger and lighter opponent. At the bell, Corbett made this advantage show as he pummeled the world champion with a flurry of well-timed blows. Dominating the fight with his "scientific" style of boxing, one that placed an emphasis on quick jabs, dodging and weaving, Corbett finished off Sullivan in the twenty-first round with a powerful right hand that brought the champion crashing to the canvas. "Gentleman Jim" Corbett was the new heavyweight champion of boxing.

The end of Sullivan's reign as champion put the final seal on boxing's emergence as a respectable American sporting pastime. The sight of Sullivan and Corbett competing in an electrically lit indoor arena in front of 10,000 spectators from all social classes emphasizes just how far boxing had come in such a short space of time. Shaking off its infamous bare-knuckle roots, boxing developed throughout the 1890s into a legitimate enterprise. Over the remainder of the decade, more and more states legalized boxing. The number of professional bouts skyrocketed. The heavyweight crown continued to change hands as British fighter and former

Eugen Sandow: The World's Strongest Man (1867–1925)

In the last decade of the nineteenth century, Eugen Sandow (born Friederich Wilhelm Mueller) rose to international prominence as the self-proclaimed "strongest man in the world." Born in the former Prussian city of Königsberg, Sandow traveled the globe as a world-renowned strongman and entertainer. Appearing in circuses and vaudeville houses throughout the globe, Sandow used his intelligence, muscular body, and business knowledge to build a fitness empire. Placing an emphasis on health and physical fitness, Sandow encouraged an American fitness craze by making exercise fashionable to all classes. Along with the heavyweight boxing champion John L. Sullivan, Eugen Sandow was probably the most famous and easily recognizable athletic figure in the United States during this period.

Gaining inspiration from the ancient statues of Greek and Roman athletes, Sandow spent his youth chiseling his muscular body with the use of early weightlifting equipment and a diet that included the consumption of over 250 grams of protein per day. By the age of nineteen, the scantily clad young muscleman began performing strongman stunts throughout Europe and North America. In 1893 Sandow appeared on stage at the World's Columbian Exposition held in Chicago. Sandow enthralled the large crowds with his extraordinary muscular poses and weightlifting feats such as the "human barbell stunt," a one-arm barbell lift of two humans. Sandow's remarkable performance made him an instant celebrity in the United States.

In an era in which prudish Victorian notions of respectability denounced the naked body, Sandow's revealing muscular displays, in which he often posed in nothing more than an oak leaf, made the natural human form more acceptable. More important, Sandow's muscular poses and emphasis toward health and fitness helped to focus the nation's attention on the poor physical condition of American men and women. Rapid urbanization, poor sanitation, pollution, and high rates of alcohol consumption had created a nation of invalids. Fearing America's physical decline, social reformers promoted Sandow as a standard of bodily perfection. As a result, Sandow's strongman shows became so popular that he ignited a fitness craze that swept the United States.

In an attempt to spread the world's interest in physical fitness, Sandow organized the first major bodybuilding competition, the "Great Competition," on September 14, 1901, in London, an event encouraging the growth of bodybuilding as a recognized sport. In recognition of Sandow's contributions toward the field of health and physical education the German-born strongman earned the title, "The Father of Modern Bodybuilding." A bronze statue titled "The Sandow" is awarded every year to the winner of the Mr. Olympia competition, the world's most prestigious bodybuilding contest. Following a successful career, Sandow died of unknown causes in 1925.

---

middleweight champion Robert Fitzsimmons defeated Corbett on March 17, 1897, in Carson City, Nevada. Fitzsimmons's success proved to be short-lived. On June 9, 1899, Ohio native James J. Jefferies (1875–1953) scored a stunning upset, beating his British opponent with an eleventh-round knockout. Jefferies ended the decade as the heavyweight champion of the world.

Cycling: An American Craze

Unlike the myriad problems facing horse racing during this period, the 1890s witnessed the dramatic growth of organized, competitive cycling. Fueled by the bicycle boom that gripped the United States during this period, cycling achieved considerable popularity as a spectator sport at both the amateur and professional level. American sports fans gathered in large numbers in cities across the nation to watch the leading riders battle for supremacy in both road and track contests. Newspapers carried extensive coverage of races on their sports pages, transforming riders, seemingly overnight, into national sports heroes. Under the auspices of the League of American Wheelman (LAW), cycling's governing body which was formed in 1880, the sport flourished in its local branches in cities across the United States. Unlike the bicycle craze that drove the middle classes toward recreational cycling, competitive amateur and professional events attracted predominately working-class and ethnic Americans. Moreover, even though American women viewed the bicycle as a symbol of liberation, cycling races remained an all-male preserve, limiting female riders to only occasional professional touring appearances.

Road and Track Races

Throughout the latter half of the 1890s, the nation's most popular cycling race proved to be the Pullman Road Race held in Chicago. Established in 1886, the race drew considerable crowds who turned out to watch the fifteen-mile contest on Chicago's South Side. In 1894 the course was shifted over to the North Side, along a nineteen-mile stretch from Chicago to Evanston. After 1895 the course was transferred back to its original location and distance. The popularity of the Pullman Road Race can be gauged by the sheer number of entries and spectators. The contest of 1893 drew 325 entries. By 1895 the affair attracted 515 entries with thousands of spectators lining the streets in support of their favorite riders. In almost every other city in the United States, road races flourished. The staging of cycling races became viewed as a form of urban boosterism, with cities battling each other to gain the nation's attention. In spite of their general popularity, road races failed to transfer into an enjoyable spectator sport. Similar to long-distance running events such as the marathon, road races had a logistical problem: spectators were unable to continuously follow the action as riders traversed the lengthy course. Furthermore, with only limited cash prizes awarded to the winners, the nation's major road races attracted predominantly amateur riders. Alternatively, professional riders focused their attentions on track contests due to the lucrative cash prizes available.

Track contests first emerged in the United States in 1883 within the confines of the Worchester Bicycle Club in Massachusetts. Held on a specially prepared track, usually a third of a mile in circumference, track contests gradually sprung up throughout the nation. Originally track races were contested among amateur riders. However, as soon as bicycle manufacturers recognized the lucrative financial rewards that promoting winning riders brought, amateurism began to disappear from the sport. Manufacturers attempted to attract the fastest riders, whom they would generously subsidize in return for the racers' willingness to ride the bicycle the company made. This marketing initiative highlights the rising commercialism that permeated American sport prior to the turn of the twentieth century. With professional riders at the wheel, spectators flooded into arenas in cities such as Chicago, New York and Philadelphia to witness the nation's leading cyclists such as the diminutive Welshman "Midget" Michael and African American champion Marshall "Major" Taylor battle for track supremacy.

As the regulation of cycling races increased and the monetary prizes awarded to riders skyrocketed, the sport underwent fundamental changes. With large cash prizes at stake, riders abandoned their old informal training regimes and unhealthy lifestyles in favor of rigorous physical workouts. Most commonly, riders engaged in weight training to enhance leg strength and muscular body tone, as well as cardio-vascular workouts to maximize lung volume. Frequently, riders also hired personal coaches—known as handlers—to design and implement individualized training regimes and to provide assistance on race strategies. Riders also placed a new emphasis on their diet, replacing cigars and alcohol, the palate of some nineteenth-century American athletes, with more wholesome foods and drinks.

Meanwhile, as riders adopted more salubrious lifestyles, the sport of cycling was improved further thanks in part to the revolutionary redesign of the bicycle. Manufacturers replaced the old rubber tires with new pneumatic tires, introduced a new lightweight frame, and made the sprocket larger in an effort to increase gearing and speed. Race organizers also improved the quality of track surfaces. The older, dusty, dirt surfaces, which hindered the growth of cycling as a spectator sport due to the creation of poor visibility as riders zoomed by, were replaced by asphalt and concrete boards. These changes drastically reduced race times and enhanced cycling as a spectator sport.

Six-Day Cycling Marathons

Despite the success of both road and track contests, "six-day" marathons emerged as the most popular form of cycling in the United States. As entrepreneurs, sports promoters were eager to find new and exciting ways to sell sport to the American public. Subsequently, in an attempt to maintain spectator interest in professional cycling, promoters conceived the six-day cycling marathon. Held in spacious indoor arenas, such as New York's renowned Madison Square Garden, riders would ride continuously for six days, or 142 hours (the races started at midnight and would conclude six days later at 10:00 P.M.), stopping only briefly for rest and refreshment. With cash prizes of $10,000 up for grabs, the rider who covered the greatest distance would be declared the winner. Eager to make a profit, sports promoters attracted large crowds by charging as little as twenty-five cents admission, allowing spectators to camp within the arena for the full duration of the race. Due to the modest entrance fee, working-class and immigrant groups made up the vast majority of race fans, turning out in large numbers to cheer on their favorite and, often, ethnically affiliated riders. Six-day cycling marathons were also strongly connected with gambling and vice. Pickpockets and hustlers frequently prayed on unsuspecting race fans. Despite the sport's tarnished reputation, six-day cycling marathons remained an important part of the American sporting scene until the mid-1930s.

Opposition to Competitive Cycling

Despite the continued growth of cycling, the sport came under attack from critics who opposed the rising presence of dirty tactics, violence, and injuries. With large cash purses up for grabs, riders would often elbow and jostle their opponents in an attempt to gain an advantage. More commonly, riders would team together in an effort to hinder the more experienced and more talented riders. Adopting a

The Bicycling Craze

In the early 1890s, a bicycle craze swept throughout the United States. The invention and production of the "safety" bicycle brought an efficient and affordable mode of transportation to most middle-class Americans. With costs ranging anywhere between $50 and $100, and manufacturing companies introducing installment purchasing plans, the number of Americans owning the "safety" bicycle quickly skyrocketed. By 1893 figures estimated that there were over one million cyclists, both men and women, in the United States alone. This number nearly quadrupled just three years later. Americans also formed cycling clubs in great numbers. By 1895, as many as 500 clubs were registered throughout the country. Prior to the early twentieth-century invention of the automobile and the electric trolley car, the bicycle represented a marvel in modern technological advances, a true testament to the industrial age.

Following the invention of the pneumatic tire in 1889, the "safety" bicycle quickly flooded American markets. With equal-sized wheels, chain gear drive, a diamond-shaped frame, and efficient coaster brakes, the "safety" proved an immediate hit with American consumers.

In an era of rapid urbanization, the "safety" bicycle represented a mode of freedom for most Americans, at least for the middle and upper classes. Urban dwellers frequently used their bicycles to escape the overcrowded and polluted city for the fresh air of the rural countryside. Medical practitioners spoke favorably of the numerous health benefits that riding a bicycle would present. For instance, the bicycle was believed to cure a whole host of illnesses ranging from depression to nervous exhaustion. Aimed predominately at sedentary urban workers and women, physicians and health advocates argued that the bicycle would help increase productivity in the workplace by helping Americans regain their strength and vitality.

For women, the bicycle served a more symbolic purpose. In an era in which Victorian social standards restricted American women in many spheres of life, the bicycle represented a form of personal freedom. By riding a bicycle, American women were able to discard their restrictive corsets and feel the invigoration of outdoor exercise. Upholders of older Victorian notions of "true womanhood" strongly opposed American women riding bicycles. Critics claimed that excessive riding could potentially cause women serious physiological damage. The list of potential harms included an unnatural curvature of the spine, pelvic damage, spinal shock, and the damaging of vital reproductive organs. More commonly, critics argued that female cyclists would experience "bicycle face," a malaise that was distinguishable by a protruding jaw, wild stare, and a strained expression.

By the turn of the twentieth century, the bicycle craze in the United States had run its course. By 1900 over 10 million Americans owned bicycles, yet the fad appeared to be over. In the coming years, the market became saturated and innovative manufacturers turned their attentions toward the production of the automobile, an invention that would soon revolutionize American society.

---

tactic known as "hemming," teams of riders would work in tandem, slowing down the pace and blocking their opponents on the inside of the track. Unsurprisingly, the use of racing strategies and physical intimidation by riders highlights the dangerous nature of cycling. For example, in 1897, in Danbury, Connecticut, one rider was killed and another seriously injured as the two riders collided at high speeds. The renowned Pullman Road Race also had a reputation for high rates of participant injuries, as riders frequently smashed into each other on the winding Chicago streets.

Similar to most American institutions, the world of amateur and professional cycling upheld de facto racial segregation. In 1895 the League of American Wheelman (LAW), the sport's governing body, voted to alter their constitution, excluding "Negroes" from membership in their organization. Nevertheless, this policy did not prohibit some blacks from racing. The remarkably talented African American rider Marshall "Major" Taylor dominated professional cycling, frequently beating his white opponents. In retaliation for their humiliating defeats by blacks, white riders attempted to intimidate their opponents. On numerous occasions, black riders such as "Major" Taylor were the victims of verbal and physical abuse.

In contrast, the experiences of Irish and Italian riders differed enormously from their black counterparts. Similar to their success in long-distance running events, Irish and Italian immigrants to the United States dominated the world of cycling. Sponsored by neighborhood organizations and social clubs, Irish and Italian immigrants entered amateur races in cities throughout the United States. Success in the amateur ranks eventually provided an opportunity for the most talented Irish and Italian riders to join the professional circuit. Ultimately, through their participation and success in both amateur and professional cycling, Irish and Italian riders were able to acculturate to American society, whilst simultaneously expressing pride in their own ethnic identity.

Horse Racing: The Battle of the Turf

Like boxing, horse racing flourished throughout the last decade of the nineteenth century. Crowds of upwards of 10,000 spectators flocked to racetracks in cities such as Brooklyn, Chicago, New Orleans, St. Louis, and New York City, the leading centers for thoroughbred racing in the United States. Unlike the vast majority of American sports, African Americans became a visible presence in horse racing during the 1890s. Overcoming widespread racial discrimination and de facto segregation, black jockeys such as Isaac Murphy, dominated professional horse racing throughout the latter half of the nineteenth century.

Although flat-course thoroughbred racing remained the most popular form of horse racing during the decade, the steeplechase, a long-distance event with fence and ditch obstacles, continued to grow in popularity among American race fans. Led by the formation of the National Steeplechase Association (NSA) on February 15, 1895, the steeplechase contributed to horse racing's prominence within the United States. Nevertheless, despite the sport's continued growth and prosperity, horse racing came under a severe attack from social reformers prior to the turn of the twentieth century. Opposing the turf's connection with organized crime, heavy gambling, and machine politics, reformers mounted a serious challenge to the presence of horse racing in the American sporting landscape. The reformers pushed cities and states to ban the popular pastime.

American Classic Series

Undoubtedly the high point of the horse-racing season was a series of races later recognized in the 1930s as the American Triple Crown. The Kentucky Derby, the

Marshall "Major" Taylor: America's Greatest Wheelman (1878–1932)

In 1899 African American cyclist, Marshall "Major" Taylor rode to victory in the famed International Cycling Association's one-mile world sprint championship in Montreal, Canada. In doing so, Taylor became the first African American to win a world title in the white-dominated world of professional cycling.

Born on November 26, 1878, to Gilbert and Saphronia Taylor, in rural Indianapolis, Indiana, Marshall Taylor developed an immediate affinity for cycling. Given his first bicycle as a child, Taylor worked in a number of bicycle shops throughout his home city where his talent became immediately apparent. In fact, one of Taylor's bosses paid him to perform bicycle tricks while wearing a military uniform on the sidewalk outside of the owner's shop. Pleasing customers and passersby, Taylor quickly acquired the nickname "Major."

In the early 1890s, at the height of the bicycle boom, Taylor's big opportunity came in the form of white bicyclemaker and former high-wheel champion Birdie Munger. Serving as a father figure, Munger supplied Taylor with expensive bicycle equipment and encouraged his entrance into competitive racing. By 1893, aged only fifteen, Taylor had already won numerous road and track races in Indianapolis and Chicago. He joined the professional ranks in 1896, making his debut at a six-day bicycling marathon held at New York's Madison Square Garden's. Taylor's natural ability, clean lifestyle, and dedication to his sport enabled him to soar to the top of the cycling world.

Regrettably, Taylor's success was met with widespread hostility throughout white America. In a sport that requires speed, skill, and intelligence, Taylor's victories against white competitors challenged notions of black racial inferiority. As a result, white riders detested him and often worked together in an attempt to block him and prevent him from claiming victory. Other riders adopted more severe methods to hinder Taylor, including verbal and physical abuse. In one instance, a white rider by the name of William Becker physically attacked Taylor, choking him into unconsciousness in retaliation for losing to the black champion.

Despite this racist opposition, Taylor's success proved that it was possible to succeed through hard work and talent. At the turn of the century, Taylor broke numerous world records and, in 1900, even won the coveted League of American Wheelman's championship. In light of these remarkable achievements, Taylor was offered substantial sums of money to compete throughout Europe. These tours established Taylor as a global sporting icon and a hero for blacks throughout the United States.

Following a hugely successful professional career, Taylor retired in 1910, but he continued to face the same racism that had hindered his cycling career when he was refused entrance to study at the Worchester Polytechnic Institute in Massachusetts. Regrettably, following a series of failed financial enterprises, Taylor ended up broke, homeless, and destitute, eventually dying in Chicago in 1932.

Preakness Stakes, and the Belmont Stakes comprised the list of classic races that captivated American horse-racing fans throughout the last decade of the nineteenth century. Inaugurated in 1875, the Kentucky Derby is still held annually in Churchill Downs, Louisville, Kentucky. The nation's leading jockeys battled for supremacy over the 1.5-mile (2.4-km) track. In 1896, however, the race distance was shortened to its current length of 1.25 miles (2 km). African American jockeys continued their widespread dominance of horse racing during this era, winning a remarkable fifteen out of twenty-eight races between 1875 and 1902. The list of

Isaac B. Murphy: The "Colored Archer" (1861–96)

Considered one of the greatest jockeys in American horse-racing history, African American Isaac B. Murphy (1861–96) rose to prominence as a sporting star in the 1880s and early 1890s. Throughout his short but highly successful career, Murphy held a staggering 44 percent winning record, amassing a remarkable 628 wins in 1,412 races, including four American Derby and five Latonia Derby victories. "The Colored Archer," as Murphy became known, was also the first jockey in American history to win the coveted Kentucky Derby on three separate occasions. At the height of his career, Murphy earned between $15,000 and $20,000 a year, a considerable amount when compared to the standard $5,000 earned by most jockeys and a prodigious amount for an African American, most of whom earned less than $150 a year. In an era of Jim Crow racial segregation, Murphy's fame and fortune helped the Kentucky native temporarily realize the American dream of social mobility and prosperity. Unlike the millions of African Americans who resided in slum ghettos in the North or the former slave plantations of the South, Murphy owned a host of luxury properties in white neighborhoods in both Lexington and Chicago.

Isaac B. Murphy was born onto a slave farm in Fayette County, Kentucky, in 1861. Following his father's death, Murphy and his family relocated to Lexington where the twelve-year-old prodigy began his apprenticeship as a prospective jockey in the fall of 1873. Due to his diminutive stature, the young Murphy quickly rose to prominence, winning his first competitive race in 1875. Murphy's presence in the white world of American sports may appear strange to contemporary observers, but during this period black jockeys were the in majority. For instance, the first Kentucky Derby, held in 1875, included fourteen out of fifteen black riders. Admired for his steady hands and marvelous sense of pace, Murphy quickly established himself as one of the most elite riders in the country, earning a reputation both at home and abroad.

A string of quick successes bought Murphy the fame and adulation awarded to American sports heroes during this period. Nevertheless, following his climatic Kentucky Derby victory in 1891 aboard the horse Kingman, Murphy's career quickly spiraled out of control. In 1892 the nation's most successful jockey only managed to win a dismal five out of forty-four races. Murphy's woes continued, as he failed to win even a single race over the course of the entire 1894 season. Because he was struggling to maintain weight and battling alcoholism, Murphy's career lay in a state of ruin. Murphy's failure can be explained, in part, by the emergence of de facto racial segregation throughout the United States. Over the course of the 1890s, as racism became more prevalent, black jockeys quickly disappeared from the horse-racing scene. White riders formed "anticolored unions," pushing the remaining black riders out of the sport altogether.

Despite Murphy's fame, "The Colored Archer" faced a similar fate. Determined to force Murphy out of the sport he had long dominated, officials frequently accused Murphy of riding drunk or not trying. Banned for considerable periods of time during the last decade of the nineteenth century, Murphy was forced to end his decorated racing career in 1895. The following year Murphy died of pneumonia on Lincoln's birthday. In 1955, as a fitting testimony to Murphy's contribution to the sport, "The Colored Archer" was inducted to the National Racing Hall of Fame in Saratoga Springs, New York.

---

black victors includes the renowned Isaac Murphy, who won aboard Kingman in 1891, and Augusta, Georgia, native Willie Simms (1870–1927), who won twice in 1896 and 1898 aboard Ben Brush and Plaudit respectively. On May 11, 1892, fifteen-year-old African American jockey Alonzo "Lonnie" Clayton from Kansas

City, Missouri, became the youngest rider in the sport's history to win the Kentucky Derby when he stormed to victory aboard Azra.

What would become the second race in the American Triple Crown series is the Preakness Stakes, held annually at the Pimlico Race Course in Baltimore, Maryland. The Preakness is the shortest of the three American classic races at a mere 13/16 miles (1.9 km). Over the course of the 1890s the Preakness fell into a state of perpetual decline due to changes in the horse-racing industry. Between 1891 and 1893 this contest was not even staged. When it did return in 1894, the Preakness Stakes was transferred away from the Pimlico track to the Gravesend Race Track in Brooklyn, New York, where it remained until 1908. Despite the event's decline, the decade still brought some breathtaking races. Most notably, in 1898 Willie Simms became the first African American jockey to win all three races when he cruised to victory aboard Sly Fox.

Completing the trio of classic American races is the Belmont Stakes, named in honor of its original financier, industrial tycoon August Belmont Sr. (1816–90). Inaugurated in 1867, the Belmont Stakes was originally held at the Jerome Park Racetrack in the Bronx, New York. Throughout the 1890s, however, the race was transferred to the nearby Morris Park Racetrack, where it remained until the official opening of its current home in 1905, Elmont, New York. In its temporary home, the Belmont Stakes staged some terrific races over the course of the decade. In both 1893 and 1894 Willie Simms continued his dominance of racing by riding to victory aboard Comanche and Henry of Navarre. Perhaps more significant in the scope of international rivalries between American and British horses, owners and jockeys, in 1898 a British horse, Bowling Brook, became only the second foreign horse to win one of America's most prestigious thoroughbred races.

Meanwhile, as the Kentucky Derby, Preakness, and the Belmont fueled interest in horse racing throughout the 1890s, the sport also witnessed the introduction of new and innovative riding styles. Led by future Hall of Fame American jockey and vaudeville performer Tod Sloan (1874–1933), the traditional riding style of jockeys holding long reins and sitting upright in the saddle with their legs dangling down was revolutionized. In 1897 Sloan experimented with short reins and stirrups while crouching on the horse's neck, a technique that reduced wind resistance and offered a better distribution of weight on the horse. Across the Atlantic, however, Sloan's new style of horsemanship was viewed derisively by British racing fans who labeled his unique technique "the monkey-crouch." In the face of British criticism, Sloan demonstrated the substantial benefits of his new technique, riding to victory in England's most prestigious thoroughbred races such as the One Thousand Guineas (1898) and the Ascot Gold Cup (1900). Due to his success, Sloan's technique revolutionized riding styles among jockeys.

Gambling, Crime, and Machine Politics in Horse Racing

Despite the aristocratic and affluent appeal of thoroughbred racing, the sport was inextricably linked with heavy gambling, organized crime syndicates, and machine politics. Throughout the latter half of the nineteenth century social reformers and religious leaders vehemently opposed the sport due to its seemingly total dependence on gambling, its abuse of animals, and its clear connections to political corruption. United together, opponents of the turf stepped up their campaign throughout the

1890s to collectively ban on-track gambling and to proscribe horse racing in the United States once and for all. In the face of virulent opposition, some of the most prominent figures in horse racing such as industrial elites August Belmont Jr. (1851–1924) and William C. Whitney (1841–1904) united with machine politicians such as New York City Tammanyites Richard Croker (1844–1922) and "Big Tim" Sullivan (1862–1913). Using their money, power, and political influence, these supporters of the turf fought to preserve the sport's legal status.

In cities across the United States, although most clearly pronounced in New Jersey, Chicago, and New York, a battle ensued over the place of horse racing and gambling in the American sporting scene. In New Jersey the Democratic-dominated legislature ignored the cries for the sport's banishment by passing the Parker Acts in 1893, an edict that legalized on-track gambling. As the state's race-tracks prospered and interest in the sport boomed, opponents of horse racing stepped up their antigambling crusade. Arousing public support, reformers in New Jersey disposed of the Democrats and handed power over to the Republicans. In 1894 the Republicans proceeded to repeal the Parker Acts, banning on-track gambling and simultaneously plunging horse racing in New Jersey into a state of decline for nearly fifty years. Meanwhile, in Chicago, a similar clash was taking place between supporters and opponents of the turf. In 1892 Chicago's Republican mayor, Hempstead Washburne (1852–1919), closed the Garfield Park racetrack, an outlaw track renowned for heavy gambling. Reformers in Chicago scored further successes when the Washington Park Racetrack closed due to negative publicity in 1894, followed into oblivion by Hawthorne Racetrack in 1895.

Despite the success of social reformers in New Jersey and Illinois, New York City set the stage for the most important battle in deciding horse racing's fate in the United States. Frustrated by the greedy track operators and the accounts of heavy gambling, reformers, clergyman and opponents of Tammany Hall united to ban horse racing in the most prominent sporting city in the country. In September 1894 opponents of the turf persuaded the State Constitutional Convention to adopt an article banning on-track gambling in New York. In retaliation, racing fans spearheaded a campaign to save the sport. Using their political influence, supporters convinced the state legislature to create a State Racing Commission, an initiative designed to save thoroughbred racing by drawing up national standards of conduct and behavior. Operating in conjunction with the Jockey Club, the nascent committee was fronted by prominent racing supporter and industrialist August Belmont Jr. For the time being, at least, horse racing in New York City continued to flourish under the scrutiny of the sport's most vocal opponents. In the early decades of the twentieth century, horse racing would be plunged into an even deeper state of despair, as reformers strengthened their attack on the sport and its affiliation with gambling, crime, and machine politics.

Golf, Tennis, Yachting, and the Country Club

As organized, competitive team and individual sports continued to gain popularity among the nation's working and middle classes, America's ultrarich shied away from institutionalized and democratic sports such as baseball and boxing. Rather, this small coterie of rich Americans, whose wealth was rooted in industrial capitalism, held an alternative sensibility about sport. For these wealthy elites, including such pioneers of industry and finance as Cornelius Vanderbilt, Andrew Carnegie, and J. Pierpont Morgan, sport was viewed as a badge of social status and prestige. Confining themselves to distinctive environments shaped for their pursuits, such as country clubs and leisure resorts, the rich used sport to distinguish themselves from the masses and the respectable middle-classes. Ultimately, their participation in exclusive sports, such as golf, tennis, polo, hunting, and yachting, served as an affirmation of both their wealth and preeminent standing in American society.

Following the construction of the Brookline (Massachusetts) Country Club in 1882, the nation's first luxury leisure destination, a wave of exclusive clubs and resorts appeared throughout the United States. Undoubtedly, the most prestigious was the Newport Country Club, in Rhode Island. Founded in 1894, by industrialist John Jacob Astor, sugar magnate Theodore A. Havemeyer, and three members of the Vanderbilt family, Newport quickly became an elite sporting haven for America's ultrarich. Adopting a strong amateur approach to sport, the wealthy classes demonstrated less commitment to the disciplined development of their abilities. Rather, viewing sport as a form of recreational leisure the rich moved from sport to sport at whim. Subsequently, the 1890s also witnessed the advent of exclusive sport-specific country clubs and resorts. For example, the Jekyll Island Club, located on the Georgia coast, emerged as the premier resort for wealthy Americans interested in hunting wild game. With a combined membership wealth of over $1 billion, Jekyll Island supplied the best turkey, deer, woodcock, quail, and duck.

In an effort to maintain the highest levels of elitism, the nation's most exclusive resorts and country clubs set both exorbitant membership rates and stringent guidelines. For instance, the renowned New York Yacht Club in Newport, Rhode Island, which was founded in 1844, kept out the lower classes by refusing to register yachts under certain tonnages, prohibiting co-ownership of vessels, and refusing membership to people without the necessary social connections. Moreover, considering that in 1891 the average daily wage of an urban industrial worker in the United States was a meager $1.69 and the average annual income for the poorest classes was only $150, a $1,400 Herreshoff and Gardner racing yacht was an extravagant luxury, affordable to only a handful of America's ultrarich. The snooty elitism of these clubs forcefully demonstrates how certain sports, such as tennis, golf, and yachting, were largely unavailable to the masses during this period.

Golf

The 1890s proved to be a pivotal decade in the development of golf in the United States. Following the game's arrival onto American shores within the confines of the St. Andrews Golf Club of Yonkers, New York, a golf craze swept throughout the country. Recognizing the sport's burgeoning popularity among the nation's ultrarich, exclusive country clubs began adding golf links to their extensive list of sporting amenities. Meanwhile, elite golf clubs were also constructed at a prodigious rate. In 1891 William K. Vanderbilt, railroad and banking tycoon and a member of the prominent Vanderbilt family, invited Scottish professional golfer William Dunn Jr. to Southampton, Long Island, to design the first professionally built golf course in the United States—Shinnecock Hills Golf Club. Vanderbilt's financial stake was quickly repaid, as Shinnecock Hills became a haven for wealthy New Yorkers. In fact, the establishment of new golf courses was so well established by 1900 that 1,040 courses were in operation throughout the entire United States.

Toward the end of the nineteenth century, America's exclusive golf clubs were comprised of four- to nine-hole courses. In 1893 short courses began to be replaced following the construction of the Chicago Golf Club, the first eighteen-hole course in the United States. With the establishment of full-length courses, organized golf began to flourish. In 1894 two unofficial National Amateur Championships were held at the St. Andrews Golf Club and Newport County Club, two of the nation's most prestigious courses. Nevertheless, under the auspices of the Amateur Golf Association of the United States (shortly renamed U.S. Golf Association), which was founded in 1894 by the Shinnecock, St. Andrews, Chicago and Newport golf clubs, an official U.S. Amateur Championship was instituted. In the first competition, held at the Newport Country Club in 1895, Charles B. Macdonald (1855–1939), chief architect of Chicago's eighteen-hole course and a major figure in the early history of golf, romped to victory, thoroughly beating his opponent Charles E. Sands (1865–1945) 12 and 11.

Following the success of the U.S. Amateur Championship event, Newport Country Club also hosted the first U.S. Open Championship, a tournament now recognized as one of the four "majors." Held on October 4, 1895, the Open attracted eleven players, including the eventual winner, Horace Rawlings (1874–1940) an English professional golfer working at the Newport Country Club. Throughout the remainder of the decade and beyond, British golfers continued to dominate the annual event, winning every single year up until 1911. Following the inception of both the U.S. Amateur and Open championships, organized golf continued to boom. In 1897 the first intercollegiate men's golf championship was held. Princeton's Louis Bayard Jr. claimed the men's title, while Yale won the overall team championship. As golf continued to attract global appeal, the sport was awarded a spot on the program for the 1900 Olympic Games held in Paris. In both the men's and women's events, the United States took first place thanks to the efforts of U.S. Amateur Championship runner-up Charles E. Sands and Chicago art student Margaret Ives Abbott (1878–1955).

Tennis

Within the confines of the nation's exclusive country clubs, tennis also enjoyed a period of unprecedented growth throughout the decade. Following the formation of the U.S. National Lawn Tennis Association (later renamed the U.S. Tennis Association) and the institution of the U.S. Open Championship in 1881, organized competitive tennis continued to thrive at the both the national and international level. Adopting a challenge system, an initiative whereby last year's winner would automatically qualify for the final of the next year's competition, the U.S. Open became tennis's showpiece event. Held on an annual basis at the prestigious Newport Casino, in Rhode Island—a playground for the nation's ultrarich—American players such as Oliver Campbell (1871–1953) and Robert Wrenn (1873–1925) dominated the event now recognized as one of the game's four "majors." Newport's hosting of the event lasted until 1915, when the U.S. Open was transferred to Forest Hills, New York. In 1900 the USTA also approved the creation of the U.S. National Men's Doubles Championship.

The success of the men's event inspired the formation of the U.S. Women's National Singles Championship in 1887. Held on an annual basis at the

Philadelphia Cricket Club, the event represented a major boost for the presence of women in the American sporting scene. New Jersey native Juliette Atkinson (1873–1944) dominated the event throughout the 1890s, winning on three separate occasions. In an attempt to ensure high social standards, the list of tournament participants was determined by invitation only. Due to the long dresses and restrictive corsets worn by upper-class American women during this period, a sport based on quick movements and mobility like tennis became extremely difficult to master. As a result, most female tennis players focused their attention on doubles competition. In fact, to mark the rising popularity of the doubles game, the U.S. National Women's Doubles Tournament was created in 1889. Remarkably, singles sensation Atkinson also dominated the doubles event, claiming victory with various partners on five occasions throughout the decade.

Unfortunately, these tournaments were severely limited to only a small group of affluent American women who played the game according to the rules of female grace and refinement. Isolated in exclusive country clubs away from the critical gaze of American society, upper-class women enjoyed the luxury of participating in gender-appropriate sports such as tennis, golf, archery, boating, horse riding, and walking. For these privileged few, sport became a positive force that promoted good health and cultivated important social values. Similar to their male counterparts, female sports were regarded as much a matter of style as of athletics. By promoting elaborate clothing styles and accessories, wealthy American women turned sport into a means of conspicuous consumption. Subsequently, fashion replaced victory as the primary purpose for female participation in elite sport. For average Americans, however, sport in the 1890s was a pastime reserved predominantly for men.

Unsurprisingly, as interest in tennis proliferated throughout the United States, the sport also gained popularity abroad. As a result, the global diffusion of tennis set the stage for the creation of international competitions. In 1891 the French Open (Championnat de France) was established for men, a tournament now recognized as another of the four "majors." The women's version of this event was formed shortly after, in 1897. Furthermore, in 1899 four members of Harvard University's men's tennis team conceived the idea of creating an international competition between the United States and Great Britain. Harvard's star player, Dwight F. Davis (1879–1945), designed the tournament format and decided to donate a special cup for the nascent International Lawn Tennis Tournament. Captained by Davis, a future U.S. secretary of war under President Calvin Coolidge, the United States surprisingly defeated their more-experienced British opponents at the Longwood Cricket Club in Boston. In honor of Davis's contributions, the tournament was shortly renamed the Davis Cup. Unlike its original two-team format, the Davis Cup is currently contested by 137 nations.

Yachting

As golf and tennis continued to prosper, America's ultrarich also actively participated in competitive yacht racing. Indeed, throughout the 1890s the sport proved to be a favorite sport of the wealthy. The America's Cup, the world's most prestigious international yachting competition, continued to attract global attention. Undefeated since the advent of the competition on August 22, 1851, American vessels continued their reign of dominance throughout the remainder of the century. In both 1893 and 1895, an Englishman, the fourth Earl of Dunraven (1841–1926), challenged for the cup against American yachts. Renowned boat designer Nathaniel Herreshoff built the American yacht that successfully defeated their British opponents on both occasions. Determined to bring the coveted cup to British shores, Scottish tea baron Sir Thomas Lipton (1948–1931) of the Royal Ulster Yacht Club of Belfast, offered a new challenge to the long-reigning American champions. In 1899, despite Lipton's efforts, his boat, *Shamrock I*, was no match for the superior Herreshoff-built American vessel *Columbia*. Despite further British challenges, American dominance of the event would continue long into the twentieth century.

Buoyed by the nation's success in the America's Cup, competitive yacht racing began to spread throughout the United States. In the Midwest, the Great Lakes became a popular venue for yacht races as cities such as Detroit, Chicago, and Toledo held organized events. The annual Chicago to Mackinaw, Michigan, race, established in 1898, provided Great Lakes sailors with their own prestigious challenge. More important, the Canada's Cup, founded in 1896 and held on the Great Lakes, brought the advent of international yacht racing contests between Canada and the United States. Meanwhile, the Pacific Northwest also had its own group of wealthy yachting enthusiasts. For instance, in 1891 Bellingham Bay, Washington, began a prestigious annual yachting contest.

RECOMMENDED RESOURCES

Baker, William J. 1988. *Sports in the western world*. Urbana: University of Illinois Press.

Cahn, Susan K. 1994. *Coming on strong: Gender and sexuality in twentieth-century women's sport*. Cambridge: Harvard University Press.

Chapman, David L. 2006. *Sandow the Magnificent: Eugen Sandow and the beginnings of bodybuilding*. Urbana: University of Illinois Press.

Davis, Richard O. 2007. *Sports in American life: A history*. New York: Blackwell.

Dyreson, Mark. 1998. *Making the American team: Sport, culture, and the Olympic experience*. Urbana: University of Illinois Press.

Gorn, Elliott J. 1986. *The manly art: Bare-knuckle prize fighting in America*. Ithaca, NY: Cornell University Press.

Gorn, Elliott J., and Warren Goldstein. 2004. *A brief history of American sports*. Urbana: University of Illinois Press.

Guttmann, Allen. 1991. *Women's sports: A history*. New York: Columbia University Press.

———. 1996. *Games and empires: Modern sports and cultural imperialism*. New York: Columbia University Press.

———. 2002. *The Olympics: A history of the modern games*. Urbana: University of Illinois Press.

———. 2004. *Sports: The first five millennia*. Amherst: University of Massachusetts Press.

International Olympic Committee (IOC) official Web site. http://www.olympic.org/uk/index_uk.asp.

Isenberg, Michael T. 1994. *John L. Sullivan and his America*. Urbana: University of Illinois Press.

Kirsch, George B., Othello Harris, and Claire E. Nolte. 2000. *Encyclopedia of ethnicity and sports in the United States*. Westport, CT: Greenwood Press.

Mrozek, Donald J. 1983. *Sport and American mentality, 1880–1910*. Knoxville: University of Tennessee Press.

Rader, Benjamin G. 2002. *Baseball: A history of America's game*. Urbana: University of Illinois Press.

Ritchie, Andrew. 1996. *Major Taylor: The extraordinary career of a champion bicycle racer*. Baltimore: John Hopkins University Press.

Riess, Steven A. 1991. *City games: The evolution of American urban society and the rise of sports*. Urbana: University of Illinois Press.

Smith, Robert A. 1972. *A social history of the bicycle: Its early life and times in America*. New York: American Heritage Press.

Smith, Ronald A. 1988. *Sports and freedom: The rise of big-time college athletics*. Oxford: Oxford University Press.

Watterson, John Sayle. 2002. *College football: History, spectacle, controversy*. Baltimore: John Hopkins University Press.

CHAPTER 4

AMERICAN SPORTS, 1900–1909

Jim Nendel

OVERVIEW

The first decade of the twentieth century witnessed both the expansion and contraction of American power, demonstrated through political imperialism, capitalistic growth, industrial development, and the growing pains of national and
international sport. Coming out of the 1890s and the American imperialistic con-
quests of Cuba, Hawaii, and the Philippines, the young nation struggled with the
challenges of ruling the land and people it had acquired as territories. Following in
the deeply entrenched racist views that continued the practices of Jim Crow and
discriminatory traditions throughout the United States, white leaders looked upon
these conquered peoples as vanquished natives in need of civilizing. The "white
man's burden" of providing political, social, and moral direction, which U.S. leaders embraced as their calling, included using sport to teach sportsmanship, fair play,
and assimilation into the American way of life. Baseball, boxing, basketball, and
other sports were introduced in these new territories to smooth the transition from
the so-called savage nature to civilized society, with its proper rules of etiquette.
However, the struggles of overseeing expanding empires quickly were realized and
American leaders pulled back in their expansionist efforts.

While American political leaders were busy expanding and contracting their
borders with the development of territorial acquisitions, business leaders were doing
the same. This decade saw the continued expansion of monopolistic capitalism as
powerful, wealthy leaders furthered their stranglehold on competitor's abilities to
challenge them. J. P. Morgan, and John D. Rockefeller, among others, continued
to monopolize railroads and steel during the decade. However, this decade also saw
efforts to curb the growing inequities and injustices brought about by such monopolistic practices, as witnessed by literary works such as *The Octopus* by Frank Norris
and Upton Sinclair's *The Jungle*.

While business and political leaders struggled to maintain and moderate the
rapid expansion that they were experiencing in this decade, industrial leaders
began to expand the production of new technological advancements. Numerous

companies were formed to produce automobiles, and the battle for supremacy between gasoline and electrically powered vehicles escalated throughout the decade. Other technological breakthroughs saw enhanced development of airplanes, helicopters, and cameras. These industrial developments, spurred on by production-line techniques, also helped advance sport, as sporting goods were now more readily available to the public at decreased prices.

The start of the twentieth century witnessed great changes in the landscape of sport. This decade challenged previous ideals of sport and set foundations for the future growth and development of many of America's favorite pastimes. The same patterns of expansion and contraction seen in the political and economic arenas would hamper sport as well. Leagues would begin, develop, and then struggle. The National League tried to assert its monopolistic hold on major-league baseball in efforts to thwart the advent of a rival league. Though this decade would not qualify as a golden age for sport, the lessons learned allowed future decades to experience monumental advances in many areas of participation and spectator involvement.

However, some groups within sport did not fare as well. African American athletes, while seeing great hope in the development of Negro league baseball and the rise of world-champion boxers, saw their opportunities severely contracted due to the success of some of their athletes, such as Jack Johnson. Women who realized new opportunities and successes also saw this athletic expansion threatened by male leaders, such as Dr. Dudley Sargent of Harvard University who warned that strenuous sports, such as basketball, were unhealthy for the supposedly weaker sex.

The years 1900–1909 became a critical turning point for international sport as well. While wars raged in Russia and Japan, many sporting events witnessed near-death experiences including the fledgling Olympic Games, the Tour de France, and American collegiate football. However, despite serious challenges to sport in general, most American sporting pastimes not only survived the scares, but established strong organizations to counter future threats.

In that respect, sport in the United States grew up and matured in this decade. Far from its infancy, it became a social force used by leaders and politicians as well as a marketing device for businesses and the media. It entered into the public mainstream in ways only dreamed of years before and helped shape American national identity.

TEAM SPORTS

Baseball

With the advent of a rival league in 1901 in the form of the American League, the major-league baseball landscape altered drastically. The upstart circuit headed by Bancroft "Ban" Johnson had risen from the Western League, a minor league with teams mainly in the Great Lakes region.

The First World Series Games

With the success of Ban Johnson's rival American League (AL), major-league baseball was forced to find a peaceful way for the two rival leagues to co-exist and remain profitable. Possibly the most significant outcome of the peace conference

The American League 1901

Ban Johnson's vision of a competitor for the National League in baseball came to fruition in 1901 as the American League declared itself a major league on January 28. The eight original franchises were the Baltimore Orioles, Boston Americans, Chicago White Stockings, Cleveland Blues, Detroit Tigers, Milwaukee Brewers, Philadelphia Athletics, and the Washington Senators. In 1900 the National League had contracted from twelve teams to eight and Johnson seized his opportunity. In 1899 he had gained approval from the National League to locate teams in Chicago and Cleveland for his then-minor league. However, when the National League dropped franchises in Baltimore, Cleveland, Washington, D.C., and Louisville in 1900 Johnson's American League filled the gap in Cleveland and established franchises in Baltimore and Washington, D.C., to replace those teams. Johnson had desired a team in New York City but the National League's New York Giants stopped those plans, forcing Johnson to place the team in Baltimore. The Giants bought stock in the Baltimore team, gained controlling interest in 1902, and began pillaging the team's talent for their own roster, including manager John McGraw. The American league stepped into the fray and took control of the struggling Orioles so that they could finish the season. The fighting continued and finally both sides sat down and had a "peace conference" to come to a solution.

The peace accord included the initiation of a Championship between the two leagues winners called the "World Series," to begin in 1903. The American League also gained consent for a team in New York City that year. The Baltimore franchise, purchased by Frank J. Ferrell and William S. Devery moved in 1903 to Hilltop Park in northern Manhattan. The Highlanders operated out of Hilltop Park for ten seasons before moving to the Polo Grounds and renaming themselves the Yankees.

between the leagues was the institution of the World Series. The owners agreed to pit their champions against each other at the end of the season. While the top two teams in the National League (NL) had competed for decades in a World Championship series, this would be the recognized beginning of baseball's "World Series." In 1903 the NL champion Pittsburgh Pirates, led by batting champion Honus Wagner, played the AL pennant winners, the Boston American League Baseball Club, also referred to as the Boston Americans.

The Boston general manager, Joe Smart, realized the potential windfall from the series and doubled ticket prices. Fans would have to pay one dollar for grandstand seats and fifty cents for a bleacher or standing-room-only seat at the Huntingdon Avenue Grounds. Charles "Deacon" Phillippe of the Pirates threw a six-hitter in game 1. Pirate right fielder Jimmy Sebring made history hitting the first home run of the World Series and drove in four runs as the Pirates beat Boston 7-3. Boston answered the next day, behind Big Bill Dinneen's three-hit pitching performance and "Patsy" Dougherty's two home runs, to even the series with a 3-0 win. Due to injuries and illness, Pittsburgh had to rely on Phillippe after only one day of rest and the twenty-five-game-winning pitcher responded with a 4-2 win. Back in Pittsburgh three days later, Phillippe would get his third victory and third complete game of the series as the Pirates, home at Exposition Park, won 5-4. The Pirates had jumped out to a three-to-one lead in the best-of-nine series.

Boston refused to quit, putting Cy Young, their twenty-eight-game winner who had also batted an impressive .321 during the year, on the mound. Young baffled the Pirate hitters, holding them to six hits while he himself drove in three runs in the 11-2 victory. In the game, Boston hit five ground-rule triples due to an over-flow crowd that had spilled onto the field.

For game 6 Boston went back to Bill Dinneen for a 6-3 victory, tying the series at three games each. The seventh game had been set for a Friday, but due to a clause that the owners arranged before the series started, Pittsburgh owner Barney Dreyfuss postponed the game until Saturday due to high winds. The postponement benefited both teams as it promised higher gate receipts, which the teams shared, but it helped Dreyfuss as it gave his ace, Phillippe, one more day of rest. It also allowed Boston's Cy Young an extra day as well, and player-manager Jimmy Collins decided to pit Young against Phillippe. The decision paid off as Young finally put an end to the undefeated run that Phillippe had in the series as Boston took its first lead in the series with a 7-3 victory.

Heading back to Boston, Collins called on Dinneen for the eighth game against Phillippe. After three scoreless innings Boston finally scored two runs in the fourth and one in the sixth to take a 3-0 lead. Phillippe and Dinneen battled, both pitch-ing complete games in the process, but Pittsburgh failed to give Phillippe any run support and Dinneen posted his second shutout of the series. Despite Phillippe's fifth complete game in the series, Boston triumphed behind Dinneen's fourth com-plete game and third victory. The American League won its fourth straight game and the first World Series.

Fears of a loss from the NL New York Giants led to the cancellation of the 1904 World Series. The Giants, who wrapped up the NL pennant early, realized the distinct potential of having to play their crosstown rivals, the Highlanders, who were leading the American League. John T. Brush, the Giants owner, had bitterly agreed to the establishment of the Highlanders in New York in 1903, but in 1904 refused to provide a potential stage for his rivals to defeat his club. In July Giants manager John McGraw announced that his club would join with the Chicago team from the National League on a world tour after the season. The teams would contribute ten players each and then travel to the Pacific Coast, Hawaii, Australia, and return via Europe playing exhibition games. The trip eventually materialized as Albert Spalding became involved, and he used the promotion as an attempt to increase the popularity of the game and as a worldwide distribution network for his sporting goods empire. For Brush and McGraw, it became a clever way to resist the reality of facing their AL rivals.

McGraw and Brush pulled their team from the series. Brush reportedly gave an ultimatum to his players to not even consider playing in a series set up outside of his authority. Rumors stated that he offered to pay players to go home after the NL season was finished and not take part in any sort of series. To counteract Brush, sport-minded businessmen interested in the game made counteroffers. Joe Ullman offered $50,000 to each team to play seven games at Hilltop Park if the High-landers won the AL pennant. In addition, if any of the Giant players received inducements to not play, Ullman stated that his group would pay them twice the amount offered to participate in the series. The battle continued as the season played out with both sides pleading their cases through the media.

Deciding game between the National and American leagues in 1903. (Courtesy of the Library of Congress)

Brush and McGraw claimed that the American League was inferior and that the series therefore proved little. Brush labeled the American League a minor league and stated that he believed that the 154-game schedule of the National League settled any disputes as to who was the best team in the United States. American League president Ban Johnson argued that baseball would benefit by maintaining its standard of skill and sportsmanship in the United States, rather than sending picked teams abroad to popularize the pastime in other countries.

Ironically, McGraw's and the Giants' fears of facing their New York rivals never materialized, as the Boston Americans rallied late in the year and won the pennant on the final day of the season in a doubleheader at New York's Hilltop Park. It marked the last time that the Boston team would defeat their New York adversaries in a pennant-clinching game until the 2004 American League Championship Series.

In the final weeks of the season both the New York and Boston American League clubs issued public challenges to Brush to play a postseason series. Brush and McGraw declined the challenge, stating there was no mandate for them to play the series in baseball's constitution. Public outcries against Brush's move led the owner to call for a meeting to resolve issues raised in regards to the organization of the title series. Brush noted that no formal agreements existed regarding payouts to teams, where games were to be played, and so on. In the off-season owners finally met and agreed on the "Brush Rules." These rules stipulated that 10 percent of all gross revenues from the World Series would go to a new bureaucratic organization called the National Commission. The two teams would split 40 percent of the remaining gross, but only from the first four games of the series. This ensured that players did not "fix" games in order to make more money by playing an extended series. The winning team received three-quarters of the money while the losers earned one-quarter. Management of the two competing clubs would then split the remaining money.

Under the Brush Rules a lottery system determined the host team for the first three games, and if a seventh game became necessary the National Commission held discretionary power to decide where to hold that game. Under this system, the World Series became compulsory and the National Commission organized the event rather than the clubs themselves.

Regardless of the failed World Series, baseball enjoyed impressive and unusual personal feats in 1904. Pitcher Jack Chesbro of the New York Highlanders pitched forty-eight complete games out of his fifty-one starts and won forty-one of those contests with his infamous spitball. However, in the first game of the team's final doubleheader against Boston, Chesbro threw a wild pitch that allowed the winning run to score, giving the Boston team the pennant.

Chicago Cubs hitter Frank Chance set a major-league record in 1904 by being hit by pitches four times in one day in a doubleheader against Cincinnati. After being knocked unconscious in the first game Chance returned to be struck by pitches in the second game as well.

The World Series returned to major-league baseball in 1905. However, even with the Brush rules, the leagues clashed and threatened the series. The National League decided that the 154-game season, which it had implemented in 1904, would continue to be its standard. Under the schedule, the National League season concluded on October 8. Ban Johnson of the American League objected to the length of the season, noting that players' contracts expired on October 15 and that they could legitimately walk away from the series on that day with no contractual obligation. Johnson favored a nine-game series but noted that even in a seven-game format, the time span allowed no days for travel between the two cities. He asked the National League to shorten its season or start it earlier so that it could conclude in time for a proper series to be played. The National League kept its schedule. In an attempt to appease players who may be asked to play beyond the length of their contract, in case the series went longer than expected, due to weather or other unexpected circumstances, the National Commission increased the amount of proceeds for the players from the previous 40 percent to 60 percent of the gate receipts. With this provision in place, McGraw's Giants earned the right to play the American League Philadelphia Athletics in the renewed World Series.

New York's Christy Mathewson delivered for the National League, as he won three games in a period of six days, all in shutout fashion. Mathewson, who had won thirty-one games in the regular season, gave up only fourteen hits and one walk while striking out eighteen batters in his twenty-seven innings of World Series action in 1905. The New York team won the series, 4-1, in a series dominated by pitching on both sides. The two teams scored only eighteen total runs in the five games. Nine of those came from New York in game 3 in a 9-0 win, the only blowout of the series.

New York had won an impressive 105 games during the regular season in addition to the world championship. In 1906 the NL Chicago Cubs eclipsed that total, winning 116 games, en route to the pennant and a showdown with their crosstown rivals, the Chicago White Sox. One of the questions that remained an issue for the National Commission was the seventh game of the series. Attempting to be fair to both teams the commission preferred a neutral site so as not to favor one team over another. In 1905 they agreed that a game 7 would have been played in Boston at the National League team's ballpark. In 1906, as the commission met to set dates for the series, the decision remained undetermined. As a result, cities vied for the opportunity to host such a game. Fresno, California, offered $25,000 to host the game. The Fresno bidders promised 40,000 spectators as well as sunshine for the game. While Fresno seemed an odd choice, it was the hometown of the Chicago NL club's manager, Frank Chance. Fortunately, the National Commission averted such a decision again as the White Sox won the series in six games, 4-2, spoiling the record-setting season of the NL club. The series was a decidedly defensive battle. The AL White Sox won while batting only .198 in the series, enough to outhit the suddenly anemic NL club, who hit only .196. White Sox pitcher Ed Walsh emerged as the star of the series winning two games, allowing only seven hits in fifteen innings for a 1.20 era, and striking out seventeen batters.

Beyond records and championships, baseball demonstrated in 1906 its connection to American society and its central role as the national pastime in a significant act of charity. After the San Francisco earthquake destroyed that city on April 18, major-league baseball stepped forward. New York temporarily suspended its ban on Sunday baseball, allowing the Philadelphia Athletics and New York Highlanders to play in a benefit game raising $5,900 for victims of the earthquake.

The 1906 season started the Chicago Cubs' dynasty, as they played in four World Series championships in five years. After losing the 1906 series the club would win three of the next four series to finish the decade as the dominant organization in all of major-league baseball.

The 1907 Cubs rose to the occasion and defeated the American League's Detroit Tigers in five games in the World Series. The Cubs had finished the season seventeen games ahead of the second-place Pittsburgh Pirates and rested their star players down the stretch. The Tigers clinched the AL pennant on the last day of the season, causing AL president Ban Johnson to attribute fatigue as a reason for the Tigers' downfall.

The Series started out strangely enough in that game 1 ended in a twelve-inning tie due to darkness. A dropped third strike by Tigers catcher Boss Schmidt allowed the Cubs to tie the game. Many felt it was the turning point of the game, and possibly even the series. The Cubs only allowed the AL team three more runs in the next four games. American League batting champion Ty Cobb only managed four hits in twenty at bats, for a paltry .200 average against Chicago pitchers. The unsung hero for the Cubs became catcher Johnny Kling, who defensively contained the Tigers' base-running prowess by consistently throwing out Detroit players as they attempted to steal bases.

Tickets for the series were priced dramatically differently for the two cities. In Chicago tickets cost $1, $1.50, and $2.00 for the highest-priced seats. In Detroit tickets sold for $1, $2, and $2.50. The difference existed because Chicago's West Side Grounds held far more fans than Detroit's Bennett Park; 78,086 fans witnessed the five-game series and gate receipts totaled $101,728.50 to be split among the National Commission, the players, and their owners. Interestingly, the losing Tigers' share of the spoils ended up being larger than the victorious Cubs, as Detroit president William H. Yawkey added $15,000 of his $18,311.13 team share to the players' $21,973,36 share, to be divided as a bonus. The Tigers players' share rose to $36,973.36, as opposed to the Cubs' share of $32,900.03. The press hailed the crowd size, but due to the small size of Bennett Park, which held around 12,000 fans, the series actually drew fewer fans than the 1905 series at 91,633 fans and the 1906 all-Chicago series, which drew 99,855.

Detroit had attempted to deal Cobb prior to the 1907 season because he created undue tension among his teammates due to his feistiness and quick temper. In an attempt to create harmony on the club, manager Hugh Jennings of the Tigers asked for offers from every team in the American League. However, when only Clark Griffith of the New York Highlanders offered a trade for Cobb, and that offer was substandard, Jennings decided to attempt to make peace between Cobb and the rest of the team. The gamble worked as Cobb led the Tigers to the pennant. Cobb would continue to win nine straight batting titles and lead the Tigers to three straight unsuccessful World Series appearances. Unfortunately for Cobb, these World Series teams were the only ones he played on in his twenty-four years in the major leagues.

Baseball held great allure for gamblers during this decade. In fact, the *New York Times* reported in 1907 that a Pittsburgh "sporting man" named Shad Gwilliam had won more than $42,000 in the 1907 series from his gambling activities. Gwilliam had bet on other series as well. The newspaper reported that he had lost $29,000 on the 1903 series, won $10,000 in 1905, and lost $30,000 in 1906.

New emphasis was placed upon off-season and spring training for baseball players held in the south. Pittsburgh established spring training facilities in Hot Springs, Arkansas. Other northern teams sought locations in the warmer south with adequate facilities to host their teams. With a lack of these facilities, Detroit in 1908 considered building its own facility, also in Hot Springs. Other northern teams took other routes. The New York Giants used a form of cross-training for their young recruits, teaching them skills in handball and basketball, utilizing the YMCA facilities in the city. The Giants eventually found facilities in Marlin, Texas, for their spring drills. With the increased emphasis on competitive levels and staying in shape, many players sought increased contracts, which would give them greater flexibility in training full-time. This led to a growing dissatisfaction among players regarding their contracts. So many were unhappy that media reports in 1908 jokingly claimed that a "Disgruntled League" could start and have plenty of teams.

Players' grievances are understandable in light of the profits beginning to roll in from major-league baseball. New York papers estimated that in 1908 the Giants' profits could climb to $240,000 after all expenses, with a World Series appearance. The Giants' payroll stood at roughly $60,000 for players or approximately $3000 per player. Players felt that they should reap more of the profit margin. Players received many extra benefits outside of their paychecks, however. The National Baseball Commission prohibited bonuses paid to players by clubs. However, the commission left open the possibility of individuals rewarding players with presents. Players, therefore, frequently received items from businesses, including suits of clothing, jewelry, overcoats, shoes, gold watches, studs, and lockets. For winning teams, these presents became more elaborate, thus increasing the importance of on-field performance.

As baseball continued to grow as a business enterprise, the National Commission realized the need to provide additional oversight to the World Series. Responding to criticism regarding different ticket prices set in the 1907 series, the commission made changes for the 1908 fall classic. They announced that the National Commission would furnish all general admission tickets for the series, one set priced at $1.00 and the other at $1.50. These prices were significantly more than regular-season tickets, which were typically twenty-five and fifty cents for the two types of seats. The commission allowed reserved seat prices to remain the province of the home teams, with the caveat that visiting players were to be given two reserved seats per player for each game.

Reserved seating or extra entrance fees for selected sections of the ballpark created one way that teams avoided splitting costs with visiting teams and possibly even the National Commission. During the regular season, teams were obligated to split the proceeds of admissions to the park 50-50 with the visiting team. The New York Giants charged a general-admission fee of twenty-five and fifty cents. Based on a daily average attendance figure of 7500 fans, the total take for the season was approximately $300,000. For regular-season games the Giants paid visiting teams half, or $150,000. However, once inside the ballpark clubs charged extra costs for admission into other sections. For the Giants this meant the lower grandstand, which cost twenty-five cents extra, or the upper pavilion that would cost an additional fifty cents per patron. In a given year, the Giants would take in around $67,500 in extra revenue, which they were not obligated to share with the opposing team. Home teams used this same concept in World Series games to withhold certain income from the potential pot, split between players, owners, and the National Commission.

Detroit, once again, celebrated winning the AL pennant, and a place in their second consecutive World Championship Series, in 1908. Reaching the series that year sent Detroit fans into a frenzy. Throughout the city people celebrated with bonfires, horns, torches, and drums amidst the cries of "Wee-ah!" made famous by Tigers manager Hugh Jennings. Mayor William B. Thompson and the Common Council issued resolutions for businesses and citizens to decorate their stores and residences for the Series, and employers to make every reasonable accommodation for their workers to be able to get time off to attend the games.

While the Tigers won the pennant on the last day of the season, in the National League the race was even tighter. For the first time in NL history a postseason play-off game determined the champion. This occurred due to a series of protests resulting from a legendary play, referred to as "Merkle's Boner." On September 23 McGraw's Giants played against Chance's Cubs in New York. In the bottom of the ninth inning with the score tied, rookie Giant first baseman Fred Merkle singled to right field with two outs and a runner on first. The next batter, Al Bridwell, singled to centerfield, scoring Moose McCormick from third base. When Merkle saw McCormick cross the plate, he headed for the Giant clubhouse in center field. Cub second baseman Johnny Evers noticed that Merkle had not gone on to touch second base as required by the rules. Evers called for the ball, tagged second, and appealed to umpire Bob Emslie, who did not see whether Merkle had actually touched second base. He appealed to home-plate umpire Hank O'Day, who granted Evers's appeal and called Merkle out on a force play. The Giants, who had left the field, were celebrating their supposed victory when O'Day declared the game a tie. A similar play had occurred the month before in a game in Pittsburgh, thus making O'Day aware of the possibility of the appeal, and alerting his attention to see whether Merkle had actually touched second base.

The Cubs immediately appealed to National League President Harry C. Pulliam that the Giants should have forfeited the game. The Giants then appealed to Pulliam, arguing that they should receive a win and the umpire should not have declared the game a tie because the rule was rarely enforced. On the last day of the 1908 season, that September game had huge implications for the pennant race. The Giants trailed the Cubs by a half game and had one more game to play against Boston. A win meant a tie between the Cubs and Giants. President Pulliam had denied both team's appeals and both appealed again to the directors for a decision. The board sustained Pulliam's decisions and ruled that the game must be made up on October 8, the day after the end of the regular season. New York beat Boston, ending the season tied with the Cubs for first. Thousands of New Yorkers tried to get into the game and were turned away because of the enormity of the crowd, some even holding tickets. Thousands of other fans watched the ticker at the *New York Times'* offices as the scores were posted outside the building. In the extra game, forced by Merkle's blunder, the Giants lost to the Cubs

New York fans reacted to the loss in an ugly manner. Police were called to the Polo Grounds to restore order. Cubs manager Frank Chance was injured by a soda-water bottle thrown from the stands while he was leaving the field. Regardless of their pregame enthusiasm, New York fans left that day disappointed and, in many cases, angry.

Fans were ruthless in their treatment of Merkle and his reputation suffered forever. Giant fans and the media hammered President Pulliam in the press, questioning his lack of courage in the affair. The criticism weighed heavily on Pulliam, who the next July would commit suicide by shooting himself in the head at the New York Athletic Club. Such were the passions now associated with the World Series.

Chicago fans were ecstatic in celebration of their team's third straight appearance in the Series. Crowds gathered outside of every telegraph line connected to New York all day, awaiting news of the game as the telegraph operators delivered it. When the team won, a collective cheer went up around the city. In Chicago, the term "repeat" emerged in the phrases of fans, while in Detroit "revenge" became the operative word.

Detroit, realizing the great demand for tickets, ordered 10,000 circus seats installed in the outfield area to accommodate fans, increasing Bennett Field's attendance potential to over 20,000. However, the Tigers were, once again, thwarted by the Cubs, four games to one. The Cubs became the first team to repeat as World Series champions and the game's first dynasty. The extra bleachers for Bennett Park never got used, however, as crowds for the games in Detroit were small. By the fifth game, when it became clear that Detroit was struggling, the local fans stayed away, creating the smallest crowd in World Series history at 6,210.

Detroit recovered and in 1909 once again won the AL title and a shot at the World Championship. The Tigers were led by Ty Cobb, who won the triple crown of hitting and led the major leagues with nine home runs, all of which were inside-the-park home runs. The Tigers were able to avoid the Cubs and played the Pittsburgh Pirates. Detroit fared better against the Pirates, and the Series, for the first time, went the full seven games. In the final game, though, Babe Adams, who had already beaten the Tigers twice in complete games in the Series, shut them out again en route to a World Series record three wins.

Chicago's Cubs ended the decade by returning to a familiar spot, the World Series. However, sports' first dynasty showed its age when the Cubs met the young Philadelphia Athletics. The A's had become the first AL team to win over 100 games in the regular season and they carried that momentum through to the Series, beating the Cubs four games to one, signaling the end of one decade's dynasty and the beginning of a new decade and a new dynasty.

Race in Baseball

The 1900s marked the second decade of African American exclusion from major-league baseball. The unwritten color line limited opportunities for black athletes in the United States. While some improvements occurred in race relations, many setbacks continued. Events such as former slave Booker T. Washington's' invitation to visit the White House, as the guest of President Theodore Roosevelt in 1901, the first for an African American, roused hope. The defeat of black congressman George White of North Carolina in the same year, just after he had proposed the first congressional legislation to ban lynching and make it a federal crime, reminded African Americans that their voices were still restricted.

Black baseball players, following Washington's advice to maintain patience and use industrious activities to fight for civil rights, began a process of developing their own teams. After a decade of exclusion, it became clear that major-league baseball was intent on continuing their policy of exclusion and, rather than waiting for white leaders in the National and American Leagues to have a change of heart, black leaders looked for new opportunities. One came in the Cuban Leagues, which in 1900 permitted black players to play. While the formalization of the Negro Leagues was still decades away, black teams did exist and played for their own world championships. In 1910 these championships even gained the attention of the *New York Times*. The newspaper highlighted the seventh game between the Royal Giants and the Philadelphia Giants at Meyerrose Park in Ridgewood, New Jersey.

During the 1900s the most popular, and arguably the best, black team was the Cuban X Giants. Other teams also had impressive runs as well, including the Philadelphia Giants. In Chicago, the Chicago Unions and Columbia Giants battled in the early part of the decade for supremacy, before both teams ran into financial problems, resulting in the split of the Unions and the demise of the Columbia Giants. Eventually, the Leland Chicago Giants arose as the dominant team in the region. Other areas also had Negro teams, such as the Algona Brownies from Iowa, who defeated the Union Giants in 1903 in a regional championship. Most of these teams played in semiprofessional leagues, many of which consisted of both black and white teams.

For black baseball, the 1900s saw the rise of black entrepreneurship. In 1907 Frank Leland attempted to form a black professional league for baseball players. Prospective teams were encouraged in Kansas City, Cincinnati, Louisville, Cleveland, Pittsburgh, Toledo, Milwaukee, Memphis, Nashville, Columbus, Detroit, Indianapolis, and Chicago. However, only Indianapolis and Leland's Chicago team made firm commitments to the league and it eventually died before becoming a reality on the field.

Black baseball executives were reluctant to incur traveling expenses in a league that was so much larger, geographically, than the regional schedules they played. Leland, however, believed that traveling teams, which could expand their influence outside of their geographical constraints, held great potential. He hired another man who shared that vision and who would establish the blueprint for such ventures. Andrew "Rube" Foster created the barnstorming model in the years 1907–10, which he would use successfully through the next decade, establishing him as the leading entrepreneur in black baseball.

As a player, the 6′4″ Foster dominated teams with his pitching. In 1902 Leland had released Foster from the Chicago Union Giants due to a performance slump. Foster joined the Otsego Independents, a semiprofessional team in Michigan whose owner, George Bardeen, was one of the first owners in baseball to allow African American players to integrate white teams. Foster reportedly won fifty-one games on the mound that season. Success followed Foster. In 1903 he pitched for

Philadelphia's Cuban X Giants and won four games in their playoff series with the Philadelphia Giants for the Eastern Black Baseball Championship. In 1904 he switched teams and led Philadelphia to victory, winning two playoff games against his former club. The Philadelphia Giants, under the direction of Sol White and with Foster as the star, continued to dominate eastern black baseball. In 1906, White embarked on a new venture, starting the International League of Independent Professional Ball Players. The league consisted of both all-black and all-white teams in the Philadelphia and Wilmington, Delaware, area. Foster, again, led the Giants to the pennant for this new league. While the Philadelphia team had great success on the field, they still struggled financially.

With financial ruin always close at the door in Philadelphia, Leland lured Foster away from White for the 1907 season with the prospect of a potential new league, and by giving the star pitcher the role of player-manager. Foster enticed seven of his Philadelphia teammates to make the move to Chicago with him, including star outfielder Pete Hill. When Leland's new league failed, the Leland Giants looked to establish themselves as more than just a regional team. Foster took over the booking of games and instituted a new policy that either split gate receipts in half or provided enticing guarantees for visiting teams, which helped attract top competitors for the Leland Giants.

The Giants also embarked on a spring barnstorming tour before their season began, becoming the first black-owned and managed club to do so. Traveling in their own private Pullman car, the team played both black and white teams in various cities in southern states such as Texas, Tennessee, and Alabama. After their barnstorming tour, the team went 110-10 during their regular season, including a streak where they won forty-eight straight games en route to winning the Chicago city championship.

The Leland Giants continued to barnstorm in the spring and dominate midwestern teams during the season. In 1908 they played for a national championship against Foster's former team, the Philadelphia Giants, which resulted in a tie, as both teams won three games in the series and no tie-breaking game was played.

In 1909 Foster and his Leland Giants gained an opportunity to play an exhibition series against the National League's Chicago Cubs after winning their league title. Foster, who had broken his leg in July of the season, realized the significance of this series and pushed to return to the mound by October for the series. However, he was not in top physical form and ended up losing a 5-2 lead in the ninth inning of the second game of the series. In fact, Foster lost the game on a controversial call when a Cub base runner scored the winning run while Foster was arguing with an umpire over a call. The Leland Giants also lost the western Black Championship to the St. Paul Colored Gophers in 1909. These two key losses inspired Foster, who determined to make changes for the 1910 season.

The first change Foster sought was to gain control of the team from Leland, whom he felt was holding back the team's potential. Foster aligned himself with Beauregard Mosley, who handled the business side of the Leland Giants Baseball and Amusement Association (LGBAA), and they forced Leland out, gaining control of his organization. Leland went to court to challenge the takeover, but lost.

With Leland out of the picture, Foster proceeded to put together what he considered the finest team ever assembled. He signed John Henry Lloyd away from the Philadelphia Giants. Foster also signed former teammates Grant "Home Run"

Johnson, who at age thirty-five would hit .397 for the Leland Giants in 1910, and catcher Bruce Petway, who reportedly threw out Ty Cobb three times in three attempts in a game in Cuba in 1910. The Leland Giants that season compiled an astounding record of 123-6. Whereas the Chicago Cubs in 1909 had answered the Leland Giants' challenge to a series, winning it in three close games, there is no record of any white major-league teams lining up to play against this 1910 team, which was loaded with players respected by their white peers as great players.

Basketball

Basketball, considered the true American game due to being invented in Springfield, Massachusetts, began to develop its organizational structure during this decade, primarily in American colleges. Leagues formed for competition around the country. The first to develop was Connecticut's Triangle League in the 1900–1901 season with Yale, Trinity, and Wesleyan. Later that season the New England League formed with Dartmouth, Holy Cross, Amherst, Williams, and Trinity creating an alliance. The Eastern League followed, with Columbia, Cornell, Yale, Harvard, and Princeton as its members. In the early years of league development, it was common for teams like Yale and Trinity to join more than one league. Other conferences also began to establish basketball competition around the nation. The Western Conference, which would become the Big Ten, started a round-robin league in 1905, although many of the teams had been playing for years without conference affiliation.

One of the innovations in the college game during this decade was the development of dribbling to advance the ball. Yale was the first to invent the technique but it quickly caught on and was mastered by Pennsylvania's Charles Keinath and Chicago's H.O. "Pat" Page.

Minnesota dominated play at the start of the decade, recording thirty-four straight victories from 1901 to 1904. As the sport grew, Spalding sporting goods realized the potential profits to be made from the game and, in 1904, introduced their first basketball sneaker, called the "suction sole."

The 1904–5 season also saw fifteen colleges gather in New York and Philadelphia to standardize rules and develop their own governing body. Possibly the most significant impact of this conference was that the colleges gained control of the game from the Amateur Athletic Union. Basketball at this time was a very physical sport without the flow of today's game. As a result, at times it fell under the same type of criticism that football received. Harvard president Charles Eliot in 1908 recommended the abolishment of basketball, as he believed it to be more brutal than football. To counteract the criticism, rulemakers established limits of five fouls per player in 1908, after which that player earned disqualification from the game.

The team of the decade was clearly the University of Chicago. Following the master plan of President William Rainey Harper to build athletic dominance to promote the school, Chicago became the first school to hire a professional coach, Joseph Raycroft, for its basketball team. While the sport's creator, James Naismith, was the head coach at Kansas University, he was a member of the faculty in physical education at the school, and not solely its coach. Realizing the trend in the sport toward professional coaches, he turned the coaching duties over in 1907 to Forrest "Phog" Allen, who would become a legendary coach at KU. Raycroft at

Chicago had set the trend, however, and his teams won seventy-eight of ninety games during the decade, including a 21-2 record in 1908. Behind All-Americans Pat Page and John Schommer, the first true center in the game, Chicago won the first national title in basketball in the first national playoff. Chicago, which had won the west regional championship in a playoff with Wisconsin, defeated the east region champions, Pennsylvania, in a best of three series. Schommer won the national player of the year award in 1909, followed by teammate Page in 1910. Schommer would also make his mark in 1910 by inventing glass backboards so that fans could see the game more easily.

Other great early players were Wisconsin's Christian Steinmetz, who became the first collegiate player to score 1000 points in his career (1903–5), and Clemson's J. O. Erwin, who scored a school-record fifty-eight points in the school's first intercollegiate game, a record that lasted the entire century.

Basketball also made its Olympic debut as a demonstration sport in this decade. At the 1904 St. Louis Games, four different Olympic basketball tournaments were held. In the Olympic College World Championship, Hiram College, Wheaton College, and Latter Day Saints University (now BYU) competed for the Olympic championship, with Hiram winning the title. In the Olympic Amateur Championships, the Buffalo Germans YMCA club won all of its games in the round-robin tournament. The other two tournaments were for high schools, in which the New York team beat St. Louis, Chicago, and San Francisco, and elementary schools, in which the New York team defeated the Chicago and San Francisco teams. Less true Olympic championships than exhibitions of the sport, the events nevertheless furthered the development of the sport in the decade.

Basketball was the one sport that gained easy acceptance with women as well. Although the rules had been altered to reflect Victorian standards of propriety to ensure the notions of female daintiness in athletic endeavors, the game grew in popularity around the country. The women played in fixed regions on the court and could not steal the ball from opponents. Regardless of the rule changes, the game proved popular as teams formed in colleges and high schools.

Football

Whereas baseball faced its greatest threat early in the decade, with the advent of a competitive major league to the established National League, it grew enormously popular throughout the decade. Football faced a much tougher road. American football existed in a unique cultural position. During this decade, it lacked a professional league and existed only as a supposedly amateur sport. It was the primary sporting vehicle for upper-class elite colleges such as Yale, Penn, Harvard, and Princeton. Yet, for a sport tied to such a seemingly refined population, it suffered from strong connections to brutality and violence. Deaths occurring during games plagued the sport. At the end of the decade football's place in American sporting life remained tenuous at best and threatened by both rugby and soccer.

Football entered the decade increasing its popularity as evidenced by the rising number of collegiate teams adding the sport to their athletic programs. The game, which had started as the province of the older established eastern universities such as Harvard, Yale, Princeton, and Penn, had spread to smaller schools in the East and across the nation. Schools as diverse as Oregon, Minnesota, Notre Dame,

Whitworth, Stanford, Auburn, Chicago, Colorado College, Arkansas, South Dakota, Texas, and Michigan all played the game at their institutions. However, as popular as the game was within these college communities, it also suffered from controversies and scandals.

Professionalism, recruiting violations, ineligible players, financial benefits, and slush funds provided ample material for the media to question the game's popularity. The use of professional coaches challenged some critics' idealism. Coaches, such as George Foster Sanford at Columbia, had received as much as $5000 to coach teams. However, as the decade began, the pressure to win, which came with these salaries, created increased violations of rules in order to produce results. These infractions led to some, like Foster in 1901, losing their positions amid scandals. However, many university leaders realized that great prestige and notoriety could come to a university through a successful football team.

This type of thinking drove University of Chicago President William Rainey Harper to hire Amos Alonzo Stagg. As head of the Department of Physical Culture and Athletics Stagg was to create a top-notch football program at the midwestern school in order to compete with the likes of Harvard, Yale, and Princeton both academically and athletically. By the 1900s Stagg's teams had become the elite of the Midwest, and other institutions emulated Harper's model. Former players from the programs at Harvard, Yale, and Princeton were in high demand as coaches. By 1901 seventy Yale graduates were coaching across the country. While scandals involving players, coaches, and the financial arrangements of those situations continued from the 1890s into the first decade of the new century, another issue took center stage in the controversies surrounding football: the style of play.

As winning became more and more important for schools, a renewed focus on tactics and strategies developed. One of these was the mass play in which teams would line up guards and tackles in the backfield and use their momentum to

A football game in the early 1900s. (Courtesy of the Library of Congress)

propel the ball carrier toward the first down, which at the time required only five yards in three downs to accomplish. As a result, football became a mass of bodies slamming into one another and, in the close quarters, many illegal acts such as punching, kicking, choking, and biting would occur, out of the officials' sight. Newspaper reports of deaths and injuries increased, raising public skepticism of the merits of the game.

To deal with the organization of the game, schools formed athletic leagues within geographic regions. These leagues began to question the rules established by the eastern elites and developed their own standards of play. One of the most powerful leagues was the Western League, which would become the Big Ten, led by Stagg and Michigan's Fielding Yost. The Western League adopted a more wide-open style of play, divorcing itself from reliance upon mass-momentum plays favored by the Big Three, Harvard, Yale, and Princeton.

Other western and southern leagues also developed their own guidelines and favored the development of the forward pass. Their games featured less ball control and greater deception in the form of fakes, end runs, and passes. As these leagues matured, claims arose as to "national championship" status. In 1901 Michigan claimed the title by recording an 11-0 record, outscoring opponents by 550-0, and defeating Stanford in the first-ever Rose Bowl 49-0. Harvard, who believed that winning the eastern championship accorded them the national title, contested the claim. Eastern schools sometimes agreed to play western and southern schools, but the stipulation was that those schools needed to travel east to play the contest. The battle over a true national champion played out in the media and between fans throughout the decade.

In 1902 Yost's Michigan team again posted a perfect record in their eleven games but slipped slightly in allowing opponents to score twelve points against them. Once again, they claimed the title of national champions, despite the fact that Yost's former team, the University of Nebraska, had a 9-0 record. Nebraska would continue its dominance in 1903, posting a 10-0 record. Princeton made its claim as the national champion that season as well, posting an 11-0 record and giving up only six points. Not to be outdone, Michigan, despite tying Minnesota 6-6, claimed it won the national title with its 11-0-1 record.

The 1904 season created even more chaos, as no less than five teams finished the season undefeated. Once again, Michigan claimed its fourth straight national title, while fellow Western Conference foe Minnesota also claimed the honor with their 13-0 record. The University of Pennsylvania laid their claim to the crown with their 12-0 record and eastern championship. Vanderbilt University and Auburn University also completed undefeated campaigns and believed that they deserved national championship honors. This debate over national prominence demonstrated that, while the eastern colleges believed that they controlled the sport, others were willing to challenge that status.

With their wide-open style of play, western teams felt they were immune to the criticisms of brutality and poor sportsmanship revolving around the eastern teams in the early part of the decade. However, with mounting deaths and serious injuries repeatedly in the media, few members of the press noted differences in playing style. As calls for the abolition of the game grew, those outside of the east felt the sting just as fiercely. In 1905 the crisis hit with full force, prompting President Theodore Roosevelt to summon leaders from the Big Three to the White House in an effort to save the game, while reigning in acts of intentional injury, brutality, and unsportsmanlike behavior.

Leaders and coaches at the Big Three set about attempts at reform, but could not agree on rule changes necessary to save the game. The 1905 season provided more fodder for those who had railed against the professionalism and commercialism of the game and now challenged it based on its abhorrent brutality.

Late in the season Union College and New York University (NYU) played in New York City where Union end Harold Moore died from an injury sustained in the game. Moore's death spurred NYU chancellor Henry MacCracken to telegraph the presidents of the Big Three, imploring them to begin a process of reform for the game. MacCracken believed that the game could be saved with rule changes. Charles Eliot of Harvard however, believed that the game itself was flawed and felt nothing short of abolishment would help. Eliot declined to assist MacCracken. With no assistance coming from the leading universities, MacCracken found himself at the front of the reform movement.

At the end of the 1905 campaign, MacCracken moved forward with discussions on whether to abolish football or to enact reforms. NYU sent letters to its opponents for the past ten seasons to meet in New York to discuss the football crisis. Of the Big Three, only Princeton had been an opponent of NYU, and Princeton president Woodrow Wilson declined the invitation. He told MacCracken that Princeton already had a solution, with a rule that prohibited blocking in front of the ball carrier. Harvard and Yale had both spurned MacCracken's earlier attempt to engage them, and continued to see the conference as insignificant. In the end, twelve schools came to the conference in December. The questions that MacCracken posed were "did the delegates believe that, in its present form the game 'ought to be played'?" and if not abolished, then "what should be done to reform it?"

One school represented at the conference had already answered that question and acted upon their decision. Columbia president Nicholas Murray Butler took advantage of the students' Thanksgiving break to announce that Columbia would abolish the game and instructed his delegates to vote in accordance to this stance. At this meeting, a vote on whether to abolish football occurred at the onset. Five of the colleges voted in support of the ban including Columbia, NYU, and Union. Palmer Pierce of West Point gathered the support of the remaining schools and stopped what could have been a decisive blow to the game. With the decision to retain and reform the game, the conference members decided to hold a second meeting and invite all football-playing colleges in America to participate. In order to enact reform, the convention also selected a new rules committee to alleviate dangerous, brutal, and mass plays.

That second meeting occurred on December 28, 1905. While the new committee was forming, the old rules committee, the Intercollegiate Football Rules Committee, headed by Paul Dashiell and controlled by its secretary, Walter Camp, held its regularly scheduled meeting. Dominated by Harvard, Yale, Princeton, and Penn, this committee struggled to find common ground for rule changes. Bill Reid of Harvard refused to support many of the changes proposed because Harvard had a special rules committee that was meeting, and Reid wanted to wait for their recommendations.

Reid understood the threat that his Harvard president Eliot posed, and heard that the Board of Regents had voted secretly to ban football. Toward the end of the season Reid and four other Harvard football enthusiasts met secretly and wrote an open letter to the Harvard Graduates Athletic Association, criticizing aspects of the game and promising that radical reforms could be made with an effective rules committee. They also released the letter to the press. The letter was designed to stave off the political will of the Regents through a grassroots campaign of athletic supporters. It was an internal political move, but Reid and his group also had an external plan. The Harvard group sent Reid to the old rules committee meeting to be held the day after the MacCracken meeting. The sixty-eight schools at the MacCracken convention formed a new organization and elected Palmer Pierce of West Point as the first president of the Inter-Collegiate Athletic Association (ICAA). This new association in five years would change its name to the National Collegiate Athletic Association (NCAA). Two weeks later the two football rules committees met separately but at the same hotel.

This provided Reid and Harvard with their opportunity to seize control of the process. Working with both committees Reid manipulated rulemakers to adopt rules demanded by Harvard's ad hoc committee. These rule changes were sent to these meetings with Reid, under the threat that if they were not adopted, Harvard would drop football. The strategy worked, and the rules committee accepted nearly all of the Harvard proposals.

Significant changes included the forward pass, a neutral zone between the opposing teams, and—Camp's favorite—the extension of a first down to ten yards. Other proposals called for stronger penalties against roughness, brutality, and insulting talk. Harvard had remained in the fold and the game received new life and Harvard greater control, at least in the East.

Noticeably absent from the ICAA's first meeting were midwestern and west coast schools. The Western Conference boycotted the meeting. Other than representatives from Colorado College, South Dakota, and Texas, western schools were not represented. For various reasons, what remained was a northeastern assembly of mostly smaller schools; however, they were strong enough to bring the Eastern powers to their knees.

The Western Conference (Big Nine) saw no reason to join the fray over the brutality of the game as they had already adopted a wide-open game that resulted in fewer injuries. However, as the crisis and the national hysteria engulfed the nation, the Big Nine schools found themselves in a crisis over the professionalism, rather than the brutality, of the game. In the final game of the season, in their traditional rivalry game with the University of Chicago, Yost's Michigan squad, which had gone fifty-eight straight games without a loss, looked to win its fifth national championship. Outscoring opponents 495-0 that season seemed to bode well for Michigan. However, Stagg's team also was undefeated and had only given up five points to opponents. In front of 27,000 fans in Chicago, Stagg's team held off Yost's Michigan men 2-0, scoring on a safety in a classic defensive Thanksgiving Day battle. That game would prove to be the last Thanksgiving Day championship, and the last traditional rivalry matchup for the Western Conference for many years, as reform hit the league with a mighty force.

Inflamed through press reports of ineligible or "tramp" athletes, illegal recruiting practices, paying players, and athletic department debt, faculty members and other reformers jumped on the bandwagon to ban the sport. Led by respectable faculty voices such as Frederick Jackson Turner from Wisconsin and William H. Hale at

Chicago, the call for reform quickly spread throughout the member institutions. In December 1905 Turner proposed a two-year suspension of football in order to discuss the need for balance between athletics and academics. The movement in the Big Nine grew outside of its boundaries as well. Presidents of sixteen Presbyterian colleges in the region met to discuss abolishment or reform.

Shortly after the ICAA and the new football rules committee announced their rule changes, Big Nine Conference members met to discuss the issue of football. Responding to faculty accusations that that football impeded academic rigor and that cheer practice and the fanaticism surrounding big games distracted the attention of students, the conference members enacted reforms, rather than the abolishment of the sport. They concluded that the season should be shortened to five games and finish before Thanksgiving, and that traditional rivalry games end. In addition, ticket prices were set at a lower fifty-cent rate, down from the two- or three-dollar price that teams could get for big games. They addressed eligibility issues by declaring freshmen ineligible. They also required the institutions to certify that all of its athletes were full-time students in good academic standing, making normal progress toward the completion of a degree.

These reforms set out to curtail the big-time nature of the commercialization of sport. The effect of these reforms would mean the loss of significant revenue for the institutions, over $100,000 a year for some schools. The reformers believed that the publicity and revenue losses were an important sacrifice in order to retain their integrity as institutions of higher learning, which were in the business of education and not of athletic promotion.

While midwestern schools approached their reforms, in the West two approaches to the crisis prevailed. The western responses paled in significance, due to distance as well as the relatively small population bases represented in the region. In the largest population area of California (the San Francisco Bay region), Stanford University and the University of California at Berkeley were the dominant educational institutions and set the standards for conduct through their actions. The Stanford-Cal rivalry in football had been bubbling since 1892. As it had in the rest of the country this rivalry took the focus off educational concerns and, in the opinions of the school presidents, Benjamin Ide Wheeler of Berkeley and David Starr Jordan of Stanford, had grown to indecent proportions in its importance. While neither wanted to do away with the rivalry, both wanted it downplayed.

Neither felt that the game had approached the evil status in the West that it had developed in the East, but both were concerned about the growing zealotry in the sport. Jordan had planned to send a representative, Max Farrand, to the MacCracken conference in December. However, as he and Wheeler watched the crisis unfold, they made a decision far more revolutionary than the reforms in the East or Midwest. Jordan canceled Farrand's trip and announced that the western schools would replace American football with rugby. While the decision barely made a ripple in the eastern landscape and had no impact upon the reform movements across the country, in California it created a dramatic change. Nearby schools such as St. Mary's and Santa Clara both made the change, as did Southern California and Pomona. Most high schools in California also decided to play rugby.

While California schools made an exodus from the American football fold, other western states did not follow suit. Schools in the Pacific Northwest stayed

Theodore Roosevelt, a Sporting President

President Theodore Roosevelt may have influenced sport during his time in office (1901–8) more than any other American leader in the nation's history. He created the National Parks System providing space for outdoor enthusiasts, promoted healthy activity and sport, and helped set in motion the development of bureaucratic structures such as the NCAA. He helped craft an image of American identity that emphasized strenuous activity with a competitive will to fight and compete with whomever and whatever would be the challenge.

Roosevelt constantly challenged and encouraged American Olympic teams to fight for victory. He interjected himself in sports debates using his authority as the president of the United States to make decisions. He selected James E. Sullivan as the head of the U.S. Olympic team in both 1906 and 1908 and injected his views in the debate between Chicago and St. Louis when both were vying for the rights to host the 1904 Olympic Games.

However, he is remembered most for his interdiction with the football crisis of 1905. In October, he gathered the leaders of eastern football powers Harvard, Yale, and Princeton to the White House and demanded that they find a solution to the brutality of the game. Realizing his limited authority over the universities Roosevelt implored the representatives to draft a statement on their train ride home. The statement released by Intercollegiate Football Rules Committee Secretary Walter Camp the next day stated that the schools would carry out the rules of the game in both letter and spirit. Because the season still exhibited numerous violations and examples of unsportsmanlike behavior, Roosevelt continued to press the issue and, in November, summoned Dr. J. William White, professor of surgery at the University of Pennsylvania, to the White House to discuss the subject. White reported that Roosevelt emphatically believed in continuing the game, but that referees should punish the brutality and foul play harshly and, if the referees would not do so, then college presidents should sanction them.

Roosevelt loved gridiron and followed his alma mater, Harvard, faithfully. Roosevelt praised the character-building elements of the game and emphasized that the rough nature of the contests were essential to the nature of American strength. To survive in a competitive international world Roosevelt believed that Americans had to develop a tough, manly demeanor and football provided a key venue for that goal. Roosevelt continued to work behind the scenes in order to move university leaders to address the issues of intentional injury, but withdrew from the public debate on the subject, believing that a form of hysteria had developed surrounding the game. Roosevelt's efforts in initiating discussions among college leaders led to the development of the Inter-Collegiate Athletic Association (ICAA) in 1906, an organization that would change its name in five years to the National Collegiate Athletic Association (NCAA).

---

true to the American version and easily adopted rule changes as they, like the midwestern teams, had already embraced the more open game that reformers in the East finally approved. Northwest teams adopted the new rules and excelled on the field. Oregon State University would complete a 7-0 undefeated season in 1907 and the University of Washington would begin an unmatched era of excellence at the end of the decade, as their 1907 season was the beginning of an NCAA-record sixty-three-game unbeaten streak that would last until 1917.

After all was said and done in the reforms, some schools made the decision to drop American football, including Columbia, Northwestern, Stanford, and California, but the majority remained in the fold. Football had survived its first major crisis in 1905. However, it would continue to struggle during this decade and would face another momentous crisis in 1909.

The reforms around the country, regardless of their results in different regions, also reflected reform movements occurring in business and industry throughout the nation. In that respect, the American public viewed these reforms not as strangely foreign concerns, but as the connection of sport to the culture at large. Abuses needed to be addressed, whether brutality in factory conditions or on the gridiron.

Ironically, the abuses in college football that led to reform movements had an unintended effect. The desire to win led teams to recruit athletes who might not have been admitted to the universities under normal circumstances. As a result, many ethnic minorities who possessed great athletic ability had opportunities to play and attend classes in schools where they would possibly not have been welcomed if not for their athleticism. African American athletes, such as Dartmouth's Matthew Bullock and Ohio University quarterback Arthur D. Carr, were sprinkled throughout college football, whereas they had been banned from professional baseball. Carlisle Indian School developed a competitive team that demonstrated the athletic ability of their teams against the national powers, producing great players such as Jim Thorpe. Hugo Bezdek, born in the Czech Republic, represented the dreams of immigrants, as he starred for the University of Chicago and would move on to coach successfully at Oregon and Arkansas.

With the crisis of the 1905–6 season averted, teams returned to the business of playing the game and trying to decide how to play utilizing the new rules. However, after a couple of quiet years in terms of injuries, eleven players died in college football in 1909, and many were at prominent eastern schools.

In the winter and spring of 1910, the ICAA committee addressed new rule changes and attempted to foresee what effects potential rule changes might have on game play. A hybrid proposal, called the Blagden Report, passed. In the report, the forward pass was liberalized to make it a more effective play. The pushing and pulling was outlawed. Backs, as well as ends, were now eligible to receive passes. The rules changed the game from the rugby-influenced style of the 1890s into the modern game of American football. The end of the decade was the dawning of a new era for American football. The game had survived two major crises and came through them not only changed but also reinvigorated.

Changes in the game included more than the rulebooks and the playing field. The gender roles represented in the game also changed dramatically. While the game had always been a male bastion on the gridiron, females played a prominent role in leading cheering sections. Progressive fears about the feminization of America altered that relationship during this decade. Schools took Theodore Roosevelt's call for masculine identity characterizing American nationality to heart. Schools with large female populations feared that they would be viewed as women's colleges. Some banned women from their campuses; others used strong football teams to proclaim their masculinity. Still others banned women from participating in the cheering sections. In 1903 the University of Washington established a separate section for women to sit and cheer, apart from the men's cheer section.

The Rose Bowl: The Granddaddy of College Bowl Games

In 1902 an American football tradition started, the Rose Bowl. The first postseason collegiate bowl game in history occurred in Pasadena, California, as one of the activities for the Tournament of Roses. The competing teams were Stanford University and the University of Michigan. Fielding "Hurry up" Yost, the Michigan coach, had led his team to an undefeated season and had accumulated 501 points against ten opponents that season. The point-a-minute offense that Yost employed was complemented by the defense, which had not allowed a point the entire year. In the matchup, Michigan fullback Neil Snow scored five touchdowns against an overmatched Stanford team as Michigan rolled to a 49-0 victory. The lopsided game failed to meet expectations of the crowd and the Tournament of Roses committee, who felt that athletic contests would add vibrancy to the festival.

Unfortunately, what they received was less a contest and more a public humiliation for the California squad. Faced with the boring nature of what promoters billed as a spectacular event, organizers decided to drop the football game and replace it with other events. In 1903 polo substituted for the football game but drew only 2000 fans. Rather than returning to football however, which had drawn more spectators than polo, organizers went a different direction, implementing chariot racing as the sport of choice. The chariot races drew upwards of 25,000 fans and lasted until 1914 when economic factors and lack of interest eventually led to the reinstatement of football as the premier attraction.

Hockey

The development of amateur ice hockey leagues in the United States began in the 1890s, and as many sports in the 1900s, hockey fought battles of sustainability. The American Amateur Hockey League (AAHL), with teams based in the New York City area, became the first amateur league in the United States in 1896. Through the 1900s, the New York Crescent Athletic Club, based in Brooklyn, dominated the league, winning eight championships between 1900 and 1910. To keep unsavory fans at bay the Crescent Club charged one dollar admission, assuring that the lower classes would not be able to attend their games.

While the teams were New York–based, the talent came from Canadian-born talent, with only a few Americans on the rosters. This provided quality hockey for New York fans. Other amateur leagues competed during the decade and met with mixed success. Minnesota, a hotbed of hockey, formed the Twin City League in 1902–3 consisting of teams from the Minneapolis and St. Paul area, and, interestingly, had no imports. Amateur leagues existed for short periods in Philadelphia, Pittsburgh, Washington D.C., Chicago, and Baltimore as well. Outside of city or regionally based teams, colleges took up the sport and developed rivalries that grew in the 1900s.

In the winter of 1900, the five-team Intercollegiate Hockey League began with Yale, Columbia, Princeton, Brown, and Harvard as charter members. In the early 1900s, Harvard supplanted Yale as the dominant team in the league. After winning the first two league championships, Yale succumbed to Harvard in 1902–3, leading to four straight Harvard league titles, until Princeton broke the streak in the 1906–7 season. The Princeton team had struggled for years with inadequate training facilities and also a scandal in 1902–3. A very successful season came to an abrupt end when, just before a postseason playoff game with Harvard, the faculty disbanded the team because of academic deficiencies. Princeton finished off the decade with its second championship in the 1909–10 season. Besides that championship, Princeton's other major victory of 1910 would be the recruitment of the one player responsible for their only defeat during that season, Hobey Baker, who entered Princeton in 1910 and would be the impetus for their success into the next decade.

Hobart Baker, from Wissahickon, Pennsylvania, began his Hall of Fame hockey career in 1906 when he enrolled at the prestigious St. Paul's School in New Hampshire. While he was a senior at the prep school in 1909–10 Baker's amazing stick work led to the only defeat that Princeton's Tigers would face that season. Baker's freshman year at Princeton in 1910 proved to be uneventful, as freshmen were ineligible for varsity sports, but the skills he developed, both at St. Paul's and during practice at Princeton, would set the stage for his emergence in the 1910s as one of the greatest hockey players of all time.

Other colleges around the nation followed the lead of the charter Intercollegiate Hockey League schools and started hockey programs. Dartmouth College entered competition in the 1905–6 season playing teams from Williams, MIT, and the schools from the intercollegiate league. Dartmouth, in 1908–9, had a remarkable year finishing second in the intercollegiate league to Harvard. They also went the entire season without registering a single penalty. Hockey, like football, had begun to struggle with images of brutality and violence. The Canadian game had turned increasingly violent. In 1907 the sport's first official fatality occurred. Players began to suffer injuries such as broken limbs, having their faces sliced open by skate blades, and their heads opened up by violent stick play.

The media, already alerted to the violence in college football, focused on the violent acts and began to question if hockey would become just another example of unregulated brutality in sport. Dartmouth's penalty-free season and relative success on the ice provided hope that hockey need not be relegated to a game of senseless violence.

Professional hockey had its debut in the United States in 1903 in the form of the Portage Lakers. In 1899 the Portage team played very successfully. On that first team, four out of the eight players were doctors. However, one of the doctors, John "Jack" L. Gibson, became the focus of the team as its captain. "Doc" Gibson was the leading scorer for the Lakers. Their 1902–3 team picture, which included "Paddy" the mascot dog, referred to the team as the champions of the United States. The team's record that season was 13-0-1 as they scored 132 goals and gave up only 26 goals. In the playoffs, they tied the Pittsburgh Bankers 0-0 in the first game before finally defeating them in the second contest 1-0 to win the U.S. Championship.

The next season James R. Dee became the club's first president and paid his players' salaries, creating the first professional hockey team. In 1903–4 the Lakers lost only two of twenty-six games, including the playoffs. Their only regular-season loss came at the hands of American Soo 7-6. In the U.S. playoffs, they lost to the Pittsburgh Victorias 5-2. However, the Lakers rebounded, winning the next two matches, 5-1 and 7-0, respectively. After their repeat victory as U.S. Champions, the Lakers hosted Canada's best team, the Montreal Wanderers at the

Amphidrome in Houghton. Over 5,000 fans watched as Portage defeated Montreal by scores of 8-4 and 9-2 to claim the title of world champions. By soundly defeating the Canadian team, the Lakers earned the reputation as the toughest team on ice. Integral to the Lakers' success was the acquisition of Joe Linder. A local high school star in not only hockey, but also in football and basketball, Linder became the key playmaker for Portage. Gibson, who had selected Linder to play for the Lakers, saw early on what others would eventually see. Linder, the first great American-born hockey player, was inducted into the U.S. Hockey Hall of Fame in 1975 joining his teammate "Doc" Gibson, a charter member of the Hall in 1973.

In 1904–5, Portage joined three other clubs to form the International Hockey League (IHL). Since Canada had yet to form a professional league, the IHL attracted many of the best Canadian players. The teams in the league came primarily from the Upper Peninsula region of Michigan but also included a team from Sault St. Marie (Canada) allowing the founders to legitimately claim international status. In 1905–6, a Pittsburgh franchise from the former Western Pennsylvania Hockey League joined after that league disbanded.

All of the communities had indoor arenas where the teams played. Houghton-Portage Lakes played in the Amphidrome on Portage Lake; Calumet's home ice was in the Palestra; Sault Ste. Marie, Michigan (aka American Soo) competed at their local curling rink named the Ridge Street Ice-A-Torium; Sault Ste. Marie, Ontario's (Canadian Soo) home ice was at the local curling rink; and Pittsburgh found a home in the Duquesne Gardens. Unfortunately, Portage would be the only IHL team to win the championship. The league operated for only three seasons and folded when competition from professional leagues in Canada lured away the top Canadian players.

As a professional league, the IHL could not compete for the Stanley Cup. Portage, however, issued challenges after both the 1905 and 1906 seasons to the Stanley Cup Board of Directors in an effort to be able to play the Ottawa Silver Seven in a championship series. Both times they were turned down. Professional teams were not allowed to compete for the Cup until after the formation of Canadian professional leagues in 1908. As a result of the Stanley Cup being given in 1908 to professional teams, a new cup for amateur clubs was established that same year by Sir H. Montague Allan to replace the Stanley Cup.

Hockey at the amateur, semiprofessional, and professional levels struggled in the 1900s. Leagues started, had limited success, and then folded with regularity. None could sustain continued growth to catapult the sport into the national consciousness into the next decade. The collegiate game, at least in the northeastern United States, had a little more stability. Regardless of the organizational struggles, hockey developed some incredible players during this period who would go on to earn Hall of Fame recognition and become idols of the game.

The Olympics

The Olympic Games allowed U.S. sporting leaders to display American superiority through athletic performances. Most other popular U.S. sports provided little opportunity to create intense nationalistic feelings. Baseball, American football, and basketball were all played nearly exclusively in the United States. Other sports, which did provide international championships such as skiing, figure skating, and cycling, were considered minor sports by U.S. fans and media. In addition, most international championships took place in European countries, and travel costs often kept U.S. athletes from participating. However, set within a four-year cycle, the Olympic Games provided organizers time to raise necessary funds for the expensive journeys. The variety of sports and the focus on track and field also helped U.S. officials justify the incredible effort to compete.

The creation of the modern Olympic Games in 1896 coincided with progressive leaders' efforts in the United States to create a sense of American uniqueness and national identity. These leaders, including James Sullivan, Casper Whitney, Albert Spalding, Luther Gulick, and Teddy Roosevelt, created a sporting republic. As the decade began at the Paris Games, American athletes sought to prove that the young nation could not only compete with traditional powers, but that due to its scientific focus on training methods and American determination, its athletes were superior. American support of the Olympics led the International Olympic Committee (IOC) to award the nation the Games for 1904. American athletes would have the opportunity to shine without traveling to Europe. American leaders believed the 1904 Games would not only allow America to demonstrate its athletic superiority but also to stake its claim as one of the leading nations in the world. While Americans embraced the Games, the opportunity to demonstrate its superiority, internationally, failed to develop.

St. Louis hosted the games in conjunction with the St. Louis Louisiana Purchase Exposition, the second consecutive Games to become a sideshow of a World's Fair. The St. Louis group, led by D. R. Francis, president of the exposition, hired James E. Sullivan as the chief of the Department of Physical Culture of the Louisiana

President Theodore Roosevelt standing with members of the 1904 U.S. Olympic team. (Courtesy of the Library of Congress)

Purchase Exposition to organize their athletic competitions. Sullivan, as secretary of the Amateur Athletic Union (AAU), held great power over amateur sport in the United States.

Regardless of Sullivan's experience and expertise, the Games flopped. European nations stayed away. Although more than forty different events gained Sullivan's Olympic sanctioning, almost all of the 9,476 participants were Americans. Of those 9,000 athletes however, many were involved in mass athletic events including Bohemian and Turner gymnastics with 800 and 3,500 participants respectively. In addition, on the program were public school championships for elementary and high school students, numerous Missouri State high school championships, and college basketball and football tournaments. Missing was the international flavor of the Games. In fact, athletes wore club or school uniforms exclusively rather than U.S. uniforms, making it hard to detect any international competitions.

For all of their failings, the 1904 Olympics did offer highlights and innovations. They were the first Games in which gold, silver, and bronze medals were awarded, and four new recognized events were included for men in the program: boxing, dumbbells, the decathlon, and freestyle wrestling. For women, archery was added to the Olympic program.

Some athletes also took the opportunity to shine in Olympic glory. Archie Hahn, "The Milwaukee Meteor," won three gold medals at these Games in track and field. In gymnastics, George Eyser won six medals. Competing on a wooden leg Eyser won the rope-climbing, vault, and parallel bar events while finishing second in the Pommell horse and the combined four event. Eyser completed his Olympic feats with a third place in the horizontal bar.

The St. Louis Games provided their fair share of controversies. In swimming Hungary's Zoltan Halmay beat American J. Scott Leary by just one foot in the 50-meter event. However, the American judge ruled that Leary had won. Halmay and Leary ended up in fisticuffs over the ruling, and the judges ordered a rematch. In the pool, Halmay once again edged Leary in the second race. In track and field, the marathon provided incredible, if not comedic, drama. Run on a very humid day with temperatures reaching over 90 degrees Fahrenheit, the runners left the stadium and embarked on a dusty, unpaved course. Mounted horsemen cleared the trail in front of the leaders. Doctors, judges, and reporters in automobiles followed the horses. The net result was a constant cloud of dust kicked up into the runners' faces.

American physical educators and scientists, including Luther Gulick and Charles Lucas, used the Olympic marathon as a platform to demonstrate science's ability to improve human performance. Lucas monitored British-born Thomas Hicks, who ran for the American team throughout the race. Using their "scientific" theories Lucas and his team helped Hicks twice during the race achieve his supposedly maximum potential through sulphate of strychnine and egg whites. When Hicks requested water, they sponged his mouth out instead. After twenty miles of running despite the heat, they bathed him in warm water from the boiler of a steam automobile along with the strychnine and a shot of brandy. Whether from the special treatment or despite it Hicks ran the race in 3:28:53.

The romantic and strange stories notwithstanding, the 1904 marathon also held significance for being the first Olympic race to include the first two black Africans to compete in the Olympics, Zulu tribesmen Lentauw and Yamasani. Americans

The Savage Games

The 1904 St. Louis Games had a unique sideshow included in the Olympic program, often referred to as the "Savage Olympics." James E. Sullivan staged what he referred to as Anthropology Days on August 12 and 13, 1904. Working with scientists, physical directors and coaches who had taken a curious interest in the debate concerning which native cultures and races created better natural athletes, Sullivan staged these games under the guise of testing these theories of superiority. He assembled a diverse group of "aborigines," mostly from the Department of Anthropology's "human zoo" in which anthropologists William J. McGee and Lewis Henry Morgan had reconstructed native villages on the site and assembled over 2000 occupants for the villages so that visitors could supposedly see the aboriginal people living in their own native environment. The variety of cultures assembled included Pygmies from central Africa, Ainus from Japan, Filipino natives, Tehuelche Indians from Patagonia, and numerous Native American Indian tribes.

Sport asserted its own programs of scientific development, which, it claimed, resulted in greater accomplishments for humanity. It seemed natural to test whether these native athletes could compete against the scientifically trained modern athlete. Sullivan and Luther Gulick staged events for the aborigines to perform and recorded their performances. Unfortunately, these events were modern athletic events such as the shot put, the 100-meter dash, and the standing broad jump, all of which were unfamiliar to the native tribesman. Having attained the results, the organizers then set out to explain and categorize the aborigines.

Sullivan, Gulick, and McGhee concluded that the myth of the greatest natural athletes existing in primitive tribes had been scientifically debunked. Noting that the times and performances of the natural athletes from the tribes could only compare with the performances of Missouri schoolboys, and not Olympic competitors, they determined that aboriginal athletes had proven to be inferior athletes. Organizers of this bizarre display failed to mention that the contestants were not specially selected athletes from their tribal cultures sent to compete. Instead, they had tested a hastily selected group of aboriginal subjects who happened to be at the exposition for the purpose of demonstrating their cultural lives and dressing up in native costume. Nevertheless, the results supported their racially motivated ideals that civilized environments created superior human beings.

---

demonstrated their prejudice in referring to the runners as the two "Kaffirs." This derogatory term, used by the media, Olympic officials, fair organizers, and fans, proved that mainstream white Americans remained unprepared to see blacks from Africa, Cuba, North America, or any place in the world as equals.

The two runners were actually on loan to the Olympic race from the fair's Department of Anthropology, where they participated in the Boer War exhibit. Ironically, both were actually students at Orange Free State in South Africa. The press was much more comfortable placing the "Kaffirs from Zululand" in more traditional roles regarding race.

1906 Athens Games

Although not considered an actual Olympic Games in the recognized history of the modern Olympic movement, these Greek games saved the movement from near failure. The Athens games were wildly successful, setting attendance records that would stand until the 1912 Stockholm Games.

The United States sent a large contingent in order to dispel rumors that their dominance at St. Louis was due to the lack of European competition. For the first time the American Olympic Committee (AOC) and the AAU consolidated control of the American team to ensure that the strongest team possible would go to Athens. Olympic organizers held local fund drives and raised $15,000 to help defray travel costs for the trip. President Theodore Roosevelt named James E. Sullivan to head the U.S. contingent in the hopes that the American team would once again demonstrate the rugged athleticism that Roosevelt advocated.

American athletes dominated in track and field events once again, and the American media declared the team the winners of the Games, even though the United States did not win the total medal count. One of the things that the Athenians did in hosting these Games was to limit the program and condense it into a manageable time frame so that the events would not go on for months as they had in St. Louis and were planned to do in Rome.

A significant development of these Panhellenic Games saw the Great Britain national team wholeheartedly embrace the Olympic movement. The large contingent sent to Athens performed very well. Great Britain, at the time, was one of, if not the leading, sport nation in the world and their full participation and endorsement of the Games boosted the young movement's prestige. In addition, they gave U.S. athletes a strong competitive challenge. The British involvement would also change the course of the Games.

Later in the year, the Rome organizing committee, which had been planning the 1908 Games, collapsed and it became evident that Rome would not be able to host the IV Olympiad. With their enthusiasm for the Games in evidence, the IOC approached the British about the possibility of London hosting the 1908 Games. They accepted, and the new rivalry between the United States and Great Britain took on renewed significance now that the Olympic Games would be contested on British soil. More than any other nation, the United States sought to distance themselves from the British, due in part to the fact that the United States had always lived in the shadow of Great Britain as one of its former colonies. For American leaders the Olympics provided opportunities to display to the world that they were as good, if not better than, their mother country. To do so in that country's home provided a great opportunity.

1908 London Games

The 1908 London organizing committee set new standards for organizational efficiency. They followed the lead of the Greeks in limiting the scope and breadth of the program to the central Olympic contests.

London held the contests in Shepherd's Bush Stadium, an 85,000-seat venue that held a 100-meter swimming pool surrounded by a five-lap-to-the-mile cinder running track and a 660-yard concrete cycling track. For the opening of the Games, organizers developed a parade of nations where over 2000 athletes and officials representing eighteen countries marched around the cinder running track carrying the flags of their countries. Unfortunately, this parade would begin a series of confrontations between the host nation and its primary competitors, the United States, as they fought for the title of the world's most vigorous nation.

In the stadium, the British displayed the flags of the participating nations with one notable exception: no American flag flew. The British explained that no suitable American flag could be found and that no ill will was meant. American athletes and officials, incensed at what they believed to be an intentional slight, decided to break Olympic protocol. The protocol called for each nation's flag bearer to dip their flag in deference to the hospitality of the organizing nation when passing in front of the host leaders. As Irish American shot putter and designated flag bearer Ralph Rose approached King Edward VII and Queen Alexandra in the royal box, Rose and the American contingent refused to dip the colors before the royal family. Rose would later explain, "This flag dips for no earthly king." The actions set the stage for a bitterly fought Olympic Games between the two nations. The media, fans, and officials representing each nation attempted to explain incidents that would occur as indicative of the weakness of the other's cultural and moral values, thus increasing their own sense of superiority.

The 400-meter track final provided a classic confrontation between the two nations. Three American runners—Robbins of Harvard, Carpenter of Cornell, and Taylor from the Irish-American Athletic Club—met in the final against Lieutenant Wyndam Halswelle of Great Britain. Coming toward the finish Carpenter passed Halswelle and teammate Robbins for what appeared to be the Olympic title. However, British judges ruled that Carpenter fouled Halswelle on the final turn. The judges stepped on the track and cut the finishing tape, thereby ruling the race invalid. When Carpenter reached the finish line there was no tape to cross and the controversy erupted. The British judges ruled a re-run and disqualified Carpenter. In the rescheduled race, the two remaining American runners refused to compete. Halswelle jogged around the track to his unchallenged victory and the only walkover in Olympic history, while the media on each side cried foul against the opposing nation.

With this controversy resounding in the press, the marathon provided an escalation of complaints regarding each nation's perspective on sport. American distance runners held low expectations. American officials believed that distance running benefited sluggish sportsmen and did not represent the vigorous American athlete who excelled in power and speed. The British had been the leading force in distance running and most people believed they would dominate this event. On race day, very hot temperatures proved destructive to the British runners not used to the unusual heat. The British runners faded trying to rein in Italian runner Dorando Pietri, who set a blistering pace. When Pietri entered the stadium, the pace had obviously affected him. He ran the wrong direction before collapsing on the sloping cycling track around the stadium. British officials ran to his aid and gave him a shot of strychnine to invigorate him. Pietri started again but soon collapsed. With officials lifting him he struggled around the track with their help. With Pietri 100 meters from the finish line the crowd roared as American John J. Hayes entered the stadium, running relaxed toward the finish. British officials quickly gathered up Pietri and literally dragged him across the finish before the hard-charging Hayes.

Refusing to disqualify Pietri, the British judges placed AOC officials in an awkward position of protesting Pietri's victory, which many had heralded as a heroic effort. The British officials finally granted the American protest and disqualified Pietri. British officials demeaned the Americans as being too concerned with winning and argued that, had it been an English runner who had finished behind Pietri, there would have been no issue as the British would have honored his supreme effort. The British press went as far as to claim that Hayes had forfeited a rare opportunity to become a beloved figure in Great Britain and wipe away the negative images of American athletes that the British people had developed. The British argued that true sportsmanship would let the race finish as it did with no protests.

After the 1908 Games American officials claimed that they had won their fifth straight Olympic Championship and heralded their sporting technology and scientific training methods along with American determination for creating the greatest athletic nation in the world.

The British took offense to these claims, attacking American attitudes of winning at all costs at the expense of fair play and sportsmanship. They also noted that American claims never reflected medal counts of all events. Americans responded by arguing that they only competed in truly athletic contests and that had they chosen to compete in what they considered nonathletic sports then they would dominate those as well.

Americans used new ideas to define themselves during this decade, as well as to separate themselves from Great Britain. Using the image of a melting pot that strengthened the old bloodlines of Europeans, the United States boasted about the racial and ethnic background of their Olympic team that included Teutons, Anglo-Saxons, Celts, Slavs, Black Ethiopians, and red Indians. While this egalitarian ideal existed on the Olympic team, it did not reflect the reality of American society at the time. Blacks remained barred from baseball, America's pastime. The Irish, Italians, and other recent immigrants still struggled in ghettoized areas of American cities. The ideal of the melting pot looked impressive on the Olympic roster but it was by no means the reality of life in America.

SPORTS FOR INDIVIDUAL COMPETITORS

Boxing

At the turn of the century, boxing entered a time of American dominance in sport. The 1900s witnessed the rise of some of the sport's most famous and colorful characters. It also witnessed American fighters laying claim to almost every world championship title in the professional ranks, and continued growth in the amateur ranks, as the AAU promoted their national championships. Boxing remained a popular sport, although a battle called the "fight of the century" between Jack Johnson and Jim Jeffries in the heavyweight class challenged the sport's already questionable reputation. As the century began, boxing had seven weight classifications. By the end of the decade boxing two more classifications would be added: the flyweight and the light heavyweight divisions.

Pugilism had always been a vehicle for social integration by ethnic minorities in the United States. While excluded in many areas of American cultural life, new immigrant populations, as well as ethnic and racial minorities, often found boxing to be a great equalizer. While many fight fans were well-dressed, well-educated, wealthy patrons, those partaking in the actual battles typically came from the lower classes of society. It provided opportunities for these marginalized groups to proclaim their equality in at least one avenue of American life. Fighters commonly came from Irish, Italian, Polish, Jewish, or black communities. In 1901 boxing allowed more opportunities to these typically oppressed groups than any other sporting venue. American football was the bastion of middle- and upper-class young men, baseball had become a whites-only endeavor, and other sports struggled to embrace diversity in the same way that boxing did. However, as this decade developed, some of those opportunities diminished as progressive leaders sought to promote a more civilized society.

Many black fighters had proven successful in the ring. George Dixon paved the way, dominating the featherweight division in the 1890s, and continued to display great skills into the new century. Abe Attell, "The Little Hebrew," fought Dixon three times and credited Dixon for helping him become a better boxer. A Jewish fighter who learned to fight on the streets in San Francisco in an Irish neighborhood, Attell decided to emulate Dixon's graceful, gliding style and used it to claim the featherweight title from Dixon in 1901 and hold onto the crown throughout the decade.

In the lightweight division, another black boxer entered the decade as the world champion. Joe Gans from Baltimore became the first native-born African American fighter to win a world championship. In 1901 Gans knocked out Frank Erne in the first round of a fight in Fort Erie, Canada, to win the world lightweight championship. Gans held the title until 1904 when he challenged Joe Walcott, another black fighter, to the welterweight championship title, which Walcott had held since 1901. Officials ordered that in order to fight Walcott, Gans had to relinquish the lightweight title, although many still regarded him as the champion nevertheless. Gans and Walcott fought to a draw, allowing Walcott to retain the title.

Gans had an opportunity in 1906 to regain his lightweight title in Goldfield, Nevada. A young promoter named George "Tex" Rickard lured Gans to fight for the title against Oscar "Battling" Nelson. Rickard owned the Northern Saloon in Goldfield and had no previous history with boxing or promotions. Rickard wanted to draw the nation's attention to Goldfield, to increase his business prospects. In the fight, the two men battled for forty-two rounds before Nelson hit Gans with a left hook to the groin and was disqualified on a foul. Gans regained the world title and Rickard, inadvertently, began a long and storied career as a promoter.

Gans defended his title over the next two years before meeting up with Nelson again on July 4, 1908, when Nelson knocked out the champion in the seventeenth round. A rematch, two months later, netted the same result, a twenty-one-round knockout. What no one realized at the time was that Gans had begun to feel the effects of tuberculosis, which would end his life in 1910.

Nelson defended the lightweight title until 1910 when he lost to Ad Wolgast in a brutally bloody fight. In the fortieth round Nelson's eyes were swollen so much that he lined up his fighting stance opposite one of the ring posts. The referee stepped in and awarded the fight to Wolgast to alleviate further injury.

Walcott, a welterweight, was born in Barbados but grew up in Massachusetts. His rise to the top took many twists and turns, demonstrating that, regardless of the opportunities seemingly provided to black boxers, there were also prices to be paid for the privileges. Walcott, like Gans, had at times thrown a fight to pacify promoters and bettors. Walcott also fought heavyweights in order to prove himself. In 1904 Walcott defended his title twice against other black fighters. The Dixie Kid–Joe Walcott fight would mark the first time in history that two black fighters would battle for a world championship. In the match, Walcott lost on a foul in the twentieth round. Later that year the two fought to a draw in a rematch. Since the

Dixie Kid exceeded the weight limit for the fight, Walcott was renamed the champion.

The middleweight division had one dominant champion. Tommy Ryan, from Irish descent, claimed the vacant title in 1898 in a battle with Jack Bonner. Ryan retained the title for ten years until he retired and vacated the title. After Ryan's dominant run, a relative newcomer claimed the vacant title. Stanley Ketchel, son of a Polish immigrant, developed his boxing skills as a bouncer in Butte, Montana. After losing only twice in his first forty-two fights, all in Montana, Ketchel decided to venture out and test his ability. He traveled to California and in 1908 earned a fight with Jack (Twin) Sullivan, knocking him out in twenty rounds and winning the vacant title. Ketchel went right to work in defending the title. In a match with Billy Papke, the two fighters met in the center of the ring to shake hands and Papke punched Ketchel in the head. Ketchel never regained full functionality during the fight and lost in a dazed performance, being knocked out in the twelfth round.

Ketchel gained a rematch eleven weeks later and pummeled Papke in a furious eleven-round knockout. With the win, Ketchel became the first middleweight boxer to regain a lost title. Ketchel, while dominating the middleweight class, sought challenges by fighting larger boxers, including heavyweight champion Jack Johnson. In the twelfth round Ketchel stunned the much-larger Johnson with a right hand that caught the champ off balance and knocked Johnson to the canvas. After sitting on the canvas for a moment, Johnson stood up and in a rage hit Ketchel in the jaw, knocking the middleweight champion out.

Recovering from the Johnson bout, Ketchel continued to dominate the middleweight division. However, in 1910 a ranch hand named Walter Dipley, who believed Ketchel attempted to steal his girlfriend while he was training at a ranch in Conway, Missouri, shot and killed the fighter. As a result, the decade ended with the title vacated.

During the 1900s boxing promoter and Chicago newspaperman Lou Houseman believed that a new classification should be added between the middleweight and heavyweight division. He proposed a new classification with a top weight limit of 175 pounds. Houseman's proposal suited his own interests as he managed Jack Root, a middleweight who outgrew the 158-pound limit, but struggled to compete against much larger heavyweights. In 1903 the light heavyweight division was established in the professional ranks, to be followed by amateur acceptance in 1906.

Root fought against Kid McCoy, who introduced the corkscrew punch, for the new title in April 1903. However, the title changed hands three times before the end of the year until Bob Fitzsimmons won the title, holding it for two years. Fitzsimmons became boxing's first triple-title holder with the victory. He had previously held both the middleweight and heavyweight titles in the 1890s and won the light heavyweight title when he was forty years old. In 1905 "Philadelphia" Jack O'Brien knocked out Fitzsimmons in fifteen rounds to take the title.

O'Brien was a successful self-promoter. In 1901 he went to England to build up his record and sent the victorious reports back to the Associated Press. The tactic proved successful as, when he returned, the mayor of Philadelphia and 10,000 fans greeted him at the docks. O'Brien was a living exemplar of the muscular Christianity movement. He traveled with prominent Philadelphian Maj. Anthony J. Drexel Biddle who, as an avid boxing fan, helped promote O'Brien on lecture circuits, so that the fighter could promote his faith and his career. In the 1905 fight with

Fitzsimmons, he won not only the light heavyweight title, but also was regarded as the heavyweight champion as well. Fitzsimmons had been assigned the vacant heavyweight title at the time of the fight. When he went down, many gave both titles to O'Brien.

In 1907 O'Brien fought Tommy Burns for the heavyweight title. Burns won a twenty-round decision over O'Brien in Los Angeles. Burns actually weighed under the light heavyweight limit and could have claimed that title as well but never did.

The true superstars of the sport were the heavyweights. Coming off his defeat of Bob Fitzsimmons in 1899, Jim Jeffries entered the decade as the reigning world heavyweight champion. Jeffries continued to knock out opponents in the first part of the decade before retiring in 1904, undefeated. Jeffries then turned to refereeing. Marvin Hart self-promoted a fight in Reno, Nevada, between himself and Jack Root, which he claimed would crown a new champion. With Jeffries overseeing the match as referee, Hart knocked Root out in twelve rounds.

Jack Johnson, Heavyweight Boxing Champion

Marvin Hart eventually lost the title to Tommy Burns in 1906. Burns, a Canadian, traveled across Europe defending the title. However, a challenger, Jack Johnson, followed him. Johnson had won the black championship title from Denver Ed Martin in 1903 and desired an opportunity for the world championship. He used the press to hound Burns around the world in an effort to get a title shot. Born in Galveston, Texas, in 1878, and the son of a former slave, John Arthur Johnson had risen from battle-royal fights in his home state to achieve prominence as a great fighter.

Burns traveled to Australia to face Aussie challengers. Hugh "Huge Deal" McIntosh was an Aussie promoter who invited Burns down under for the bouts. McIntosh realized that when President Theodore Roosevelt ordered his Great White Fleet in the Pacific to travel to Australia for maneuvers that the potential for profits from a championship fight when the fleet landed would be enormous. After a couple of successful defenses McIntosh promised Burns enough of a purse that race became a secondary concern. With a guarantee of $30,000, Burns agreed to fight Johnson. On Christmas day 1908 Johnson and Burns fought in an oval-shaped stadium built for the occasion, which would become the model for American football stadiums in the future.

Scientific theories of the period held that blacks were inferior to whites in their endurance levels and had weaker abdominal strength. It quickly became clear that Johnson was not inferior physically to the white Burns. From the outset, Johnson battered Burns. Police who entered the ring in the fourteenth round finally stopped the fight and Johnson was awarded the championship, turning the world of boxing upside down.

While in lower classifications, black champions, if not accepted, were tolerated. In the heavyweight division, which held much greater prestige, Johnson's victory brought great consternation. Johnson refused to play the role of the subdued Negro who knew his place as an inferior in society. Whites considered him "uppity" and a threat to the status quo. Immediately, there was a call for white fighters to step up and face the new champion.

A series of white hope fighters faced Johnson, including "Philadelphia" Jack O'Brien, Al Kaufman, and Stanley Ketchel. When none of the fighters could dethrone Johnson, white promoters enticed Jim Jeffries to come out of his six-year retirement to uphold the dignity of the white race and fight Johnson in the fight of the century.

News media coverage of the Johnson-Jeffries fight was like none before. Magazines and newspapers sent correspondents to cover the fight for weeks before the event. These correspondents were often celebrities including Jack London, John L. Sullivan, and Rube Goldberg. Throughout the nation, actors portraying the fighters recreated the fight blow by blow in auditoriums. Crowds gathered outside telegraph offices to hear the play-by-play read by to them.

Young promoter Tex Rickard won the bid to host the fight with a promise of a $101,000 purse. Rickard planned to stage the fight in San Francisco, but pleas from reformers around the country and the threat of congressional leaders pulling support for a 1913 Panama-Pacific exhibition, caused California governor J. N. Gillett to outlaw the fight in the state just two weeks before the date. Rickard moved the fight to Reno, Nevada, with promises by city officials that they could build a stadium and stage the fight with only two weeks preparation.

Before a crowd of 22,000 fans, in an arena built solely for the bout in downtown Reno, bands played songs such as "All Coons Look Alike," and the crowd chanted, "Kill the Nigger." This event became a symbolic battle over racial superiority. Despite racial catcalls, Johnson kept his poise and responded by knocking down Jeffries twice, something the undefeated former champion had never experienced. In the fifteenth round Jeffries' cornermen called the fight, before their man was knocked out by the much stronger Johnson.

Johnson's victory inflamed tensions, and race riots broke out across the nation. White fight enthusiasts, confronted by the celebratory attitudes of black fans, resorted to violence. Race riots led to numerous deaths and injuries across the nation. Johnson became a larger-than-life hero in the nation's black community.

"The Fight of the Century": A Black Man Refuses to Learn His Place

Jack Johnson and Jim Jeffries fought on July 4, 1910, in Reno, Nevada, in what was termed "The Fight of the Century." Although fought on a symbolic day of American unity representing the ideals of the Declaration of Independence signed 134 years before, which stated that "All men are created equal," the circumstances of this fight spoke to the contrary. In 1910 many citizens of the United States believed that the color of one's skin made one inherently unequal, and in the ring that day was a man who embodied that white sense of hatred toward African Americans, Jack Johnson. Whites regarded his opponent as "The Great White Hope." Jeffries came out of retirement convinced by American fight supporters that Johnson represented a threat to the reputation of boxing and to American notions of proper society. Jack Johnson won the fight in the fifteenth round.

Johnson not only rejected the idea that African Americans accept their low status in American society but also flaunted his opposition. In the ring, Johnson mercilessly pummeled his white opponents, showing no mercy whatsoever and fighting with a seeming rage. Outside of the ring, Johnson dated white women, showed off his wealth driving his prized cars around town, and generally disregarded the racial boundaries of the age.

Whites saw him as a racial symbol who threatened the American social order. Calls for the abolishment of the sport rang out, even from boxing's most ardent and famous supporter, Theodore Roosevelt.

Cycling

After the bicycling craze of the 1890s, the sport settled down into a comfortable existence. In the wake of the recreational boom came increased interest in competitive racing. Sprints, touring, and endurance events all became immensely popular. An African American led the way in American cycle racing, Marshall "Major" Taylor. The powerful track-racing sprinter won his first world championship in 1899 and collected numerous national and world titles in his career. He proved to be enormously popular on both sides of the Atlantic and won races around the world on numerous tours. He was a devout Baptist, however, and refused to compete on Sundays, which initially proved troubling for promoters. However, when they realized Taylor's tremendous popularity and the profit potential in the huge crowds he drew to events, they quickly adapted their race schedules to accommodate the young American. (For more on Taylor, see sidebar in chapter 3.)

Long-distance races also proved popular. Six-day races at Madison Square Garden drew massive crowds. When in 1898 the New York legislature passed an ordinance forbidding riders from staying on the bike for more than twelve hours at a time, race organizers quickly adapted, making the event two-man team races. The new format proved even more popular as fans could interact with racers while they took their breaks for food and rest. The jams, or quick sprints to steal a lap in a mad dash, kept fans enthralled in the event.

Motorpace racing also became popular. Racers would draft behind an automobile, which acted as a pace car. The racers were able to reach speeds of fifty miles an hour in these events and fans loved the speed. Bobby Walthour Sr., the "Dixie Flyer" from Georgia, excelled at these dangerous events. At high speeds, tires were prone to bursting, often leaving riders with broken bones and other injuries. Walthour was an accomplished six-day rider and very popular internationally as well.

Cycling internationally grew incredibly and opportunities to compete in international events in cycling outpaced any other sport besides possibly boxing or the Olympic Games. During this decade the world's most famous international cycling event began, the Tour de France. The inaugural event in 1903 ran flawlessly. Villagers lined roadways to watch the excitement of the race. However, in 1904, the event suffered scandals and riders went to extreme measures to win including spreading nails out on the road behind them, having gangs of thugs mug other riders, and hopping trains to get to the next checkpoint. Fortunately, officials punished offenders and the event recovered and continued to grow in scope and popularity through the decade.

Women also competed in competitive cycling events, including modified six-day races, track races, and some tour races . While these races provided opportunities to compete, formal titles and championships were not awarded, however, in keeping with the moral beliefs at the time that the fairer sex should not be subjected to the corrupting influences of win at all cost mentalities, which came with championship titles.

Cycle racing during this period provided great opportunities for financial gain for both the cyclists and the promoters. Professional cyclists could earn up to $15,000 a year in prize money and appearance fees. Even lesser cyclists were guaranteed $5,000 to $7,000 a year for competing.

Skiing

While skiing was seen as the national sport of Scandinavian countries, American enthusiasts developed the sport in the United States during this decade. In the nineteenth century downhill ski racing had flourished in California's Sierra Mountains, but the sport barely survived the opening of the twentieth. Replacing it were ski jumping competitions, which became popular throughout the country. Jumping competitions used manmade structures that could be built anywhere. Downhill racing relied upon natural features, which were typically far away from major urban centers of turn-of-the-century America. New York's Central Park was a hotbed, and in Chicago authorities erected running platforms for ski jumping in the parks that had no hills.

The downhill races of La Porte, California, remained a popular event, but with the death of the gold-mining industry, the races declined in popularity and eventually stopped completely, with the last race held in 1911. However, these races used techniques that remain familiar today. Using long skis and unique concoctions of "dope," a type of wax that allowed the skis to glide better, speed was the key factor for these racers. With downhill speeds of eighty miles per hour, the races created great local pride. The festivals held numerous races and provided opportunities for children to race in a Tom Thumb division. Women's racing style was different from the men's crouching technique that resembles today's tuck in racing. The women had to adopt an upright style to keep their skirts from flying up over their heads while racing. Races for Chinese laborers, who were viewed as socially and athletically inferior to the white racers, were included in the program as well.

While the La Porte races provided thrills through the pure speed of racing down a mountain, other ski enthusiasts found excitement in regions where mountains were unavailable. Ski jumping became immensely popular throughout the country, attracting up to 15,000 spectators to events. The heart of this craze was Ishpeming, Michigan, where in 1904 members of the local ski club founded the National Ski Association of America (NSA). They held the first National Ski Jumping Tournament that winter. This group would continue to organize and sanction events around the country and host the national championships throughout the decade.

The winter of 1904–5 also witnessed the rise of the nation's first winter sports and ski resort as the Lake Placid Club decided to stay open for the winter season. The resort imported forty pairs of skis and single poles from Norway in order to provide skiing opportunities. The gamble paid off, installing the resort as a leader in the skiing movement.

Five years later an avid skier and young college student at Dartmouth started the Dartmouth Outing Club. Fred Harris began the club so that students could take advantage of winter sports and in 1909, the club held its first winter meet, which would be the forerunner to the famous Dartmouth Winter Carnival. From these intramural competitions intercollegiate skiing competitions developed in the next decade.

Surfing

In a new U.S. territory in the South Pacific, surfing—a sport unfamiliar to Americans—emerged. For Native Hawaiians, surfing held religious significance and had been a popular sport for centuries. However, Christian missionaries had made surfing taboo in the nineteenth century due to its religious connections. But the start of the twentieth century saw the loosening of bans on the activity. As the islands developed a growing tourist trade as a U.S. territory, the commercial prospects of the sport became clear to white promoters.

Publisher Alexander Hume Ford, while in Hawaii, watched native Hawaiians display their skills at riding the waves on their handcrafted boards. The surfboards, measuring up to sixteen feet long and weighing 150 pounds, were mastered by these young natives on the beaches of Oahu. Ford befriended these young surfers, who helped him learn how to surf.

Ford arrived in Hawaii in 1906 just before another famous tourist, Jack London, arrived in the islands. Ford took London to observe the surfers in action and introduced him to the locals. London tried the sport and loved the experience enough that he featured it in his work "A Royal Sport," which, when published, introduced surfing to the world. London's article highlighted the surfing abilities of George Freeth, who was of Hawaiian and Irish descent.

Ford viewed the sport as a way to promote Hawaii and leased land on the beach at Waikiki to start the Outrigger Canoe Club in 1908, the first club devoted to surfing. He and Freeth organized the beach boys in establishing the club as they held competitions in surfing, canoe riding, and other aquatic events. Ford also started a magazine promoting Hawaii called *Mid-Pacific Magazine*. On his first cover, he featured a photo of a young surfer named Duke Paoa Kahanamoku, who would become regarded as the father of modern surfing. The magazine regularly featured articles on surfing to promote the sport. Ford took Freeth with him to the mainland United States where Freeth provided demonstrations of surfing at Huntington Beach, California. Rail baron Henry Huntington, after witnessing Freeth's displays, hired the young Hawaiian to perform exhibitions and teach the sport at his resort hotel at the beach. Freeth consented and began to spread the sport throughout California.

Back in Hawaii, Kahanamoku and others formed another surfing club called the *Hui Nalu* in which they competed against the Outrigger and other surf clubs as the decade ended. Kahanamoku would emerge in the next decade as the world's premier swimmer, winning Olympic gold medals and introducing surfing around the world.

Tennis

Tennis consisted of two styles of play at the turn of the century. The first was court tennis, an indoor game played almost exclusively by wealthy Americans who had the resources to build their own court or belong to exclusive clubs that had courts. The game, played in an enclosed court where the walls and even the roof are in play, is a complex game where the chase is the heart of the game. The greatest court tennis player of the decade was also one of the best ever. Jay Gould, famous financier, won his first singles title in 1906 and was defeated only once in singles in his career spanning from 1906 to 1926.

Jay Gould II, holding tennis racket. (Courtesy of the Library of Congress)

The second style was amateur lawn tennis, which contrary to the limited access of court tennis was played by multitudes of people in the United States. Tennis at this time remained an amateur sport, however, with professional status still two decades away. Its international competitions grew stronger with the new century. In 1900 American Dwight F. Davis established a cup in his name for play between England and the United States. In 1907 the competition opened up to other nations and Australia became a formidable foe for the Davis Cup. The winner of the cup from the previous year would act as the host for the Cup championships the next year.

Both men and women participated in tennis. It provided an acceptable competitive outlet for women. In fact, at Wimbledon, the greatest international tournament, a woman was the only American to win at the championships. May G. Sutton won the women's singles title in 1905 and 1907.

The U.S. Lawn Tennis Association held national championships in a number of disciplines, including men's and women's singles and doubles, mixed doubles and all-comers singles and doubles for men. In addition, they held National Intercollegiate Championships. At the national level, Hazel Hotchkiss Wightman began an impressive playing career at the end of this decade as she won singles, doubles, and mixed doubles titles in both 1909 and 1910. Wightman would later donate a trophy for international competition between women, in 1923, as a complement to the Davis Cup.

SUMMARY

As the first decade of the twentieth century ended, sport in America saw its influence on culture strengthened. Regardless of the struggles that sport had encountered, it had become a powerful tool used by progressive leaders to develop and construct images of American identity. Through the encouragement of Theodore Roosevelt who, as president, promoted a strenuous life, evidenced through rugged American sport and physical activity, the role of games and play in American society became of paramount importance.

Although the decade experienced the constant ebbs and flows of contraction and expansion that growing organisms typically witness, it is undeniable that during this decade sport became entrenched in the mindset of Americans. Baseball as the national pastime grew ever more popular, and the World Series established a tradition for the sport that would continue to build upon its mythical imagery. Other sports, such as football and hockey, while challenged due to the brutality evidenced in the games, still were able to overcome serious threats to their development and build on the foundations that they had established. Basketball continued to grow in popularity as leagues were formed across the nation, and even soccer and rugby developed fan bases as they were examined for potential replacements for American football.

Individual sports such as cycling, skiing, and tennis built on their growing popularity and established important international competitions during the decade. Boxing became an American stronghold, as many champions originated in or moved to the United States as the young nation developed a reputation for toughness, evidenced by the boxing prowess, especially, of its immigrant and ethnically diverse populations. The Olympic Games, while challenged due to the unhealthy connections to World's Fairs, not only survived the decade, but developed a competitive stage for American leaders to put forward their notions of the strength of the melting pot of American culture, and prove American superiority through scientific training methods and determination. Track and field athletes and officials, in particular, utilized the Games to challenge other world powers, especially European nations, regarding national prowess.

While sport grew and developed in American culture during this decade, not all Americans were included in that growth and development. African Americans and women were the most notable exceptions. African American athletes remained outside of the scope of baseball's major-league system. Although the development of Negro league teams had its nexus during the decade, the fact that race issues pervaded the opportunities to play sport in America is significant. While African Americans did, at times, find opportunities in sports such as football, it remained a rare event. In boxing, which witnessed a large number of African American world champions during the decade, by the end of the decade opportunities became non-existent, due to Jack Johnson's impact in and out of the ring.

Women also saw very little growth in opportunities available to them. Olympic venues had minimum sporting competitions for women throughout the decade and colleges saw little growth in the development of women's sports. Only in figure skating, where a woman won the world title, beating all of the men, do we see women's opportunities enhanced. American culture still viewed women as the frail sex and sought to protect them from the unhealthy pursuit of savage competition and rugged athletic endeavors. Both women and African Americans would have to wait a few more decades before seeing sporting opportunities develop for them in the same ways that white males experienced during this decade.

Sport seemed poised to take a leading role in American culture at the end of the decade. Some people viewed it as the answer for William James's "Moral Equivalent of War," that is, a healthy and moral way to determine nationalistic disputes without bloodshed and bullets. Newspaper and media coverage of events blossomed during the decade. Realizing not only the cultural significance, but also the potential profitability of sport, many newspapers developed sports pages and even sports sections in their daily coverage of local and national events. Sport had arrived in the twentieth century and, even in its young developmental stages during this decade, it is easy to see the foundations of what would become a national obsession and love affair with sport through the rest of the century.

RECOMMENDED RESOURCES

Abrams, Roger I. 2005. *The first World Series and baseball fanatics of 1903*. Boston: Northeastern University Press.

Anderson, David. 2000. *More than Merkle*. Lincoln: University of Nebraska Press.

Barnett, C. Robert. 2004. St. Louis 1904. In *Encyclopedia of the modern Olympic movement*, ed. John E. Findling and Kimberly D. Pelle. Westport, CT: Greenwood Press.

Baseball Almanac. 2008. http://www.baseball-almanac.com/.

Bjarkman, Peter C. 2000. *The biographical history of basketball*. Chicago: Masters Press.

Cohen, Stan. 1985. *A pictorial history of downhill skiing*. Missoula, MT: Pictorial Histories Publishing.

Dyreson, Mark. 1998. *Making the American team: Sport, culture, and the Olympic experience*. Urbana: University of Illinois Press.

Fry, John, ed. 1972. *America's ski book*. New York: Charles Scribner's Sons.

Guttmann, Allen. 1984. *The Games must go on: Avery Brundage and the Olympic movement*. New York: Columbia University Press.

Heaphy, Leslie A. 2003. *The Negro Leagues: 1869–1960*. Jefferson, NC: MacFarland.

Henry, Bill. 1976. *An approved history of the Olympic Games*. New York: G. P. Putnam's Sons.

Herlihy, David V. 2004. *Bicycle*. New Haven, CT: Yale University Press.

Hietala, Thomas R. 2002. *The fight of the century: Jack Johnson, Joe Louis, and the struggle for racial equality*. Armonk, NY: Sharpe.

Hubbard, Kevin, and Stan Fischler. 1997. *Hockey America*. Indianapolis: Masters Press.

Lester, Robin. 1995. *Stagg's university: The rise, decline, and fall of big-time football at Chicago*. Urbana: University of Illinois Press.

Lomax, Michael. 2004. Black entrepreneurship in the national pastime: The rise of semiprofessional baseball in black Chicago, 1890–1915. In *Sport and the color line: Black athletes and race relations in twentieth-century America*, ed. Patrick B. Miller and David K. Wiggins, 25–43. New York: Routledge.

McCallum, John D., and Charles H. Pearson. 1973. *College football U.S.A., 1869–1973*. New York: Hall of Fame Publishing.

McGurn, James. 1987. *On your bicycle: An illustrated history of cycling*. New York: Facts on File Publications.

Menke, Frank G. 1969. *The encyclopedia of sports*. 4th ed. South Brunswick, NJ: A. S. Barnes and Co.

Oriard, Michael. 1993. *Reading football: How the popular press created an American spectacle*. Chapel Hill: University of North Carolina Press.

Riess, Steven A. 1995. *Sport in industrial America, 1850–1920*. Wheeling, IL: Harlan Davidson.

Roberts, James B., and Alexander G. Skutt. 2006. *The boxing register: International Boxing Hall of Fame official record book*. New York: McBooks Press.

Roberts, Randy. 1983. *Papa Jack: Jack Johnson and the era of white hopes*. New York: Free Press.

Smith, Robert A. 1972. *A social history of the bicycle: Its early life and times in America*. New York: American Heritage Press.

Smith, Ronald. 1981. Harvard and Columbia and a reconsideration of the 1905–6 football crisis. *Journal of Sport History* 8 (Winter): 5–19.

Watterson, John Sayle. 2000. *College football: History, spectacle, controversy*. Baltimore: Johns Hopkins University Press.

CHAPTER 5

AMERICAN SPORTS, 1910–1919

Sarah Bair

OVERVIEW

The 1910s marked a period of economic growth, technological advancement, and rising consumerism for many Americans. Perhaps nowhere was this more visible than in the automobile industry. Led by the Ford Motor Company, which developed the moving assembly line to produce the Model T in 1913, American automakers had produced two million cars by 1920. Economic expansion led to an increased need for global markets and to more international economic ties, a significant factor in U.S. policy regarding World War I. Members of the middle class, who had begun to feel some of the benefits of industrialization and mass production, enjoyed greater freedom and more time for leisure activities. Innovations such as x-rays, airplanes, audio recordings, and moving pictures, as well as advances in medicine and transportation, led to a sense of optimism and possibility. At the same time, rising urbanization, immigration, economic disparity, and social problems created feelings of uncertainty and danger that galvanized reformers.

From 1880 to 1920, 23 million immigrants came to the United States and by 1920, 40 percent of New York City residents were foreign born. The 1920 U.S. Census showed that for the first time, the percentage of Americans living in cities outnumbered those in rural areas. In addition, depletions in the labor force due to men being drafted to fight in World War I caused a greater number of women and African Americans, many of whom moved out of the South to northern cities in what became known as the Great Migration, to seek industrial jobs. The social upheaval and urban problems caused by these changes led many Americans to embrace a variety of reform movements that developed in the late nineteenth and early twentieth centuries.

Although loosely connected under the *progressive* umbrella, reformers in the 1910s had different priorities and used a range of strategies to achieve their goals. Some lobbied Congress and pushed for legislative reforms. In fact, the 1910s saw the passage of four constitutional amendments calling for the direct election of senators, a federal income tax, women's suffrage, and prohibition of alcoholic beverages. Other reformers, such as Jane Addams, formed clubs and organizations designed to help the poor and to provide healthy forms of recreation. Finally, some reformers advanced the social efficiency movement with its emphasis on order, stability, and effective management of public institutions by credentialed experts working for the public good.

Both advocates for the welfare of the poor and those more interested in social order saw the potential of recreation, and sports in particular, for alleviating stress and for controlling crime and violence that often erupted due to boredom, despair, and pent-up physical energy. As cities became more crowded and work life more regimented, sports provided an outlet for both middle-class and working-class Americans. Games and contests were something to look forward to and brought a degree of pleasure to what were otherwise bleak daily lives. This same philosophy applied to the newly developing comprehensive high schools. Sports were viewed as a vehicle for social control that would alleviate both adolescent sexual urges and tensions between immigrant groups. High schools became community centers and sources of shared pride, identity, and purpose for neighborhoods.

Even as the 1910s were marked by reforms and social upheaval at home, Americans were forced to confront their changing place in the world and to endure a world war and an influenza epidemic that devastated people of all social classes. By the time World War I broke out in Europe in 1914, the United States was already becoming a global economic power, and the war, despite its human costs, provided business opportunities for American banks and companies. It also greatly increased the number of women and African Americans in the workforce, a trend that was not entirely reversed after the war ended and that contributed significantly to the passage of the Nineteenth Amendment granting women the right to vote in 1920. The United States, which did not enter the war in force until the spring of 1918, suffered far fewer casualties—100,000 deaths with half attributed to disease—than most of the other countries involved in the war, but the effects of the war were felt by all.

When the United States declared war on Germany in 1917, the largest numbers of American immigrants were from Germany. These individuals, as well as immigrants from the other Central Powers countries, were subjected to constant suspicion and questions regarding their loyalty. The Wilson administration sought to stamp out dissent and criticism of the war through a variety of means, including passage of the Espionage and Sedition acts in 1917 and 1918, which attempted to restrict free speech in opposition to the war. In his efforts to promote nationalism and increase support for the war, Wilson demanded conformity on all fronts and used government agencies to control economic conditions, transportation, and communication. Teaching the German language was outlawed and those who failed to comply with the new guidelines were considered traitors. Sauerkraut was even renamed "Liberty Cabbage." Although many Americans came to accept an increasing role of government in their lives during the 1910s, Wilson's wartime policies undermined First Amendment rights and intentionally created fear in the populace.

The last two years of the 1910s were difficult ones in the United States. In addition to the war, Americans and people from around the globe confronted an influenza epidemic in 1918 that killed 675,000 Americans and 20 to 40 million people worldwide. American deaths in a single year were greater than those incurred by Americans in all of the wars of the twentieth century combined. Then, in 1919, just as the epidemic was beginning to wane, President Wilson, embittered from his battles with Congress over the Treaty of Versailles and the League of Nations, suffered a severe stroke from which he never fully recovered. In addition, 1919 brought major strikes by workers who had put their grievances on hold during the war as well as race riots in several major cities around the country. The general fear of uprisings and unrest led Americans in 1920 to elect Warren G. Harding who had run on a platform of healing and normalcy.

In many respects, sports during this period of promise and turmoil can best be described as setting the stage for the Golden Age of sports in the 1920s. This does not suggest that the decade did not have its own share of heroes and great athletic moments. There were, for instance, many firsts in American sport in the 1910s, including the first Indy 500 automobile race in 1911, the first American Stanley Cup ice hockey winner in 1917, and the first thoroughbred horse-racing Triple Crown in 1919. More important, many of the trends that fully emerged in the 1920s had roots in this decade. These trends included a greater belief in the social value of sport and in the level of interest and participation among Americans, a growing shift from amateurism to professionalism, and a desire to curb brutality and injury in sport, especially in football and boxing.

Theodore Roosevelt, president of the United States for much of the first decade of the twentieth century and a great athlete himself, was perhaps the most visible advocate of competitive sports for men and a champion of the idea that sports had value beyond recreation. Roosevelt, like many others of his generation, believed that a late-nineteenth century "crisis of masculinity" had diminished the strength, vitality, and competitive spirit that men needed to lead. For Roosevelt, the rigors of organized sport provided the ideal training ground for the kind of mental and physical toughness that he believed men should possess. The notion that sports could be instrumental in developing courage as well as a variety of other physical and mental skills, prevalent throughout the 1910s, reached a peak during preparations for World War I.

According to historian Wanda Wakefield (1997, 13–19), sports played an important and tangible role in the lives of U.S. soldiers during World War I. First, athletic training was considered an effective tool for improving fitness and relieving stress. In fact, there was a general concern about the fitness level of military recruits and a belief that improving one's physical fitness was a patriotic duty. Soldiers preparing at bases around the country for deployment to the war participated in football, boxing, tug of war, volleyball, baseball, and basketball. Raymond Fosdick, chairman of Commissions on Training Camp Activities, argued that participation in these sports before the war made soldiers more effective once they got to the front. Wakefield suggests that military leaders placed special emphasis on sports that encouraged aggression and that had American origins. This emphasis on the connection between sport and military preparedness continued once the troops got to Europe. According to sports historians Elliott Gorn and Warren Goldstein (1993), when American troops were deployed to Europe in 1917, they were joined by 12,000 YMCA workers who were expected to promote health and fitness among the troops.

In addition to the physical benefits, military leaders saw sport as a way to help soldiers deal with fear and to promote a team spirit within the ranks. Wakefield suggests that sports helped soldiers cope with fear in two ways. First, they could be used as a distraction. Second, sports provided a way for military leaders to make the tasks of war seem more familiar and, therefore, less frightening. Despite all evidence to the contrary, war became a game. Tactics could be equated to football strategy.

Throwing a grenade was like throwing a baseball. Relying on one's fellow soldiers to hold a position was just like relying on one's teammates to stop the opposition. The link between the language of war and the language of sport greatly expanded in World War I. The use of sports metaphors in war and the subsequent use of war metaphors in sport became, in many respects, the language of "real" men.

Finally, sports became a unifying agent for American soldiers who, by World War I, were an extremely diverse group. Men were expected to know and understand the language of sport, whether or not they played sports prior to the war. This provided common ground for men from different parts of the country with different religions, languages, and cultural backgrounds. In order to help them bond with each other and to feel a sense of American pride, U.S. soldiers routinely competed against European teams throughout the war. Military leaders encouraged a feeling of superiority among American soldiers and nurtured the belief that success as a team on an athletic field would translate into success on the battlefield. When soldiers with these experiences finally returned home, many had become hooked on sports. This, in turn, strengthened the country's emphasis on athletics as a form of recreation. It also opened the sports arena to a broader range of young men.

The linking of sport with masculinity and war often had negative implications for women athletes who were seen as a threat to men or as an affront to established gender roles. Despite the fact that women had always engaged in hard, physical labor working on farms and rearing children and, more recently, working in factories, they were still viewed as more delicate than men. This perspective was bolstered by changing economic roles in the early twentieth century. For most of human history, the family formed an economic unit, one in which men and women labored together for the family's economic well-being. The maturation of the industrial economy, especially the ability of workers to buy many of the goods that they helped to mass produce, created "separate spheres" for men and women. Men went to work and women stayed home. Athletics could help to prepare men for the rough-and-tumble public sphere, but would be unnecessary and inappropriate for women. Doctors gave credence to this point of view by warning that strenuous exercise would endanger women's reproductive development and health.

In addition to being viewed as a preparation for manhood, sports in the 1910s were valued for other reasons, too. At a time when the United States was changing rapidly and becoming increasingly involved with the rest of the world, sports strengthened local communities, created a bridge between different social classes and ethnic groups, and provided working-class men with upward mobility. Average guys, including immigrants in many cases, could, through ability and hard work, make a living and become local heroes if not always national figures. In short, sports were seen as a reflection of emerging American values.

One indication of the increasing role of sport in American culture was the level of interest by Americans, young and old. An unprecedented number of Americans were participating in and following organized sports during the 1910s. The growth of the sports pages in newspapers throughout the country contributed to the popularity of sports among fans as they were able to follow their teams' progress even when they could not attend games. In the decade preceding 1910, some of the largest newspapers reached the one-million mark for number of copies of a single issue. This growth continued through the 1910s, and the sports page became a staple in all major American newspapers.

Another trend that emerged in conjunction with the growing interest in sport was the shift from amateurism to professionalism. This was especially true in base-ball, which had professional national leagues by this period, but it applied to foot-ball, basketball, and golf as well. When a football league of national scope emerged in the 1920s, it was partially a result of the success of professional football in Ohio, especially star player and Olympics gold medalist Jim Thorpe's Canton Bulldogs in the 1910s. In basketball, professional teams and leagues were being formed by the turn of the twentieth century, but there was little stability or loyalty among players to a particular team. The strength and innovative play of a few teams in the 1910s, such as the New York Celtics and the Philadelphia SPHAs, both formed in 1918, helped to set the stage for professional basketball on a national scale in the 1920s and 1930s. In golf, Walter Hagen, who won the U.S. Open Golf Championship in 1914, promoted professionalism by earning money on tours, endorsing products, and hiring a business manager by the name of Robert "Bob" Harlow who became known as the "founder of professional golf."

Not surprisingly, another trend during this reform-minded progressive era was the desire to "clean up" problems that had developed in the early years of sport, especially in baseball, football, and boxing. In the 1890s, baseball games were often characterized by inebriated crowds as well as the use of obscenities and poor behavior among players. Reformers in the 1910s wanted baseball games to be family events enjoyed by the community, and they supported the efforts of managers such as Connie Mack of the Philadelphia Athletics who tried to improve the image of the game by requiring play-ers to dress professionally and to behave appropriately on the field. The primary con-cern in football, which will be discussed more fully later in the chapter, was the prevalence of violence, injuries, and death among the players. A number of rule changes were put into effect in the 1910s in order to stem the violence and improve the image of the game. Unfortunately, reformers made little progress in this period to reform boxing, which was still illegal in many states and had long been viewed as little more than backroom brawling. Efforts to change this image throughout most of the 1910s were overshadowed by race issues within the sport, and it was not until after World War I that it became more popular and acceptable.

TEAM SPORTS

Baseball

Baseball's hold on the American imagination grew in the 1910s. The deadball style of play, with its emphasis on power pitching and protecting a small number of runs through short hits and stolen bases, continued throughout the decade, but it was being challenged by a new approach to the game. The innovative cork-centered ball, introduced in 1909, allowed for greater offensive production and the emer-gence of great hitters. During the 1911 season, for example, fans were treated to Ty Cobb's astounding .420 batting average and "Shoeless Joe" Jackson's impressive .408. This shift in style of play coincided with the rise of big-park stadiums and growing attendance. According to baseball historian David Voigt (1983), in 1911 as many as 10 million fans enjoyed games in major-league parks for every team. The success of these parks caused promoters in other cities to follow suit and attendance, with a couple of exceptions, held steady throughout the decade.

Ty Cobb, Detroit Tigers, American League.
(Courtesy of the Library of Congress)

Economic and Legal Issues in Baseball

The 1903 Agreement, forged between the National League (NL) and the American League (AL) and credited with bringing order and stability to baseball, gave professional teams more control over their players and created a National Commission to serve as a judicial body that would resolve disputes within the sport. Immediately after this agreement, the owners cut salaries. Although they rose at a slow and steady pace after that, salaries did not go up in proportion to the owners' profits. In 1910 the average salary for a professional player was $3000. This led the players to form a union known as the "player's fraternity" in 1912. Counting minor-league players, the union had 700 members and was able to win a number of concessions from the National Commission.

Part of the union's leverage came from the creation of a third league that served as a threat to American and National League owners. Formed in 1914 by James A. Gilmore, a Chicago businessman, and other members of the business community, the Federal League offered better salaries than either of the other two leagues. In 1914, one-third of the AL and NL players were enticed to join the new league. Although they were blacklisted in the two original leagues, the defections of these players caused most AL and NL owners to raise salaries. Eventually the Federal League owners were bought out by the major leagues and the players' union lost some of its bargaining power.

Baseball and Ethnicity

The earliest Negro leagues were formed in the late 1860s in response to segregation, but these regional leagues were often transitory, and players, who had no formal contracts, switched teams often. Ironically, most of the early teams were centered in the North even though the vast majority of African Americans still lived in the South. Over the years, there were some efforts to create a national league for African American players, but it was not until 1920 that a viable Negro League on a national level was established. In 1911 two former members of one of the Negro teams, the Cuban Stars, signed with the Cincinnati Reds in the National League, giving some hope that further integration in the major leagues would follow. Outfielder Armando Marsans and third baseman Rafael Almeida were light-skinned and considered Latinos, not blacks, which at that time made them more accepted, but many players and the Negro press hoped that these two would break down the barrier for all African American players. Unfortunately, this did not happen. Almeida played in the major league for three years and Marsans played for ten, but they remained isolated exceptions.

By 1915, in conjunction with the Great Migration of African Americans to northern industrial cities, participation and interest in Negro baseball was growing.

New York Giants manager John McGraw and Chicago Cubs manager Frank Chance, in 1911. (Courtesy of the Library of Congress)

In the second half of the 1910s, most major cities in the North and West had Negro teams and some, in places like New York and Chicago where there were large African American populations, actually made money. Because there were fewer teams in the South, many players looked to move north where there were more opportunities. In fact, in 1916, one whole team, the Duval Giants of Jacksonville, Florida, moved north and became the Bacharach Giants of Atlantic City. Players on the team believed that they would be paid more, would have more fan support and better facilities, and would have more opportunities for themselves and their families in New Jersey.

Negro teams played each other, but they also played local white teams, including some major-league teams. In some areas, such as Chicago, big-league teams were reluctant to play Negro teams because they figured that they had nothing to gain and everything to lose. Major-league teams in the East were more willing to play Negro teams. In 1915, for instance, Negro teams played eight games against big-league teams and won four of them. Two of the most consistently successful Negro teams during the decade were the Chicago American Giants, led by the great pitcher Andrew (Rube) Foster, and the Lincoln Giants of New York. Formed in 1911 by Jess McMahon, a white boxing promoter, the Lincoln Giants played at Olympic Field located at 136th Street and Fifth Avenue in Harlem. Playing semi-pro and major-league all-star teams several times per week, the team drew crowds numbering in the thousands. To add to the festivities, McMahon added burlesque to baseball with a pregame show that included juggling and acrobatics. Behind the pitching of Joe Williams ("the Cyclone"), the Lincoln Giants were one of the best independent teams in the East during this period.

Perhaps the most ethnically diverse team during the 1910s was the All Nations Club, organized in the second half of the decade by J. L. Wilkinson, a Kansas City white man who later operated the Kansas City Monarchs. The team played with considerable success and had players from a variety of ethnic groups. Several African American men played on the team, including two of the best Negro pitchers, Jose Mendez and John Donaldson, along with a Japanese player, a Hawaiian, an American Indian, three whites, and one or two Latin Americans.

Women's Baseball

Baseball first took hold for women in the last half of the nineteenth century at women's colleges such as Vassar, Smith, and Wellesley, all of which played an important role in the development of women's athletics generally. Women loved baseball from the start and it did not take long for women's college teams to emerge. As in other sports, pioneers in women's baseball struggled to find suitable clothing to perform successfully. Barbara Gregorich (1993), who has written much of the history on women's baseball in the early period, describes how, after hitting the ball, a female player would have to put down her bat, gather up the train of her long skirt, and throw it over her arm before running to first base. By the 1890s, some women took advantage of Amelia Bloomer's newly designed trousers for women, but others, wanting to avoid the controversy provoked by wearing "bloomers," continued to do the best they could in skirts. By 1910, many women's professional teams, typically known as Bloomer Girl teams, had been established around the country.

Maud Nelson, an Italian immigrant who began her baseball career in the late 1890s, played an important role in the development and promotion of these early teams. Remembered for her incredible durability and longevity, Nelson played the game well into her thirties and made a guest appearance for the Boston Bloomer Girls at the age of forty-one. While best known as an outstanding pitcher who rarely gave up more than a couple of hits in any given game, Nelson also played third base in the late innings and contributed to her teams with solid hitting. In 1911, at the age of thirty, Nelson and her first husband, John B. Olson Jr., formed the highly successful Western Bloomer Girls. Nelson sold her interest in the team to her fellow player and co-owner, Kate Becker, in late 1912, but not before ensuring the team's long-term success—a feat that she accomplished with several additional teams during her long career in baseball.

Another outstanding women's player in the 1910s was Mary Elizabeth "Lizzie" Murphy, who made her living playing on semipro men's teams. The daughter of a French Canadian mother and an Irish millworker who also played baseball, Murphy grew up playing the game with her father and brothers in Warren, Rhode Island. She began her baseball career in earnest when, in her late teens, she was offered five dollars a game to play for a semipro team in Warren. After moving up to the more successful Providence Independents, she was ready, in 1918, to sign as an infielder with Ed Carr's Boston All-Stars, another semipro team. Although he took some criticism from those who thought he was corrupting and exploiting a young woman, Carr exulted in having Murphy on the team and credited her with improving the team's performance and with selling more tickets. Throughout her years playing in the man's world of semipro baseball, Murphy earned respect as a tough competitor

Bloomer Girl Baseball

Bloomer Girl baseball teams existed in the United States from the mid-1890s until 1934. Dubbed "Bloomer Girls" because many of the players chose to wear the loose-fitting trousers designed by Amelia Bloomer when they played, the teams were comprised mostly of women, but they generally had at least one man on the team to play catcher and often two or three additional men. Unlike most men's teams, the Bloomer Girl teams did not have a set location, but instead played exhibition games against men's amateur and semipro teams around the country. While there were hundreds of these teams throughout a forty-year period, the Western Bloomer Girls, formed in February 1911 by Maud Nelson and Katie Becker, was one of the most successful.

The Western Bloomer Girls began touring in May 1911 with Nelson pitching and playing third base and Becker pitching and playing second base. From the beginning Nelson recruited the best players she could find whether they were from rural areas in Michigan and Illinois or from large cities such as her own Chicago. With some of her later teams, Nelson recruited throughout the country, which was unusual at the time. She was well known for her ability to spot talent among men or women players and also worked as a scout during most of her career. The Westerns fielded six women and three men for games. Nelson typically put the men at catcher, shortstop, and center field, but occasionally she had one of them play pitcher. Over time, she also figured out the best strategy for placing men in the batting order.

Nelson sold the Westerns to her partner, Kate Becker, in October 1912 once they had completed their first two seasons, but her departure did not hinder the team's success. The same could be said of her second team, the American Athletic Girls, when she sold her share to co-owner Rose Figg. Nelson's ability to build stable and successful teams that continued to thrive after she moved on proved to be one of her greatest contributions to women's baseball.

and an excellent first baseman. She was the first woman to play for a major-league team in an exhibition game which she did in 1922 and again in 1928.

Baseball and World War I

When the United States entered World War I in April 1917, baseball owners decided not to cancel the 1917 and 1918 seasons. The 1917 season was already under way, and for the next several months the season continued normally. Attendance remained high throughout the summer, and baseball owners hoped that the government would consider baseball essential to national morale and would exempt players from the draft. By the end of 1917, however, the situation was bleak and owners worried about the 1918 season. It turned out that baseball was not what Secretary of State Newton Baker meant when he released the government's "Work or Fight" slogan. Despite arguments used by baseball officials about the importance of keeping people's morale high during the war, baseball was not considered essential war work. There was also a growing sense that these strong, male athletes had a patriotic duty to fight for their country. A failure to do so was seen, in some quarters, as cowardice.

After the 1917 season 227 players ended up joining the armed forces, while others turned to draft-exempt industries such as shipbuilding and farming.

STAR BLOOMER GIRLS BASE BALL CLUB
627 W. MICHIGAN ST. INDIANAPOLIS, IND.

Star Bloomer Girls' baseball club, 627 W. Michigan St., Indianapolis. (Courtesy of the Library of Congress)

Eventually more than 500 current or future players served in the military. Not seeing a viable alternative, the owners pressed on with the 1918 season and filled in their rosters with retired players or with ones brought up from the minor leagues, a necessity that greatly weakened the minor leagues during this time. When Secretary Baker declared that after September 2, 1918, baseball players would be officially eligible for the draft, he allowed a two-week delay so that the World Series could be completed, but the Series was poorly attended and marked the end of a dismal financial year for baseball.

Baseball's image suffered for a number of reasons during the war. While teams sought to show their patriotism by holding parades, performing drills before games, giving out free tickets to servicemen, and encouraging fans to purchase war bonds, baseball generally was accused of not sacrificing enough for the effort. Owners tried to deflect some of this criticism by providing equipment to military teams in Europe as well as sending some major-league players to teach baseball skills to soldiers. Few players, however, initially volunteered to serve in the armed forces, and they continued to demand high salaries throughout the period. In fact, during the 1918 World Series, players, knowing that tickets sales were down and fearing that owners would respond by docking their pay, threatened to strike for more money. According to Voigt (1983), it was only after appeals to the players' patriotism that they were convinced to play the final game of the Series. In addition, baseball was marred by corruption during the war years. In a widely publicized case, Hal Chase of the Cincinnati Reds, in August 1918, was suspended for betting and trying to bribe a pitcher to throw a game. All of these factors, combined with financial losses from the war and the influenza epidemic of 1918, led to a general sense of pessimism in baseball going into the 1919 season.

The Chicago White Sox Scandal

Despite this pessimism, tides shifted and 1919 turned out to be a banner year for baseball. Attendance and profits rebounded as war-weary fans welcomed the return of a more normal day-to-day life. After exciting pennant races, spectators relished the prospect of a World Series between the Chicago White Sox and the Cincinnati Reds. No one could have guessed that the series would end in one of the most notorious scandals in sports history. The White Sox, who had been a dominant team over the previous two years, were favored to win based on their overall balance and the strength of their pitchers, especially Eddie Cicotte and Lefty Williams. Chicago's success, however, did not cure a number of problems that plagued the team going into the 1919 World Series.

To begin with, Charles Comiskey, the White Sox owner and manager since 1901, managed his team shrewdly and left many believing that he had a greater interest in profits than in his players. Comiskey began his long career in professional baseball in 1882 as a player with the St. Louis Browns, but by 1919 he was known best as a hard-driving owner who took advantage of the no-free-agency rule for players and cut costs wherever he could. For example, most teams allowed players four dollars per day to cover the cost of meals, but Comiskey expected his players to make do with three dollars per day. As a result of his efforts to cut laundry costs, the White Sox often played in filthy uniforms. More significantly, Comiskey's players earned well below what players of comparable talent earned with other teams.

In 1919 owners across the country cut players' salaries because they feared a continuation of the low attendance that had plagued baseball during 1918. Despite strong attendance in 1919, Comiskey did not raise salaries, a decision that almost caused the players to strike in July of that year. In addition, Comiskey routinely went back on promises for bonuses if the team or individual players reached specified levels of success. Some baseball historians have noted that the general dissatisfaction of White Sox players in the late 1910s, as well as the limited options available to them for having grievances addressed, contributed to a climate that made cheating for money more likely.

In addition to their frustration with Comiskey, White Sox players were often at odds with one another and this, too, played a role in conditions leading to the scandal. The low morale resulted in part from class differences among the players. Whereas most of the players were poorly paid, one, Eddie Collins, was awarded a $14,500 annual salary when he came to the White Sox from the Athletics in 1915. This was almost twice the amount paid to any other player on the team, a fact that caused considerable resentment among his high-performing, underpaid teammates. Collins, a graduate of Columbia University, was one of a small group of educated players on the team who tended to live a more refined lifestyle than most of the group. Arnold "Chick" Gandil, who ended up initiating the Series fix, hated Collins and everything that he represented. It was not difficult for Gandil to convince some of his teammates that they, in fact, deserved more money.

When the Series actually began, the Reds came out of the gate strong, winning four of the first five games. The Sox came back to win the next two and were scheduled to play the final games of the series at home in Chicago. In the eighth and what turned out to be final game, however, the Reds won by a score of 10 to 5. In the aftermath of the game, rumors spread that the Series had been "fixed," but the stories did not immediately gain strength. Many, including the editor of the respected *Spalding Guide*, dismissed them and noted the considerable strengths of the Reds.

The story may have ended there had it not been for the investigative journalism of Hugh Fullerton, who wrote for the *Chicago Herald and Examiner*, and Christy Mathewson, the great ex-Giant player and Braves' manager who wrote for the *New York World*. Having heard of rumors within the gambling community even before the Series began, both agreed to compare notes on any questionable plays during the Series. In the months following the Series, Fullerton began a relentless effort to dig up the truth. He eventually wrote a series of articles that described the fix and identified the names of those involved as well as their payoffs. Mathewson added to these accounts by providing Fullerton with detailed diagrams of each questionable play throughout the series. Although Fullerton's accusations were not immediately believed, his work, combined with renewed allegations against the White Sox and other teams during the 1920 season, led to a grand jury investigation in September of 1920.

Investigators produced evidence against eight players and seven confessed before the grand jury to receiving from $5,000 to $10,000 to throw the Series. Those implicated in the conspiracy and dubbed the "Black Sox" included the great hitter and outfielder Joe Jackson, pitchers Ed Cicotte and Claude "Lefty" Williams, infielders Buck Weaver, Swede Riseberg, Fred McMullin, and Chick Gandil, and outfielder Oscar "Happy" Felsch. It is generally believed that Gandil, who retired in 1920 and who received the largest pay out of $35,000, was the chief instigator in the conspiracy. Weaver, who never confessed guilt, said that he played no part in the plot, received no money, and exercised only poor judgment by not reporting the scheme. Comiskey, who suspected the plot and actually offered a reward to anyone providing information on it, did not directly punish the players because he hoped to keep his stars for the 1920 season.

After the grand jury investigation, a conspiracy trial was scheduled for June 1921 in Chicago. Baseball historians point out that the trial turned out to be a farce for two reasons. First, records of the grand jury testimony as well as the confessions of Cicotte, Jackson, and Williams mysteriously disappeared before the trial began. This sudden lack of evidence allowed all of the defendants to recant their original confessions. Second, both the jury and the spectators at the trial were extremely friendly to the players from the outset. When the jury announced its predictable "not guilty" verdict on August 2, 1921, spectators cheered and shouted praise for their "clean sox." Although the players were absolved of legal wrongdoing, they soon paid a heavy price for their association with the scandal.

Comiskey's failure to make an example of his players by sanctioning them and by publicly condemning their corruption undermined AL president Ban Johnson's authority and baseball's National Commission system of rule. Thus, in 1921, a single commissioner replaced the commission system. Judge Kenesaw Mountain Landis, the first person to take on this role, considered it his duty to restore honor, decorum, and integrity to baseball, a view that caused him to rule with an iron fist during his twenty-five-year tenure. Landis, deciding that the court's verdict should not be used to exonerate the players, banned the eight "Black Sox" from professional baseball for life. Today such a ruling would be viewed as a violation of the players' civil liberties. Even in 1921, there were those who opposed it on these grounds, but Landis had the support of baseball owners and the general public who wanted to restore baseball's image.

"Shoeless Joe" Jackson (1888–1951)

Born on July 16, 1888, in the mill town of Greenville, South Carolina, Joseph Jefferson Jackson, nicknamed "Shoeless Joe," began playing baseball at the age of thirteen for the Brandon Mill team, which played in the Textile League. The league was formed by mill owners as a way to keep workers and to build community spirit. Jackson distinguished himself as a great player immediately and by the time he was sixteen had become a local hero. In his early days as a player and later during his professional years, Jackson was known as a great natural hitter, but he excelled in all aspects of the game and thrilled fans with his stellar play both at bat and in the outfield.

In 1908, at the age of nineteen, Jackson began his professional career with the Carolina Association's Greenville Spinners and averaged an impressive .350 for the year. It was while playing with the Spinners that he earned his "Shoeless Joe" nickname. Apparently after developing a severe case of blisters from wearing a new pair of shoes in a game the day before, Jackson decided to play the next day in his socks, a decision that did not go unnoticed by the perceptive fans. He never played without shoes after that day, but the nickname stuck. His success with the Greenville team caused Jackson to be picked up the following year by Connie Mack's Philadelphia Athletics. After one season with the Athletics, he was traded to Cleveland where he played until 1915 when he joined the Chicago White Sox.

Before he was implicated in the 1919 Black Sox scandal, Jackson had been a star on every team he played on and was well on his way to gaining legendary status. He hit a total of 54 home runs, had 785 RBIs, and batted a career average of .356, an accomplishment that places him third on the list for Highest Career Batting Average, behind Rogers Hornsby and Ty Cobb. Although evidence indicates that Jackson played no direct role in the Black Sox scandal, a point reinforced by his near-flawless performance in the 1919 World Series, he ended up being indicted during the 1920 grand jury hearings. He was found not guilty during the 1921 trial, but he was still banned from baseball for life by newly appointed baseball commissioner Kenesaw Mountain Landis, who said that he should have notified his teammates of the plot.

Jackson continued to play in semipro and exhibition games every chance he got and remained popular with the fans, but he was never reinstated into major-league baseball. He stopped playing baseball altogether in 1933 at the age of forty-five and spent the rest of his life working in other industries. Since Shoeless Joe's death in 1951, fans have continued to push for his reinstatement so that the way might be cleared for him to be inducted into the Baseball Hall of Fame. So far, this has not happened.

Some, such as baseball historian David Voigt, have argued that Landis's ruling, and the willingness of people to accept it, was part of a larger effort to perpetuate the myth that the "Black Sox scandal" was a lone exception in an otherwise pristine and virtuous sport. The evidence does not support such a myth, but the power of baseball as a symbol of America's emerging values was well entrenched by 1920 and needed to be protected. For the eight banned players, this meant years of trying to play under assumed names for semipro teams. Inevitably, they would be detected and ousted. Most soon gave up the hope of ever playing again. Buck Weaver, however, continued to fight the ban. Maintaining his innocence to the end, he appealed to Landis to be reinstated six different times, including once with a petition containing 14,000 signatures, but each time the commissioner rejected his pleas. The eight "Black Sox" were not the only players in the 1910s to risk their careers for financial gain, but they were the ones who paid the price both in their own day and in history.

Baseball Through the Decade

The American League dominated the decade, winning eight out of ten World Series from 1910 to 1919. The Philadelphia Athletics won in 1910, 1911, and 1913; the Boston Red Sox won in 1912, 1915, 1916, and 1918; and the Chicago White Sox won in 1917. The National League's most dominant team was the New York Giants. Although they never won the World Series, they won the NL pennant four times from 1911 to 1913 and again in 1917. The Chicago Cubs won the pennant but lost the World Series in 1910 and 1918, the Philadelphia Phillies in 1915, and the Brooklyn Dodgers in 1916. The only NL teams to win in the decade were the Boston Braves "miracle team" in 1914 and the Cincinnati Reds in 1919.

Basketball

Basketball grew in popularity during the 1910s, but the game was still in its infancy compared to baseball. Invented in 1891 by James Naismith, basketball developed in conjunction with the Playground movement in the early 1900s. Urban reformers hoped that city playgrounds would attract idle youth and keep them occupied in healthy recreation. Basketball, a sport well suited to concrete surfaces and requiring little space or equipment, became an ideal city sport. It could easily be played on playgrounds, in churches and schools, and even on rooftops. It also worked well in regions with colder climates because it could be played indoors. As with baseball, reformers and educators viewed basketball as a way to organize and Americanize immigrant youth. It, too, became a sport of choice in working-class, ethnic communities and spread across the United States with amazing rapidity.

In many respects, basketball served as an ideal vehicle for urban reformers to reach immigrant children and their families. It gave urban recreation programs structure and staying power that probably would not have existed otherwise. Like baseball, basketball became a tool for Americanization and community building. Ethnic neighborhoods took pride in their teams, and leagues were often organized to allow for the naming of ethnic champions.

College and Amateur Basketball

By the turn of the twentieth century, basketball was being played in high schools and colleges as well as in YMCA and American Athletic Union (AAU) leagues and tournaments. Although many men disapproved, the sport caught on almost immediately with women and was played regularly at the high school level and at all-women's colleges such as Smith, Vassar, Wellesley, and Mount Holyoke. The first national rules for women were published in 1901. The National Collegiate Athletic Association (NCAA) assumed control of college rules for men in 1908, and, in 1915 YMCA, NCAA, and AAU representatives formed a joint committee on basketball. In the second half of the 1910s, when the Playground movement was beginning to wane and funding was drying up, as the country prepared to enter World War I, Naismith and others pushed to have basketball incorporated as widely as possible into the newly emerging comprehensive high schools. This push carried the sport well beyond its urban roots.

College basketball by 1910 was gaining momentum and had extended to most regions of the country. The Southwest Conference was formed in 1915 and the Pacific Coast Conference followed in 1916. New York teams performed well during the decade with Columbia winning the unofficial national championship in 1910, St. Johns in 1911, and Syracuse in 1918. Wisconsin won twice in 1912 and 1916 and the West Coast team, Washington State, won in 1917. The AAU also sponsored national tournaments through much of the decade and approved the use of the first open-bottom nets for basketball for the 1912–13 season.

Professional Basketball

The formation of a professional National Basketball League had been attempted in 1898, but it lasted only two years. Pro basketball in the 1910s still lacked formal organization on a national level. There were, however, many professional teams and leagues, particularly in the mid-Atlantic and New England regions. Often, players played for more than one team in a single season and switched teams when they could earn more money. Owners issued contracts by the game rather than by the season. Early professional teams such as the Buffalo Germans, who turned pro in 1905 and played successfully well into the 1930s, often started out as local club teams. The year 1918 proved to be a turning point in the development of professional basketball because two important professional teams were formed that year: the New York Celtics and the Philadelphia SPHAs.

The New York Celtics, or the Original Celtics as they were known at the time, had their roots with a pre–World War I Irish settlement-house team from the Hell's Kitchen area of New York City. The team, which was reorganized under the direction of James Furey in 1918, combined many of the Original Celtics from the settlement-house team with new players from other parts of the city. After a mediocre first year, Furey recruited more talented players and began to build his team around the first of many outstanding Celtics, Henry "Dutch" Dehnert. A 6'1" guard, Dehnert became known for perfecting the pivot play in basketball. In the 1920s, the Celtics recruited more top players and revolutionized the game of basketball by playing as a team, rather than as a group of individuals responsible only for single players on the opposing team.

At the same time that Furey was establishing the Celtics as a pro team in New York, Eddie Gottlieb, Harry Passon, and Hughie Black organized the Philadelphia SPHAs. They acquired their name because the team was funded and equipped largely through the efforts of the South Philadelphia Hebrew Association and until the mid-1920s all of the players were Jewish. Although they got their start as an amateur team, early success against top teams in the region earned them a spot, first in the Philadelphia League, and later, in the Eastern League. Like the Celtics, the SPHAs came into their own in the 1920s and 1930s, but they were one of the few longstanding professional basketball teams who got their start in the 1910s.

As an institution in Philadelphia, the SPHA team promoted ethnic pride and proudly claimed their Jewish heritage by wearing the Star of David on their uniforms and adorning their uniforms with Hebrew letters (Riess 1998, 27). The team

Playing basketball at the 1919 Inter-Allied Games, Pershing Stadium, Colombes, France. (Courtesy of the Library of Congress)

was part of a long line of Jewish teams and players to distinguish themselves in basketball. The 1910s marked a period when Jewish players began to transition from playing on settlement teams in major East Coast cities to playing in college and on professional teams. One of the most successful Jewish players to move from the college to professional ranks in the 1910s was Barney Sedran, who played for City College of New York and then went on to play for numerous professional teams from 1911 to 1938.

Football

Prior to 1910 football was an extremely violent game. Players dealt with numerous injuries, and deaths were not uncommon. In fact, eighteen college players died playing football in 1905 alone. With the support of President Theodore Roosevelt, whose son played for Harvard during these years, many rule changes were implemented between 1905 and 1910 (see chapter 4). Still, football fatalities continued, with 113 between these years. In 1910 additional changes were made. Seven men were required on the line of scrimmage and the flying tackle was outlawed. In addition, teams were no longer allowed to run interference by interlocking arms or to advance the ball by pushing and pulling the ball carrier. To make the game more humane, play was divided into four fifteen-minute quarters with a one-minute

Barney Sedran (1891–1964)

"The Mighty Mite of Basketball" was one of the early "greats" among little men in professional basketball. Born January 28, 1891, on the Lower East Side of New York City to Russian Jewish immigrant parents, Sedran grew up playing basketball on the playgrounds and in the settlement houses of his neighborhood. Despite his small stature—he stood 5'4" tall and weighed 115 pounds as an adult—Sedran chose basketball because it was the one sport that was easy to play in the area where he grew up. As a youngster, he developed his game at the University Settlement House under coach Harry Baum, who encouraged his young charges to develop a new style of play. Sedran and his teammates were expected to master all aspects of the game, to move well with and without the ball, to master man-to-man defense, and to play intelligently on the court. This early tutelage served Sedran well throughout his career.

As a student at DeWitt Clinton High School, Sedran failed to earn a tryout for the high school team because he was considered too small, so he continued to play with the settlement house team. He and several of his teammates from this team—the "Busy Izzies" as they were known—went on to play with great success at the City College of New York (CCNY). Although Sedran became a highly respected college player, he was not expected to move on to professional basketball because of his size. His prospects changed when another of the former "Busy Izzies," Marty Friedman, called Sedran to join him on a professional team in Newburgh, New York. That team went on to win the Hudson River League championship in 1911–12 with Sedran leading the league in field goals. This effectively launched a professional career that spanned close to fifteen years and that included play on a variety of New York teams, on one Indiana team, and, finally, on the Cleveland Rosenblums in the American Basketball League (ABL) formed in 1925. After retiring as a player, Sedran went on to coach professional basketball for another twenty years. A member of the International Jewish Sports Hall of Fame, Sedran was elected to the Basketball Hall of Fame in 1962 and still holds the distinction of being the smallest player ever inducted.

break between the first and second and third and fourth quarters and a thirty-minute break between halves. Two years later brought the establishment of four downs to achieve a first down, the creation of an end zone behind each goal line, and the increase of five to six points for a touchdown's value. Finally, a number of improvements in protective gear were introduced during the 1910s. All of these changes eventually led to a decrease in the number of serious injuries and deaths over the course of the decade.

College Football: A Training Ground for Business

On college campuses, football was becoming a bit of a spectacle by 1910. Serious recruiting had taken hold and many coaches and players viewed the game with a "win at all costs" attitude. A regimented, military-style approach to practice, perfected by Walter Camp during his many years (1876–1909) as head coach at Yale University, became the norm. Players, viewing the demanding drills as a test of their physical and psychological strength, bonded with each other, seeing themselves as brothers and comrades. These young men had limited exposure to women during their college years because most of the schools that had football were all-male institutions. Football, in a sense, served as a measure of masculinity and a training ground for leadership. The ranks of early football teams were filled largely by men from elite backgrounds; they expected to be the leaders and powerbrokers in their communities when they reached adulthood.

Successful college coaches, replicating Camp's approach at Yale, learned to apply business principles to football and to market football as an ideal way to prepare privileged young men for business leadership. Camp, a successful clock manufacturer, climbed to the top of college football at the same time that Frederick Winslow Taylor's scientific management movement gained momentum in the business world. Camp applied Taylor's regimented efficiency to football, including the notion that tasks should be broken down into component parts with individuals mastering their assigned parts for the good of the greater whole. In their *Brief History of American Sports*, Gorn and Goldstein include a passage from one of Camp's 1920 writings that illustrates this connection. Camp wrote:

> Finding a weak spot through which a play can be made, feeling out the line with experimental attempts, concealing the real strength till everything is ripe for the big push, then letting drive where least expected, what is this—an outline of football or business tactics? Both of course. (1993, 158)

At Yale, Camp worked with elite young men from all over the country, and he made it his business to mold them into an efficient machine. His efforts resulted in Yale's complete dominance of college football during the late nineteenth and early twentieth centuries, but by 1910 other coaches had perfected Camp's techniques and new powerhouses emerged.

The Geography of College Football

In the 1910s the Ivy League continued to reign supreme in college football, but among the Ivy schools Harvard took the mantle from its rival Yale. The transition began with Harvard's hiring of Percy Haughton in 1908. Haughton used the Camp model to bring order and structure to Harvard's program. Between 1908 and 1916, Haughton's team amassed a 71-7-5 record and won the national title in 1910, 1912, and 1913. Harvard and Yale played eight times during the decade (the 1917 and 1918 games were not held due to World War I), and Harvard won five times, tied twice, and lost once. In 1912 Harvard defeated both Yale and Princeton, spoiling their attempts at undefeated seasons, and won the mythical national championship. There was no championship game at the time and there were other undefeated teams, including Wisconsin, which won all seven of its games in 1912 and claimed the Western Conference title. There was a push that year for Harvard and Wisconsin to play in a true national championship game, but the idea never gained sufficient momentum. In 1915 Harvard humiliated Yale with a 41-0 victory and then lost its own bid for a perfect season by losing to Cornell University 10-0. Cornell went on to win the national championship that year.

While football teams at elite eastern schools within the Ivy League captured a lot of attention in the 1910s, programs at schools in the Midwest, West, and South continued to grow in strength and prestige during the decade. This was the decade, for example, that led to the rise of Notre Dame, a team that would be a major national contender throughout the twentieth century. In 1913, after completing

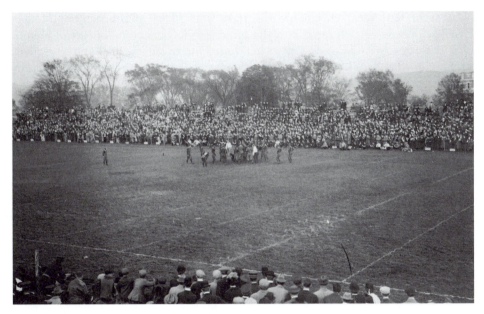

Army-Yale at West Point, October 19, 1912. (Courtesy of the Library of Congress)

two straight undefeated seasons, Notre Dame earned a secure place in college football history when, under coach Jesse Harper, the team perfected the use of the forward pass. Knute Rockne, who was a receiver on the team in 1913, was a perfect
target for quarterback Gus Dorais. Rockne went on to become a chemistry instructor at Notre Dame and an unrivaled coach of the football team throughout the
1920s. Other midwestern teams to excel in college football in the 1910s included
Illinois, Minnesota, and Ohio State.

In the South, Georgia Tech led by coach John Heisman dominated the decade
of the 1910s and emerged as a national power. From 1915 to 1919 Georgia Tech
enjoyed a thirty-two-game winning streak that included the most lopsided game in
college football history, a 222-0 win over Cumberland College in 1916. Heisman
coached at Georgia Tech until 1919 when he became coach of the University of
Pennsylvania, his alma mater. On the West Coast, the University of Washington,
under the leadership of coach Gilmour Dobie who arrived at Washington in 1908,
dominated the decade. In fact, during Coach Dobie's tenure, from 1908 to 1916,
the Washington Huskies did not lose a game. During the run, they won fifty-six
games and tied three. The team's total win streak from 1907 to 1917 included
sixty-three games. This record still stands as the most wins without a loss for any
college football team. Football also became popular in California during the 1910s
with a "re-introduced" Rose Bowl being held on New Year's Day in 1916.

The incredible rise in the popularity of college football in all sections of the
country in the early twentieth century led to an increased level of tension on college campuses between academics and athletics. The fact that football players saw
themselves as special, set apart and united by what they were forced to endure on
the field, much as veterans were set apart by their battlefield experiences, caused
consternation among many college faculty members. It seemed to them that football was taking precedence over academics with students who often expressed more

interest in festivities surrounding the next game than in the content of their courses. This perception grew with the increasing influence on colleges of alumni, many of whom were large donors with a vested interest in football and who themselves viewed college more as a socialization experience than as an intellectual pursuit. In addition, as college football began to generate increasing fan interest, even among those who would never attend college, and began to earn significant revenue for colleges, the power and influence of coaches, players, and alumni grew. Many of the tensions between athletics and academics observed in the 1910s could be seen throughout the twentieth century.

Professional Football

Although some players began to receive pay for playing football as early as the 1890s, professional football remained unorganized and regional until the 1920s. Most of the early teams were situated in Pennsylvania, Ohio, or Illinois and were associated with local athletic clubs. The teams typically played for city championships and sometimes played other teams around the state, but there was no national league and most football fans were inclined to follow college football. In contrast to the ranks of college football, which tended to be filled with privileged young men, many of the early professional teams attracted ethnic and working-class players.

A number of problems hampered professional football in the 1910s. Perhaps most important, there were no uniform rules, which made it difficult for teams to compete with each other on fair terms. The leagues that did exist were weak and teams often refused to join them. Because many of the players used football as a means to put food on the table for their families, they switched teams often in search of the best pay. Gambling and related scandals were common. Recognizing the potential of professional football and wanting to tackle the problems at hand, a group of representatives from several of the Ohio teams met in Canton, Ohio, in 1920 to draft a plan for stabilizing, improving, and marketing pro football. It was from this meeting that the National Football League (NFL) emerged in 1922.

Although professional football, like the college game, was dominated by white players, one of the best known professional players of the period was a Native American named Jim Thorpe. Thorpe is perhaps best remembered as a track star, but after the 1912 Olympics, he spent many years playing professional sports, including football. In 1915 he was offered $250 per game by the Canton Bulldogs. According to Thorpe biographer Bill Crawford (2005), this was considered quite an enormous sum at the time, especially to play in an informal league that kept no statistics. Thorpe was known for both his running ability and his defensive tackling skills. In order to take advantage of his name recognition, the group who first met in Canton in 1920 named Thorpe the first president of the NFL, a position for which he was poorly suited and only held for one year. In 1923 Thorpe played for a professional team of his own making, "Jim Thorpe's Oorang Indians," and then played with various other professional teams until his retirement from football in 1928 at the age of forty-two.

Some African American players also participated on the early professional football teams. One of the best known was Fritz Pollard, who was a standout player at Brown University during this decade and who was the first African American player to be named to the first team of Walter Camp's All-American team. From

Jim Thorpe (1887–1953)

In 1912, Sweden's king Gustav V, who was serving as host of the Stockholm Olympic Games, called Jim Thorpe "the world's greatest athlete," a title used to describe him more than once over the course of his career as a football player and international track star. Born in 1887 on the Sac and Fox Reservation in Indian Territory (in present-day Oklahoma), Thorpe entered the Carlisle Indian Industrial School in Carlisle, Pennsylvania, in 1904. Here, under the tutelage of famed football coach Glenn Scobey "Pop" Warner, Thorpe began to make a name for himself as a football player and track athlete. In 1911 he led his team to an 11–1 record, including an 18–15 upset of powerhouse Harvard, a game in which he scored all of his team's points. The following year, Carlisle won the national collegiate championship behind Thorpe's 25 touchdowns and 198 points.

While football was Jim Thorpe's favorite sport, he became most famous for his performance in the 1912 Olympics where he won gold medals in both the pentathlon and decathlon and competed for fourth- and seventh-place finishes in the high jump and long jump respectively. His Olympic record of 8,413 points for the decathlon stood for almost two decades. Thorpe had his medals and his official records taken away in 1913, however, after several newspapers published accounts that Thorpe had played two seasons of semi-professional baseball for which he received wages, albeit meager ones. Although this practice was common among college players at the time, there were strict rules against amateur Olympic athletes playing sports for pay, and Thorpe's request for an exception on the grounds that he did not know he was doing anything wrong went unheeded. His medals and records were finally reinstated posthumously in 1982.

After the Olympics, Thorpe spent the next ten to fifteen years playing professional baseball and football and even spent two years (1927–28) barnstorming with his "World-Famous Indians" basketball team. His greatest success was in football where he played most of his career for the Canton Bulldogs, which won team titles in 1916, 1917, and 1919, and in 1920 joined with thirteen other teams to form the American Professional Football Association (APFA). The APFA became the National Football League two years later. Thorpe played an instrumental role in the formation of the league as well as in developing and coaching the Oorang Indians, an all–Native American team in the early 1920s. Thorpe, who was married three times and had eight children, spent his later years working various jobs and struggling to stay out of poverty. He died of a heart attack in 1953. In 1950 he was selected as the most outstanding athlete of the first half of the twentieth century by American sports writers.

1919 to 1926 Pollard played for four different professional teams and was the first African American to become a pro coach when he served as a player-coach for two different teams, Akron and Hammond. In time, football would become a much more inclusive sport and would shed its more elite beginnings, but this was not yet the case in the 1910s.

Olympics

Because the 1916 Olympics were canceled due to World War I, the only Olympic competition held during this decade occurred in 1912 in Stockholm, Sweden, with 2490 men and 57 women representing twenty-eight different countries. By all

Osage Indian School football team, circa 1910. (Courtesy of the Library of Congress)

accounts this fifth modern Olympiad was an overwhelming success. This is not to say that the 1912 Games, and Olympic competition in general, did not have detractors. Many were quick to point out a host of problems associated with international athletic competition of this magnitude, but, by and large, the Stockholm games were well organized, and the Swedes showcased outstanding athletic facilities. The host country was especially pleased with its 30,000-seat stadium built in the form of a medieval castle.

Athletes from England, the United States, Sweden, and Finland generally outperformed those from other countries throughout the 1912 Olympics. The host country, fielding an enormous team of some 600 athletes, won the largest number of total medals. England and the United States focused most of their efforts on track and field. Both countries competed extremely well in what was becoming the signature sport of the modern summer Olympics, but the fact that American track athletes bested many of their British counterparts increased an already well-developed rivalry between the two countries. American dominance also revealed a growing tension over different ways that one could view the purpose of sport, competition, and training.

Throughout the nineteenth century, British athletes performed well in small-scale international athletic competitions and they did so using relatively low-key training methods and traditional techniques. The British valued the notion of the "gentleman amateur" who competed as much for recreation as anything else. The Stockholm Games revealed that international competition, especially at the Olympic level, was no longer considered play. From the British point of view, Americans had made a business out of it. American track and field athletes in Stockholm, referred to by the British press as "professional gladiators," had in fact reaped the benefits of a major shift in the way Americans were coming to view sport in the early twentieth century. The U.S. athletes of 1912 had grown up being coached at the high school, college, and club levels and had benefited directly from a growing American interest in the science of sport and athletic training. According to Olympic historian John Lucas (1980), the entire American team trained three to five hours a day while traveling on board the *Finland* from the United States to Sweden. They were under the supervision of coaches and specialists throughout the trip. By contrast, British athletes were largely on their own in Stockholm.

Just as many British officials were disgusted by the Americans' newfound training methods and technical innovations, they felt threatened by the racial makeup of the U.S. team. Adding to their argument that Americans would do anything to win, the British press pointed out the "exotic racial mix" of U.S. athletes and argued that the United States was violating the spirit of the Olympic Games by relying on African American and American Indian athletes as well as those from various immigrant groups. The success of individual athletes such as pentathlon and decathlon winner, Jim Thorpe and sprinter Howard Drew added to British discontent and caused some, like writer Sir Arthur Conan Doyle, to suggest that in the 1916 Berlin Olympics all those living under the British Empire should compete under one flag (Lucas 1980). As it turned out, however, neither the British nor anyone else competed in Berlin in 1916 because World War I led to the cancellation of the Games. Olympic competition resumed in Antwerp, Belgium, in 1920.

SPORTS FOR INDIVIDUAL COMPETITORS

Boxing

Prior to 1910 boxing was illegal in most parts of the United States. Some states passed specific laws that banned prizefighting and others applied existing laws against riots, assaults, and betting to curtail its practice. Despite these legal restrictions, by the late 1800s boxing in many parts of the United States was becoming increasingly popular. Part of this popularity reflected a growing interest in sports and recreation generally, especially among urbanites who longed for ways to escape the tedium of factory work and a more regimented way of life. Boxing also benefited from a growing desire to see American athletes compete against the best sportsmen around the world and an increasing tendency to equate physical strength with power and race superiority. The emergence of John L. Sullivan in the last two decades of the nineteenth century added to boxing's momentum. (See chapter 4.) Sullivan's preference for fighting according to the Marquis of Queensbury rules, which required boxers to wear gloves, his support among respectable athletic clubs, and his increased attention from the press made boxing seem more modern and respectable. Even in places where boxing remained illegal, promoters could often work around the laws by disguising prizefights as sparring exhibitions.

Despite these gains, boxing continued to have many detractors, both individuals and organizations such as the United Society of Christian Endeavor, who spoke out against the sport and pushed legislation to ban it or to limit its influence. A landmark bout in the history of boxing on July 4, 1910, added fuel to the fire for boxing critics. On that day Jack Johnson, an African American man known for his flamboyant lifestyle, defeated James Jeffries, the former heavyweight champion in fifteen rounds in Reno, Nevada. Johnson's victory and subsequent actions, until he lost the title to Jess Willard in Havana, Cuba, in 1915, dominated the boxing world in the 1910s, and added to the racial tension that engulfed the nation at this time.

Boxing and Race

Johnson was not the first African American fighter in the United States. In fact, historians of boxing generally believe that, on some level, slaves participated in the sport. Several lighter-weight African American boxers found success in the late 1800s in matches against both African Americans and whites, but there was considerable resistance to having an African American fighter challenge for the heavyweight crown. Some boxing enthusiasts viewed such a challenge as a threat to white supremacy. For many, the holder of the heavyweight crown symbolized national and racial superiority. That this title might be held by an African American man was unthinkable for most whites in the early years of the twentieth century. For working-class African Americans, Johnson's success became a source of immeasurable racial pride and inspiration.

Like many boxers who moved West around the turn of the century in response to reform efforts in the East, Jack Johnson began to make a name for himself fighting on the West Coast. By 1908 when Johnson was finally allowed to challenge Tommy Burns, the reigning heavyweight champion, in a bout in Australia, he was well known among boxing fans and the press. Many in the press supported the idea of Johnson taking on Burns, some because they believed that sport was sacred and should not be tarnished by racial problems in the larger society and others because they assumed that Johnson would lose and that white supremacy would be symbolically affirmed. Even the prospect of a Johnson victory did not trouble many sportswriters because Burns, a German Canadian, was a lackluster champion, and they knew that a Burns/Johnson bout would bring much-needed publicity to the sport.

Johnson's victory over Burns in the fourteenth round may not have caused as much of a stir as it did had it not been for his demeanor in the ring, his personal lifestyle, and his string of victories over white challengers in the year immediately following his title victory. Johnson taunted and belittled Burns, wanting to make clear his personal superiority, if not the superiority of his race. He celebrated his win, as he would after future bouts, with fancy parties and in the arms of white women, a fact that raised the ire of many whites. Johnson further alarmed racist whites by dominating the American boxing scene in the two years following his 1908 victory. The other heavyweight to gain some notoriety during this period was another African American man, Joe Jeanette. All of these factors combined to create a sense of urgency among white sports enthusiasts. Cries for the return of former champion James J. Jeffries reached a crescendo by the end of 1909.

In December 1909 Jeffries, who was promised significant financial rewards, finally agreed to take on Johnson. George "Tex" Rickard, who would become one of boxing's earliest and most well-known promoters, organized the fight. Rickard, known for his moneymaking prowess and for his willingness to exploit any advantage to sell tickets, billed the fight as a black-versus-white affair. What started out as an athletic event in a relatively minor and still widely criticized sport became front-page news and symbolic of tensions and hostilities that were tearing the country apart. Rickard's tactics may have raised publicity for boxing but they had also pushed racial conflict to the breaking point by the time Jeffries and Johnson finally met in Reno,

Nevada, on July 4, 1910. It took Johnson fifteen rounds to knock out the former champion, but the outcome of the fight was never in question (see chapter 4).

Not surprisingly, Johnson's success and the African American pride that it evoked caused many to begin looking for the "Great White Hope"—someone who could defeat Johnson and restore white supremacy. At the same time, Johnson's lifestyle choices, combined with a desire among many white leaders to find a way to get rid of him, made Johnson a target for criminal investigation. In 1913 authorities charged Johnson with violating the Mann Act, a law passed in 1910. The act, named for James Robert Mann, the Republican congressman who introduced it, primarily targeted commercialized sexual vice, but it was worded in such a way that any man who crossed state lines with a woman other than his wife and had sex with her could be prosecuted. Johnson, who had made many trips between Chicago and Pittsburgh with a woman named Belle Schreibner, was convicted by an all-white jury and sentenced to a $1000 fine and one year in jail.

Boxing historians point out that the prosecutors produced no hard evidence in the case, but that the desire to remove Johnson from the public eye and to quiet racial tensions outweighed the need to prove guilt beyond a reasonable doubt. Johnson, who was released on bond, ended up escaping to Canada and then moving to Europe. While pleased to have him out of the country, white supremacists would not be fully satisfied until Johnson's heavyweight title once again resided on a white man. Johnson, after spending two years in Europe, barely supporting himself by fighting second-rate boxers, agreed in 1915 to fight white challenger Jess Willard in Havana, Cuba. Willard, a 6'7″ tower of muscle, trained hard for the fight; Johnson, now pudgy and past his prime did not and was defeated on April 5, 1915 in the twenty-sixth round.

Johnson later stated that he had lost the fight on purpose in hopes of receiving a lighter prison sentence when he returned to the United States, but most doubted the truth of this claim. Willard defended his title in 1916 and then did not fight again until 1919 when he lost to William Harrison "Jack" Dempsey who went on to dominate American boxing in the first half of the 1920s, a period when the sport fully emerged as an acceptable form of entertainment for all social classes.

Other Weight Divisions

While much of the boxing world focused its attention on Jack Johnson and the heavyweight crown during this decade, other boxers fought for supremacy in the lighter weight classes. In 1909 the Queensbury rules had been modified to define eight traditional weight classes. Thus, the decade of the 1910s saw the implementation of the following competitive weight classes: Heavyweight—176 pounds and over; cruiserweight/light-heavyweight—175 pounds maximum; middleweight—160 pounds max.; welterweight—147 pounds max.; lightweight—135 pounds max.; featherweight—126 pounds max.; bantamweight—118 pounds max.; and flyweight—112 pounds. max. Like today, boxers typically made a name for themselves in one weight class, but it was not uncommon for them to fight in several different classes over the course of their careers.

In the bantamweight class, a Danish immigrant named John Gutenko distinguished himself throughout the decade. After spending his early teens in a tough, working-class section of Baltimore, Gutenko fought his first professional match in

1910 at the age of sixteen. After winning the fight with a knockout, Gutenko took on the name Kid Williams and began a career that included more than 200 bouts over a span of almost twenty years. In 1914 Williams, who stood only 5'1" tall, officially won the world bantamweight title with a decisive victory in three rounds over reigning champ Johnny Coulon. In the decade after his first title win, Williams faced top talent in both the bantam and featherweight classes and only lost seventeen official contests over the course of his career. Considered by many to be one of the top bantamweight fighters of all time, Williams was elected to the International Boxing Hall of Fame in 1996.

The featherweight division in the 1910s was dominated by Johnny Kilbane, a native of Cleveland, Ohio, who made his boxing debut in 1907 at the age of eighteen. Kilbane captured the featherweight world championship on February 22, 1912, when he defeated Abe Attell, a Jewish fighter from San Francisco, in a twenty-round bout. Attell had won the featherweight title in 1903 and, after losing it briefly, put together a streak where he defended the title eighteen times in a row. Attell, who was known for his use of dirty tactics, tried to hold off Kilbane in the title fight by grabbing his arms and butting him with his head, but Kilbane out performed Attell and prevailed when the referee called the fight in his favor. Kilbane fought 140 matches in his career and only lost four of them. He held the featherweight title from 1912 until 1923. No one in any weight class has held a title for that long without interruption or temporary retirement. Kilbane and Attell were both inducted into the International Boxing Hall of Fame, Attell in 1990 and Kilbane in 1995.

While he held the featherweight crown, Kilbane also went up against heavier boxers, including lightweight standout Benny Leonard, who captured the lightweight title from Freddie Welsh in 1917. Leonard, a New Yorker who turned pro in 1911 at the tender age of fifteen, defeated Kilbane in three rounds in his first title defense and then went on to defeat several additional challengers. Leonard and Kilbane were also challenged in the 1910s by the durable Johnny Dundee. Known as the "Scotch Wop," Dundee fought in both the featherweight and lightweight divisions during the 1910s before winning the junior lightweight title as well as the featherweight title in 1923. Over the course of his long career, Dundee fought 343 bouts, including nine against Leonard.

In the welterweight division, boxing fans in the 1910s were treated to one of the great boxing rivalries of the period between American Jack Britton and the British great, Ted "Kid" Lewis. Lewis won the world welterweight title in 1915, but lost it to Britton in 1916. Lewis regained the title in 1917 in a twenty-round decision only to lose it again to Britton in 1919 in a knockout. Britton then held the title until 1922 when he lost at the age of thirty-seven to Mickey Walker. He did not retire from boxing until the age forty-four by which point he had fought in a total of 344 bouts.

Golf

Despite a growing interest in golf in the United States between the late 1880s and 1920, the American game, particularly the U.S. Open, tended to be dominated by British players until 1910. Spurred on, in part by President Taft's interest in the sport and the press's coverage of his many golf outings, Americans began to take to the game in earnest in the 1910s and both private and public courses grew in number. The success of American golfers in major tournaments during the decade heightened fan interest and greatly increased the number of average people who took up the sport. According to one estimate there were 350,000 American golfers in 1913. By the early 1920s, there would be close to two million. With its emphasis on etiquette and its elite roots, the sport especially appealed to businessmen who could afford club memberships and who often used golf outings both as a distraction from work and as a vehicle for conducting business with fellow players.

In 1911, for the first time since its inception in 1895, an American-born player, former caddy John J. McDermott, won the U.S. Open title. Using his excellent iron play, he repeated the feat in 1912 and thereby ended British supremacy in the event, but his promising career was ultimately cut short by mental illness. Whereas McDermott and others golfed as professionals in the 1910s, most top American golfers in the early 1910s competed as amateurs. One important American golfer in the period was Jerome D. Travers from Long Island, who added a U.S. Open title in 1915 to his five U.S. Amateur championships. The following year, the Open was captured by another prominent American amateur, Charles "Chick" Evans Jr. On route to victory, Evans shot 286, a record-low score that was not broken until 1932. In addition, Evans won the 1916 National Amateur event, and this marked the first time that both tournament titles were held by the same golfer in the same year.

Joining Travers and Evans, in what some called the great amateur triumvirate of American golf, was the gifted Francis Ouimet, who actually paved the way for his compatriots by being the first amateur to win the U.S. Open in 1913. Considered one of the greatest U.S. Opens in golf history, Ouimet played at the Brookline Country Club in Massachusetts in front of at least 3000 American fans. He scored an upset victory by defeating two prominent British professionals in a dramatic, eighteen-hole, playoff round. It was also the first year in U.S. Golf Open history that a large number of entrants required tournament officials to schedule a qualifying round. In many respects, Ouimet's 1913 victory in the U.S. Open marks the real beginning of American golf as it developed in the twentieth century.

Social Class and the Rise of Professional Golf

While Travers, Evans, and Ouimet can be credited with strong roles in bringing American golf to prominence, it was another American golfer, Walter Hagen, who had the most lasting impact on the game. Hagen dominated golf in the United States through much of the 1920s, but he made his initial mark at the U.S. Open held at the Midlothian Country Club near Chicago in 1914. He won the Open that year, defeating several outstanding British golfers as well as his fellow American Evans, who was golfing as an amateur. It was not Hagen's victory, however, that was most significant. Rather, it was the role he played in helping to make professional golf a viable and respectable occupation.

Before Hagen, most top American golfers were amateurs and those who did play professionally were not only poorly paid, but they also were considered socially inferior to amateurs who often came from upper-class backgrounds and enjoyed the privileges of memberships in private country clubs. Given the paltry amount paid to tournament winners and the lack of product endorsement opportunities, pro golfers struggled in their efforts to gain some level of economic security and social standing. As an added insult, professionals were generally banned from clubhouses during open events. Hagen, a generally well-liked and respected golfer, decided to challenge these social strictures directly during the 1914 Open.

In what became known as the "Midlothian Incident," Hagen, acting as if he knew no reason not to, joined the amateurs in the Midlothian clubhouse and locker room. Noting the ease with which Hagen moved among the more socially elite players and wanting to avoid a showdown with one of the top golfers in the country, the country club failed to endorse its own rules, and Hagen effectively knocked down one of the sport's strongest barriers. Hagen continued to break through social barriers during the course of his career and revolutionized the pro game by turning to product endorsements in order to supplement low tournament earnings. Hagen's business manager, Robert "Bob" Harlow, made the most of his golfer's popularity to ensure Hagen's financial success through both endorsements and golf tours around the country. Harlow has often been considered the "founder of professional golf."

Hagen and Harlow were not the only ones pushing for the professionalization of golf in the 1910s. Several early professionals who, like Hagen, were interested in improving financial conditions for pro golfers and in building popular support for the sport joined together in 1916 to form the Professional Golfers' Association (PGA). The initial meeting to discuss forming an association was hosted in New York City on January 17, 1916, by Rodman Wanamaker, of the department store family. From this meeting an organizing committee was formed that eventually drew up bylaws and elected a first president, Robert White. Later that same year, the PGA began hosting its first professional tournaments with Wanamaker donating a significant amount of prize money. PGA tournaments, like most other golf events, were suspended after the United States entered World War I in 1917, but they resumed soon after the war ended. Several patriotic fundraising tournaments were held in 1917 and 1918.

No Time on the Course: Women and Golf

American women participated in golf from the time the game first came to the United States in the nineteenth century, but their involvement was limited by a number of factors. First, while golf, unlike many other sports, was considered an acceptable ladies' game and was often promoted by early country clubs as healthy, moderate exercise for men and women of all ages, women were not expected to play competitively. Rather, they were viewed more as occasional companions for their husbands or fathers and as adornments that would make club life more pleasant. In the early years, including the decade of the 1910s, female golfers were clearly considered women first and golfers second. According to golf historian Herbert Warren Wind, "The early golfers liked to find pretty women lounging on the verandas of their clubhouses, but they were not in favor of women playing the game" (Chambers 1995, 12). Throughout the 1910s, women golfers struggled to maintain their socially defined femininity while challenging the widely held view that women were not meant to be competitive athletes.

This point of view led to a second factor that limited the development of the women's game. While husbands, fathers, and brothers were happy to have women occasionally join them on the club's golf course, they saw no reason for them to golf on their own. As a result, women were often restricted from playing on club courses except during a very small number of hours set aside for women (Chambers 1995, 27–41). For instance, at the Garden City Golf Club in New York women could only play on Monday and Friday mornings, and they had to tee off by 11:00 A.M. At the Merion Cricket Club on Philadelphia's Main Line, rules prohibited any woman from playing on the course unless she could prove a familial relationship to a male member. These types of restrictions were not at all uncommon, and they severely hampered the development of the women's game.

In addition to social proscriptions and lack of practice times and spaces, women golfers, like their counterparts in many other sports, were severely restricted by the accepted female clothing of the day. Even competitive golfers wore long dresses over top of several petticoats. In order to see the ball before hitting it, women had to wear an elastic strap around the knees to hold their skirts out of the way and often elastic around their left arms when fashion dictated voluminous sleeves that blocked their vision. By today's standards it may seem silly for women athletes to maintain strict fashion guidelines, but for many women in the 1910s maintaining a feminine sense of propriety was extremely important. Female identity and fashion, both in and out of sports, would begin to shift fundamentally in the 1920s.

Despite the limitations, women did compete in golf in the 1910s. At the time, there was only one major championship for women, the U.S. Women's Amateur, but it drew a healthy number of competitors from around the country and large crowds of local spectators. One of the most successful competitors during this period was Dorothy Campbell Hurd. Originally from Scotland, she settled in the United States in 1909 at the age of twenty-six. That year she won the women's national championship in four countries—the United States, England, Scotland, and Canada. She repeated her win in 1910 and began to write a column on the women's game for *The American Golfer*. She offered advice to other women golfers and pushed club manufacturers to make and market women's clubs. Too often, according to Hurd, women golfed with their husband's cast-off clubs, which tended to be worn and too heavy for them to be effective. Hurd was one of the few women of her generation to score under 70 on a regulation course. She and other lesser known golfers in the 1910s paved the way for Marion Hollins and Glenna Collett in the 1920s.

Horse Racing

Prior to the 1910s, horse racing in the United States was not an especially lucrative sport for the owners. The purse money for races came only from admissions, which meant that it was unpredictable. During this decade, however, major tracks started requiring owners to pay entry fees for stake races which increased the prize money considerably. Races that grew in popularity during the 1910s included the Saratoga Cup, the Belmont, the Champagne, the Alabama, the Preakness, the Withers, and the Kentucky Derby. These races generated excitement within the sport and brought in more fans. At the same time, though, progressive reformers cracked down on gambling, which had a major impact on the sport and its followers.

Economics and Betting

By 1910, betting was a firmly established aspect of the horse-racing world, a reality that created widespread concern among reformers who sought to eliminate

Horse-racing racetrack, Saratoga, July 1913. (Courtesy of the Library of Congress)

gambling and its related vices. Most racetrack betting was conducted through bookmakers who paid a fee to track owners in exchange for the privilege to handle racetrack betting. Bookmakers, of course, guaranteed themselves a cut of the payouts before distributing the money. In 1908, concerned with the potential problems associated with gambling in general and bookmaking in particular, Kentucky legislators passed a law that prohibited bookmaking. A similar law was passed in the same year in Maryland.

Because Kentucky and Maryland were dominant states in horse racing, track owners got around the laws by allowing pari-mutuel betting. In this system, all bets are placed together in a pool and odds are determined by sharing the pool among all placed bets. As a result horse racing actually thrived in these two states in the early 1910s. Pimlico Racetrack in Baltimore, which was already considered one of the top tracks in the East by 1910, became a leader in daily purse distribution by the 1920s. In an effort to capitalize on the popularity of racing in the Baltimore area, several new racetracks were built during this period. These included Laurel in 1911, Havre de Grace in 1912, and Prince George (later Bowie) in 1914.

Maryland, Kentucky, and several western states also benefited in the first years of this decade from antiracing developments in New York State. In 1910 antigambling legislators with the support of New York governor Charles Evans Hughes passed an especially strict antibetting law that effectively ended racing in the state for two years. This was especially damaging to the sport because New York had a long and rich tradition in horse racing and boasted one of the best tracks in the country at Saratoga Springs. When racing was reinstituted in 1913, only Saratoga and three other tracks were able to begin holding races right away. In the second half of the 1910s, the popularity and stability of the sport grew in New York and around the country.

Great Horses of the 1910s and the Emergence of the Triple Crown

Three horses from the 1910s deserve special mention. Horse racing is typically dominated by male horses. This was certainly true during the 1910s with one notable exception. In 1915 Regret became the first filly to win the Kentucky Derby. The Derby has been run more than 130 times, and Regret is only one of three fillies to ever win it. The second victory by a filly did not come until Genuine Risk won in 1980. Born in 1912 in New Jersey, Regret was bred by Harry Payne Whitney, a successful American owner. She was sired by Broomstick, the leading sire from 1913 through 1915, and was out of the Hamburg mare Jersey Lightning. After racing lightly, but making a name for herself, in her two-year-old season, Regret began her three-year-old season with the Kentucky Derby. Picked as a favorite over the outstanding colt, Pebbles, she did not disappoint and led wire to wire. Perhaps most important, Regret's groundbreaking win focused the attention of Americans on the Derby and greatly increased its popularity. In fact, some have noted that it was Regret's 1915 victory that established the Kentucky Derby as an American institution. The filly finished her career with nine wins and one second in eleven starts, earning just over $35,000. She retired a legend and became a successful broodmare.

In the last few years of the 1910s, Exterminator played a major role in American racing. A gangly gelding who made his three-year-old debut with a win in the Kentucky Derby in 1918, Exterminator went on to race for eight seasons in more than 100 races. He won fifty of those races and became known for his stamina over long distances and for his ability to win carrying heavy weights. Horses who won were handicapped with more weight in subsequent races. Twenty times he won carrying more than 130 pounds, sometimes as much as 138 pounds. Exterminator had several trainers over his long career and won races in Canada and Mexico as well as in the United States. He amassed earnings of $252,996 before retiring in 1924 after seven starts as an eight-year-old. He retired to the stable of Willis Sharpe Kilmer in Binghamton, New York, and died in 1945 at the age of thirty.

While Regret made her mark by winning the Kentucky Derby and Exterminator impressed by racing successfully for so many years, Sir Barton earned his place in history by being the first horse to win the American Triple Crown. At the time, the Kentucky Derby, the Preakness, and the Belmont Stakes were not known collectively as the Triple Crown, but each was considered a premiere race. Given how closely together the races were run as well as their varying lengths, no horse had ever won all three in a single season. This feat, along with his five other victories in 1919, made him an easy choice for Horse of the Year honors. Sir Barton and Exterminator, however, were about to be eclipsed by the legendary Man o' War, who began his illustrious career in 1919 and went on to become one of the greatest racehorses in history.

Tennis

Like golf, Americans viewed tennis in the early twentieth century primarily as a country club sport for wealthy families on the East Coast. This was still largely true

Sir Barton, the First Horse to Win the Triple Crown

In 1919 Sir Barton, a Kentucky-bred, chestnut colt won the Kentucky Derby, Preakness, and Belmont Stakes to become the first horse to win America's Triple Crown, an honor that was not formally recognized in the racing world until 1948. Sir Barton had an impressive pedigree. He was sired by Star Shoot, an English stallion who came to the United States to stand stud in 1901 and who had been sired by English Triple Crown winner Isinglass. In 1912 Star Shoot was purchased by John E. Madden, who owned a farm near Lexington, Kentucky. Madden bred Star Shoot to Lady Sterling who foaled Sir Barton in 1916.

Madden raced two-year-old Sir Barton six times in 1918 with limited success and then sold him to J. K. L. Ross, a Canadian businessman, for $10,000. Ross employed H. Guy Bedwell as Sir Barton's trainer and Johnny Loftus as his jockey. Bedwell, who initiated a new training program for Sir Barton, decided on the Kentucky Derby as the colt's first test in 1919. Rainy weather and a muddy track favored Sir Barton who, like many of Star Shoot's offspring, suffered from chronic sore hooves. Showing speed out of the gate, Sir Barton led the race from start to finish and defeated his stablemate, Billy Kelly, and the favorite, Eternal. Four days later, Sir Barton bested Eternal again in the Preakness and then came back to win at the Withers Stakes in New York just ten days after that. Ross's colt completed the Triple Crown by winning and setting a new U.S. record of just over 2:17 for 1 3/8 miles in the Belmont Stakes. In a feat that would be unparalleled today, Sir Barton captured these four stakes victories over the course of thirty-two days. He was rewarded by being named the 1919 Horse of the Year, American racing's highest honor.

Sold to Audley Farm in Virginia in 1922, he stood stud until 1933, but showed only moderate success as a sire. He spent the remaining days until his death in 1937 on a U.S. Army Remount ranch in Douglas, Wyoming.

through the 1910s, but by the middle of the decade tennis was becoming more popular, and asphalt, cement, and clay courts, which were more accessible to average people, began to supplement the traditional grass courts. The U.S. Lawn Tennis Association (USLTA) governed tennis in the United States throughout the decade. In 1915 the USLTA championships were moved from elite Newport, Rhode Island, where they had been held for thirty-four years, to Queens, New York. This move symbolically began the transition from tennis as a sport for the wealthy to one that was adopted by the middle class and enjoyed by a wide range of fans. Because tennis's popularity at this time was increasing around the world as well as in the United States, the International Tennis Federation (ITF) was formed in 1913 to serve as a liaison between member countries and to standardize the game worldwide. Thirteen countries joined the ITF in the first year, but the United States did not join until 1923 when it became an affiliated member.

One player during this period who helped to raise the profile and popularity of American tennis was Maurice E. McLoughlin. Known as the "California Comet," McLoughlin took over the reins of men's tennis in the U.S. from William A. Larned, who had dominated the sport in the first decade of the twentieth century, winning the U.S. Championship singles division in 1901–2 and again for five consecutive years from 1907 to 1911. While Larned was a good all-around athlete and one of the "big three" to win the U.S. Championship seven times (along with Dick

Sears before him and Bill Tilden after him), he was not a particularly exciting player. Relying on a cautious serve and lob game, Larned rarely scored an ace and seldom ventured into the forecourt. He typified the moderately paced game of tennis as it was played at the turn of the twentieth century.

McLoughlin, on the other hand, brought speed, style, and a ferocious serve to tennis. He had developed his game on the public courts in California, and by 1910 he was starting to make a name for himself. When he brought his tennis to the East Coast and to Europe, he impressed fans with his unconventional approach to the game. Unlike most players at the time, "the Comet" followed his powerful serve with a rush to the forecourt and used a smashing overhead shot or a nifty volley to throw his opponent off balance. As his biography in the International Tennis Hall of Fame reads, McLoughlin "opened the eyes of the public to tennis as a demanding game of speed, endurance, and skill." He won the U.S. Championship in 1912, the first year that the champion was required to play through the tournament rather than just meet the survivor of tournament play in a challenge match, and again in 1913. He also played at Wimbledon in 1913, and, though he lost in the final to defending champ Tony Wilding, he thrilled British fans with his new style of play. William M. Johnston, another Californian with a pleasing personality, succeeded McLoughlin in the tennis arena by winning the U.S. Championship in 1915 and 1919 and by continuing to draw new fans to the sport.

If McLoughlin transformed men's tennis in the 1910s, Hazel Hotchkiss Wightman did much the same on the women's side. She too grew up in California and brought a unique style of play to the game. Over the course of her long career, Wightman won numerous championships in singles, doubles, and mixed doubles while serving as an outspoken advocate for women's tennis and as a mentor to younger players. The women's game was also advanced by the play of Molla Bjurstedt. A Norwegian who captured a bronze medal in women's singles at the Stockholm Olympics in 1912, Bjurstedt was the first foreign woman to win the U.S. Championship. She captured her first U.S. crown in 1915 and then won the next four straight years. By the time she retired from tennis in the mid-1920s, she had won eight U.S. singles championships.

Track and Field

When the modern Olympics were revived in 1896, track and field not only became a cornerstone of Olympic competition; it also took on a more central place in national and international athletic competition. Track and field, though lacking the publicity of team sports, especially baseball, was firmly established in the United States and in many other countries around the world by 1910. The International Amateur Athletic Federation was formed in 1912 to govern the sport. The decade of the 1910s saw many American standouts both in national competitions and in international events such as the 1912 Olympics. Several innovations in track and field were also introduced during this period.

America's long reputation for producing outstanding male sprinters can be traced to the 1910s. Since women did not compete internationally in track and field until the 1920s, the emergence of outstanding American women sprinters came later. The dominant American male sprinter in the 1910s was Howard P. Drew. Drew competed consistently throughout the decade in the sprints and lowered the world record for the

Hazel Hotchkiss Wightman (1886–1974)

Hazel Hotchkiss Wightman is the mother of American women's tennis. A lifelong advocate of the sport, she dominated women's tennis in the 1910s, winning sixteen titles overall at the U.S. Championships, including four singles titles in 1909, 1910, 1911, and 1919. From 1909 to 1911, she swept the competition in women's doubles and mixed doubles as well as singles. Wightman was also the key organizer behind the formation of the Ladies International Tennis Challenge between British and American women's teams. Better known as the Wightman Cup, this annual competition began in 1923 and was held until 1989. Wightman played for the American team for five years and served as its captain every year from 1923 until 1948.

Wightman's future tennis prowess never would have been predicted when she was a child. She was small and physically weak. In fact, it was her doctor who first suggested that she take up a sport in order to build her strength. She practiced hitting the ball against her home in Berkeley and then perfected her game on the courts at the University of California at Berkeley. She practiced first against her four brothers and then played against the Sutton sisters. May Sutton, who went on to win the singles title at the U.S. Championships in 1904, became one of Wightman's chief rivals. Together, they helped to shape the future of women's tennis.

Although Wightman only reached the adult height of five feet, she moved extremely well on the court and became known for both her strong volleying and her outstanding sportsmanship. She temporarily retired from tennis in 1912 after marrying Bostonian George Wightman and stayed away from the courts during the early days of her motherhood. She returned in 1915 to win the women's doubles and mixed doubles at the U.S. Championships, but she lost the singles title to Molla Bjurstedt Mallory. After 1919, when she won her fourth singles title, she continued to play for many years, but achieved most of her success in doubles play. This included Olympic gold medals in 1924 in doubles and mixed doubles. Remarkably, she won her last U.S. title in 1943 at the age of fifty-six when she and Pauline Betz Addie won doubles at the U.S. Indoors. Wightman was inducted into the International Tennis Hall of Fame in 1957.

100-yard dash on several occasions. In middle-distance events during this period, Americans were led by James "Ted" Meredith who won an Olympic gold medal in the 800-meter race in 1912. He set a new world record in the event with a winning time of 1:51.9. Meredith also helped the United States to win gold in the 1,600-meter relay and to establish a new world record of 3:16.6. After the 1912 Olympics, Meredith enrolled at the University of Pennsylvania and became a stand-out middle-distance runner throughout the decade. Among many other honors, he won a total of five collegiate titles in the 440- and 880-yard events between 1914 and 1916.

While the United States does not have the same strong tradition of exceptional male distance runners as it does sprinters, three strong milers ran for the United States in the 1910s. In 1913 John Paul Jones, a collegiate star who ran for Cornell University, established the first officially recognized world record in the mile run with a time of 4:14.4. England's Walter George, clocking a time of 4:12.8, had set a professional record in the mile in 1885, but this was not recognized as an official world record. In addition to Jones, the United States boasted two other exceptional milers during this period, Abel Kiviat and Norman Taber. Taber ran for Brown

Howard P. Drew (1890–1957)

Dubbed the "fastest man alive," track and field standout Howard P. Drew dominated the sport in the 1910s and began a century of great achievement for African American sprinters on the international stage. Drew first garnered attention in 1910 and 1911 when he won national junior championships in the 100- and 220-yard dashes. Drew qualified for the 1912 U.S. Olympic team and was considered a favorite in the 100 yard event. Unfortunately, he pulled a muscle during his 10.7-second win in the 100 semifinal and never made it into the final. The Olympic committee recognized Drew with an honorary medal and certificate, an honor received by no other Olympic athlete.

Howard Drew was born in Lexington, Kentucky, in 1890. His father, a Baptist minister, did his best to support the family, but money was always tight. The Drews moved to Springfield, Massachusetts, around 1900 and Howard began his track career soon after. According to Drew's profile in the African American Registry, he won his first race wearing homemade shorts and nonspiked shoes. He later fashioned his own spikes by putting six nails through the bottoms of his regular shoes. By the time Drew reached high school, he had become a national track sensation. His family's economic circumstances caused him to drop out of high school in order to work, but he eventually re-enrolled and graduated in 1910. After the 1912 Olympics, Drew attended the University of Southern California and excelled as an athlete and as a student. In 1914 he tied the world records of 9.6 seconds for 100 yards and 21.2 seconds for 220 yards. He also won gold in both events at the Tournament of Roses Track and Field Meet in 1914. Drew was one of several runners who lowered the 100-yard record during this period, but no one did it more consistently. He was clocked between 9.3 and 9.5 on numerous occasions.

Drew graduated from USC in 1916 and enrolled in law school at Drake University in Des Moines, Iowa. When the United States entered World War I, Drew enlisted as a private in the U.S. Army. While in Europe, he continued to run when he could and coached the Army track teams in Nice, France. He was honorably discharged from the army in 1919 and returned to law school. Although Drew was unable to make the Olympic team in 1920, he graduated from Drake and passed the bar exam in both Connecticut and Ohio that year. Drew, who married Dora Helen Newcomb and had two children, practiced law in Hartford, Connecticut, and became justice of the peace there in 1924. He died in 1957 after a long career as a lawyer and a civil rights activist.

University and tied Jones in the 1912 collegiate mile. Kiviat, a Jewish runner who competed for the Irish American Athletic Club, dominated the AAU circuit and in 1912 covered the 1,500-meter distance in 3:55.8, establishing a world record. The American team went into the 1912 Stockholm Olympics with three milers who had legitimate chances to win, but to their collective disappointment the gold was captured by Britain's Arnold Jackson.

The 1910s was a great decade for American high jumpers and pole vaulters. Not only did an American, Alma Richards, win the Olympic high jump in 1912 with a leap of 6′4″, but he was joined by fellow American and world-record holder, George Horine, who established the world record earlier in 1912 with a jump of 6′6 1/8″ and had improved it to 6′7″ prior to the 1912 Olympics. Horine's place in track and field history was assured by his development and use of the "western roll." Abandoning the scissor's-style approach, which required jumpers to maintain an upright position while cutting their legs through the air, Horine "rolled" over the bar with his body parallel to the ground. Another American high jumper, Clinton Larson, added to the new techniques available to jumpers by introducing an approach similar to the "flop" popularized by Richard Fosbury in the 1960s. As Larson approached the bar, he turned his body so that he would be back-to-the-bar and went over face up. He used the technique effectively and won the 1917 AAU high jump event.

As Horine and Larson revolutionized the high jump during this period, so too did Marcus Wright set a new course for the pole vault. He used a thirty-meter run-up, a prolonged swing, a single-hand release, and an arch position over the bar. Wright established the world record in pole vault in 1912 with a vault of 13′2½″ and held it until 1919 when it was broken by Frank Foss. Despite his success throughout the decade, Wright only earned a bronze in the 1912 Olympics. Fellow American Harry Babcock brought home the gold.

OTHER SIGNIFICANT SPORTS: AUTO RACING

The growing fascination that Americans had with the automobile in the 1910s carried over into the sport of auto racing. One of the most important events to occur during this period was the first running of the Indianapolis 500 in 1911. The Indianapolis Motor Speedway Complex was built in 1909 by Carl Graham Fisher, an automobile dealer and ex-bicycle racer. Fisher envisioned a track that could be used by automobile manufacturers to test the safety and performance of cars at increasing speeds while also serving as a site for occasional races between cars made by different manufacturers. Fisher and his partners, Jim Allison, Frank Wheeler, and Arthur Newby, purchased 328 acres of farmland outside of Indianapolis and built a 2.5-mile rectangular track. Sadly, the first race held on the track, a five-mile event on August 19, 1909, ended in tragedy as the track surface broke up resulting in the death of six people, including two spectators. This rocky start coupled with a few more disappointing events caused Fisher to change plans and focus on one major event per year.

In order to prepare for the first running of the Indianapolis 500 on May 30, 1911, Fisher and his partners had the original surface paved with 3.2 million bricks in order to improve safety conditions. More than 80,000 spectators, each paying a one-dollar admission, attended the first running of what was soon to become a great tradition in American auto racing. Forty drivers competed in the race, which was officially won by Ray Harroun in a time of six hours and forty-two minutes (average speed of 74.59 mph). While Harroun is listed as the official winner of the first Indianapolis 500, the results have been disputed. Some claim that the actual winner was Ralph Mulford, the 1911 national driving champion. Mulford protested Harroun's victory, saying that he (Mulford) had been given the checkered flag first, but that he took three extra laps just to be sure that there would be no dispute over his lap total. Mulford's claims were discounted and Harroun remained the official winner.

In some respects, Ray Harroun's place in auto-racing history was secured as much by his work as an engineer and designer as it was by his racing victories. In 1910 he joined the Marmon automobile company in Indianapolis as chief engineer. Company owners asked Harroun to design a car for the upcoming Indianapolis 500. The result of Harroun's work was the Marmon Wasp. Up to this point, race

Auto racing in or near Washington, D.C. (Courtesy of the Library of Congress)

cars were built to hold two people, a driver and a mechanic whose job was to monitor oil pressure and to assist in navigating traffic on the course. Harroun built the Wasp to hold only a driver, which meant that the car would have less weight to carry and could be streamlined in design. To help the driver navigate, Harroun invented the rear-view mirror. He also designed the car with a pointed tail and a stabilizer. After his success with the Wasp at the Indianapolis 500, Harroun went on to invent the carburetor and to develop a kerosene-burning race car in 1914 that became a mainstay on American tracks until the late 1920s.

SUMMARY

Although the 1910s cannot match the Golden Age in sports history that came to characterize the 1920s, the decade certainly saw its share of great athletic moments and milestones as it helped to establish athletic trends that characterized much of the rest of the twentieth century. One of the most important of these trends was a significant increase in the level of interest and participation among Americans, both men and women, in a wide variety of sports. Baseball continued to capture the American imagination throughout the decade, and football and basketball, the two other major team sports that generated widespread participation and large fan followings after 1920, began to take hold at the professional level in the 1910s. The shift from amateurism to professionalism, another significant theme during this decade, could also be seen in individual sports such as golf, tennis, boxing, and auto racing.

As in all periods, sports in this decade both reflected and influenced the larger culture. Progressive reform movements that characterized the early twentieth century were visible in several sports arenas—particularly in efforts to make football safer, to curtail boxing in many parts of the country, and to outlaw betting in horse racing. The rise in sports participation during this decade also reflected the full emergence of an industrial economy and the resultant increase in leisure time for many American families. President Theodore Roosevelt's emphasis in the previous decade on the importance of strong masculinity and his linking of athletic prowess to fitness for combat and leadership were also manifested in the 1910s. This connection was visible in the way that soldiers were trained for World War I and in the way that male college graduates strived to compete in the growing industrial economy. For women, the tendency to link athletic prowess with masculinity had negative effects as women athletes were often viewed as unnatural and as a threat to established gender roles.

Finally, sports in the 1910s, for better or worse, helped to define what it meant to be American. Within athletic clubs, urban settlement houses, YMCAs, and new public high schools, sports teams served as vehicles for assimilation and for community and national identity. In a period marked both by optimism and by uncertainty in the face of industrial growth, urbanization, and immigration, sports provided a means of social control and an avenue for promoting upward mobility, hard work, and competitive spirit as emerging American values. These values continued to be reflected in American sport and culture throughout the twentieth century.

RECOMMENDED RESOURCES

Print Sources

Chambers, Marcia. 1995. *The unplayable lie: The untold story of women and discrimination in American golf.* New York: Pocket Books.

Crawford, Bill. 2005. *All American: The rise and fall of Jim Thorpe.* Hoboken, NJ: John Wiley and Sons.

Gorn, Elliott J., and Warren Goldstein. 1993. *A brief history of American sports.* New York: Hill and Wang.

Gregorich, Barbara. 1993. *Women at play: The story of women in baseball.* New York: Harcourt.

Lucas, John. 1980. *The modern Olympic Games.* New York: A. S. Barnes and Company.

Peterson, Robert W. 1970. *Only the ball was white.* Englewood Cliffs, NJ: Prentice-Hall.

Riess, Steven A., ed. 1998. *Sports and the American Jew.* Syracuse, NY: Syracuse University Press.

Sammons, Jeffrey T. 1988. *Beyond the ring: The role of boxing in American society.* Chicago: University of Illinois Press.

Voigt, David Quentin. 1983. *From the commissioners to continental expansion.* Vol. 2 of *American baseball.* University Park: Pennsylvania State University Press.

Wakefield, Wanda Ellen. 1997. *Playing to win: Sports and the American military, 1898–1945.* Albany: State University of New York Press.

Ward, Geoffrey C. 2005. *Unforgivable blackness: The rise and fall of Jack Johnson.* New York: Knopf.

Watterson, John Sayle. 2000. *College football: History, spectacle, controversy.* Baltimore: Johns Hopkins University Press.

Web Sources

African American Registry. http://www.aaregistry.com/african_american_history/category/12/sports_outdoors. Includes information on many African American athletes from the 1910s including track star Howard Drew.

Chicago Historical Society. http://chicagohs.org/history/blacksox/joe2.html. Contains infor-
    mation on the "Black Sox" scandal and Joe Jackson, including several photographs.
Eastland Memorial Society. http://www.inficad.com/~ksup/landis0.html. Includes articles on
    the "Black Sox" scandal and Kenesaw Mountain Landis.
Jews in Sports Online. http://jewsinsports.org/. Uses archival materials from the American
    Jewish Historical Society to trace the achievements of Jewish athletes including Frank
    Basloe and Barney Sedran.
Jim Thorpe c/o CMG Worldwide. http://www.cmgww.com/sports/thorpe/photo.htm. This
    official Jim Thorpe Web site includes biographical information, career highlights, and
    statistics. It also has a nice collection of photos.
West, Elizabeth. http://www.eduwrite.com/baseball.html. Includes several Bloomer Girl
    postcards with captions and brief information on the early women's leagues.

Films

Eight Men Out. 1988. Dir. John Sayles.

CHAPTER 6

AMERICAN SPORTS, 1920–1929

Murry R. Nelson

OVERVIEW

The United States had grown to 106 million by 1920, and during the decade the population would rise to just over 123 million. The 1920s were a marked contrast to the decade that had just ended. World War I had been extremely destructive for Europe, but the United States escaped unscathed and was now, clearly, the world leader in economics and was almost as powerful as Great Britain and its enormous empire. With the onset of the 1920s two great social changes took place with the implementation of the Eighteenth and Nineteenth amendments to the U.S. Constitution, which mandated legal prohibition of alcohol for consumption in the United States (Eighteenth) and prohibited denial of the franchise (voting) on the basis of gender (Nineteenth).

Prohibition remained in effect for fourteen years, finally being overturned in 1933 with the passage of the Twenty-first Amendment. During the 1920s the consumption of alcohol actually rose as its distribution was no longer regulated by the government. Many people turned to distilling, distributing, or selling alcohol, thus making a large number of criminals in the American populace. Alcohol was brewed by some people who did not understand, or care, about safety in the distilling process. As a result many people who consumed this improperly brewed product died. The trafficking in illegal alcohol brought organized criminal gangs into the alcohol business. Such gangs were led by people like Al Capone, who made millions from such illegal businesses, but wound up in jail after being convicted of income tax evasion. Most alcohol was served in speakeasies, secret clubs that were hidden within cities and towns. Since it was hard to keep their locations secret because customers needed to know where to find the clubs, speakeasy owners often had to bribe police or public officials to "look the other way" and pretend that they were unaware of the presence of these drinking establishments. Such scenarios were carried out across the country, creating a whole new breed of "scofflaws," people who openly failed to follow laws with which they disagreed.

Though the public consumption of alcohol was illegal, the lack of sales at sports venues, especially baseball games, seemed to have little effect on attendance. Sports were entering what has been termed a golden age in the 1920s since people had peace, leisure time, and more disposable income. Spectator sports, especially baseball, horse racing, boxing, and college football, were the biggest draws and beneficiaries of the new, nationwide interest in sports.

The Nineteenth Amendment gave women the right to vote for the first time in federal elections. Some states had granted the franchise as early as 1869 when Wyoming granted women the franchise. Colorado followed in 1893. The motives of the voters of these states were not totally altruistic. Most of the West was very rough and undeveloped and there was a decided lack of single women. The entice-ment of being able to vote was seen as an inducement to gain a larger female popu-lation in these states.

Women had not been given the right to vote in the Constitution when it was first ratified in 1788. Women were not often well educated since only the poorest women would actually have worked outside the home. Women were often idealized by the ruling classes, but that idealization included neither education or decision-making. Basically, the society of the time was sexist, denying women almost every basic human right under the pretext of protecting them. It certainly would have been difficult for a woman to be successful on her own at that time, since society was not structured in a way to allow it.

As more and more women received basic education, there were more opportuni-ties for women to go on to academies and, for some, even higher education, though these instances were not usual. By 1900 most middle- and upper-class women had completed elementary school and were certainly capable of making informed deci-sions, at least as informed as many men who might not have attended school at all but were still allowed to vote because of their gender. When female suffrage finally was passed in 1920, it was not without a great deal of resistance. In 1920, the first federal election for which they were eligible, fewer than half the eligible women voted, and in 1924 the estimate was that one-third of eligible women voters had gone to the polls, as opposed to two-thirds of eligible male voters. The percentage of women voting slowly increased throughout the decade, particularly as women began to identify with, and be courted by, the political parties.

This initial reticence by many women to go to the polls was also seen in their reluctance to attend major sporting events. Of course, most men were attending such events with other male colleagues and, in the case of baseball, many came to games directly from their places of employment for games beginning at 3 P.M. Horse racing and boxing saw more women attendees, although women were initially barred from the latter events in many states because of the violence.

The election of 1920 pitted Republican senator Warren G. Harding against Democratic governor James Cox, both of Ohio. Harding promised a "return to normalcy" (though there was no such word; the proper word was "normality") and he appealed to people who had grown weary of the war in Europe and longed for a quieter time. Harding won in a landslide, with 60 percent of the vote, but he was not a very engaged president. He appointed some excellent Cabinet secreta-ries, but he also was largely unaware of corruption in his administration. Many scholars consider him the worst U.S. president and he died suddenly of a heart attack in 1923.

Harding was succeeded by his vice president, Calvin Coolidge, a former governor of Massachusetts. Coolidge was a laissez-faire president, that is, he didn't see any reason for the government to be deeply involved in the business of the nation. In fact, he said, "the business of America is business." Some link this view and practice to the resultant Depression of the 1930s. Coolidge was very popular and seen as a real populist, like one of the "regular" people, and he swept to victory in 1924 with 54 percent of the vote versus 29 percent for Democrat John Davis and 16 percent for progressive Robert M. LaFollette. Coolidge was known as "Silent Cal" because of his taciturn nature. In 1928 he chose not to run for re-election and former Secretary of Commerce Herbert Hoover became the third Republican victor in a row when he defeated Democrat Al Smith of New York in that year. Many Americans feared voting for Smith because he was a Catholic and they thought that American policies might be subject to approval or scrutiny of the Roman Catholic Church and its leader, the pope. This mistrust was still evidenced until 1960 when John F. Kennedy won the presidency.

The prejudice toward Catholics (as well as Jews and African Americans) was widely publicized and practiced by a number of hate groups, the most widely known being the Ku Klux Klan (KKK). The Klan had begun in the mid-nineteenth century, but had largely vanished until it was resurrected in 1915. At its peak in the early 1920s, membership was about 15 percent of the nation's eligible male voters, or about 4–5 million men.

The decade also had great technological changes, which altered the way people received information. Most specifically, the radio became a medium for citizens, with the first regular broadcasts during this decade. Radio helped transform many areas of American society, among them sport. The first radio broadcast was on November 2, 1920, when the returns of the Harding-Cox presidential election were carried on KDKA, Pittsburgh. Radio usage started slowly but accelerated astronomically in mid-decade. In 1926 the National Broadcasting Company (NBC) was formed through the connection of twenty-four stations. The Columbia Broadcasting System (CBS) followed in 1928. Congress passed the Radio Act of 1927, which established the Federal Radio Commission, which would create and police regulatory guidelines for broadcasting in the United States. Television broadcasting was first experimented in the late 1920s, but it would not be until after World War II that television would become a common broadcasting medium.

The radio became the medium of choice for many sports fans during the 1920s. The radio created new fans and increased casual fans' interest as play-by-play coverage of baseball, boxing, and college football became commonplace. Certainly the creation of the biggest sports heroes of the period was the result of the adulation by radio announcers, many of whom, like Graham McNamee, became heroes in their own right.

Automobile ownership grew tremendously during the decade and this influenced the construction of better roads, subsequently making it possible for Americans to be more and more mobile. Henry Ford's Model T was an assembly-line model that allowed few deviations, but drove costs way down. This made automobiles affordable to many families and the 1920s became the first automobile decade. By 1927 more than 15 million Model Ts had been sold in the United States. By 1929 nearly half of all American families owned a car.

The automobile allowed many fans to attend games more easily; the biggest beneficiary was probably college football. Alumni and other football fans could now drive to big games and return in the same day. The best examples were the enormous followings that Red Grange and the University of Illinois squad and Coach Knute Rockne and his University of Notre Dame teams inspired. Fans from Chicago, Cleveland, Detroit, and Indianapolis (just to name a few urban centers) now regularly drove to the games in Champaign or South Bend, backing up the highways for miles. New stadiums were built, reflecting both increased popularity of sport and the ease of access, such as the University of Illinois's Memorial Stadium, the University of Michigan's Stadium, and that of the University of Notre Dame. All were opened between 1923 and 1930 with capacities of more than 50,000 and were filled each football Saturday.

Still, trains were the most efficient way to travel any great distance. Railroads criss-crossed the eastern half of the United States; the northeastern quadrant had the most track and rail systems. Long-distance travel was dominated by the railroads since roads were not universally well maintained and commercial airplane travel did not really become established until the 1930s. Most airline companies were formed for and carried U.S. mail. Pan American World Airways began in the 1920s with passenger service, but that was limited.

Almost all sports teams traveled by train, which was far more comfortable than other modes of travel at the time. Train compartments were spacious and the food good. Players had room to stretch out and there were cars where they could play cards, eat, and smoke (which many of them did). Not until the late twentieth century, and the onset of charter or privately owned team planes, would teams begin to fly.

One of the greatest American heroes of the period was Charles Lindberg, who became the first person to fly solo, nonstop, across the Atlantic in 1927. His feat did not send people clamoring to fly to Europe, but it did show that long-distance air travel did have a commercial future in the United States and the world.

Cities had extensive trolley systems that linked much of an urban area and allowed citizens to travel easily within the urban confines to attend various sports events. Most immigrants lived in urban areas and many of their children became caught up in sports, often mystifying their parents, who had little leisure time for sports in their native countries and were unlikely to engage in those in the United States.

The U.S. economy seemed to be constantly on the upsurge during most of the 1920s. The early years of the decade saw job cuts and strikes, but as the 1920s continued, the economy grew, corporate profits increased dramatically, taxes were cut, the building trades boomed, and the forty-hour workweek was instituted. The greatest economic gains were by the wealthiest Americans. For the poorest workers, gains were minimal, if seen at all.

During this time sports stars' salaries rose dramatically against that of the average worker and some of the greatest stars like Babe Ruth were paid what were seen as astronomical sums. Ruth's $80,000 salary in the early 1930s exceeded that of the president and astonished the fans, though most did not begrudge the Babe receiving this enormous amount. Red Grange's entry into professional football also entailed an enormous amount of money, previously unheard of for a pro football player. Fans flocked to the stadiums to see these superstars who were receiving super salaries.

The collapse of the stock market in October of 1929 brought American prosperity to a halt. Unemployment rose from 500,000 in October to more than 4 million in December and it continued to worsen into most of the 1930s.

Arts in the 1920s were exciting and innovative. George and Ira Gershwin created hundreds of wonderful songs and musicals including *Strike Up the Band*, *Funny Face*, *Girl Crazy*, and *Pardon My English*. Of more renown were George Gershwin's fabulous *Rhapsody in Blue*, *An American in Paris*, and the opera *Porgy and Bess*. Irving Berlin wrote classic songs and Martha Graham produced creative dances. The Harlem Renaissance flourished at this time, which provided for a wealth of innovative African American art, music, dance, and literature. Langston Hughes, James Weldon Johnson, Paul Laurence Dunbar, and Zora Neale Thurston were the best-known writers, while jazz/blues greats like Bessie Smith, "Jelly Roll" Morton, Duke Ellington and Louis Armstrong began their careers. The first talkie movie was made in 1927, *The Jazz Singer*, starring Al Jolson. The Gershwins, Jolson, and Berlin were all the children of Russian Jews who had emigrated to escape the pogroms of Eastern Europe and sought the freedom of the United States.

Three sports dominated fans' interest during the 1920s: baseball, boxing, and college football. Horse racing, tennis, and golf also had some significant appeal. Both professional basketball and professional football were in their infancy at this time, but they had some rabid adherents.

One general comment on the media is necessary. Radio was new in the 1920s, but was amazingly common in most homes by the end of the decade. There were far more newspapers than today, especially in big cities, where there might have been five to ten daily papers, many of which had three or four editions printed per day. One of the most common sources of information, particularly providing images, was the movie newsreel, short films of various events shown in movie theaters with new films each week. Though the stories were short and sometimes a bit quirky, these newsreels were the only time that most Americans would have actually seen and heard moving images of politicians and sports heroes. Babe Ruth, Red Grange, Bobby Jones, Knute Rockne, top boxing matches, major horse races, and the World Series were all subjects in these newsreels. In addition, short films were sometimes made featuring top sports stars like Babe Ruth. These, too, made such figures more familiar to Americans, often more so than the president.

TEAM SPORTS

Baseball

Without a doubt baseball was "king" in the 1920s. The game had reached stability in that the sixteen franchises had been established for at least a decade, the World Series had become institutionalized since its onset in 1900, and minor-league baseball teams at levels from Class AAA to Class D were located in almost every town of more than 10,000 (or so it seemed) throughout the eastern United States and much of the western. The sixteen major-league teams were all in the Northeast, where the majority of the population was situated. This was also where the major U.S. industries were located. Teams were located from Boston to Washington, D.C. The southwestern limit was St. Louis where two teams, the Cardinals of the National League and the Browns of the American League, were established. The northwest limit was Chicago with its two squads, the Cubs and the White Sox. Major-league baseball was given extensive coverage in one of the newest and most popular sections of daily and weekly newspapers, the sports pages. Local minor-league teams were also well covered. Thus, it was easy for most of the nation's baseball fanatics (shortened to "fans" about this time) to follow the progress of their favorite teams.

Baseball maintained its dominance because every lad seemed to have a nearby ball field, whether it was a grassy field or a sand lot. Baseball was both a rural and urban game, though it would have been challenging to play the game in the squalid sections of many of the inner cities populated by the newest, poorest immigrants. Nevertheless, the game was popular in schools and municipal play areas and one that many fathers had played, so there was an intergenerational captivation with the game that could be shared in families.

All major-league baseball games were played during the day (the first major-league night baseball game was not until 1935) and the starting times were usually 3 P.M. Thus, most of the fans who could attend would have not been working class, but rather management or so-called white-collar workers, since they had some latitude in leaving their workplace early enough to attend a game. Men attended games in suits and white shirts, since most had come directly from work and that was the accepted dress for this level of worker. Women were not frequent attendees unless they were accompanied by a male; there were no restrictions as such, but sporting events were seen as not refined enough for women to attend on their own. Most women would have been at home tending to families or at low-paid jobs; there were simply no women in management at the time. Thus, it would have been unlikely that many "respectable" women would have or could have gone to baseball games alone. Seeking more business, many teams promoted "Ladies Days," where a woman was given free admission (and would have been accompanied by a man, who paid).

Ethnicity and Baseball

Organized baseball was segregated. It had not always been so, but no African American had appeared on a major league roster since 1889 when Moses Fleetwood Walker had played in the International League, then considered a major league (see chapter 2). Baseball did serve as a societal entrée for many white, first-generation immigrants from throughout Europe. Many played under assumed names in order to seem more "American" or, in some cases, to retain their amateur status for college sports. Baseball was a very assimilative sport, that is, there was less tolerance for diversity than in some other minor sports and this was likely the reason that players altered their "foreign" surnames.

Shut out of so-called organized baseball, African Americans formed and played in their own leagues, including a few major-league-level leagues, the Negro National League and the Eastern League. Both of these collapsed later in the decade, but in 1924 the first Negro League World Series was held with the Kansas City Monarchs defeating the Hilldale club of Philadelphia, five games to four. Earlier in the decade Negro League teams had played a number of major-league clubs in exhibition games after the regular season ended, but this was stopped by the new commissioner of baseball, Kenesaw Mountain Landis, in 1924. Games featuring white and black players continued, but the white players could no longer compete in their major-league uniforms and the games were, thusly, promoted as a particular Negro League team against a team of white "all stars."

Andrew "Rube" Foster was considered the "father" of the Negro Leagues. He was a fantastic pitcher in the early part of the century and then formed the Negro National League and helped form the Eastern League. Some of the top players in the Negro Leagues, such as John Henry Lloyd, Oscar Charleston and Biz Mackey (all eventually elected to the Baseball Hall of Fame), played for Foster, but then left his league to make more money in the Eastern League. The Negro Leagues were well covered by the African American press such as the *Chicago Defender*, the *Pittsburgh Courier*, and the *Amsterdam News*. Segregation in the 1920s extended to major- and minor-league baseball and led to the growth of outstanding Negro league teams. The development of a separate group of newspapers that drew mostly on African American readers provided the exposure necessary for the Negro Leagues to succeed.

Economics and Legal Issues

Players were not usually middle class, unlike most of the attendees of games, who were. Most players were working class, with few skills and education, happy to be paid to play baseball. There were exceptions, however, with a small, but significant number of players having attended or graduated from college. The owners had all of the power to keep players under contract and prevent their movements to other teams. Salaries were relatively low, just above that of a middle-management wage earner.

The owners' power was legally sanctioned by the U.S. Supreme Court in 1922, in a case that had been brought by a baseball club in the Federal League. This league had operated in the latter years of the 1910s before the National and American Leagues offered financial inducements to some Federal League owners to drive the league out of business and maintain the monopoly that the established major leagues had on players and player salaries. One Federal League owner, instead, brought a lawsuit against the National League under U.S. antitrust laws, claiming, essentially, that the major leagues were an illegal monopoly that restrained trade and led to illegal higher prices for customers.

In a case that would have impact for the next seventy-five years or more, the Court decided that baseball was not as much a business as it was a sport or entertainment, and the antitrust laws did not apply to baseball for that reason. Such a finding meant that the reserve clause, which bound players to one club until the team might decide to release the player, was not illegal. Player salaries were artificially contained for more than fifty years until the reserve clause was found to be an unfair restraint of trade. Even with that handicap, there were still a few players whose salaries rose enormously in this period. The most noted was Babe Ruth, the player credited with making baseball more popular than ever and whose name was synonymous with baseball excitement and accomplishment.

Ruth's emergence as a national hero came at the same time that the throwing of the 1919 World Series by members of the Chicago White Sox (often referred to as the Black Sox scandal) became known and led to baseball hiring its first commissioner, Judge Kenesaw Mountain Landis. Since sports have been played, there are references to observers betting on the outcome of contests. The early Olympics in ancient Greece were the subjects of betting, but that did not also involve what was the issue with the 1919 World Series, that is, players taking money from

Babe Ruth (1895–1948)

George Herman ("Babe") Ruth was born in Baltimore, Maryland, on February 6, 1895. He was a difficult child to control and his parents briefly placed him in St. Mary's Industrial School for Boys School at the age of seven and was incarcerated there from the age of ten until the age of twenty. There he learned to read and write and to play baseball, though he had obvious natural ability.

Ruth began as a left-handed pitcher and he was excellent. He was purchased by the Baltimore Orioles, a top minor-league team, in early 1914, where he excelled, before he was sold in July of that year to the Boston Red Sox. In nearly six years with the Red Sox, Ruth won eighty-nine games and lost only forty-six and he was one of the top pitchers in baseball. But it was his astounding hitting that was the talk of baseball and he began to pitch less and play the outfield more. In 1919 he went 9–5 as a pitcher, but hit twenty-nine home runs, an astonishing total for the time. The next highest total was ten.

In 1920 Ruth was sold to the Yankees by the Red Sox owner, Harry Frazee, for $125,000, the highest amount ever paid for a player. It turned out to be a bargain as Ruth led the league in home runs numerous times on his way to setting what was the record for career home runs of 714. He also compiled a lifetime batting average of .342. More important was the fact that Ruth led the Yankees to seven pennants and four World Series titles in his fifteen years as a Yankee. He was one of the first five players elected to the Baseball Hall of Fame in 1936.

Ruth also was the most well-known figure in sports and appeared in films, had his own basketball team in the off-season, and was famous for just being himself. He was a prodigious consumer of food, drink, cigars, and good times. In the early years of the Great Depression he had a salary of $80,000, more than the president of the United States, and his overall income was much higher. When questioned about this by a reporter, Ruth said, "I had a better year." He is still one of the most recognizable of sports figures, sixty years after his death in 1948.

---

gamblers to influence the outcomes of games. Baseball had had various players who were either known or rumored to have accepted bribes to "fix" games for many years, but this was the biggest, most complex plot ever known. The perceived sanctity of the World Series made the crime seem all the more despicable.

The case against the players was not fully investigated and brought to trial until 1921. Because of various errors in retaining evidence, the eight players were acquitted, despite confessions (some of which were retracted or "lost"). The verdict was not convincing to Judge Landis, however. A federal judge, he had been hired by organized baseball to provide order to a nearly anarchic enterprise, largely magnified by the Black Sox trial. Following the trial, Landis banned all eight players from organized baseball for life. The most well known was "Shoeless" Joe Jackson, who left the game with a lifetime batting average of .356, the third highest of all time. Because of his banishment from baseball, he has been barred from election to the Baseball Hall of Fame (see sidebar in chapter 5).

Baseball and the Media

As noted earlier, sports pages became an integral part of the major newspapers only in the early twentieth century. By the 1920s, a few sportswriters had begun to make names for themselves, enhancing the various sports through their reporting. Among the best known were Grantland Rice, Paul Gallico, Ed Sullivan, Damon Runyon, Ring Lardner, Walter "Red" Smith, and Alison Danzig. Runyon, Lardner, and Gallico went on to become well-known novelists and short-story writers in other areas besides sports, but their writing lifted the respect given to sports journalism. Sullivan went from sport reporting to "gossip"/entertainment writing (not a huge transition was needed), before moving to radio and then television as the host of a top-ranked variety show, which aired from 1948 to 1971.

After graduating from Notre Dame in 1927 Smith covered baseball and boxing. He wrote for the *St. Louis Star* (and its successor the *Star-Times*) and the *Philadelphia Record* before becoming a writer and columnist for various papers in New York City, beginning in 1945. He won a Pulitzer Prize for his *New York Times* writing in 1976 at the age of seventy-one.

Rice was more known for his college football coverage and as an early radio reporter. Radio was invented in the late 1800s, but commercial radio did not become cheap enough to make feasible until 1920 and the first station on the air with actual licensing was KDKA in Pittsburgh, which covered the election returns for the 1920 presidential election between Cox and Harding. The next year one game of the World Series between the Yankees and the New York Giants was broadcast; the following year the entire series was broadcast on two stations in Baltimore and Schenectady, New York. Grantland Rice was the announcer. Radio amplifiers were set up in the ballpark, so listeners could hear the sounds of the game and imagine that they were right there. By the end of the decade, every top sports event would be broadcast on the radio as 50 percent of all American households had a radio. The World Series was the most listened-to baseball event, but many major- (and minor-) league teams began regular broadcasts of the teams' games during this era. At first, it was feared that radio broadcasting would lower regular attendance at games, but, in fact, the opposite occurred. Radio made fans of more people and attendance rose during the 1920s.

Baseball through the Decade

The decade began with the Cleveland Indians and the Brooklyn Robins meeting in the 1920 World Series, a series most noted for the fact that Bill Wambsganss of Cleveland made the only unassisted triple play ever in World Series history as the Indians won the series in seven games. During the regular season, while at bat, Indians' shortstop Ray Chapman was killed by a ball pitched by Carl Mays. Chapman was and is the only major leaguer even to have been killed in a contest. His death was not an incentive to find more protective headwear for players, and batting helmets did not become mandatory for major-league use until 1971.

Beginning in 1921, the New York Yankees became the dominant team in baseball. Led by Babe Ruth, they won pennants in 1921, 1922, 1923, 1926, 1927, and 1928. The 1927 team is often called the greatest team of all time and the term "Murderers' Row" was coined to describe their hard-hitting batting order, which featured Ruth, Lou Gehrig, and Bob Muesel at the middle of a lineup that led the league in batting average, triples, home runs, and slugging percentage and scored 70 more runs than the next closest team in the league. They also had four of the top starting pitchers in the league and won the American League pennant by nineteen games, then swept the Pittsburgh Pirates in the World Series in four games.

Shown from left: Babe Ruth, Lou Gehrig, circa 1927. (Courtesy of Photofest)

Ruth and Gehrig were seen as the top two hitters in the game, one or the other consistently leading the league in runs batted in and/or home runs. Ty Cobb was just ending his Hall of Fame career, but still hit .357 at the age of forty to finish fifth in the league. Despite the Black Sox scandal being exposed in the early part of the decade, Ruth's mammoth home runs and the new power-hitting of baseball overall drove attendance astronomically higher, from 52 million in 1910–20 to more than 86 million in the 1920s.

The National League pennants were won by the New York Giants more than any other team of the decade (four), but the St. Louis Cardinals and the Pittsburgh Pirates were also outstanding with two pennants each. John McGraw, a short, gruff man, was the Giants' manager and helped fuel the New York rivalry between the Yankees and the Giants. Until Yankee Stadium was completed in 1923, the Yankees shared the Giants' home field, the Polo Grounds, from 1913 to 1922.

The National League was not without its heroes and great future Hall of Fame players including Rogers Hornsby (nicknamed "Rajah"), Paul and Lloyd Waner (known as "Big and Little Poison"), Grover Cleveland "Pete" Alexander, and Chuck Klein. In the American League, Walter Johnson (the "Big Train") was the top pitcher, and Al Simmons, Harry Heilman, and Robert "Lefty" Grove were also future Hall of fame players, among others.

Baseball was transformed in the 1920s from a game where singles and adept base running were the dominant mode to one where home runs became the key to success. In 1921 Babe Ruth hit fifty-nine home runs; the next highest total was twenty-four. By 1929 Ruth led again with forty-six, but the next highest totals were forty-three and forty-two. The game was more popular than ever, and baseball players, especially Ruth, were recognized heroes throughout the country.

Basketball

Basketball was a recent invention (1891), but by 1920 it was well established in colleges and professionally. Like football, there were significant differences between the quality of play and the fan base for pro and college basketball. Many of the professionals never went to college and some even eschewed the completion of high school. The result was a much rougher professional game, with mostly lower- and working-class fans thriving on the rugged action. College play did not elicit the same type of excitement that professional basketball did. Many newspapers would not cover pro basketball because they did not feel that their readers would find it appealing. For much of the decade this was true of the *New York Times*, even though there were many professional leagues in the region and the top pro basketball team was located and associated with the city, the Original New York Celtics.

The rules of the game were still in flux and court size, for example, was not standardized. Foul shots were taken by one designated player on a team, though this began to change in the 1920s. During this time, the professional game was

The Original New York Celtics, 1916–1928

The New York Celtics began as a local team in the Hell's Kitchen area of New York City and were mostly composed of Irish immigrants or their children. The name of the team indicated their roots. During World War I, the ownership of the team changed hands and the squad was transformed into a powerhouse that attracted the best players of the day. The Celtics' manager, Jim Furey, got the best players to sign exclusive, high-paying contracts with the Celtics, and they played as many as 200 games per season. The Celtics won almost every league that they played in, so they were often either kicked out or forced to leave because their success brought ruin to the league. They often played throughout the country as an independent squad, playing local teams or other professional squads following the same pattern of traveling, often called barnstorming.

The Celtics were led by a number of future Hall of Fame players. Johnny Beckman, sometimes called the Babe Ruth of basketball, the leading scorer in a game that had little scoring, was one of the Celtics from the Hell's Kitchen area. Nat Holman, was one of the rare college graduates playing professional basketball and he also was the coach at City College of New York (CCNY). He was known as one of the smartest and most fundamentally sound of the pro players. Henry "Dutch" Dehnert was a wide player with deft hands, who perfected a new play called the pivot play, in which he came into the center lane (then only six feet wide) and then received the ball. Teammates would cut by him and Dehnert would move the ball quickly, faking to some and delivering the ball to one of the cutting players moving toward the basket. The last Hall of Fame player was Joe Lapchick, who joined the team in 1923 as a 6'5" center, considered a giant at the time. In a game that emphasized winning tipoffs (one was done after every basket or made free throw and for tie-ups on the court), Lapchick was the master and helped the Celtics dominate play in a time when there was no shot clock.

The Celtics won two Eastern League titles, then won two American Basketball League titles, before being disbanded in 1928 because of their superior play.

played in a cage, usually of wire mesh, to both protect the players and make the game faster, since the ball was always in play, even off the cage itself. The cage had been developed in New York State in the early 1900s, but was phased out in the late 1920s. Retained, however, was the term "cagers" to designate players on a basketball team.

The Celtics were the dominant team of the 1920s, winning many league titles and playing games throughout the nation. They brought many regions their first opportunity to see the swiftness of pro basketball and they were real pioneers of the game. Traveling mostly by train, they would often play two games in a day at two different sites, usually winning both contests. They learned to keep games close in order to make sure that there would be interest in their games the next time they came to town.

Most pro basketball leagues were regional and many players played in more than one league since only the Celtics had exclusivity clauses in their contracts. Players were able to renegotiate contract terms with teams, sometimes on a daily or weekly basis. Pro basketball was wildly disorganized, but games often drew large crowds of more than 10,000 to armories or arenas where the games were played.

The Eastern League, mostly centered around the Philadelphia region, was the longest-lived league, lasting from 1909 to 1923 (then reappearing as a lesser league in 1925–26). Other top leagues were the New York State League, which ran from 1911 to 1924 (with a hiatus for World War I); the Pennsylvania State League, which ran from 1914 to 1921 in the Wyoming Valley area in the northeastern part of the state; the Interstate League, which moved its location and franchises frequently from 1915 to 1923 (with various stoppages), and the Metropolitan League, which went from 1921 to 1928, when it suspended operations for three years.

The first truly, national professional basketball league was the American Basketball League (ABL), which began operations in 1925 in nine large cities, stretching from Boston to Chicago. In 1926 the Celtics were "forced" to join the league because the league members would no longer play teams outside the league. The Celtics won the league titles in both 1926–27 and 1927–28, before the league disbanded them and the players were redistributed among other ABL teams. In what was their final season in the league, the Celtics went 40–9, with the next-closest league team having a record of 30–21. In 1928–29 and 1929–30, the Cleveland Rosenblooms, with former Celtics Joe Lapchick, Henry "Dutch" Dehnert, and Pete Barry, won the ABL titles.

Ethnicity in Pro Basketball

African Americans began playing basketball soon after its invention, with players in New York and Washington, D.C., the best organized and dominant in most play. Edwin Henderson, an outstanding player in the Washington area in the early twentieth century, became an outstanding coach and promoter of the game into the 1960s. The Harvard-educated leader died in 1977 at the age of ninety-three.

In 1923 Robert "Bob" Douglas formed a team that played its initial home games on the floor of the Renaissance Casino in Harlem and became known as the Renaissance Big Five or the New York Renaissance. By 1927 the Rens were the acknowledged top African American team in basketball and they became one of, if not the top, professional team of the 1930s. The top Renaissance stars of the 1920s were Clarence "Fat" Jenkins, James "Pappy" Ricks, Eyre "Bruiser" Saitch (also a top-ranked tennis player), Hilton "Kid" Slocum, and Charles "Tarzan" Cooper.

There were a number of excellent African American teams barnstorming during this decade, most notably the Harlem Globetrotters (actually from Chicago) who began in 1927 and rivaled the Rens for success during the 1930s and 1940s. In the 1950s the Globetrotters would become more "entertainment" than a legitimate team, after the National Basketball Association came into being and began signing African American players. The African American squads received excellent media coverage in the black press. The *Chicago Defender*, the *Pittsburgh Courier*, the New York *Amsterdam News*, among many others all covered the various teams in the newspapers' weekly publications.

In the 1920s there were many teams composed of players of similar ethnicity and the team names often reflected this such as the Brooklyn Visitation (Irish Roman Catholic) and the South Philadelphia Hebrew Association squad. The latter team was one of the top teams of the late 1920s and 1930s, chief rivals to the Celtics and the Rens. The SPHAs played in a number of leagues, but mostly barnstormed in the 1920s and perpetuated an early stereotype that Jews were good in basketball through their cleverness and sleight of hand.

George "Horse" Haggerty of the Palace Club holding basketball upside down with one hand. (Courtesy of the Library of Congress)

Basketball Transportation

Pro basketball in the 1920s was successful largely because of the U.S. railroad system. Most of the top pro players were essentially independent contractors who played for the highest bidder on a regular basis. They were able to do this because of the ability to get to the various sites of games swiftly and easily. Almost every town had a rail connection. The Pennsylvania State League, for example, was composed of cities located on the Pennsylvania, the Philadelphia and Erie, and the Delaware, Lackawanna and Western railroads, which went through the Wyoming Valley and on to Philadelphia, where lines connected to the Eastern League teams around Philadelphia. Heading north from Philadelphia, players could join with the New York Central or the Delaware and Hudson to get to New York City or beyond to the teams of the New York State League. Many players would meet in Grand Central Station in New York City and compare game salaries and destinations with their peers. This made pro basketball a seller-driven economy, in that the players had greater economic leverage than the owners, the buyers of the players' services. This would change by the end of the decade.

Some barnstorming teams, like the New York Rens, purchased a bus and traveled in that manner, beginning late in the decade. This gave them the flexibility to go to any town, even those not on rail lines. It also gave them a place to eat or sleep in case they faced either Jim Crow laws or hotels or restaurants that would not serve African Americans.

Basketball was one sport that attracted women early on, and not just as spectators. Shortly after the invention of the game, interscholastic and college teams were formed and women enjoyed the game greatly. Senda Berenson of Smith College created a set of rules that adapted the men's game for women's "more delicate" constitutions (see sidebar in chapter 3). Players had assigned areas on the court and could not go to other areas. The game had three zones and players could only play in two contiguous zones. The game became a six-person game with play at each offensive end, three on three. Over time, the playing on a competitive basis was altered to emphasize sportsmanship, exhibited at "play days."

College Basketball

The college game was different from the professional basketball game. It was not as rough and had a limited number of fouls allowed before a player could be disqualified. There were no national tournaments, but there were some top teams. In the Northeast, Nat Holman, the Celtics' star, was also the coach of the City College of New York team. CCNY was a top squad in the New York region, as was New York University, where Howard Cann starred and later coached. In the Midwest, a number of legendary coaches led top teams. In the Big Ten, Justin "Sam" Barry and his Iowa Hawkeyes won the Big Ten title in 1923, but Barry left at the end of the decade to coach on the West Coast. Everett Dean was a top player and coach at Indiana University, leading them to the 1926 Big Ten title. The dean of these Hall of Fame coaches was at Wisconsin, where Walter "Doc" Meanwell had a twenty-two-year coaching career from 1912 to 1934. During the 1920s, his Badgers won Big Ten titles in 1921, 1923, 1924, and 1929.

Because there was no playoff system (the National Invitation Tournament [NIT] began in 1938, the National Collegiate Athletic Association [NCAA]

Tournament in 1939), various teams might claim national titles because of strong seasons. The University of Pittsburgh, coached by Cliff Carlson, was undefeated in 1928 (21–0) and was acclaimed as the national champions by most writers and coaches. Pitt received similar honors for 1930. In 1923 and 1924 Forrest "Phog" Allen, another Hall of Fame coach, from the University of Kansas, led his Jayhawks to national championships, as proclaimed by the Helms Athletic Foundation. Allen was also a founder of the National Association of Basketball Coaches in 1927 and served as its first president.

College Football

By 1920, just over 20 percent of Americans were high school graduates and only 8 percent were college graduates. Nevertheless, college football was enormously popular with the nation's populace. People attended games and huddled by their radios to follow the action on Saturday afternoons. The game had nearly been outlawed in the late 1800s because of the high number of injuries and deaths on the field, but President Theodore Roosevelt helped push for needed changes in the game regarding equipment and rules and, by the 1920s, college football was more popular than ever. Many colleges had greatly increased enrollments following World War I and there was a parallel boom in new stadium building on a number of campuses during the decade of the 1920s.

The top eastern teams were in the Ivy League like Penn, Yale, and Harvard, as well as services teams like Army and Navy. In the Midwest Michigan, Illinois, and Ohio State were the top squads in their conference, but Notre Dame moved

Georgetown-Navy game, Georgetown bulldog and Navy goat. (Courtesy of the Library of Congress)

upward through the decade to take top honors in the region and the country. Georgia, Alabama, and Tennessee were top squads in the South. The University of Southern California did not begin football until 1922, but became one of the top teams in the country during the decade, going undefeated three years in a row in the early 1920s. Other top teams on the West Coast were Stanford University and the University of California.

Most college teams played within their own region, because of the time and money needed to play farther from their own campuses. Beginning in the early 1900s some schools began trying to extend their geographic parameters, but they were still limited by the fact that the only way to travel was by train and this meant more class time would be missed as teams traveled farther than they

Knute Rockne of Notre Dame (1888–1931)

The most famous college football coach of the 1920s was Knute Rockne, who was born in Norway and immigrated to Chicago with his parents when he was just five years old in 1893. Rockne's parents were working class and could not afford college, so after high school he worked for four years for the U.S. Postal Service in Chicago, saving money to attend college.

In 1910 he enrolled at the University of Notre Dame majoring in chemistry and intending to play on the football and track teams. He set a school record in the pole vault during his sophomore year, and became a starting end on the football team. He combined with his roommate, Gus Dorais, who was the quarterback, to set passing/receiving records for the Irish team. Dorais is sometimes credited with "inventing" the forward pass, but that was not the case. He and Rockne perfected the pass play, however, to such a degree that both of them received All America recognition and the Notre Dame team went undefeated for three straight years.

Following graduation in 1914, Rockne, who was a top student, accepted a position as a graduate teaching assistant in the chemistry department and helped coach the football team. In 1918 he became the head coach of the Fighting Irish. The first year he was coach, the team played only six games, losing one, but over the next six years Rockne led Notre Dame to fifty-five wins and only three losses, going undefeated three times and winning the Rose Bowl and being named national champions for the 1924 season. Over the next four years, however, Notre Dame went 28–12 and lost four games in 1928, the most losses in a season for an Irish team since 1905. There were some questions about whether Rockne had lost his coaching touch, but in the next two seasons Notre Dame went undefeated and was voted national champions both years.

Following the 1930 season, Rockne traveled to California to assist in the film production of *The Spirit of Notre Dame*. He traveled by airplane, stopping in Kansas City to visit his sons. He boarded a plane for Los Angeles, but it crashed in a wheat field near Bazaar, Kansas, on March 31, 1931. Rockne was just forty-three years old.

Rockne's overall coaching record was 105 wins, 12 losses, five ties, and six national championships. His winning percentage of .881 leads all college and professional football coaches. Rockne was popular because of his great record, but also because of his poor immigrant beginning, similar to so many in the United States. He managed to rise to the top of his profession and was seen as illustrative of the American Dream that anyone could succeed, no matter how humble one's background.

normally had done. One school that successfully expanded their schedule and, in the process, became the most popular school in the country, was the University of Notre Dame, led by their dynamic coach, Knute Rockne. With Notre Dame and the Big Ten schools like Michigan and Illinois, the Midwest became a real rival to the northeastern teams for football supremacy in the college ranks.

In the battle for better teams, amateur rules were often not followed precisely by many college programs. Professionals were hired to play, illegally, on some college teams and some students on the football team hardly showed up in their classes, belying the notion of "student athletes." George Gipp, the Notre Dame star, was one such player, but there were many since there was little standard regulation of college football. The NCAA had been formed in 1910, but it had a small staff and few rules, relying on individual institutions to police themselves honestly. It was during this decade that football coaches became stars themselves and most no longer had the additional duties of coaching other sports or teaching a class or two. The coach was only the coach and some were paid more than university professors or the university president, unheard of practices until then.

One of those coaches was Glenn "Pop" Warner, who began his coaching career at the University of Georgia when it had only 248 students, then coached at Cornell and Carlisle Indian Industrial School in Pennsylvania. Jim Thorpe, of Sac and Fox American Indian descent, who went on to be called one the greatest athletes of the twentieth century, was the star of that squad in the 1910s (see chapter 5). In 1915 Warner went to the University of Pittsburgh, leading them to thirty-three straight victories before being hired in 1922 to coach at a salary of over $5000 at Stanford University. He was still employed by Pitt until 1924 and could only help Stanford in the spring until his Pitt contract expired. His 1926 team went undefeated and he coached one of the all-time great football players in Ernie Nevers. He moved to Temple University where he coached from 1933 to 1938. Warner won 313 games and lost only 106, with 32 ties, but his greatest contribution was probably the youth football program that bears his name. He began this in 1929. Now over 240,000 players and 160,000 cheerleaders take part in these programs nationwide.

Economics of the Game

Some of the other highly paid and well-known coaches were Fielding Yost of the University of Michigan, Amos Alonzo Stagg of the University of Chicago, Bob Zuppke of the University of Illinois (often credited with inventing the huddle), Andy Smith of the University of California, and Howard Jones of the University of Southern California. The top coaches got from $4000–$7000 and many had no obligations other than coaching the football team. Veteran professors might have gotten as high as $4500 and the average annual salary in the United States, as noted earlier, was about $1500. Tickets for the games might run as high as three dollars, but most were less. Most of the stadiums that were built cost less than $100,000 to complete. Thus, a new stadium could be paid off within the course of a season. Players, of course, were not officially paid, but there were numerous instances where college players were hired by towns to appear in a high school game in order to ensure that the high school would win a game from a bitter rival. Some of the college players would also get $25–$50 a game to play for semiprofessional teams, usually playing under assumed names in order to maintain their amateur eligibility.

Geography of the Game

As noted earlier, most teams played within their region because of the time and expense of travel. Ivy League teams played within the league and would play some eastern independents like Army, Navy, or one of the liberal arts colleges that had a strong program, such as Washington and Jefferson College. The latter team, from Washington, Pennsylvania, played in the 1922 Rose Bowl, but by the end of the decade the larger universities dominated college football, forcing smaller schools to lower their expectations and recruitment efforts.

Most of the Big Nine (now Big Ten) schools played six games against other league squads, then two games against nonconference foes from the region, such as other midwestern state schools, not part of the Big Nine, like Western Michigan, Northern Illinois, or Ohio University. The same was true in the South, where most of the top football schools were still not affiliated with a league until the Southern Conference formed in 1922. It consisted of twenty-two teams, stretching from Virginia to Florida and west to the Mississippi River.

On the West Coast the Pacific Coast Conference (PCC) had six members at the beginning of the decade and ten by 1929. Leagues were changing almost from year to year, but the core of the PCC remained stable with Oregon, Oregon State, Stanford, California, Washington, and Washington State. The Missouri Valley Conference was based solely in Iowa, Missouri, Kansas, and Oklahoma with eight schools, but in 1928 that conference was reconstituted the Big Six with Iowa State, Oklahoma, Oklahoma State, Missouri, Kansas, and Kansas State forming that league.

One of the biggest exceptions to this regionalism was Notre Dame. They started their football excellence a bit later than other universities, becoming most prominent under Coach Knute Rockne. Most leagues were relatively set and Notre Dame did not want to get tied into a weak league so they remained independent. That made scheduling games a challenge and Rockne ended up scheduling games not only in the Midwest, but in the Northeast and Southeast as well. In 1926 Notre Dame traveled to the University of Southern California and began one of the most storied of intersectional rivalries, still existent today.

The Media and College Football

No sport received as much of a boost from the media as college football. Radio became the great communicator for the sport. Some of the greatest sports announcers were identified with college football broadcasts. Nevertheless, newspaper sportswriting was the most popular way to find out about college football in this

Knute Rockne in 1930. (Courtesy of the Library of Congress)

era. Grantland Rice often covered games of the U.S. Military Academy (Army) as well as Ivy League games and, later, Notre Dame. Rice was responsible for giving the nickname "Four Horsemen" to the 1924 Notre Dame backfield in an article for the *New York Herald Tribune* in reference to the Notre Dame victory over Army. Rice was interested in creating heroes for his readers and the 1920s had many of them. Besides Red Grange, the Four Horsemen, and Frank Carideo of Notre Dame; Benny Friedman and Bennie Oosterbaan of Michigan; Ernie Nevers of Stanford, and Bronko Nagurski of Minnesota were among the most colorful of the college stars of the era. They made for great copy for the eager sportswriters like Rice, Ring Lardner, Walter Eckersley, Paul Gallico, Arch Ward, Shirley Povich, and Red Smith.

The first national broadcast of a football game was in 1922 when Princeton defeated the University of Chicago. The Four Horsemen were soon joined by Fordham's "Seven Blocks of Granite," which referred to their strong linemen. One of those linemen was Vince Lombardi, a future Hall of Fame coach of the Green Bay Packers.

Harold "Red" Grange, carrying football in Illinois-Michigan game, 1925. (Courtesy of the Library of Congress)

Law, Ethics, and College Football

Many of the same issues plagued college football that dogged other sports, including gambling, the legality of players, and contract issues. Player eligibility was difficult to police because many teams operated out of the scrutiny of anyone in the college other than the football coach. Gambling seemed to be less common on college football games because the point spread had not been developed and "perfected" by this time. The "spread" was a number of points that seemed to separate two opposing teams. Gamblers set a point spread and those betting on the favored team would only win if their team "beat the spread." In the 1920s the betting was mostly straight up, that is, on one team or another, with no points given and that seemed to make football a less attractive sport to wager on for big-time gamblers.

The question of who was eligible to play was a thorny one, and it was addressed by different colleges in different ways. There was no question that a player had to be a student at the college for which he played, but the definition of an "eligible" student varied. Was one class enough to be considered a student and what happened if a student failed to pass that class or a number of classes? Who should determine such eligibility, if not the college's faculty? In some cases college presidents overrode the faculty and made decisions, often on the basis of economics rather than academics. Could a school be punished for having professionals on their roster, and who administered such punishment? In the midst of this discussion, a new wrinkle appeared when Red Grange signed with the Chicago Bears immediately after his senior season ended, rather than after graduating from college, which was the accepted norm. There was a great outcry about the notion of professionals raiding the college ranks, and the fledgling National Football League agreed to not sign college players until after their class had graduated, but this would have no effect on players who never attended college. The NCAA, provided with more enforcement powers by its constituent member colleges, tried to address the concerns of an overemphasis on football and the professional impact on colleges. Two of the biggest concerns were illegal recruiting and subsidies to college athletes.

Red Grange Scores Five Touchdowns, Four in the First Quarter, 1924

The date was October 19, 1924, a lovely fall day for football. In 1923 both the University of Illinois and the University of Michigan had been undefeated with records of 8–0, but, despite being in the same league, the teams did not meet that year. Both were undefeated when the two teams met on the third Saturday in October, but within fifteen minutes the game was essentially over. A crowd of 60,000 was in Memorial Stadium to see Harold "Red" Grange (1903–91), the star running back of the Illini, try to break through the rugged Michigan defense.

Grange was from Wheaton, Illinois, just southwest of Chicago, and he had worked in the summers delivering ice, often carrying fifty-pound blocks up two or three flights of stairs. At this time the electric refrigerator was quite new, having been patented only about ten years before (in 1913) and most people had iceboxes to keep food cold, but they required regular deliveries of ice. Grange became known as the "Wheaton Iceman" because of his summer job. Soon after the 1924 Michigan game, however, he acquired a new nickname, "the Galloping Ghost."

Grange took the opening kickoff on the five-yard line and returned it ninety-five yards for a touchdown. Michigan took the ball, but turned it over on downs, and the Illini got the ball back four minutes into the game. Shortly after that, Grange broke through the Michigan defense and ran sixty-seven yards for his second touchdown of the day. On their next possession, the Illini began another march, culminating with Grange sprinting fifty-six yards for his third touchdown. Just before the end of the quarter, at the twelve-minute mark of the game, Grange wove his way through the entire Michigan defense to go forty-four yards for his fourth score of the day. At the end of the quarter, the score was Illinois 27, Michigan 0.

Coach Bob Zuppke took Grange out for the entire second quarter, but he returned in the second half to score once more, leading the Illini to a rout of the Wolverines by a score of 39–14. The five touchdowns were more amazing because Michigan was one of the strongest defensive teams in the nation and finished the year with a record of six wins and two losses. The game was the first to be broadcast by WGN radio in Chicago, with one of the strongest signals in the country and the largest station in the Midwest. Thus, thousands attended the game, but likely millions heard Grange's feats as they occurred via the radio.

During the 1920s, then, a number of schools were often dominant in their play and the recognition that they received from the media. In 1920 many teams went undefeated, but Notre Dame had the most victories and was 9–0 in the regular season. The University of California finished 9–0 after defeating Ohio State, who finished 7–1 with this loss, in the Rose Bowl. (The other major bowls did not exist until the 1930s.) In 1921 California and Washington and Jefferson, who had finished at 9–0 and 10–0, respectively, tied 0–0 in the Rose Bowl. Iowa of the Big Ten, finished at 7–0. Many teams were undefeated in 1922, among which were Princeton, California, Iowa, and Michigan. The next year Yale, Illinois, Michigan, and Cal were again among the undefeated teams. In 1924 Notre Dame went undefeated, defeated Stanford in the Rose Bowl, and was acclaimed the number 1 team in the nation. The next season the University of Alabama went undefeated, including a defeat of previously unbeaten Washington, by a single point in the Rose Bowl. Alabama returned to the Rose Bowl after the 1926 regular season to meet Stanford. Both teams were undefeated, tying 7–7 in the Rose Bowl. In 1927 Illinois, Minnesota, and Texas A&M all went undefeated, but had ties on their records. Georgia Tech, undefeated, untied, and victorious in the Rose Bowl, was the top team of 1928. Notre Dame and Purdue were the only undefeated and untied teams in 1929, with Notre Dame voted number 1. The Fighting Irish refused all bowl invitations because of time away from campus for their students.

Professional Football

At the beginning of the 1920s, professional football was viewed as an inferior game to college football in many ways. It was seen as rougher, not as well played, and the players were seen as low-life reprobates, not the educated young men that college football claimed to produce. There was some truth to this, but was also more a stereotype. Pro football teams had begun in the late nineteenth century, mostly out of clubs, but an actual pro league began in 1902, and by 1915 a number of pro leagues had come and gone. The Canton Bulldogs made some headlines in 1915 by signing Jim Thorpe to their team, but in 1919 the long-established Ohio League (begun in 1903) folded and the 1920s began with the birth of the new American Professional Football Association (APFA). The teams were drawn from the old Ohio League cities, plus Illinois, Indiana, Wisconsin, Michigan, and New York. Fourteen teams began the season and the Akron Pros were voted league champion after the end of the season. After the 1921 season, the league changed its name to the National Football League.

Initially, most of the APFA and NFL games were played on the weekends and players held other jobs. Practice time was after work and equipment was not great. The league(s) were barely holding on, hoping that professional football would catch on with a larger segment of the population. Despite the disdain with which some people viewed pro football in comparison to college football, a surprisingly high number of pros had attended college. The 1920s were economically a time of growth and it was hoped that some of the "discretionary" money that Americans now had would be spent on pro football. The league had as its first president Jim Thorpe, the Carlisle Indian School football star and Olympic decathlon champion, who was chosen for his name recognition, not necessarily for his administrative ability.

Ethnicity in the 1920s NFL

The 1920 season saw Akron proclaimed league champion and they were led by Fritz Pollard, the first African American in the league. Pollard had starred at college at Brown University; the next year he was joined by Paul Robeson, who had starred at Rutgers. They were a powerful running tandem. In 1923 Robeson played for the Milwaukee franchise, before leaving pro football for endeavors in musical theatre and opera. Pollard became the co-coach of the Akron Pros for the 1921 season, but remained an active player. He remained with Akron through that season, then went to Milwaukee for 1922, Hammond in 1923 and 1925, and back to Akron as player coach before the franchise folded. In 1928 Pollard organized and coached an independent all–African American team, the Chicago Black Hawks, a team that played into the 1930s. Pollard was inducted into the Professional Football Hall of Fame in 2005.

By 1926 there were five African Americans in top pro football leagues, but pressure from some NFL management, most notably the New York Giants, convinced teams to no longer sign black players because of the fear that they would "disrupt the game." There was only one, Duke Slater of the Chicago Cardinals, in 1927, and beginning in 1934 the NFL executed an unofficial ban on black players, which was not lifted until 1946.

In 1922 the Marion (Ohio) squad was composed of all Native Americans, led by Jim Thorpe, Joe Guyon, and Pete Calac, all former teammates at the Carlisle Indian School. The players were getting older and only compiled a record of two wins and six losses, but they were highly popular, and came out on the field wearing war bonnets and buckskins over their football pants. The next year, the Oorang Indians went only 1–10 and disbanded. The three Carlisle players remained in the league on different teams.

The Seasons of the 1920s

Overall, pro football had a small but loyal following, which meant that most clubs did not make a profit, but managed to eke out an existence, constantly hoping that things would improve. That would not happen until after World War II, however. The new NFL had seventeen teams at the beginning of 1922 and twenty teams in 1923, but the number of league games being played varied. The Canton Bulldogs won the title in both 1922 and 1923. The Chicago Bears were one of the few teams to make a profit and, after the 1922 season, the Green Bay Packers were in financial straits. Their coach and quarterback decided to sell shares to the citizens of Green Bay, who responded eagerly, purchasing shares at five dollars and getting a box seat in addition. The Packers remain the only community-owned professional team today.

In 1924 the Canton squad moved to Cleveland because of money problems and won the championship, once again, as the Cleveland Bulldogs. At the end of the 1925 college season, the Chicago Bears signed Red Grange of Illinois to their team and he finished the season with the Bears, only the second-best team in Chicago, as the Cardinals compiled the best record in the league.

In 1927 the league was reduced to twelve teams, because of the continual financial losses, and in 1928 the number of teams was reduced further, to ten. The circuit increased back to twelve in 1929 and the Packers went 12–0 to secure the league title. Led by halfback Johnny Blood and defensive lineman Cal Hubbard (later a respected major league umpire), the Packer players usually played sixty minutes a game, even though they sometimes played twice a week. Pro football in the 1920s was not a game for the faint of heart!

Professional Hockey

The National Hockey League (NHL) was formed and began play in 1917 so the league was in its earliest years during the 1920s. Unlike the other major professional leagues in the United States during that period, the NHL was relatively small and largely Canadian. Not until 1924 did an American team (the Boston Bruins) enter the league, and they were joined by the New York Americans and the Pittsburgh Pirates in 1925. In 1926 the NHL expanded to ten teams with the addition of the New York Rangers, the Chicago Blackhawks, and the Detroit Cougars. The league remained at ten teams, in two sections of five, until 1931. American interest in the league was minimal except in the franchise cities of New York, Boston, Chicago, Detroit, and Pittsburgh. Even there, coverage was not extensive. Players were almost all Canadian so there was little "hometown" identification for local American fans.

The Olympic Games of the 1920s

The modern Olympic movement was begun in the latter part of the nineteenth century and finally culminated in the first modern Games, held in Athens in 1896. Eight nations, seven from Europe, sent teams to the Games. Twenty-nine nations participated in the 1920 Olympiad, held in Antwerp, Belgium, with less than a year to really prepare. There had been a hiatus from the four-year cycle because of World War I; the Games had last been held in 1912. There was great excitement in the athletic world with the announcement in 1919 that the Games would be held, but preparation was rather impromptu. Finland was competing for the first time as a completely independent nation, having gained its independence from Sweden in 1917. The Finns won thirty-four medals, fourth highest behind the United States, Great Britain, and Sweden. Paavo Nurmi of Finland won the 10K race and the 10K cross-country race (no longer held). A. G. Hill of Great Britain also won two gold medals in middle-distance races (800 and 1500 meters). Charlie Paddock of the United States won the 100-meter race, giving him the title of world's fastest man, with American winners in seven other track and field events.

Duke Kahanamoku of Hawaii and Norman Ross of Chicago won gold in swimming, Ross with three, Kahanamoku two. American women swept the swim sprints, led by Etheda Bleibtrey, as well as the fancy diving events, and the Americans were strong in shooting events, winning eight golds there and numerous other medals. The American press provided minimal coverage of the Games and there was far less overall publicity for winners than today. Most of the winners returned to regular jobs (if they hadn't lost them by competing and being away so long). There was little coverage of the athletes upon their return to the United States other than in their respective hometown newspapers.

Olympic athletes were true amateurs and any of them who made any money on being an Olympic athlete lost his or her amateur standing and was considered a professional. This made them ineligible to compete in further amateur events, which, of course, included the Olympics. This was true of athletes in all sports and nations, so most of these athletes were happy to find jobs that allowed them some flexibility to train for their events. Unlike today, however, when athletes train every day, all year round, most of these athletes just trained "in season" each year.

In 1924 there were two Olympic Games, the Summer Games of Paris and, for the first time, Winter Games, held in Chamonix, France. The Winter Games were almost exclusively European nations and the United States and Canada, among the sixteen competing countries. At the Winter Games, the United States won a total of four medals and finished fifth in medal competition, which was dominated by Norway and Finland. There were only sixteen events. There was little interest in the Games in the United States.

The Summer Games in Paris, by contrast, had 126 events, 44 countries competing, and over 3,000 athletes. The U.S. team dominated in the games with Finland, France, and Great Britain next highest in medals, but far behind the U.S. total of forty-five gold medals and ninety-nine total medals. The increased number of nations, the longer time for planning, and the increased attention by the American media made some Olympic winners American and/or world heroes. The increased media coverage still pales by comparison to today's multimedia and, often, live or tape delay broadcasts. Though coverage increased, it rarely, if ever, got off the sports pages to the first page of the papers.

The biggest star of the Games was Paavo Nurmi, the "Flying Finn," who won four gold medals in track at various long distances. American track and field results did have ten gold medal winners (one gold was shared in the pole vault), but no American star emerged in this area. As a team, the U.S. men took first and second in the broad (now long) jump, the high jump, the shot put, the hammer throw, the 200 meter, and the decathlon. Johnny Weissmuller of Chicago took gold medals in both the 100- and 400-meter freestyle swimming events. In the 100, the United States had a sweep with Duke Kahanamoku second and Sam Kahanamoku third. In all, the United States took thirteen gold medals in men's and women's swimming and diving. Helen Wills and Vince Richards of the United States took gold medals in singles tennis as well as combining with others to win the men's and women's doubles titles.

The Americans returned directly after the Games to welcomes in New York and some other smaller celebrations, but most returned to their training or their jobs with little fanfare. Being an Olympic hero was not yet a stepping-stone to fortune, and fame seemed rather fleeting.

The final Olympic Games of the decade were held in 1928. The Winter Olympics were in St. Moritz, Switzerland, and again American impact at the Games and interest at home were minimal. Twenty-five nations and 464 athletes competed, a marked increase from Chamonix four years earlier, but there were only fourteen events. Surprisingly, the United States took gold medals in one- and four-man bobsleds and totaled six medals (four in bobsleds) to finish second in medal totals to Norway's fifteen. Still, the U.S. population hardly noticed.

By contrast, the 1928 Games in Amsterdam were much better covered and there was increased interest in the United States and worldwide. There had been strong consideration of awarding the Games to Los Angeles, but finally, that city was awarded the 1932 Games. Countries from South America (Argentina, Chile,

Johnny Weissmuller (1904–1984)

Born in Hungary (though today it is Rumania) in 1904, Johnny Weissmuller and his parents moved to the United States when he was seven months old. They lived briefly in Windber, Pennsylvania, before settling in Chicago where Johnny began his swimming career at the age of fifteen. In 1924 Weissmuller was chosen for the U.S. Olympic team, although he did not have American citizenship. He and his younger brother (who was born in the United States) essentially traded identities and birth-dates in order to make Johnny eligible for the Olympic team.

Johnny Weissmuller was recognized as an American hero after winning five gold medals in two Olympic Games. He also held fifty-two American swimming championships at various distances from 1921 to 1928. He is credited with inventing the American crawl swimming stroke. Following the 1928 Games, Weissmuller signed an endorsement contract with BVD, manufacturer of swimsuits and men's underwear. He was paid almost $200 per week, a princely sum in the late 1920s. He also appeared in two motion pictures. In 1931 Weissmuller was asked to play the role of Tarzan in the filmed version of Edgar Rice Burroughs' books, but in initially refused. Following some negotiations, he signed a contract for a beginning salary of $250 a week that rose to $2000 per week. This was in the early years of the Great Depression and was one of the largest salaries in the nation.

In 1932 *Tarzan the Ape Man* was released, with Weissmuller as the lead and Maureen O'sullivan as "Jane," his "mate." Weissmuller reprised the role through sixteen years of filming. Tarzan swam, swung on vines, and dived off cliffs and Weissmuller was the man to play such a role. Following his Tarzan career, he made films and a syndicated television series as *Jungle Jim*. The series was shown for many years after its production in 1955.

Weissmuller was the founding chairman of the International Swimming Hall of Fame in Fort Lauderdale, Florida, and was named to the American Olympic Hall of Fame. He was also voted the greatest swimmer of the first half of the twentieth century and died in 1984 at the age of seventy-nine.

Uruguay), Africa (Egypt, South Africa), Asia (Japan, Philippines, India), and Australia/New Zealand competed and won medals. The U.S. victories now were seen as truer world victories, rather than just European and North American triumphs. And the United States did, indeed, triumph in the Amsterdam Games with twenty-two gold medals and fifty-six total medals. Germany, now dramatically recovered from the devastation of the world war, had thirty-one medals, including ten gold.

There were repeat winners at these Games, most notably Paavo Nurmi, who took another gold and a silver medal to end his fabulous Olympic career. Following the Olympics, Nurmi toured Europe and the United States, but was deemed a professional for taking too much money for his expenses in Germany. He and the Finns appealed, but he was denied and was unable to compete in the 1932 Games. He finished his Olympic career with nine gold and three silver medals in twelve events. Another repeat winner was Johnny Weissmuller, who won the 100-meter freestyle, once again.

The continued American success at the Olympic Games and the anticipation of hosting the 1932 Games created greater interest in the Olympic Games in the

United States, but the amateur restrictions made it hard for the athletes and the American public to maintain long lasting relationships.

One great feat that was connected, somewhat, to the swimming of the Olympics was long-distance swims. The most noted of the decade was the swimming of the English Channel. This was accomplished, initially, in 1895, but no woman mastered the distance until 1926. Gertrude Ederle, winner of two bronze medals for the 100- and 400-meter freestyles and a gold medal as part of a victorious U.S. relay team at the 1924 Paris Games, swam from France to England in 14 hours, 30 minutes, a record for men or women. Ederle, a native of New York City, was welcomed home with a tickertape parade on Broadway in New York.

SPORTS FOR INDIVIDUAL COMPETITORS
Boxing

The "manly art of boxing," seemingly ingrained in many cultures and introduced in the original Olympics in about 688 BCE, adopted the Marquis of Queensbury rules in the late 1800s and made the sport less violent. In 1892 gloves were first used in a heavyweight fight and have been standard equipment ever since. There are at least eleven weight classes, which negate the different weights that opponents might have and make fights decided upon skill rather than size. Boxing was done at various levels, both in an organized and less organized manner. Mining camps, lumber camps, and other "rough" places often had contests for the amusement of the workers, who were interested in demonstrations of strength and skill. In cities, boxing was often engaged in by lower-class or working-class youngsters, and it could serve as a way to gain fame and wealth. Until the 1920s, many states did not allow organized bouts because they deemed it too dangerous.

Ethnicity, Sexism, and Boxing

Many ethnic groups were prominent in boxing in the 1920s, most notably lower-class groups, often more recent immigrants. At the lower weight classes Italians and Jews were very prominent. Many of these fighters were from inner-city neighborhoods and the young men fought on the street from their early years. Such fights would have been especially common where there was some ethnic "overlap" and more than one ethnic group "claimed" the neighborhood. This still occurs today, but at that time fists predominated, rather than guns.

One of the greatest fighters was Benny Leonard, whose actual family name was Leiner. The son of very observant Jews, he used the name Leonard to prevent his parents from finding out about his boxing. Eventually they did so, anyway, and they were hurt and perplexed, noting that Jews were scholars rather than fighters. Nevertheless, Leonard was amazingly successful. He became the lightweight champion of the world in 1917 and held the crown until 1923. Except for a disqualification in 1922, Leonard did not lose a fight for twenty years from 1912 to 1932. He had retired in 1925, but returned to the ring in 1932 after losing his fortune in the stock market crash of 1929.

Many of Leonard's top rivals were Irish, indicative of the great Jewish-Irish rivalry in boxing at the time. Despite not being a recent immigrant group, the Irish were often discriminated against in many ways into the twentieth century, and their social progress was often impeded by this discrimination. In boxing, however, there was no such prejudice and the Irish were also dominant in heavier weights.

From the time of the first American heavyweight world champion, John L. Sullivan, who was champ from 1888 to 1892, Irishmen dominated the weight class. Jack Dempsey (1919–26) and Gene Tunney (1926–28) were the world champions in this decade. (The championship was open after Tunney's retirement in 1928, until 1930.)

Dempsey came out of the West and was "discovered" by promoter George L. "Tex" Rickard fighting in mining towns in Colorado. Before being a fighter, Dempsey, who was from a large Mormon family (ten brothers and sisters) in Manassa, Colorado, was a hobo who found work as a peach picker and a ditch digger, among a number of low-paying jobs. He defeated Jess Willard in 1919 for the heavyweight championship and became an instant hero, particularly to the working class. His rise to fame and fortune made it seem possible for many of the downtrodden, uneducated masses to hope for similar success. Dempsey was a bruising 6'1" and weighed 190 pounds, but could take a punch; he was only knocked out once in his sixty fights, and lost seven total fights.

Tunney, by contrast, from New York City, was a nondrinker, quite articulate, and a college graduate. He was also from a working-class family, but served in World War I as a Marine, and also became light-heavyweight champion of the American Forces in Europe. He fought as a light heavyweight upon his return,

---

The Long Count, Tunney vs. Dempsey, 1927

On September 22, 1927, heavyweight boxing champion Gene Tunney met former champion Jack Dempsey in a rematch of their fight in 1926 in which Tunney upset Dempsey, who had reigned as heavyweight champion of the world for seven years. The rematch, held in Chicago's Soldier Field, drew 105,000 fans to the stadium on Chicago's lakefront. Tunney, an articulate ex-Marine who had fought in World War I, was from New York City, while Dempsey was a rough fighter from the mining camps of the West who had captured the heavyweight title at twenty-four and was still seen as the hardest puncher in boxing, now age thirty-two, though he had slowed a bit.

The fight was scheduled for ten rounds, and the first six were largely controlled by the champion. Then, in the seventh round, Dempsey floored Tunney with a combination of punches that had Tunney clinging to the ropes. Dempsey, rather than retreating to a neutral corner, as is required by the rules, hovered nearby, and the referee kept signaling for him to retreat, yet failing to begin the count on Tunney. After at least five seconds, Dempsey crossed the ring and the referee, Dave Barry, began the count. Given the extra time to recover, Tunney was able to right himself and rose at the count of nine to continue the fight, which he then won in ten rounds.

The fight was heard by millions on the radio and the exciting account, including announcer Graham McNamee's pleading for Dempsey to go to a neutral corner, made Dempsey a tragic hero, and this fight one of the most famous in history.

Dempsey opened a restaurant across from Madison Square Garden in 1935 and it remained open until 1974, keeping Dempsey's name and memory in the public eye for fifty more years.

winning the world title in 1922, then losing it to a middleweight Harry Greb. He then defeated Greb four times in very bloody contests. In 1926 he decided to move up to heavyweight and fought Dempsey, defeating him twice before retiring from the ring in 1928 with a record of sixty-five victories, one loss, one draw, and forty-seven knockouts.

Racism in boxing made it difficult for African American fighters to compete for world titles and a so-called Negro circuit developed in which the top African American fighters fought each other, often many times. Sam Langford and Harry Wills, two top African American fighters, battled at least fourteen times over a five-year period. Wills, in particular, was a savage puncher and no top white heavyweight was inclined to face him. Besides the fear of losing and being battered, there was another fear of having another African American champion, like Jack Johnson had been in the previous decade (see chapter 5). Johnson was an outstanding fighter who flaunted his excellence and his blackness, much to the chagrin and anger of many whites. Anything resembling a repeat of that was simply unacceptable to whites who wanted to perpetuate the myth of black inferiority.

Reinforcing this fear of black fighters flaunting their "blackness" after winning a championship was "Battling" Siki, born in Senegal (a French colony) as Baye Phal in 1897. After serving with valor in the French army in World War I, he returned to his fighting career and in 1922, defeated Georges Carpentier in Paris for the light-heavyweight championship of the world. Following his victory, in which the referee tried to disqualify him but was overruled by the ringside judges, Siki made a career of partying and carousing. He fulfilled the worst fears of white men by marrying two white women and he soon was woefully out of shape for fighting. He lost his title in 1923 in Ireland, then moved to the United States where he compiled a mediocre record before he was shot in the back and killed in New York City. The crime went unsolved.

Women gained the right to vote via ratification of the Nineteenth Amendment to the Constitution in the United States in 1920, but that right hardly extended to boxing. There were records of females boxing in the 1880s; there is scant record of this being replicated. In fact, women were prohibited from even attending prizefights until the late 1890s. Some boxing promoters tried to get women accepted as spectators at fights because they felt that it would make boxing look more respectable and would allow it to be publicly allowed in the many states that had prohibited public bouts. These included New York. Tex Rickard, Dempsey's promoter, made arrangements for a special section for women spectators at the Dempsey-Willard fight in Toledo, Ohio, in 1919, and this was helpful in convincing New York State to sanction bouts beginning in 1920.

This newfound interest of women in boxing led to the first female journalists covering prizefights, often for the reporting of who attended and what they wore, but also for accounts of the fights themselves. Often distinctions were drawn between men and women spectators and what their real interests were in attending and observing fights.

The World Geography of Boxing

Because of the various state regulations that sanctioned or allowed boxing, fights, even championship fights, were staged in some very unusual or obscure locations. In addition, boxing was, more than almost any American sport, truly international in the nationalities of the participants and fans of the sport. Some weight classes were dominated by men from countries other than the United States, so many championship fights in those weight classes were fought in other countries. Within the United States, the "checkerboard" laws governing the sport led to championship bouts in mining camps, such as the 1908 bout that pitted Jack Johnson against heavyweight champion Tommy Burns, born as Noah Brusso, in Canada. The champion had been avoiding Johnson, but a fight was finally accomplished in Sydney, Australia, where Johnson won and became the champion. Seven years later, Johnson lost the title to Jess Willard in Havana, Cuba. Prior to that he had fought bouts in France, Spain, and Mexico.

The first heavyweight champion of the 1920s, Jack Demsey, fought throughout the West before winning the championship in 1919. His first defense was in Benton Harbor, Michigan; subsequent defenses were in Madison Square Garden; Jersey City, New Jersey; Buffalo, New York; Shelby, Montana; Philadelphia and Chicago. The fight in Shelby (against Tommy Gibbons) is known mostly for nearly bankrupting the town, which staged the contest. It was hoped that Shelby, flush with the discovery of oil in the region, would become a destination for tourists and industry as a result of the fight, but the difficulty in getting to Shelby by rail and the expensive cost of seats meant that fewer people traveled there than anticipated and local people could not afford to view the fight. There were fewer than 8000 attendees (in the new 40,000-seat arena) and, as a result of the guaranteed amounts that each fighter received, four banks in Shelby subsequently went bankrupt.

Traveling to boxing matches would have been by train, except within the confines of a large city, where trolley cars were generally ubiquitous, i.e. most common. The developed rail system that linked major-league baseball easily in the Northeast also allowed for fights and fans to travel almost anywhere within the country. Two problems in attracting fans were price and time to travel to the designated location.

Media and Boxing in the Decade

For those who could not go to the fights, there were two ways to get up-to-the-minute accounts of the contests. One was through teletype machines, which used the telegraph/telephone wires to transmit accounts to various places such as Times Square in New York. The accounts of the round, sometimes even the blow-by-blow details, were then posted for large crowds to read and follow the fight. A second way was through radio broadcasting, though that was difficult when the fight was in a relatively obscure location like Shelby, Montana. In that particular case, one station in Minneapolis hooked up teletype contact, then had an announcer broadcast an account of the fight, complete with fake crowd noises and other sound effects like the bell at the end or beginning of rounds. In larger cities, radio broadcast was easier and became more and more common through the 1920s as radio networks were formed and made the broadcasts more available.

Graham McNamee, the broadcast announcer for the second Dempsey-Tunney fight became famous for his radio tones immediately recognizable to fight fans. He had begun his career as an actor and singer in New York, but, in 1923 he was chosen as an announcer for WEAF in Newark after a tryout and rose to prominence as the most well-known sports announcer of the decade. He first covered the

Greb-Wilson bout for the middleweight title in 1924 and also did color for Grant-land Rice's announcing of the 1923 World Series. By 1925 McNamee was receiving 50,000 letters and telegrams a year from listeners.

A number of famous journalists were regular boxing reporters, including Ring Lardner, Paul Gallico, and Westbrook Pegler. Gallico, in particular, was responsible for enhancing boxing through his writing. He covered Jack Dempsey for the *New York Daily News* at his training camp in 1923 and convinced Dempsey to let him spar with the champion. Gallico was knocked out within two minutes, but his account of this was well received and he was then assigned regular sports stories, especially boxing. He was named sports editor of the *New York Daily News* later that year and had a daily sports column. He also was credited with inventing and organizing the Golden Gloves amateur-boxing competition, which was held throughout the United States. Paul Gallico went on to have a successful career as a writer; among his most famous books were *The Snow Goose* (1941) and *The Poseidon Adventure* (1969).

Boxing and the Law

From its earliest inception, boxing was the subject of fervent interest on the part of some fans, and they often expressed their belief in their favorites by placing bets on the outcome of fights. These wagers were often followed by various "side bets" on the outcomes of rounds as people, intrigued with gambling, found lots of ways to carry out that interest. Most of the bets were relatively small amounts, but as boxing and gambling became more and more popular, larger amounts were bet and figures from organized crime were often involved in this gambling.

The entrance of organized crime and criminals into the mix also altered the entire sport of boxing. As more money was bet on fights, gamblers found it profitable and more "secure" to bribe certain fighters to "take a dive," that is, to lose the fight intentionally, but not obviously. In some cases, a fighter might leave himself open for a powerful punch from his opponent and then take a full count from the referee and lose. In others, a fighter might not punch as well or not block punches as well and allow punches to hit him, thus losing on a judges' decision. Sometimes the rumor of a "fixed fight" would cause the judges to rule a "no decision." Boxers could be suspended or lose their licenses to fight if there was proof or strong indications of them throwing a fight, so there was a real risk involved. Nevertheless, boxing was notorious for having crime figures involved with the sport.

In the 1920s the biggest legal battles for boxing were simply to have the sport legalized in all states. It was recognized that boxing was often linked to gambling, but the prevailing notion was that if the sport was regulated in all states, there might be tighter controls on fights and potential fixes, and the game might have more overall "decorum." When New York State decided to legalize and regulate professional boxing in 1920, many formerly reluctant states followed and allowed prizefighting. The result was that boxing commissions had tremendous authority to regulate the sport in each state. It was believed that this would make the sport "cleaner," but that depended on the integrity of the individuals involved, as well as the temptations that they would face in trying to regulate the sport. Promoters and gamblers had vested interests in having top fights in their states. Boxing commissioners also saw the economic benefits for their respective states, so there were often times that rumors or incidences of bribery or questionable ethical conduct were ignored, so that a fight might be staged in a particular locale. Legalizing prize-fights made a huge economic impact. In 1922, for example, more than $5 million in gate receipts were taken in at prizefights in New York State at a time when the average American income was $1500 per year. Boxing had become an important industry and promoting a fight became significant, especially when the fight was not likely to be very close. In fact, it was great promotion by Tex Rickard that made Jack Dempsey such a big hero to millions of Americans in the 1920s, even though Dempsey had managed to avoid serving in the military in World War I by claiming that he was the sole support of his mother.

Boxing's Decade in Summary

The "glamour" title of boxing, heavyweight, was held by only two boxers during the 1920s, Jack Dempsey and Gene Tunney. African American fighters such as Harry Wills were never allowed to fight for the title. Other top fighters in this dec-ade were Harry Greb, who held both the light-heavyweight and middleweight titles during the decade; Benny Leonard (Leiner) who was the lightweight champion for six years; Mike McTigue of Ireland, who was light-heavyweight champion during this decade; Battling Siki (mentioned earlier), another light-heavyweight cham-pion; Pancho Villa from the Philippines, who was their first world champion when he won the flyweight title in 1923; and Jack Sharkey, a heavyweight who defeated Tommy Loughran in 1928 for the National Boxing Association's heavyweight title. This match was not universally recognized as a title bout, needed when Tunney retired in 1928. The undisputed title was not decided until 1930 when Sharkey lost to Max Schmeling of Germany for the open title.

Golf

Golf was an almost exclusively upper-class sport in the 1920s. There were rela-tively few public courses and private clubs were too expensive for almost anyone but the rich to join. It would seem that golf was not a sport that resonated with the American public, but that was not entirely true. Three golfers symbolized golf in the 1920s and they were so colorful that millions (most of whom had never played golf) followed their exploits. Two were professionals, Walter Hagen and Gene Sarazen, and the third remained an amateur, Robert Tyre "Bobby" Jones.

Jones was more typical of the nation's golfers. He was from a wealthy Atlanta family and began playing golf at a very young age. He won a children's tournament at age six and played in the top amateur tournaments from his early teen years. He also graduated from Georgia Tech University with a degree in mechanical engi-neering and later received a degree in English from Harvard. He read for the law and was admitted to the Georgia bar and practiced law while playing in the world's best golf tournaments. Beginning in 1923 at age twenty-one Jones was the domi-nant figure in golf for seven years, winning the U.S. Open four times, the British Open three times, the U.S. Amateur five times, and the British Amateur once. He retired from competitive golf after winning the Grand Slam of the time in 1930. Jones was a well-spoken, courtly southerner, who was gracious in his dealings with the public. He came into prominence when weekly newsreels were first being shown at the movie theatres each week. With the advent of talking movies in 1927, fans were able to both see some of Jones's play and hear him speak after winning tournaments, enhancing his popularity. He also made some short films on golf, which were shown in theatres.

After retiring as a competitive golfer, Jones practiced law, designed golf clubs, and founded both the Augusta National Golf Club and its fabled tournament, the Masters. He was confined to a wheelchair in 1948 as a result of a rare disease of the central nervous system. Nevertheless, he continued to host the Masters tournament until his death in 1971.

Jones's chief rivals for attention in golf were Hagen and Sarazen, whose lives contrasted greatly with that of Jones. Hagen was the son of a blacksmith in Rochester, New York, and he learned the rudiments of golf by practicing in a field while herding cows. He caddied at an exclusive country club where the professional taught him the finer points of the game. He also worked as a taxidermist. A great natural athlete, Hagen turned down a tryout with the Philadelphia Phillies at age twenty-one in order to play in the 1914 U.S. Open, which he won.

At that time there was a stark difference between amateurs and professionals in golf. At some private clubs, especially in England, professionals were allowed on the golf course, but not in the locker room, because they were not considered "gentlemen." This class distinction was reflective of American society at that time, but Hagen's success and insistence on better treatment of professionals was a large factor in breaking down some of the class barriers in golf. Hagen wore dashing outfits and was outspoken, but polite. He garnered a huge following among "common people" who had previously had no interest in golf. Hagen won the U.S. Open again in 1919 and the British Open four times in the 1920s as well as five PGA championships (he cofounded the PGA in 1916). He designed golf clubs, played in tournaments and exhibitions well into his sixties. He was one of golf's greatest ambassadors and died in 1969 at age seventy-six.

A rival to Hagen, though ten years his junior, was Gene Sarazen (born Eugene Saraceni, the son of a carpenter), from Harrison, New York. Sarazen won the U.S. Open in 1922 and 1932, three PGA championships, one British Open, and a Masters championship. Sarazen became more Hagen's rival in the 1930s and was too young to play much against Jones, but Sarazen was a popular player because of his outgoing nature and because he came from such a humble background. Sarazen played golf into his eighties, was a golf commentator on television for decades, invented the modern sand wedge, and, along with Hagen, made golf seem like something for more than just the very rich.

Horse Racing

Thoroughbred horse racing became wildly popular at the end of the nineteenth century and that popularity carried over into the twentieth century. Harness racing, in which a driver rode in a small cart, called a sulky, was also staged, but was only very popular in pockets of the United States A number of states, most notably New York in 1913, outlawed legalized gambling, as part of the same reform movement that led to Prohibition. By 1919 attendance at racetracks was at a twenty-year low. By 1922 that trend had been reversed, largely because of the performance of one horse, Man o' War. In 1920 the Kentucky Derby did not have the exalted status that it has today. As a result, the owner of Man o' War decide to skip that race, feeling that it was too early in the racing season for a three-year-old to race $1^1/_4$ miles. That omission cost Man o' War the opportunity to win what today is called the Triple Crown of racing, the Kentucky Derby, the Belmont Stakes, and the Preakness. Man o' War raced in the latter races and won both convincingly. He also entered nine other races that season and won each of them. That record combined with his two-year-old record of entering ten races, winning nine and losing the one race by one length. His record of twenty victories in twenty-one races charmed the many people who followed racing at that time and also drew thousands into the sport. At the height of his popularity, his owner decided to end his career and put him out to stud. Over the next twenty-seven years, more than 500,000 visitors came to the farm to see him, and at his death in 1947 at age thirty, over 500 attended his funeral, which was broadcast on the radio.

No other racehorse had Man o' War's dynamism, but both Jolly Roger and Equipoise were outstanding enough in their careers in the 1920s to be elected to the Racing Hall of Fame.

Tennis

Tennis was first developed in France, by French royalty, beginning in the 1500s. It was known as the sport of kings and its exclusivity persisted until late in the nineteenth century. In the United States, the game became popular in the 1800s, first as court tennis and later as lawn tennis, though it was still largely a game for the rich. The Olympics included tennis in the first modern Olympiad in 1896 and it was an Olympic sport through 1924, when two Americans, Helen Wills and Vince Richards, won the singles gold medals. In 1900 the first British-American Davis Cup competition was staged with the Americans winning the first two Davis Cups. A similar prize for women, the Wightman Cup, was established in 1923.

Men's tennis was dominated in the 1920s by "Big" Bill Tilden, who was from the Philadelphia area. He won the national mixed doubles title in 1913 and 1914 and became the number 1 ranked tennis player in the United States in 1920, a distinction that he held until 1930. During the 1920s, Tilden, who was also a playwright and actor, won Wimbledon three times and won seven U.S. singles championships. He often defeated "Little" Bill Johnston, who had defeated Tilden for the 1919 U.S. Championship. Tilden and Johnston combined to play as doubles partners, as well as singles players for the U.S. Davis Cup team. They won seven consecutive Davis Cups in the 1920s, a record that still stands.

In the early 1920s, Molla Mallory was the dominant U.S. player, but she was overshadowed by Suzanne Lenglen of France. In 1923 Helen Wills won her first U.S. championship, and she was the outstanding female tennis player of the 1920s. Besides her Olympic medals, Wills won six U.S. championships, three Wimbledon titles, and two French championships in the 1920s. She married in 1929 and, as Helen Wills Moody, won five more Wimbledon titles, two French championships, and one U.S. championship in the 1930s.

Despite the popularity of Tilden and Wills, tennis was still largely restricted to wealthier classes. There were few public courts and all the championships were strictly amateur; any player who made any money from tennis was considered a professional. The game was international in scope, but few ethnic groups in the

United States other than wealthy, established Western Europeans could afford to play competitive tennis.

SUMMARY

The 1920s were a time of great growth in the United States, economically and socially. This being said, there were also many obstacles to continued social growth, the most obvious being racism and ethnic prejudices. Certainly there was continued sexism, but the granting of suffrage to women allowed for some small admission of the rights of women and recognition of their potential. It would take another generation before that growth and recognition continued, when women became vital cogs in the war effort of World War II. Incomes continued to rise for the wealthy, but the lower classes saw much less economic growth, and that was reversed in the last years of the decade. Immigration, which had peaked in the previous decades, now slowed greatly, though nearly half the American populace was first- or second-generation American.

Sport was one avenue for many immigrant groups to pursue and achieve social and economic recognition. Sports were aided greatly by the media, particularly the radio, which became a standard in almost every American home by the end of the decade. Transportation infrastructure continued to improve within urban areas and the railroads provided more flexibility for the travel of fans and teams. The assembly-line process made the auto more affordable and stimulated the improvement of thousands of miles of American roads, another factor in greater travel of sports teams.

The media coverage of more events and the increased interest of Americans led to the first great pantheon of sports heroes. These included Babe Ruth, Rube Foster, Red Grange, Knute Rockne, Jack Dempsey, Gene Tunney, Bill Tilden, Bobby Jones, Johnny Weissmuller, Chick Hagen, Gertrude Ederle, Helen Wills, and Man o' War. Subsequent stars would have a difficult time measuring up to the greats created in this decade by writers like Grantland Rice, Paul Gallico, Red Smith, and Ed Sullivan.

The stock market crash of 1929 plunged America and the world into a deep economic depression from which it took nearly an entire decade to escape. The emergence of sport as a popular diversion would carry into the 1930s as an important factor in Americans finding something "stable" to hold on to in a careering world. The sports heroes of the 1920s created a foundation that American sports continued to build on, even into the twenty-first century.

RECOMMENDED RESOURCES

Allen, Frederick Lewis. 1964. *Only yesterday: An informal history of the 1920s*. New York: Perennial Library.

Carroll, John M. 1999. *Red Grange and the rise of college football*. Urbana: University of Illinois Press.

Creamer, Robert. 1974. *Babe: The legend comes to life*. New York: Simon and Schuster.

Evensen, Bruce. 1996. *When Dempsey fought Tunney: Heroes, hokum and storytelling in the Jazz Age*. Knoxville: University of Tennessee Press.

Gallico, Paul. 1938. *Farewell to sport*. New York: Knopf.

Gems, Gerald R. 1997. *Windy City wars: Labor, leisure and sport in the making of Chicago.* Lanham, MD: Scarecrow Press.

Grimsley, Will. 1971. *Tennis—Its history, people and events.* Englewood Cliffs, NJ: Prentice-Hall.

Holway, John. 2001. *The complete book of baseball's Negro Leagues: The other half of baseball history.* Winter Park, FL. Hastings House Publishers.

Inabinnet, Mark. 1994. *Grantland Rice and his heroes: The sportswriter as mythmaker in the 1920s.* Knoxville: University of Tennessee Press.

Jones, Bobby. 1966. *Bobby Jones on golf.* New York, Doubleday.

Neft, David. 1991. *The football encyclopedia: The complete history of NFL Football from 1892 to the present.* New York: St. Martin's Press.

Nelson, Murry. 1999. *The originals: The New York Celtics invent modern basketball.* Bowling Green, OH: Bowling Green University Press.

Peterson, Robert W. 2002. *Cages to jump shots.* 2d ed. Lincoln: University of Nebraska Press.

Riess, Steven A., ed. 1998. *Sports and the American Jew.* Syracuse, NY: Syracuse University Press.

Robinson, Ray. 1999. *Rockne of Notre Dame.* New York: Oxford University Press.

Tilden, William. 1948. *My story: A champion's memoirs.* Philadelphia: Hellman-William.

Voigt, David Quentin. 1987. *Baseball: An illustrated history.* University Park: Pennsylvania State University Press.

Weissmuller, Johnny. 1930. *Swimming the American crawl.* New York: Houghton-Mifflin.

Films

Baseball: Fourth inning, a national heirloom. 1994. Dir. Ken Bums. PBS Video.

Galloping ghost. 1931. Dir. Reeve Eason and Benjamin H. Kline. Alpha Video.

Knute Rockne, All-American. 1940. Dir. Lloyd Bacon. Warner Home Video.

Knute Rockne and the Fighting Irish of Notre Dame. 1989. Direct Cinema Limited.

There was always sun shining someplace: Life in the Negro baseball leagues. 1989. Dir. Craig Davidson. Refocus Films.

CHAPTER 7

AMERICAN SPORTS, 1930–1939

Mark Dyreson, Chad Carlson, John Gleaves, and Matthew Llewellyn

OVERVIEW

In 1930 baseball, the American national pastime, enjoyed its most prosperous season yet recorded. More than 10 million customers pushed through the turnstiles of major-league baseball stadiums. Just four years later, in 1933, fewer than six million people showed up at major-league ball parks, a 45 percent decline. The huge fall-off in baseball attendance represented just one of the consequences of the Great Depression. Throughout the 1930s an economic disaster gripped the United States of which the calamitous stock market crash of 1929 signaled just the beginning. This collapse of the nation's financial markets was just one of many causes of the Depression. A litany of other problems, including uneven distribution of wealth, overproduction, inadequate regulation, frenzied speculation, poor banking policies, and a general failure to perceive the nature of the twentieth-century industrial economy at many levels of American society contributed to the downward spiral.

Throughout the 1930s every sector of the nation's vast commercial system faltered. In fact, not until 1940, when the economy began to gear up to fight World War II, did a measurable recovery begin. During the Depression loan defaults reached record highs, credit evaporated, and banks collapsed. Factories shut down assembly lines as the market for consumer goods shrank dramatically. By all key measures, industrial production plummeted. By the winter of 1933 one-quarter of the nation's workforce had drifted into the unemployment lines. Those still employed faced shrinking paychecks. Massive insecurity wracked the nation. Breadlines and soup kitchens popped up. Millions of homeless people flocked to dingy shantytowns or made epic journeys to find work. The national suicide rate rose. The national marriage, birth, and divorce rates fell. Radical alternatives to capitalism from every ideology on the political spectrum drew growing numbers of adherents. In rural America farmers sometimes took up arms to prevent foreclosures on their lands. In urban America city governments desperately sought to make jobs for the growing numbers of economic refugees. In the nation's capital military veterans of World War I marched on the seat of government to demand aid. The republic, many believed, was in grave peril. Fear of mass starvation stalked the land, a new terror in a nation that for more than a century had been known to the rest of the world for its material abundance. There was a significant rise in the number of Socialists and Communists registered as party members as people turned to these parties in the face of hopelessness.

The Great Depression crept into every fiber of the national fabric. Even the national pastime suffered. While major-league attendance fell dramatically, minor-league baseball saw the collapse of entire leagues. By the 1933 season, the nadir of the Depression, several major-league franchises were rumored to be on the verge of bankruptcy. Teams slashed salaries and cut roster sizes. Even Babe Ruth, the icon of the American national game, took a pay cut. At the beginning of the Depression the New York Yankees paid Ruth $80,000, a salary that the press gleefully noted was higher than that of U.S. president Herbert Hoover. Ruth, in a probably apocryphal but widely repeated story, allegedly defended making more money than the president by observing that he had enjoyed a better year than Hoover. By 1934 that quip seemed no laughing matter. The voters had replaced Hoover with Franklin Delano Roosevelt and Ruth earned just $35,000 from the Yankees.

Not only baseball but every other sport in the vast American recreational industry suffered during the Depression. Revenues from intercollegiate football games

---

Babe Ruth's "Called Shot"

In Game 3 of the 1932 World Series, New York Yankees slugger Babe Ruth blasted a home run over the 440-foot wall in deep centerfield of Wrigley Field. The titanic clout, the Yankee star's second home run of the game off Chicago Cub's pitcher Charlie Root, quickly became part of American baseball lore as Ruth's famous "called shot." Whether or not Ruth actually pointed to a specific spot and then hit a home run to it, as the legend claims, remains shrouded in the mysteries of interpretation, the ground where all good myths flourish.

Some of the facts of the "called shot" are not in dispute. Ruth hit the huge home run off Root as the Cubs' dugout heckled him. The home run proved a decisive blow in the series, leading to a Yankee victory in that game and paving the way for a four-game sweep by the New York club. Newsreels and an amateur film discovered in the 1970s of the event show that during the at-bat Ruth made repeated gestures toward the Cubs players, or the pitcher, or, perhaps to centerfield. Eyewitnesses all agree that Ruth shouted something at the pitcher before his famous hit. Did Ruth, however, actually call his shot? The films are not clear enough to determine that "fact" with any clarity and the contemporary media accounts of the event vary widely.

The "called shot" tale initially emerged from the typewriter of Scripps-Howard sports editor Joe Williams, who in a widely circulated wire-service story claimed that Ruth had responded to the Cubs' taunting by calling his shot and then delivering the baseball to the very spot in the stands to which he had allegedly pointed. Ruth, in interviews immediately following the game, did not make any such claim. When the story proved popular, however, Ruth later claimed in a host of interviews and in his own biography that he had in fact called his shot. Ironically, Joe Williams, the reporter who started the legend, in later decades came to believe that Ruth had not actually called his famous shot.

declined markedly. Athletic departments struggled to remain solvent and some cut entire sports to keep afloat. Women's intercollegiate and interscholastic sports, already under attack in the 1920s by female physical educators who objected to the male model of elite, competitive athletics as an assault on femininity, proved especially vulnerable. The Women's Division of the National Amateur Athletic Foundation (established in 1923) spearheaded the assault on women's competitive sports, closing most intercollegiate programs by the beginning of the 1930s. The Women's Division, dominated by female physical educators from the nation's colleges and universities who favored gender separatism and eschewed highly competitive athletics for women, continued their assault by turning their attention to competitive interscholastic sports for girls. Aided by the financial crises of the Depression hanging over school systems, fourteen states terminated their girls' high school basketball tournaments during the decade.

Canceled competitions, eroding budgets, salary cuts, and declining attendance each testified to the Depression's impact on American sport. For some, the maladies of the economic collapse extended beyond fiscal nightmares. As John Tunis (1934), one of the era's leading sportswriters, lamented, the Great Depression seemed to diminish the luster even of the competitors that the nation loved to cheer. In the 1920s, the "golden age" of American sport, Tunis observed that athletes had been "gods" who stood atop the national pantheon of heroism. In the grim 1930s they became, in Tunis's words, "just ordinary mortals."

In spite of declining attendance and falling profits, the Depression did not kill the American sports industry. Indeed, in the midst of the economic woes, signs abounded that American interest in sport actually expanded. Sport provided temporary escape from the economic misery and promised that hard times could be overcome. Baseball and intercollegiate football continued to bring in revenue. Prizefighting plugged along as new champions were crowned. The young National Football League built a stronger foundation. Interest in basketball grew. Golf courses, tennis courts, and bowling alleys still drew customers. Most scholastic, youth, and college sports programs, especially for boys, survived. In the midst of the Depression a race horse captured the national imagination and brightened spirits. In this same decade the United States hosted a winter and a summer Olympic Games. Through the Olympic Games and other international competitions, especially prizefights and baseball tours, Americans also made sport into a part of their foreign policy efforts in the decade during which the international community descended toward a second world war.

Indeed, so firmly were Americans wedded to the belief that sport could help them triumph over the Great Depression that Franklin Delano Roosevelt, elected president in 1932, made it a central feature of his New Deal programs. Roosevelt's recovery bureaus such as the Civilian Conservation Corps, the Works Project Administration, and other "alphabet agencies" created not only jobs but vast new networks of recreational opportunities in the nation's forests, deserts, and cities. Federal laborers built parks and playgrounds in urban areas, constructed camping facilities and cut trails through national parks, and promoted national interest in sport and recreation. According to federal calculations, the U.S. government between 1935 and 1941 spent $941 million on recreational facilities and an additional $229 million to underwrite community recreation programs. The government built thousands of athletic fields, gymnasiums, parks, and playgrounds, and dug hundreds of pools. In addition, the Civilian Conservation Corps (CCC) dramatically improved the nation's outdoor recreation opportunities. The federal agency proudly noted that between 1933 and 1942 it blazed more than 100,000 new miles of hiking and horse-riding trails, and improved thousands of acres of beachfront, campgrounds, and picnic grounds. The CCC insisted it had radically expanded the recreational freedoms of the American public. Roosevelt also used sporting analogies in his famous "fireside chats," speeches broadcast from the White House over the radio designed to urge Americans to fight the Depression. Following a tradition that dated to the early twentieth century, President Roosevelt sought to restore American spirits by continuing to appear every April on major-league baseball's opening day to throw out the first pitch of the season. He not only threw out first pitches throughout the Depression but in 1935 flipped a switch at the White House that sent electricity all the way to Cincinnati to power up the lighting system for the first night game ever played in the major leagues. President Roosevelt clearly understood that baseball could help him connect with American voters and sell his New Deal to the public. In spite of the Depression, sport remained a powerful force in American culture.

TEAM SPORTS

Baseball

Decline and Innovation in Baseball

The Great Depression hit baseball hard, slashing attendance and profits dramatically. The national pastime's economic decline mirrored the general decline of many other American industries, revealing roots that stretched before the Depression Era. During the 1920s baseball lost some of its market share in comparison to other forms of entertainment. Though gross attendance numbers grew a bit throughout the 1920s, the number of paying customers did not grow as quickly as the national population. The 11.5 percent rise in attendance at major-league stadiums paled in comparison to 75 percent rise in attendance at movie theaters during the 1930s. Competition from other leisure industries and a flattening demand for baseball tickets indicated that even before the Depression the baseball business had problems.

The Depression exacerbated baseball's woes, as the plummeting attendance and failing minor leagues illustrated. In 1933, the Depression's most severe year, only 80,000 fans turned out to see the struggling St. Louis Browns over the franchise's entire home schedule of seventy-seven games. The Browns and several other teams appeared to be headed toward bankruptcy. To combat the dismal economic conditions several of the struggling franchises suggested a profit-sharing plan. The wealthier clubs rejected the proposal. "I found out a long time ago that there is no charity in baseball," New York Yankee's owner Jacob Ruppert scoffed at the failed attempt to enact baseball socialism (Voigt 1983, 251).

The major leagues tried other schemes to bring fans back to ballparks. Borrowing an innovation from the Negro Leagues, the Cincinnati Reds introduced night games, with President Roosevelt at the White House flipping the switch to light the major league's first evening contest. The Reds' general manager, Larry Mac-Phail, tried a host of other innovations. He bought bright red uniforms to replace the traditional dour pinstripes in shades of white and grey. MacPhail also resorted to marketing sex appeal, employing cigarette girls clad in skimpy satin pants and enticingly garbed usherettes to bring fans back. Other teams quickly followed Mac-Phail's innovations, at least in regard to night baseball. The owners took austerity measures as well. They cut salaries significantly. In 1933 major-league salaries averaged $7000. By 1936 that figure had been slashed to $4500. Front offices reduced roster sizes from twenty-five to twenty-three players while the leagues cut the number of umpires so that most games were umpired by two-man rather than three-man crews.

Franchises also searched for new sources of revenue. Owners increasingly looked to radio. Most teams initially resisted the new medium when it first appeared in the 1920s, fearing it would cut attendance. The Depression, however, made owners more willing to gamble, particularly as stations discovered they could sell commercials and pay rights fees for broadcasts. The Chicago Cubs and St. Louis Cardinals led the way in developing radio markets, building strong regional networks to carry their games to fans. Baseball commissioner Kenesaw Mountain Landis signed a huge $400,000 contract for the radio rights to the World Series, a deal that initially garnered sponsorship from the Ford Motor Company and then, after 1936, from Gillette shaving products. Bucking the trend toward beaming games to radio audiences, the three teams in the New York metropolitan area, the Yankees, Giants, and Dodgers, kept baseball off the airwaves in the nation's largest market for most of the 1930s through a mutual agreement to a broadcast ban. When in 1939 Larry MacPhail moved from Cincinnati to take over the Dodgers, he broke the agreement and sold the Brooklyn club's rights for $70,000. The Yankees and Giants then procured their own radio contracts. By the end of the 1930s all sixteen major-league franchises had joined the radio age.

Teams discovered other sources of sponsorship money in addition to selling radio rights. Fourteen of the sixteen teams had contracts with General Mills to promote Wheaties cereal. Baseball targeted the male adult audience as well as children's breakfast habits. When prohibition ended in 1933 and the sale of alcohol once again became legal, reopened beer breweries clamored to sign deals with major-league teams. By the end of the 1930s teams derived approximately 10 percent of their total revenues from radio and other commercial sponsorships.

Major-league baseball tried a few other innovations in addition to radio broadcasts, deals with corporations, and night games. In the early 1930s Chicago sportswriter Arch Ward proposed an annual midsummer All-Star game. In 1933 Ward's idea came to fruition as the major leagues staged their first annual All-Star Game at Chicago's Comiskey Park. The All-Star contest became a fixture thereafter. In 1936 the leagues founded the Hall of Fame in Cooperstown, New York, a shrine to the game's power in the nation's social fabric. Both innovations heartened devoted fans and intrigued those with less passionate commitments, bringing new customers while increasing the fervor of loyal consumers. The new innovations helped a bit. By 1935 attendance started to climb again, though in very slow increments. By 1941 the number of paying customers at major-league baseball games finally reached the record level established in the 1929 season, before the Depression had fully gripped the United States.

On the field, baseball flourished during the 1930s. Continuing a long pattern in the history of professional baseball, teams in the largest metropolitan areas, especially New York and Chicago, generally fared better than small-market teams. The one exception to this general rule was the St. Louis Cardinals. Stocked with good players developed by general manager Branch Rickey's innovative "farm system" of minor-league affiliate clubs—an invention the rest of the major-league clubs soon copied—the Cardinals rose to prominence in the National League. By 1940 the Cardinals had thirty-two minor-league affiliates and more than 700 players in their system. Bolstered by this innovative system, the Cardinals won the World Series in 1931 and 1934. The press labeled the Cardinals the "Gas House Gang" in honor of the many colorful characters who populated the St. Louis dugout, including their stellar pitcher, Jerome "Dizzy" Dean, their great hitter Joe "Ducky" Medwick, and their colorful third baseman, Johnny "Pepper" Martin.

In the American League the New York Yankees continued the dynasty that they built during the 1920s. Babe Ruth's 1935 retirement barely dimmed the Bronx Bombers' star power as they replaced the "Bambino" in 1936 with the "Yankee Clipper," the elegant Joe DiMaggio, who would reign, in the estimates of most experts, as the game's outstanding player of the 1930s and 1940s. The Yankees won five World Series during the 1930s, including four straight from 1936 to 1939.

Baseball stars remained national heroes during the Great Depression; the product on the field remained strong, even as Babe Ruth's magnificent career came to an end in 1935. Though Ruth's skills declined greatly in his last few seasons, the public continued to adore him. While Ruth proved irreplaceable as the most popular icon of the national pastime, other stars emerged in the decade. Carl Hubbell, Lefty Grove, and Dizzy Dean earned reputations as dominating pitchers during the 1930s. Great hitters such as Hank Greenberg, Ted Williams, Joe DiMaggio, and Ducky Medwick started their stellar careers in the midst of the Depression. In an era of intense anti-Semitism both in the United States and abroad, Greenberg, the greatest Jewish star in the major leagues, served as an important symbol of pride for the Jewish community as well as for opponents of all forms of bigotry. Playing in the same city, Detroit, where the notorious radio commentator and Catholic priest Father Charles Coughlin regularly broadcast charges that an alleged international cabal of Jewish financiers had caused the Great Depression, Greenberg slugged home runs and tried to shatter racial and religious stereotypes. Indeed, at least for European ethnic groups during the era, baseball became a symbol of the promises of success and inclusion in American life, with Joe DiMaggio's success serving as a source of great pride for Italian Americans.

The Negro Leagues

In the shadows of the whites-only major and minor leagues, the Negro Leagues struggled through the Great Depression. Just as the economic collapse hit African Americans, most of whom lived at the economic margins of U.S. society, proportionally harder than it hit the majority, so too did black baseball suffer more than its white counterpart. The original Negro National League, founded in 1920, suffered from shaky finances from the beginning and collapsed in 1930 at the beginning of the Great Depression.

In 1933 entrepreneur Gus Greenlee resurrected the Negro National League from his base in Pittsburgh, a hotbed of African American baseball. While most of the teams in the new circuit rented stadiums from major-league clubs, Greenlee spent

$100,000 to build a stadium for his own team, the Pittsburgh Crawfords. The second installment of the Negro National League also included teams from New York, Newark, Philadelphia, Washington, D.C., and Baltimore. In 1938 a second black circuit, the Negro American League, sprang up, featuring teams from the South and Midwest.

The Negro National League represented the strongest association of black baseball teams throughout the 1930s. The two dominant clubs in the league were both in Pittsburgh where Greenlee's Crawfords usually fought for the pennant against Cumberland Posey's Homestead Grays. The Crawfords had the most famous player in the history of the Negro leagues, Leroy "Satchel" Paige, as their pitching ace. Paige was the one African American player known to the vast majority of white as well as black fans. The Grays also had great players, including outfielder James "Cool Papa" Bell, catcher and Pittsburgh native Josh Gibson, and first baseman Buck Leonard.

Negro League players earned much less than their white counterparts. Even the best players such as Bell, Gibson, and Leonard made only about $2500 a season. On such meager salaries they could not afford to support their families and so they played throughout the year, spending the late spring and summer months in the Negro National Leagues, barnstorming the United States, including the segregated South, in the fall and early spring, and spending winters playing in Latin American leagues.

While the color line remained firmly in place in baseball's major and minor leagues, Negro League and white major-league players occasionally squared off in direct competition. Satchel Paige in the 1930s was, by some estimates, next to Babe Ruth, the second-biggest draw in baseball. In 1932 he and St. Louis pitcher Dizzy Dean organized two teams for a barnstorming tour of the American South. The squads, segregated by race, played a series of contests to enthusiastic fans who packed local stadiums and sat in seats segregated by race—neatly mirroring the racial dynamics on the diamond. The tour clearly revealed that African American players could compete with white major leaguers. The African American press, led by Wendell Smith of the *Pittsburgh Courier*, Frank "Fay" Young of the *Chicago Defender*, and Sam Lacy of the *Baltimore Afro-American*, pushed for integration. Some white sportswriters also joined the campaign. Baseball commissioner Kennesaw "Mountain" Landis and major-league owners ignored the cries of the integrationists, however. The efforts to open baseball to all Americans, regardless of skin color, would not bear fruit for another decade. During the 1930s, with the anomalies of a few barnstorming tours, the national pastime remained firmly segregated.

Even though baseball divided the United States by race, some promoters of the game thought it the perfect institution for promoting American influence around the globe among peoples of all races, creeds, and cultures. Continuing policies first developed in the 1920s, the U.S. Departments of State and Commerce advocated the spread of baseball to further American diplomatic goals, particularly in Latin America and East Asia. Recognizing that baseball had gained a strong foothold in those regions, federal officials were convinced that the game could increase the success of American foreign policies. Baseball diplomacy played an especially important role in U.S. relations with Japan, the major rival during the 1930s to the expansion of American power in the Pacific. Indeed, baseball ranked as the Japanese as well as the American national pastime. Americans hoped the game might bridge the growing rifts between the two nations.

Major-league baseball, eager to expand its market as well as to help the federal government, participated in the campaign to spread the game by sending traveling all-star teams to East Asia even in the midst of the Great Depression. In 1931 New York Yankee slugger Lou Gehrig captained a squad of major leaguers who toured Japan and other Pacific Rim nations. In 1934 the biggest star in the game, a legend in Japan as well as in his own homeland, Babe Ruth led an American League All-Star team on another Asian sojourn. The American press applauded both tours, claiming that the ballplayers did more to ease Japanese-American tensions in their brief exhibitions than diplomats had accomplished in decades. Ironically, one of the American players on the team, Moe Berg, a major-league infielder and catcher from 1923 to 1939, surreptitiously filmed Tokyo during one of the tours. His films were used during World War II to plan bombing raids of Japan's largest city. Shortly after Ruth's squad returned from Japan, however, major-league owners announced a ban of future tours in response to growing unease with Japanese aggressions in China and other areas of the Pacific.

The effort to spread baseball included the amateur as well as the professional versions of the game. In 1936 Babe Ruth, recently retired as a player, led an American committee dedicated to adding baseball to the program of the Olympic Games. The United States succeeded in getting Nazi Germany to stage a baseball exhibition as one of the two demonstration sports at the 1936 Olympics. In Berlin a crowd of more than 100,000, the largest to that point in history ever to witness a baseball game, was, depending on the viewpoint of the observer, either completely enamored or totally befuddled by a clash between two American teams composed mainly of collegians. With the 1940 Olympics scheduled for Tokyo, the Japanese promised to make baseball an even more significant part of their Olympian spectacle. Japan lobbied the International Olympic Committee (IOC) to sanction a proposed multination baseball tournament as a medal sport.

Over the next few years the Tokyo Olympic baseball jamboree evaporated as the world lurched toward war. When Japan invaded China in 1937, Americans concluded that although the Japanese had adopted baseball they had failed to learn any of the lessons of "fair play" that the game allegedly taught. The chorus concerning the Japanese failure to adopt the true spirit of baseball grew even greater after the attack on Pearl Harbor in 1941 drew the United States into World War II.

In the growing climate of nationalism in the late 1930s, Americans reasserted their belief that baseball was really their own national pastime, even if other nations had taken to the game. The tradition of singing the "Star-Spangled Banner" to begin games started in that era. It spread quickly and became standard practice at every level of the sport, from local summer-league games to the major leagues by 1940. That same year, with U.S. entry into the war appearing increasingly likely, major-league baseball demonstrated its patriotism by encouraging all of its players to register for the draft and promising the nation that it would cancel operations if entry into the conflict required such a sacrifice.

At the grassroots level, where baseball flourished during the Depression among children playing on sandlots, an initially little-noticed but very important development in the long-term transformation of youth sport in the United States appeared. The invention of Little League baseball in 1939 rapidly speeded the transformation of the child-organized games of an earlier era into the adult-controlled recreational activities common to the second half of the twentieth century. This new version of

Hotchkiss School baseball. (Courtesy of the Library of Congress)

children's baseball sprang to life in Williamsport, Pennsylvania, where a lumber company worker named Carl Stotz created the new organization in response to his own youthful experiences with the anarchy of children-controlled sandlot games. Stotz provided teams with uniforms, diamonds, and drafts modeled on the major leagues. His innovation rapidly spread across the nation, part of a long process of increasing levels of adult control of child's play that signaled a profound change in twentieth-century American social patterns.

Basketball

Innovation and Modernization in Basketball

While football and baseball reigned as the American national pastimes, basketball established strong footholds in the 1930s at the local level. In 1939 the "father of American basketball," James Naismith, a Canadian by birth, passed away. The game he had invented just five decades earlier in 1891 had spread throughout the United States and into the world beyond. The Great Depression did not destroy the enthusiasm the nation held for basketball, as rule changes, innovations in styles, and the rise of two new national intercollegiate tournaments and the expansion of the Amateur Athletic Union (AAU) championships reveals. Particularly at the grassroots level, basketball remained a powerful force in local American cultures. The game thrived in high schools and on playgrounds in every region of the nation. By the year of Naismith's death, 95 percent of the nation's high schools sponsored interscholastic teams.

The Depression, however, clearly had an impact on basketball, as it had on American society as a whole. In Indiana, where the game had already become a part of the state's folklore, sociologists Robert and Helen Lynd revisited the site of their earlier landmark study of an "average" American town they had dubbed "Middletown" (Muncie, Indiana, in reality) in order to see the impact of the Great Depression on the nation. The Lynds discovered that the economic collapse had changed American life. In 1931 "Middletown" had won the state high school boys championship. City officials, in spite of budget shortfalls, purchased gold watches to reward the players. By 1935, however, economic realities caught up even with hoops-crazed "Middletown." The town struggled to pay off the debt incurred in building a 9000-seat gymnasium during better times. Ticket sales plummeted and what once had been hailed around the state as a cutting-edge basketball palace became Middletown's "financial white elephant" (Lynd and Lynd 1935, 291–92). (Not even Indiana high school basketball could entirely escape the impact of the Great Depression.)

Basketball had a powerful a grip on cities as well as on the small towns of Indiana and other states. Indeed, in urban areas in the Northeast, the game thrived despite the Depression. The city version of the game offered an important venue for the shaping of religious and ethnic identities. The American-born offspring of recent immigrant groups dominated urban play at the highest levels. The Catholic Youth Organization (CYO) was founded in 1930 as an alternative to Protestant sporting institutions such as the Young Men's Christian Association (YMCA), where Naismith had invented basketball. The CYO sponsored thriving leagues in Chicago and other cities. The Young Men's Hebrew Association, a Jewish alternative to the YMCA and the CYO, encouraged basketball in Jewish neighborhoods throughout the nation. Indeed, in New York City and in other major metropolitan areas, the success of Jewish teams made basketball and important vehicle for shaping Jewish identities both within and across religious boundaries. Many sportswriters during the 1930s depicted basketball as a "Jewish game," simultaneously offering positive affirmations of Jewish masculinity while reinforcing vulgar stereotypes about how alleged Jewish "craftiness" gave the group advantages over players from other backgrounds.

Professional Basketball

While local versions of basketball grew more popular in spite of the challenges of the Great Depression, the professional game languished. American professional basketball of the 1930s did not resemble the global enterprise that has developed in the twenty-first century. Professional basketball consisted of ragtag teams playing in leagues that regularly teetered on the edge of financial oblivion. Professional teams toured through eastern and midwestern towns and cities taking on any quintets interested in any gymnasium available. The professional game drew rowdy, mostly working-class fans to crowded, smoke-filled armories and converted warehouses, offering a brief winter alternative to the more popular spectator sports on the national menu. Before the 1930s, the deliberate, ball-possession style of the American Basketball League, dubbed the "Northeastern style" and typified by the "Original Celtics" of New York City, produced a unappealing brand of basketball (the Celtics were deliberate, sometimes dull, and almost always won) which doomed the organization to extinction as the Great Depression began.

A variety of professional leagues also came and went during the economic hardships of the 1930s. The American Basketball League, the top conference of the 1920s, succumbed to fiscal instability in 1931 and then reorganized, under the same name, as an eastern regional league in 1933. The National Basketball League, centered in midwestern cities, went under after 1933, resurfaced as the Midwest Basketball Conference from 1935 to 1937, and reorganized once again as the National Basketball League in 1937. Professional teams increasingly drew collegiate veterans in the 1930s. Players from working-class backgrounds used basketball to raise themselves to middle-class incomes and status. Businesses looking to promote their products sponsored many teams, such as the Akron Firestones. The Indianapolis Kautskys, named after the grocery store magnate who owned the team, reigned as a top Midwestern Basketball League squad with former Purdue University All-American John Wooden leading the squad. Jewish players dominated the American Basketball League, making up the majority of the roster of that conference's superior team, the Philadelphia SPHAs, sponsored by the South Philadelphia Hebrew Association.

Arguably the finest professional basketball team of the 1930s was the New York Renaissance Big Five, or Rens as they were commonly known, a barnstorming

---

Basketball's "Barnstorming" Champions: The New York Rens and the Harlem Globetrotters

Before the NBA debuted in 1949, the best professional and amateur players displayed their skills in regional, upstart leagues or on barnstorming teams that often sensationalized basketball to draw bigger crowds and make more money. Unlike the modern NBA, professional basketball players of the 1930s often played more than 150 games in a season—in high school gymnasiums, municipal armories, second-floor social halls, and even drained swimming pools—to stay afloat financially.

By the late 1930s, arguably the best two teams in the United States made their livings in a very difficult way. The New York Renaissance Five (Rens) and the team that is now known as the Harlem Globetrotters (although originally from Chicago, they played under the guise of a New York name) rose to the top of the professional ranks in spite of the fact that both squads consisted entirely of African American players who were excluded from the existing leagues. To play basketball in an era of intense segregation and strident racism, the Rens and Globetrotters were consigned to barnstorming, traveling constantly to American towns and cities in search of exhibition games against any team, black or white, willing to play them.

The Rens and Globetrotters overcame off-court racism, such as being denied housing at public hotels and food at public restaurants, as well as on-court racism, such as blatantly biased officiating, to become the top two teams in the country. From 1932 to 1936 the Rens won at least 120 games each season. They remained dominant through the end of the decade as their victory in the 1939 at the first World Tournament of Basketball in Chicago testified.

In 1940 the Globetrotters, although often prone to the chicanery and comedy for which they remain famous to this day, maintained a greater focus on winning games rather than entertaining the crowds. The Globetrotters avenged their 1939 defeat to their unfriendly rival by winning a tight 37–36 quarterfinal game on their way to the tournament title. The Globetrotters squeaked past the hometown Chicago Bruins, 31–29, in the final game.

The Globetrotters went on to entertain the world for the rest of the twentieth century, earning global fame for both their basketball skill and their comedic talents. The Rens declined after their world championship, disbanding in 1949.

squad from the nation's biggest city led by two great stars, Charles "Tarzan" Cooper and William "Pop" Gates. The organized professional leagues did not allow African Americans on their squads, so black players found roster spots on all-black touring teams such as the Rens and their major rivals, the Harlem Globetrotters. White professional teams regularly scheduled exhibition matches against the Rens, Globetrotters, and other African American squads. Given the Rens' and the Globetrotters' sterling records against white teams during the Depression, the barnstorming squads deserved their reputations as the best professional basketball players in the United States. In 1939 a Chicago newspaper, the *Herald American*, began to sponsor a World Professional Basketball Tournament which allowed both white and black teams to enter. The Rens won the 1939 tournament and the Globetrotters captured the 1940 crown.

At the professional, collegiate, and scholastic levels, the Depression era witnessed several rule changes and technological innovations that eventually sparked a much more exciting version of basketball. The limit on offensive players to three seconds in the lane rule unclogged the area around the basket. The rule allowing teams just ten seconds to advance the ball past mid-court sped up the action, as did the replacement of the center jump after every made basket with a simple inbounds pass. A new manufacturing method developed a smaller, rounder, molded ball that allowed for better dribbling, shooting, and passing. New styles of play also enhanced the basketball's spectator appeal, in particular the one-handed shot and the fast break. The innovations in basketball flair developed mainly in the American West as a lively counterpoint to the staid "Northeastern style."

College Basketball

The best American basketball during the 1930s may not have been played by the professionals, but by intercollegiate teams and by the industry-sponsored squads that battled on a fiercely competitive AAU circuit. The game's founding organization, the YMCA, also remained a hotbed of quality competition. Though the college and AAU teams sometimes played intersectional matches, they mainly produced strong regional centers of the game. Though the Northeast and Midwest remained important basketball areas, the game also thrived in the South, the Rocky Mountain region, the Great Plains, and the West Coast. Indeed, the regional variations in style made for dramatic intersectional clashes in college and AAU basketball.

The regional structure of the game was highlighted in 1936 by the celebrated arrival of Stanford's great one-handed jump-shooter, Hank Luisetti, at New York City's Madison Square Garden, a building that served as basketball's mecca. Luisetti's West Coast flair and creativity thrilled the huge crowd of more than 17,000 as well as the throngs of New York reporters who turned out for Stanford's matchup against local powerhouse Long Island University, a team that possessed a forty-three-game winning streak. Luisetti's marksmanship led Stanford to an upset win and demonstrated that the slow, deliberate "Northeastern style" that favored the two-handed set-shot was no longer effective for either winning games or pleasing fans.

At the intercollegiate level, while innovative and athletic styles such as Luisetti's jump-shot advanced the game, a group of legendary coaches known for their strategic genius, typified by Clair Bee at Long Island University, Nat Holman at

City College of New York, Hank Iba of Oklahoma A&M (now Oklahoma State), Adolph Rupp of Kentucky, and Phog Allen of Kansas remained in charge of the game. The coaches enjoyed great success through their ability to manipulate virtually every move their players made. Although these coaches had terrific players on their teams, the coaches, and not their athletes, were the true icons of 1930s college basketball.

Despite some of the best basketball being played in the heartland of the country by teams led by Iba, Rupp, and Allen, New York City, with its extraordinary event facility, Madison Square Garden, remained the hub of American basketball. Collegiate teams from around the nation made the pilgrimage to "the Garden" if they wanted recognition for being among the nation's best. In 1938 New York's Metropolitan Basketball Writers Association created the National Invitation Tournament (NIT) in the Garden to determine the best college team in the country at the end of the season. Although the NIT still exists (and is now owned by the NCAA), it does not have nearly the prestige it had throughout its first decades. Temple University won the inaugural NIT tourney. Long Island University triumphed in 1939, and a western upstart, the University of Colorado, took the 1940 crown.

In 1939 the National Association of Basketball Coaches, led by Kansas's Phog Allen, created a rival postseason tournament to the NIT. The first NCAA championship final pitted Ohio State University against the University of Oregon in a game played at Northwestern's Patten Gymnasium in Evanston, Illinois. Oregon won the game and became, without the glitz and glamour that accompanied the NIT, the first NCAA basketball champion. Indiana University beat the University of Kansas in the final of the 1940 tournament. The proximity of the nation's major sportswriters to Madison Square Garden made the NIT more prestigious than the NCAA championships during the first few years of the rivalry between the two tournaments.

When basketball players graduated from college in the 1930s, they did not have many options for full-time employment playing basketball. Professional basketball leagues offered a nomadic lifestyle with little pay and little stability. The most popular alternative was the AAU model. Independent businesses and companies sponsored teams in the AAU leagues and, to avoid the professional label and preserve amateur status, hired basketball players to work for their companies. Although many companies received scorn for supposedly giving their basketball players a high salary for working short hours at cushy jobs, many ex-college basketball players accepted this model as an opportunity to develop a trade or to make business connections while continuing to play competitive basketball. Indeed, perhaps the highest level of basketball during the 1930s was played by AAU teams comprised of ex-collegiate stars.

The AAU had begun sponsoring a national tournament in 1921. The event drew some of the best squads in the nation, particularly those from west of the Mississippi River, to Kansas City every March. In 1935 Denver swiped the AAU tournament away from Kansas City. Denver offered a breath of fresh air for the stagnant tournament and became the permanent host thereafter. Industrial teams from the Great Plains, Rocky Mountains, and West Coast such as the South Kansas Stage Lines and Healey Motors of Kansas City, Missouri, the Globe Refiners of McPherson, Kansas, the Phillips 66ers of Bartlesville, Oklahoma, the Safeway

Stores and the Nuggets of Denver, and the Universal Pictures of Hollywood, dominated the AAU tournaments of the Depression era. The AAU tournament peaked in popularity during the late 1930s and early 1940s before the National Basketball Association, born in 1949, began its slow rise to dominance, luring away many of the great amateur players with more money and fewer responsibilities outside of basketball.

During the 1930s the AAU's model of the player/worker appealed to many ex-college athletes for its value to their futures. The scheme also allowed them to maintain their amateur status, making them eligible for the Olympic Games. When basketball won a spot on the roster of medal sports for the 1936 Berlin Olympics, many players found an additional incentive to preserve their amateur status and play for their country.

In 1936 the American Olympic Committee (AOC) held an Olympic trials basketball tournament that included the top AAU, college, and other amateur teams to decide which players and coaches would comprise the American team. AAU powerhouse Hollywood Universal Pictures won the eight-team tournament and placed a coach and seven players on the American roster. The runner-up, another AAU squad, the McPherson Globe Refiners of McPherson, Kansas, placed a coach and six players on the roster. A center from the University of Washington was the only collegiate player selected for the team.

At the 1936 Berlin Olympics the United States easily dominated competition and took home the gold medal. The American squad won all four of its games and beat Canada in a final matchup played on an outdoor court in a driving rainstorm. The poor playing conditions in Berlin reflected the relative apathy of the rest of the world toward the American-invented game in the 1930s. In spite of U.S. superiority, the seeds of a future basketball boom were sown in other nations. Frank Lubin, a star of the U.S. Olympic team who was of Lithuanian descent, was approached by Lithuanian officials in Berlin. His countrymen asked him to tutor Lithuanians in the intricacies of basketball. The Californian accepted, changed his name to Pranas Lubinas, and led Lithuania to the 1939 European championship title while developing his legacy as "the Godfather of Lithuanian Basketball."

Adaptation and Expansion in Football

College Football

American football developed its own adult-controlled youth organization, the "Pop" Warner League, named after the longtime coach of Carlisle Indian School and Stanford University, in 1929, a decade before Little League baseball appeared. Naming the new program after a famous college coach indicated that the intercollegiate version of football served as the most important arena for the game. While baseball declined in the Great Depression, college football actually increased its market share in spite of the dismal economy.

The 1920s had witnessed a boom in intercollegiate football as attendance doubled and gate receipts tripled. By the beginning of the 1930s, more than 400 colleges from every locale in the nation fielded teams. During that era every "big-time" football program had stadiums that sat more than 30,000 and eight campuses boasted coliseums with capacity for more than 70,000 fans. "King football" reigned on campuses and drew enormous attention in newspapers, magazines, radio, and the newsreels. Indeed, in the 1930s college football rivaled major-league baseball as the nation's most popular sport.

Public adoration did not, however, make football invincible to the ravages of the Great Depression or to the excesses that plagued the intercollegiate game. Less than two months before the stock market crash of 1929, Howard Savage, a former college English professor and higher education researcher, and his team of investigators released a report licensed by the Carnegie Foundation documenting the prolific rule-breaking and unethical behavior of college football programs. Savage's investigative squad visited more than 130 campuses across the country, documenting the serious maladies afflicting college football.

The report did not mince words, declaring college football programs inherently corrupt. Almost all of the schools Savage's investigators reviewed had participated in illegal behavior, particularly in the recruitment and subsidization of players. Colleges routinely provided illegal financial inducements, procured jobs for players that involved no work, housed teams in plush living quarters, and built gigantic slush funds. The report concluded that winning football games and making money mattered more than maintaining academic standards and ethical integrity at the nation's institutions of higher learning.

Savage's report garnered headlines across the nation. University presidents and college football coaches issued irate denunciations of the Carnegie findings. The timing of the report, however, guaranteed it would ultimately have little impact on intercollegiate sport. After a few weeks in the national spotlight the deadly dive on Wall Street extinguished public furor at the revelations. Indeed, instead of encouraging university presidents to take control of their athletic programs to avoid further harmful excesses, the report ended up collecting dust on their bookshelves.

Though the Great Depression pushed the Savage report on the scandals that had spread throughout college football into obscurity, the financial crisis itself had a significant impact on the game. Colleges and universities across the country struggled to stay afloat. The economic hard times kept many families from sending their children to college, forcing a sharp decline in enrollment at most institutions across the nation. Administrators made manifold budget cuts. Freezes on professor salaries and reallocations of building improvement funds produced some savings, but, on most campuses, not enough to balance budgets. Many leisure-time activities, including sports, were abolished. The cost-cutting measures generally eliminated less popular sports, especially women's competitive athletics, while intense pressure from students, alumni, and the media kept football programs a vital part of campus life.

Despite the economic hardships, college football survived. Only a few schools dropped their programs. Most responded to the Depression by lowering ticket prices and forcing coaches and athletic directors into better stewardship of resources. Still, college football actually fared much better than professional baseball in the Depression. While attendance fell in the early 1930s it rebounded quickly and rose sharply. In 1937, 20 million fans attended college games, more than double the number who bought tickets for the 1930 season.

As college football produced more money for institutions and drew more support from the media, it became increasingly difficult to enact the reforms suggested in the Carnegie report. The cult of the coach, a phenomenon that had developed in the

"Big-Time" Football and Higher Education at the University of Pittsburgh

The University of Pittsburgh made a name for itself on the gridiron during the 1920s and 1930s, rising to a status as a "big-time" college power. Off the field the football program was mired in scandals as Pitt's athletic dreams came into conflict with the school's academic priorities. During the early 1920s legendary coach Glenn "Pop" Warner built the foundation for Pitt's football prowess during that decade. Warner was one of the best-known coaches in the history of college football, as his attachment to the youth football organization (founded in 1929) known ever since as the "Pop" Warner League, reveals. Warner's best player at Pitt, All-American John "Jock" Sutherland, became a coach at Lafayette College after his playing days at Pitt. After a few monumental wins over his mentor, Sutherland in 1924 succeeded Warner at Pitt. Sutherland inherited a strong program and sought to make it even stronger. He won national championships in 1936 and 1937. Sutherland succeeded for more than a decade before claims of illegal payments to his players created a major scandal that led to his dismissal from Pitt in 1938.

As Pitt's football team prospered, the university struggled. Pitt's academic reputation hardly matched its football prowess. Chancellor John Bowman dreamed of erecting a towering Cathedral of Learning, a skyscraper in downtown Pittsburgh that would house classrooms, laboratories, and offices, but had great difficulty finding donors to complete the project. At the same time, the football program easily found the money to build an enormous new stadium. While Chancellor Bowman's Cathedral of Learning, which was finally completed in 1937, slowly rose skyward, Pitt's football program fell victim to illegal payments to players, a scandal that mushroomed after Pitt's second national title in 1937. Newspaper accounts during the 1930s revealed that Pitt's gridiron players received illicit financial stipends roughly equal in per-hour wage rates to Pittsburgh steelworkers, even though the mill laborers worked fifty- to sixty-hour weeks in brutal blast furnaces. The revelations rocked the institution that had gained such national fame from its football team. Documentation of illegal payments dated from 1924, the year of Sutherland's hiring, to 1936. Reporters even discovered that the Depression-induced hard times actually forced Pitt to cut players' salaries after 1933 as the financial crisis worsened. The resources lavished on the football program at a time when Pitt's academic mission, as symbolized by the great difficulties in erecting the Cathedral of Learning, highlighted the power of athletic departments in higher education at Pitt and across the nation (Watterson 2000,180–81).

1920s and flowered in the 1930s, made the chief administrator the star of the game rather than the athletes. Though Notre Dame's pioneering Knute Rockne died in a 1931 plane crash, other long-time field generals such as the University of Chicago's Amos Alonzo Stagg and Stanford's Glenn "Pop" Warner continued their dominions, while new field generals such as Dana X. Bible at the University of Texas and Bob "The General" Neyland at the University of Tennessee emerged. Successful coaches became the most recognized public representatives of their schools and wielded enormous power. They often had more clout on campuses than college presidents and earned more money than any other employees in their states, even governors.

The Carnegie report, the cult of coaches, and continuing scandals led but a single major football power to get rid of the sport. The story of how Stagg's university,

Chicago, dismantled its program in 1939 had as much to do with the team failing to have a winning season since 1924 as it did with President Robert Maynard Hutchins's long campaign to convince the university trustees and alumni that football was inherently corrupt and had no place on a university campus. In spite of college football's financial travails, ethical debacles, and endless hypocrisies, no other big-time football school followed the University of Chicago's course. Instead, most institutions aspired to be more like Notre Dame, the formerly obscure, small midwestern Catholic college that Knute Rockne turned into a national sensation on the gridiron.

Notre Dame's program set the standard for big-time college football success in the 1930s. Notre Dame, Army, and Navy were the only teams with truly national followings during an era in which the United States was still highly "sectionalized." Football helped to shape local, state, and regional identities, as the growing focus on intersectional games revealed. Notre Dame, under Rockne and his successors, played a national schedule as they traveled from coast to coast playing the best teams in the country. The "Fighting Irish" drew hordes of "subway alumni," Catholic fans from all over the United States, most of whom never actually attended the institution but found in the school's football fortunes a powerful force for celebrating their religious and ethnic identities. Many other public and private universities followed Notre Dame's lead in the 1930s in efforts to raise their national profiles.

Radio represented a key component in Notre Dame's formula for football and public relations success. During the 1930s Notre Dame built a huge audience through regional and national radio networks. While some teams and conferences believed that radio broadcasts posed a financial threat to their interests by threatening ticket sales, others followed Notre Dame's lead and plunged into the new market. Notre Dame sought wide exposure rather than lucrative payments for its games. Other schools, however, discovered they could make a great deal of money from radio. The University of Michigan sold football broadcast rights in 1934 to WWJ in Detroit for $20,000. In 1936 Yale sold radio rights for the same amount to a consortium of East Coast stations. In 1937 Walter Cronkite, who would later become a legendary American newscaster, began broadcasting football on WKY out of Oklahoma City. Radio broadcasts of college football did, in fact, diminish ticket sales at college games but only at the smaller, less prominent schools that played in the shadows of big-time programs. For Notre Dame, Michigan, Yale, Pennsylvania, and the other football powers in the nation, radio, and later television, only increased public enthusiasm for their product.

Public enthusiasm was also generated by new scheduling priorities. Although conference rivalries continued to garner great interest among fans of geographic proximity, intersectional games escalated state and regional pride. While the old "Big Three" of Harvard, Princeton, and Yale had dominated football's early years, the upsurge of universities with successful teams pulled the locus of power from the Northeast to the rest of the nation, democratizing the nation's gridiron geography. USC, UCLA, and California-Berkeley proved that the West could field solid teams, while Michigan, Minnesota, and Ohio State in the Midwest, and Georgia, Tennessee, and Southern Methodist in the South did the same. A series of victories during the 1930s by these teams over the historically elite programs of the Northeast proved that the South, Midwest, and West could more than hold their own on the football field.

California-Stanford football game, Berkeley, California, November 22, 1930 (Courtesy of the Library of Congress)

The hunger for more intersectional games led to the creation of season-ending bowl games staged in newly constructed stadiums in the South. The Orange Bowl (1935) in Miami, the Sugar Bowl (1935) in New Orleans, the Sun Bowl (1936) in El Paso, and the Cotton Bowl (1937) in Dallas joined the original postseason game, the Rose Bowl (1916) in Pasadena, California, during the Great Depression. The bowls flourished in spite of the Depression as southern cities courted tourist dollars to boost their economies and fans across the nation eagerly anticipated the chance to see how their teams stacked up against those from other sections. The growing phenomenon of intersectional play did not take away from the intensity of regional and local rivalries. Georgia and Georgia Tech's annual matchup, for example, escalated in importance along with many other in-conference battles.

During the 1930s college football developed the ability to produce and promote geographic identities like no other American sport. Games between neighboring institutions became more than just football contests. Victories validated a region's or a state's pride, power, and identity. Interscholastic football, on a smaller geographic scale, performed the same function, pitting neighboring town against town in contests for local prowess. High school football teams across the country built community bonds on Friday nights and Saturday afternoons. Media coverage of prep football increased markedly in the 1930s as local sportswriters followed high school teams on the road and games began to be aired on local radio stations.

Chicago's Prep Bowl best exhibited the intensity of high school football during the Depression. The championship game, initiated in 1927, pitted Chicago's top Catholic high school against the city's top public school (with mainly Protestant enrollments). This championship game reached its apex in 1937 when 120,000 fans jammed into Soldier Field to see the two league champions play. The bowl represented not only Catholics versus Protestants but also showcased ethnic rivalries. Chicago's Catholic teams consisted of mainly Italian, Irish, and Polish American players while the public school teams fielded more players from English, German, and Scandinavian backgrounds.

Ethnicity played a key role in highlighting the increased democratization of college as well as high school football. European ethnic groups took enormous pride in producing nationally recognized college players. By the 1930s football had evolved from the game of the white Anglo-Saxon Protestant elite to a multiethnic scrum that supposedly symbolized a growing American egalitarianism. Notre Dame's Italian American stars Joe Savoldi and Frank Carideo, Michigan's star Jewish quarterback Harry Newman, and many others were hailed as ethnic heroes. Bronko Nagurski may have been the most interesting case of all early non-Anglo football heroes. The Minnesota Gopher standout running back was hailed by the Polish American press throughout his career as the greatest representative of the nation's Polish community. However, in 1935 the press discovered that Nagurski was, in fact, not of Polish but of German descent.

At the same time that players from new European ethnic groups surged into big-time collegiate football, African American players gained ground as well. The most notable of these in the 1930s were Oze Simmons of Iowa, and Kenny Washington and Jackie Robinson of UCLA. Robinson, who would become more famous in the next decade when he broke the color line in major-league baseball, starred at running back for the Bruins. Segregation and racism, however, remained embedded on the college gridiron. Throughout the 1930s, many teams north of the Mason-Dixon Line scheduled games against all-white teams in the South. By the terms of the "gentlemen's agreements" that governed college sport in that era, integrated squads had to leave their black players at home when traveling to play in the segregated South.

Professional Football

Racism and segregation plagued professional as well as intercollegiate football in the 1930s. The professional game was dwarfed by the vast college football industry, playing mainly on Sunday afternoons to much smaller crowds than the amateurs drew. Professional football found a niche mainly among the working-class Catholic communities of northeastern metropolises and Great Lakes region cities. The National Football League (NFL), organized in 1922, saw franchises appear and disappear at a rapid rate. The Depression exacerbated the financial instability of the league, killing teams in all the small cities with the exception of Green Bay, Wisconsin. From 1929 to 1932 the NFL shrank from twelve to eight teams.

Professional football had historically struggled to attract college stars to play or the media to cover games. While the NFL did sign more collegians and did garner a bit more media coverage in the 1930s, the public adoration for the professional game paled in comparison to the national infatuation with college football. The game itself was plagued by a lack of innovation and scoring. Professional teams generally ran rather than threw the ball, and defense dominated the league. In 1931 half of the NFL's franchise averaged seven or fewer points a game for the entire season.

The NFL also retreated from racial progress during the 1930s. Several African American players, most prominently Fritz Pollard, had starred in the NFL during the 1920s but in the 1930s the owners, led by George Preston Marshall of the Washington Redskins, drew a color line that prohibited blacks from competing. Under Marshall's leadership the NFL moved backwards and joined major-league baseball, and many other sporting institutions, in prohibiting more than one-tenth of the nation's citizens from equal participation in American society.

A reactionary on racial matters, Marshall proved a great innovator in other areas. He pushed the league to make the game more high-scoring and more exciting by promoting the forward pass. He pushed through the adoption of a more aerodynamic football that was easier to throw. Under Marshall's leadership, substitution rules were eased, coaches increasingly sent plays directly to the quarterback, and aerial attacks grew more sophisticated. In 1937 Marshall drafted the greatest passer of the era, Samuel "Slingin' Sammy" Baugh out of Texas Christian University, and made him the NFL's new star. With Baugh on board the Washington Redskins quickly joined the Chicago Bears, New York Giants, and Green Bay Packers as the Depression era's strongest teams.

Off the field Marshall pushed the NFL teams to upgrade the entertainment quality of their product, adding college-style marching bands and scantily attired usherettes to produce more colorful pageants to supplement the action on the gridiron. In 1938 Marshall created the Pro Bowl, an annual season-ending contest that initially pitted the NFL's champions against a team of NFL all-stars. In 1940, the Mutual Broadcasting System paid $2500 to broadcast the NFL championship to a national audience. The Chicago Bears obliterated Marshall's Redskins by a score of 73 to 0 in the contest. In spite of the lopsided loss, Marshall's success in promoting the entertainment and commercial aspects of the NFL allowed the league to survive the Great Depression.

Regional and Immigrant Pastimes—Hockey and Soccer

While the American pastime of basketball began to spread around the globe during the 1930s, two team games invented elsewhere developed strong regional and ethnic followings during the decade. Hockey during the Depression era stood as a popular game in the regions bordering Canada, particularly in the Great Lakes and New England. Recreational hockey games thrived on frozen ponds and on indoor and outdoor ice rinks. Interscholastic and intercollegiate teams from Massachusetts to Minnesota played to large throngs of frost-belt fans. Professional franchises from Boston, Chicago, Detroit, New York, Philadelphia, and St. Louis competed in the U.S. and Canadian-based National Hockey League (NHL). During the decade American teams dominated the NHL on the ice. Detroit won the Stanley Cup, the emblem of the NHL championship, in 1933, 1936, and 1937. Chicago earned the 1934 and 1938 Stanley Cup. Boston triumphed in 1939 while one of the two New York teams, the Rangers (the Americans were the other Gotham squad), won the 1940 title.

At the box office the Great Depression had a major impact on the NHL, shrinking the league from ten to seven teams from 1931 to 1938. In spite of a loyal fan base in both Canadian and American cities, hockey teams fared poorly in the dismal economic climate. Both Canadian and U.S. franchises struggled financially. The Philadelphia Quakers and Ottawa Senators went under in 1931. The Ottawa squad reappeared a year later but then moved to St. Louis the next season. After just one year in their new American home the St. Louis Eagles went bankrupt and were taken over by the NHL. The league promptly disbanded the squad and dispersed its players to the remaining teams. The New York Americans went into receivership the same year. The NHL also took over the Americans but kept operating them for several more years before finally giving up and folding the franchise in 1942. Even in hockey-mad Montreal the Maroons, along with the Canadiens, one of the city's two franchises, went under just a few seasons after winning the 1935 Stanley Cup.

Soccer had a broader geographic appeal than hockey but also faced serious financial problems at the professional level during the Great Depression. By the 1930s, soccer had become firmly established as the "world's game," if not a hugely popular American game. Soccer reigned as the leading sporting pastime throughout most of the globe, especially in Europe and South America. This position was further enhanced with the creation of a "World Cup" tournament, scheduled to be held for the first time in Uruguay in 1930 as a fitting testimony to that nation's gold medal successes in soccer at both the 1924 and 1928 Olympic Games.

The United States, a member of the Fédération Internationale de Football Association (FIFA) since 1913, managed in spite of the Depression to send a team to Uruguay for FIFA's first world championship. The American team made an impressive run in South America, reaching the semifinals before succumbing to Argentina 6-1. In front of a crowd of 90,000 spectators, the host nation Uruguay became the first ever World Cup winners, defeating their South American rivals Argentina 4–2.

Though soccer in the United States did not enjoy the popularity in the 1930s of the American version of football, the "world's game" did garner fanatical support in many U.S. immigrant communities. As early as 1921, the United States had a professional league. Centered on the East Coast in industrial areas with large European immigrant populations, such as Bethlehem, Pennsylvania, and Fall River, Massachusetts, the early professional soccer league drew roughly equal numbers of fans as the early National Football League (founded in 1920)—which made both groups minor leagues when compared to major-league baseball or college football. American squads recruited European, especially British professionals, as well as incorporating U.S. born-players on rosters. The Depression wreaked havoc on the professional teams, dependent as they were on the struggling corporate sponsors, such as Bethlehem Steel, which sponsored soccer teams. By 1933 the professional league had failed. Amateur and semiprofessional leagues took its place. In certain urban hotbeds with large immigrant populations such as Chicago, St. Louis, Newark, Trenton, New York, and Philadelphia, soccer continued to thrive even after the collapse of the professional league.

The professional league and the amateur and semiprofessional leagues that replaced it provided players for the United States to mount international competitions. Throughout the 1930s the United States sought international matches. An American team played in the second World Cup, held in 1934. FIFA granted the next World Cup to Italy, a nation under the grip of Benito Mussolini's brutal fascist regime. Hoping to use the 1934 soccer World Cup as a vehicle for projecting a favorable image of Italy to the rest of the world, Mussolini set about ensuring his nation's success. "Il Duce," as the Italian leader became known, promised rich rewards for Italian players if they won the World Cup on home soil, while simultaneously threatening them with severe punishments if they were to lose. The U.S. team failed to repeat their earlier success in Uruguay. Though the Americans won an impressive 4–2 victory against their Mexican neighbors in the tournament's preliminary stages, in their next match the United States was routed 7–1 by the host Italians. The Italian team then swept through the tournament, winning the World Cup final 2–1 on an overtime time goal against Czechoslovakia. The Italian team repeated as champion in the third World Cup, held in 1938 in France, while the U.S. failed to qualify for the 1938 tourney.

The United States also sent a team to the 1936 Olympic soccer tournament in Germany. The American team had the misfortune to draw powerhouse Italy in the opening round of the single-elimination tournament. Playing the same basic squad that won the 1934 and 1938 World Cups, the United States turned in a very credible showing, falling by a score of 1 to 0. Italy went on to defeat Austria in the Olympic final. Though many Americans ignored soccer in the 1930s, the United States managed to field some respectable national teams.

An American, a "Nazi," and a Canceled Olympic Games

During the 1930s the United States managed not only to get basketball included on the Olympic program but also staged Winter and Summer Games. In the midst of the Great Depression the United States hosted the Olympics, an event that by the 1930s had become the world's most significant sporting competition. Since the inception of the modern Olympics in 1896, the United States had used the games as a test of national superiority. To many Americans U.S. dominance in medal counts during the 1920s had confirmed their new superpower status. The nation eagerly embraced its role as host for the Olympic spectacle. In 1932 the Olympics found a cozy winter home at Lake Placid, New York, and a glitzy summer mansion in Los Angeles, California.

Lake Placid beat out several California locales, including Yosemite and Lake Tahoe, and a variety of other American towns including Denver, Salt Lake City, Duluth, and Minneapolis, as well as foreign cities including Montreal and Oslo, to win the Winter Olympic Carnival. The third Olympic Winter Games were the first held outside of Europe. The Lake Placid Organizing Committee, led by Dr. Godfrey Dewey, sought to use the Winter Olympics to boost national interest in snow and ice sports. Dewey and his fellow residents of the Adirondack resort hoped the Winter Games would make them the nation's foremost skiing, sledding, and skating destination. They were optimistic that Lake Placid might broaden the appeal of snow and ice sports beyond its small base among northern European immigrants and elite dilettantes interested in imitating the winter recreations of European aristocrats.

The state of New York, led by Gov. Franklin Roosevelt, saw the Lake Placid Olympics as an opportunity to create jobs and pump an infusion of capital into the region's depressed economy. The state government provided significant funding for preparations and infrastructure. The third Winter Games opened on February 4, 1932, with Governor Roosevelt, at the beginning of his campaign for the U.S. presidency, presiding. The Depression limited the number of competitors, with only 364 athletes making an appearance in Lake Placid. Seventeen nations, including the U.S. team, dipped their national colors to the governor at the opening parade. Plagued by bad weather, disagreements over interpretations of rules, fears the bobsled was too dangerous, and the general skepticism the American press normally exhibited in that era toward snow and ice sports, the Lake Placid Olympics nevertheless captured for a February fortnight the American public's attention. The U.S. team turned in an exceptional performance. By the media's unofficial count, the American team won the medal count over Norway, with Canada, Sweden, and Finland trailing. The United States won all of the speed-skating and bobsledding contests but failed to medal in any skiing event. The U.S. hockey team managed a silver medal, losing to Canada in the final. The fact that the global Depression limited foreign entries certainly tarnished the American triumph.

Despite the successes of the U.S. team, the third Winter Games failed to have a major impact on the sporting habits of the American public. The U.S. media mainly portrayed the games as an oddity, focusing on spectacular bobsled crashes and the exotic atmosphere of the events rather than on competition and athleticism. Lake Placid, which spent more than $1 million on the Olympics, failed to sell enough tickets to pay for the cost of the Games, forcing the shortfall onto the region's taxpayers. The Olympics also failed to transform Lake Placid into the

Presidential Politics and the Olympic Games

Much like today, in the 1930s being associated with the Olympics brought notoriety and public attention. Recognizing the public relations value inherent in the Olympics, the governor of New York, Franklin Delano Roosevelt, used the 1932 Winter Games in Lake Placid to gain national exposure and public support for a soon-to-be-announced presidential bid. Governor Roosevelt convinced the New York legislature that the Lake Placid Olympics represented an opportunity to start a public works project to stimulate the region's economy. The New York legislature, spurred on by Roosevelt, unanimously passed a resolution to aid Lake Placid's bid for the III Olympic Winter Games. Roosevelt's insistence and the New York Legislature's speedy action in providing funding for the Olympics revealed the common belief that the Lake Placid games promised a substantial return for the state.

The press covered Roosevelt extensively during his Olympic visit to Lake Placid to open the Games. Although the bobsled course had taken on an infamous reputation as one of the most challenging and dangerous tracks in the world and had already sent many athletes to the hospital, Roosevelt decided it would make a great story if his wife braved the run. Guided by the captain of the U.S. bobsled team, "Eleanor's Wild Ride," as the media dubbed it, helped to create a favorable image for the first couple from New York. While there was much campaigning left in 1932 for Roosevelt before he would win the presidency, his use of the Olympic Games to launch his presidential campaign illustrates the growing popularity and public interest in the Olympics. By contrast, his opponent in the race for the White House, President Herbert Hoover, refused an invitation to open the 1932 Olympics in Los Angeles, forfeiting a great opportunity to earn public adulation. Clearly Roosevelt understood better than Hoover that power of sport in attracting voters.

---

nation's premiere winter resort, as more spectacular ski areas in the western United States, such as Idaho's new Sun Valley resort, captured the fancy of most skiers. The Lake Placid Games did, however, stir the public's interest for Los Angeles' summer spectacle.

The Olympics came to Los Angeles after the city's aggressive boosters spent years trying to acquire the games to polish the image of the California metropolis. Los Angeles won the Games of the Tenth Olympiad at a meeting of the IOC held in Rome in 1923, a surprising result given that at the time the city was only the tenth-largest urban area in the United States and that it was separated from the major European nations that dominated the Olympic movement by more than 6000 miles. William May Garland, an American member to the IOC and a prominent California real estate baron, led the campaign for the Olympics to return to the United States for the first time since the 1904 St. Louis Games. The effective promotion of Southern California by Garland and the region's boosters and their construction of Los Angeles Coliseum, the largest stadium in the United States with seating for more than 100,000 spectators, overcame the IOC's trepidations, including the imposing distance of the site from Europe and the low rank of Los Angeles on lists of the world's important cities.

After winning the right to host the games, Garland served as chair of the Los Angeles Organizing Committee (LAOC). He and his organization sold the Olympics to Californians as a way to boost tourism, encourage migration, and promote business throughout the West Coast. The Depression severely hindered their attempt to put Los Angeles on the map. Economic prosperity quickly turned to despair, and the Los Angeles Games faced major problems. Confronted by the global economic decline and record unemployment rates, the LAOC worked tirelessly to protect the games from cancellation. President Herbert Hoover and the federal government refused to offer any financial assistance. Many critics thought it senseless to stage an Olympics as the U.S. and global economies imploded. In spite of the obstacles, the LAOC persisted. Los Angeles' rapid growth helped insulate the region from the harshest consequences of the Depression—between 1920 and 1930 the city's population expanded from 576,000 to 1,238,000, raising the metropolis from tenth to fifth largest in the nation. Significantly, the Coliseum, completed in 1924, and some other structures had already been built before the American economy collapsed. The LAOC also enjoyed a $2.5-million bond that California voters approved in 1925, a more prosperous and optimistic time, to underwrite the spectacle.

On July 30, 1932, 105,000 spectators converged on the Los Angeles Coliseum for the opening ceremony of the 1932 Olympics. Over the next two weeks of competition, the Olympics proved a remarkable success. Attracting a record field of 1,332 athletes from thirty-seven nations in spite of the Depression, the Los Angeles Games helped establish the Olympics as a truly global sporting mega-event. Connecting the Olympics with the glamour of Hollywood helped draw more than 1.25 million spectators from across the world, leaving Los Angeles with an economic surplus of over $1.5 million after the Olympic bills had been paid. The Hollywood connection allowed the LAOC to license four newsreel companies to film the Los Angeles games. Millions around the world enjoyed the motion-picture footage the newsreels shot. Millions more heard Olympic recaps on the radio, though the LAOC barred live broadcasts of events. In a new innovation, the LAOC housed male athletes in an Olympic Village built on 250 acres in the undeveloped Baldwin Hills section of Los Angeles. The 160 female athletes stayed in the Chapman Park Hotel in the trendy Wilshire district.

In Olympic competition, American athletes swept the medal count, winning a total of 103 medals, 67 more medals than their nearest rivals, Italy. Gender and race played significant roles in U.S. media interpretations of their Olympic triumph. The most remarkable performer at the games was Mildred "Babe" Didrikson, a multitalented sportswoman from Port Arthur, Texas. Limited by the Olympic rules for women's track to only three events, Didrikson won gold medals in the 80-meter hurdles and the javelin throw, and a silver medal in the high jump. While lauding her athletic prowess, the press frequently commented on Didrikson's supposed lack of femininity, making her a controversial figure in the American understandings of gender during the 1930s. The American women swimmers and divers overwhelmed their competitors. Treating the American "mermaids" much differently than Didrikson, the press turned American swimmers such as Helene Madison and Eleanor Holm into stars both for their performances and for their sex appeal.

Ethnic and racial tensions surfaced in a variety of Olympic venues. The Japanese men's swimmers dominated proceedings in the Olympic pool. With Japan locked in a struggle against the United States during the 1930s for dominance of the Pacific Rim, Japanese dynamism in the Olympic pool made many American observers quite uneasy. In an era where legal segregation still flourished, particularly in the American South, the notable performances of African American competitors in track and field stirred a great deal of comment. Edward Gordon won the high jump. Eddie Tolan ran to victories in the 100- and 200-meter sprints. Another African American, Ralph Metcalfe finished second in the 100-meters and third in the 200-meters. The successes of African American men and American women made many white men nervous, as the humorous Will Rogers revealed when he joked that "Every winner is either an American Negro or an American white woman. Wait till we get to golf, bridge or cocktail shaking, then the American white man will come into his own" (Will Rogers Remarks 1932).

The Los Angeles Games provided a stunning showcase for both California and the United States, making it clear that the Olympics played a major role in shaping the world's perceptions of host nations. As the Los Angeles Olympics ended, the world turned its attention to Berlin, the site for the 1936 Olympics. The IOC had awarded the games to the German capital city at its 1931 Olympic Congress when Germany was still under the leadership of the Weimar Republic. The 1933 seizure of power by the National Socialist Party (Nazi) and its leader, Adolf Hitler, placed serious question marks over Germany's hosting of the Olympics Games. Reports of racial and religious discrimination in Germany led many nations to question their own participation in Berlin. Most notably, in the United States, widespread opposition from religious, trade, and civic organizations created a powerful movement to boycott the Olympics. Attending the 1936 Olympics became a major political issue. In spite of widespread opposition, in December of 1935, against a backdrop of mass rallies and signed petitions advocating a boycott, the AAU, led by its secretary Avery Brundage, who also served as the president of the AOC, narrowly voted to send an American team to the 1936 Olympics.

Nazi leader Adolph Hitler embraced the Olympics as an opportunity to promote a favorable image of Germany to the rest of the world while also demonstrating the supremacy of the Aryan race. Pledging his nation's full financial support, Hitler charged Carl Diem, a German member of the IOC, with the responsibility of making the Berlin Olympics the greatest athletic spectacle in human history. Hoping to exceed the spectacular success of the Los Angeles Games, Diem conceived of the idea of an Olympic torch relay. In a remarkable twelve-day, 3000-kilometer journey, runners carried a flame-lit torch from Olympia, the birthplace of the ancient Greek games, to the newly renovated Olympic stadium in Berlin.

Before the Summer Games reached Berlin, however, the towns of Garmisch-Partenkirchen in the German Alps hosted the fourth Olympic Winter Games. Opening on February 6, 1936, the Winter Games not only provided the Nazi government with an opportunity to showcase the "new Germany," but also allowed the German government a chance to test their policies and organizations in anticipation of the upcoming Summer Games. Twenty nations sent more than 600 athletes to the winter installment of the Nazi Olympics. Knowing they were under a microscope, the German government prepared to market its "new culture" to the world. In order to make foreign observers more comfortable, off-duty military personal were barred from wearing their military uniforms, anti-Semitic literature was removed from public places, and price gouging was prohibited. Moreover, the German government ensured that local taverns had a good selection of beer, a clear difference from the Lake Placid Olympics where U.S. prohibition laws prevented spectators from having a drink.

At Garmisch-Partenkirchen, the U.S. team, which had dominated the previous Winter Games they hosted, did not perform to the same standards. While the

Norwegian and German teams took control of the events, the United States faltered. Managing just one gold medal and four total medals, the United States finished near the bottom of the standings in the unofficial medal count. The introduction of alpine ski racing at the 1936 Winter Games helped the Germans who were the pioneers of the sport, boost their medal totals; U.S. downhill skiers were hopelessly outclassed.

Garmisch-Partenkirchen provided a fitting prelude for Berlin. Despite boycott threats from many Western nations and continued German racial and religious persecution, the Berlin Olympic Games went ahead as scheduled. Held from August 1 to August 16, 1936, the Games proved a great success. Attracting over 3 million spectators and 3,963 athletes from forty-nine nations, Berlin easily surpassed the turnout in Los Angeles in staging the largest sporting event in history to that time. Hitler and the Nazi Party went to extreme lengths to convince international visitors, especially Americans, that Germany was a safe, friendly, and prosperous nation. During the Olympics Jews were no longer openly excluded from restaurants, blacks were allowed to mingle with whites, and churches and synagogues were briefly permitted to operate freely.

To Hitler's delight, German athletes dominated the 1936 Olympics, winning a remarkable eighty-nine medals, followed by the United States with fifty-six medals. The defeat marked the first time since 1912 that the United States had not won the most medals at a Summer Olympics. In fact, many in the world press corps interpreted the results of the Berlin Olympics as confirming the superiority of totalitarian regimes over Western liberal societies since not only did Nazi Germany defeat the United States but Fascist Italy won more medals than France and militaristic Japan beat Great Britain.

In spite of losing the overall medal count, many Americans cheered that Hitler's theories of Aryan racial supremacy had been disproved by African American sprinter Jesse Owens. In claiming four gold medals in the 100-meter and 200-meter sprints, the 4×100 relay and the long jump, Owens emerged as the hero of the Berlin Games. Several other African American athletes, or "black auxiliaries" as the German press labeled them, also earned laurels including gold medal performances by Archie Williams in the 400-meter race, John Woodruff in the 800-meter run, and Cornelius Johnson in the high jump. While much of the U.S. press celebrated Owens and other African Americans for triumphing over Nazi bigotry, a few voices in the American media pointed out that given widespread segregation in the United States racism was not exclusively a German malady. They observed that had Owens lived in the American South, he would have been barred from the qualifying meet for determining the U.S. Olympic team.

Other notable American performances included Helen Stephens' double gold medal performances in the 100-meter dash and 4×100-meter relay. Thirteen-year-old Marjorie Gestring's victory in the three-meter springboard diving competition made her the youngest female to ever win an Olympic gold medal. The U.S. men's team, competing in the first-ever Olympic basketball tournament, cruised easily to victory. In spite of sterling individual performances, the final medal count from the 1936 Olympics disturbed Americans. Shaken by the defeat, the American press attributed German victories to a variety of violations of Olympic rules that went unpunished, including allegations that the Nazi's state-supported athletic system violated amateur standards and that Nazi athletes were the robotic slaves of a perverted nationalism.

Jessie Owens (1913–80)

At the 1936 Olympic Games in Berlin, African American track star Jessie Owens rose to international fame as the fastest man in the world following his superlative gold medal performances in both the 100- and 200-meter sprints. Owens added to his incredible performance by claiming two additional gold medals in the long jump and 4×100-meter relay events. On American shores, Owens's performances were viewed by the national media as a devastating blow to Nazi myths of Aryan supremacy. Despite his success at the Olympics, however, Owens's career exemplified the restrictions imposed upon black athletes in the United States during the Depression era.

Born James Cleveland Owens in Oakville, Alabama on September 13, 1913, the young "Jesse," as he later became known, experienced the harsh realities of a nation divided by racial segregation. Following World War I, Owens's family joined the Great Migration northward and moved to Cleveland, Ohio, where young Jesse blossomed into a national track and field star. In 1930 Owens enrolled in Cleveland's East Technical High School, determined to earn the necessary vocational training that would give him the qualifications to escape the clutches of Depression-era poverty. To the benefit of the sporting world, Owens shunned his academic training in favor of developing his prodigious athletic talents.

A host of big-time colleges coveted Owens's sprinting and jumping abilities. After initial interest from the University of Michigan, Owens enrolled at Ohio State University. Arriving onto the Columbus campus, Owens experienced the harsh realities of a segregated America as he was barred from the dormitories by the color line and kept out of public view in his job as a freight elevator operator in the state government office complex. Owens ignored the racial slights and continued to focus his energies on developing his blossoming athletic skills. The Alabama native's hard work soon paid off as he claimed an unprecedented eight NCAA titles from 1935 to 1936. The "Buckeye Bullet's" greatest intercollegiate athletic achievement came in May 1935, at the Big Ten Championships held in Ann Arbor, Michigan. In the span of forty-five minutes, Owens set three world records and tied another.

After the 1936 Olympics, he returned to the United States a hero but quickly realized the limitations of race in translating his fame into material and social success. Lucrative financial offers failed to materialize, forcing Owens to humiliate himself by racing horses at county fairs and fronting a swing band. Although racism certainly limited his opportunities, Owens still made good money, by Depression-era standards, in his entertainment pursuits. Through various failed investments, Owens lost most of his earnings. Nevertheless, over the remainder of his life Owens achieved success as an envoy for the Republican Party and as a corporate "pitchman" for a variety of products. Later, Owens became the leader of the U.S. Olympic Committee (USOC). On March 31, 1980, following an incredible career, sixty-six-year-old Jessie Owens succumbed to lung cancer.

Seeking to build upon a Berlin Games that many interpreted as a huge success, the IOC awarded the 1940 Olympics to another controversial host, the Japanese capital city of Tokyo. The rise of militant totalitarianism in Japan, the Japanese seizure of the Chinese province of Manchuria in 1931, and Japan's subsequent invasion of China in 1937 aroused widespread international concern. Many nations reconsidered their commitments to participate in the 1940 Olympics. Boycott movements once again began to organize, especially in the Western liberal democracies, including the United States. In July 1938 Japan defused this potentially explosive controversy by renouncing their right to host the 1940 Olympics. The IOC transferred the games to Helsinki, Finland. The outbreak of World War II in 1939 scuttled the IOC's plans and forced the cancellation of the 1940 Olympics, though the United States, which would not enter the war until 1941, briefly flirted with the idea of staging a smaller-scale version of the 1940 Olympics, mainly for the nations of the Western Hemisphere, in Detroit, Michigan.

Though the 1940 Olympics did not relocate to the United States, two "Olympic"-style sports carnivals were staged on American soil during the Depression. In 1936 at a year-long fair celebrating the centennial of Texas' war for independence from Mexico, Dallas held a "Centennial Olympics" composed of a multitude of sporting events, highlighted by a June 19 track meet at the Cotton Bowl that included performances by 1932 American Olympic heroes Eddie Tolan and Ralph Metcalfe in a field comprised mainly of black and white collegians from segregated southern universities. The event represented a remarkable exception to the thorough racial segregation during the 1930s of sporting events in the states that had seceded from the union during the Civil War. P. D. Whitted, the sports editor at the *Dallas Express*, the city's African American newspaper, heralded the "Centennial Olympics" as a precedent-setting event. "Mark my word, athletics will break down more racial prejudice than any other single factor," Whitted predicted. "It was a great day and sometime in the future we who witnessed the event will sit back in our rocking chairs and say we saw the 1st one," Whitted concluded (1936).

Though the "Centennial Olympics" did not lead to the immediate dismantling of racial segregation in Dallas, in Texas, or anywhere else in the South, it was not a one-time anomaly. In 1937 Dallas staged the "Pan American Olympics" as part of an international exhibition that extended the centennial celebration of independence for an additional year. A U.S. national team competed in track and field, boxing, and soccer against athletes from Argentina, Brazil, Canada, Chile, Colombia, Cuba, Peru, and Uruguay. Texas law barred interracial boxing, requiring the U.S. team to leave two national champions who were African Americans off the "Pan American Olympics" roster but Latin American and U.S. athletes of African descent once again competed in the track and field competitions. Though Jesse Owens had forfeited his amateur status and could not compete in Dallas, several of his fellow "black auxiliaries" from the 1936 Berlin Olympics, including Cornelius Johnson (the gold medalist in the high jump), David Albritton (the silver medalist in the high jump), and John Woodruff (the gold medalist in the 800-meters), competed in the "Pan American Olympics" in the heartland of the segregated South.

SPORTS FOR INDIVIDUAL COMPETITORS

A Color Line Falls in Boxing

The Olympic Games of the 1930s, and the two imitations in Texas, revealed battles over racial segregation in American sport. So, too, did the prizefights of the Depression decade. During the 1920s prizefighting had transformed from a scandalous pastime controlled by nefarious promoters with links to gambling rings and organized crime that catered to the vulgar tastes of the rabble into a respectable, multimillion-dollar entertainment that attracted both the masses and glamorous celebrities. Though colorful characters and rumors of fixes still swirled around the edges of the sport in the 1930s, it increasingly became a drama that showcased the nobility of the common man. The decade began without the superstars who in the 1920s dominated the fight game. Heavyweight champions Jack Dempsey and Gene Tunney decided they were too old for the ring while promoter Tex Rickard, who presided over the grand million-dollar fights of the 1920s, passed away in 1929. As the Great Depression seized the nation, prizefighting searched for new stars, particularly in the heavyweight division.

In spite of the lack of great heavyweights in the early 1930s, boxing flourished. The amateur ranks witnessed the expansion of the Golden Gloves tournaments. In 1932 the national title fights, which had initially pitted the champions of New York City and Chicago against one another, expanded to include teams from thirty-eight different cities. Boxing also flourished on college campuses, ranking as the second most popular spectator sport behind football at many schools. In professional prizefighting, African American pugilist Henry "Homicide Hank" Armstrong compiled a stellar record. Armstrong, the son of Mississippi sharecroppers who migrated in during his childhood to St. Louis, became in 1938 the only fighter ever to hold titles in three classifications simultaneously ranking as the featherweight, lightweight, and welterweight champion of the world.

During the first half of the 1930s, however, the most glamorous title in boxing, the heavyweight crown, was unavailable to African American challengers due to a firmly drawn color line. The crown remained in the hands of journeymen fighters such as Jack Sharkey, Primo Carnera, Max Schmeling, Max Baer, and James Braddock, who did not particularly thrill the public with their pugilistic skills. In this climate the nation discovered a boxing hero in the unlikely figure of Joe Louis. The racial dynamics of prizefighting made Louis an unlikely hero in an era in which the specter of Jack Johnson still hung over the prizefighting industry (see chapter 5). The proud, provocative Johnson, who reigned as heavyweight champion from 1908 to 1915, had played to the worst stereotypes of white racism. Arrogant, vain, boastful, and stubborn, Johnson intentionally transgressed every racial boundary he could find, bragging about his pummeling of white challengers, partying with abandon, and reveling in breaking the era's taboos regarding relationships between white women and black men. Johnson became a lightning rod for white racial hatred. When he triumphed over white challengers in the ring, whites erupted in violent spasms, rioting in African American neighborhoods. The upwelling of white violence destroyed lives and property, and clearly communicated to the African American community that they needed to stay in their subservient roles in American society regardless of Johnson's challenges to the commonly accepted racial hierarchy of the era. When Johnson in 1915 finally lost, under what some thought were suspicious circumstances, the heavyweight title, the white public, the white press, and white fight promoters promised to never again allow an African American a shot at boxing's most significant championship.

That twenty-year-old tradition seemed guaranteed to prohibit Joe Louis, the son of an African American sharecropping family from Alabama that migrated to Detroit in the 1920s in search of better economic opportunities, of a shot at the heavyweight title. The Great Depression hit the Louis family and other African Americans, both in the industrial North and the agricultural South, especially hard. In the racial climate of that time, African American factory workers were generally the first laid off and the last rehired. African American farm laborers, already the nation's poorest group, suffered even greater hardships in the Depression era. Many state and federal programs designed to relieve the miseries of the Depression discriminated against African Americans.

During the early 1930s young Joe Louis exhibited tremendous skills but seemed destined to exclusion based on skin color to the highest levels of the fight game. The white press routinely depicted him through the standard racial stereotypes of the time as an animalistic brawler who triumphed through brute strength and entirely lacked mental agility. The African American press depicted a much different Louis, a well-spoken, well-mannered, intelligent young man who appeared destined to be denied an equal opportunity in his chosen profession by the pernicious patterns of American racism.

Following an amateur career in which he won fifty fights, lost only four, and earned an AAU national heavyweight championship, Louis turned professional in 1934. He initially battled in the obscure bottom rungs of the heavyweight division. He quickly learned that he had to beat his mainly white opponents by knockouts to earn victories. Leaving decisions to white judges was a recipe for defeat. His manager, John Roxborough, a Chicago machine politician with ties to the underworld, taught him to avoid the boastful displays that had made Jack Johnson the most reviled man in white America. Louis learned to retreat quickly to his corner when he knocked down an opponent rather than gloating over a prostrate white fighter and providing a potential signal of arrogance. His handlers made sure that Louis did not imbibe or womanize in public, and that he studiously avoided liaisons with white women. His humble demeanor and the careful crafting of his image worked. The white press, while generally portraying him in unflattering racial stereotypes, nevertheless labeled him a "credit to his race," the polar opposite of Jack Johnson.

Throughout the mid-1930s, Louis kept beating his opponents while hoping for a title shot. The American media, white and black alike, recognized he was a superbly talented fighter in an era of mediocre heavyweights. Pressure began to build to erase the color line drawn and grant Louis a shot at the heavyweight title. The only blemish on his ring record was a shocking, twelfth-round knockout in 1936 at the hands of German boxer Max Schmeling (the heavyweight title-holder from 1930 to 1932), a huge upset that disheartened millions of African Americans while allowing Hitler's Nazi regime to trumpet the superiority of Aryans over other races.

Louis, overconfident and poorly trained for the Schmeling bout, quickly recovered. He would never again lose a fight. In 1937 he finally received a title shot and quickly dispatched James Braddock to earn the heavyweight crown. The next year, in a much anticipated rematch with Schmeling that the press and public viewed as a referendum on the rivalry between American democracy and Nazi totalitarianism, Louis easily avenged his sole setback in the prize ring with a first-round knockout. Celebrated after the fight as a national hero to white as well as black Americans, Louis became the most visible African American in the world. Even in Mississippi, the heart of the Jim Crow South, whites heralded Louis's triumph as a public drubbing of Nazism.

For Depression-era African Americans who had little to cheer from their places at the bottom of the American socioeconomic ladder, Louis became the most important hero of his generation. African Americans throughout the nation huddled around radios to listen to his fights. Victory celebrations in African American neighborhoods in northern cities drew tens of thousands into the streets. Death row inmates in southern prisons invoked his name as they went to their deaths, pleading for Louis to help them. African American musicians composed dozens of songs about him, African American writers lionized his achievements, and African American leaders enlisted him in their campaigns for racial justice. Louis became, particularly to the most impoverished African Americans, the "Black Messiah," a symbol of hope for redemption against racism's enormous travails.

Louis defended his crown successfully twenty-five more times before he retired in 1949. He used his fame in the late 1930s and after to fight for civil rights causes such as greater access to employment and better educations for the nation's disenfranchised minority. For African Americans, from the black elites to those at the impoverished bottom of American society, the white celebrations of Joe Louis's prowess served as a portent that segregation might be sooner rather than later overcome. In the troubled Depression decade Louis rose to hero status in American culture, in the white as well as the black community.

Setting New Standards in Track and Field and Swimming and Diving

While Joe Louis won the hearts of white as well as black Americans for his triumph over Max Schmeling and the Nazis, the dramatic stage of international competition also made Jesse Owens and other African American track and field stars into national heroes. Indeed, as the Olympics and the major meets in Texas indicated, track and field provided an important arena during the Great Depression for challenging color lines. Track and field was a popular spectator sport during the 1930s, drawing tens of thousands of fans to major meets. The sport thrived on college campuses and at a national circuit of AAU events. For American audiences, it also stood as the most important sport at the Olympics. Track and field functioned during the era as an amateur sport, though promoters of major AAU events and intercollegiate programs offered financial inducements to star athletes. Indeed, the money involved was an open secret and the media often condemned the "shamateurism" system of pretend-amateurism that dominated the highest levels of track and field.

At the Olympic Games of the 1930s U.S. athletes dominated the sprints, jumps, throws, and middle-distance races. In the decathlon, the ten-event contest generally considered the greatest all-around test of track and field skills, a former University of Kansas football star named James Bausch began at the 1932 Olympics a streak of U.S. gold medal performances that would last for the next three decades. American Glenn Morris won the 1936 Olympic gold medal. In the sprints and jumps, African Americans replaced Irish Americans as world-dominating athletes. Indeed, on college campuses and at the Olympic Games track and field represented one of the leading areas of integration in American society. While the vast majority of American intercollegiate track and field athletes were white, African Americans starred at the highest levels of competition. Eddie Tolan and Ralph Metcalfe set the standard by carrying off the lion's share of sprint medals at the 1932 Olympics. Jesse Owens turned in the first four-gold-medal performance in Olympic history in 1936, winning the 100-meter and 200-meter dashes, anchoring an American victory in the 4×100-meter relay, and taking the top prize in the long jump. In addition to Owens, John Woodruff won a gold medal in the 800-meters, Archie Williams won a gold medal in the 400-meters, and Cornelius Johnson won a gold medal in the high jump. In 1935 Owens turned in what many track and field experts still consider the greatest individual performance in history. Representing Ohio State University at the Big Ten Championships, Owens set three world records and tied another in the span of a single hour. In women's track and field, African American star Alice Coachman, who in 1948 would become the first black woman to win a gold medal for the U.S., won in 1939 the first of her ten national championships in the high jump.

Babe Didrikson Transforms Women's Sport

During the Great Depression, track and field, and other sports, showcased challenges not only to racial boundaries but to gender stereotypes. The nation witnessed the rise of Mildred "Babe" Didrikson Zaharias. Arguably the best female athlete in American history, she received the Associated Press award of "Best Woman Athlete of the Twentieth Century." Babe, as she was known to everyone, stood out in several sports. She made her first mark on the national stage in basketball. In 1930, during her senior year of high school, the Golden Cyclones, a Dallas-based AAU semiprofessional team sponsored by women's sports promoter and Employers Casualty Insurance Company owner Melvin McCombs, recruited Didrikson to play on their squad with the promise of a lucrative job. On the court, Didrikson stood out for her exceptional talent and for her fierce competitiveness. From 1930 to1932 she led her team to two AAU tournament finals and one national championship. She made the AAU All-American basketball teams in 1931 and 1932.

Didrikson's ego nearly outshone her immense talent. In an era during which the public expected athletes, especially female athletes, to be humble and self-effacing, she made bold and brash pronouncements about her skills and never hesitated to make her accomplishments known. Both her opponents and her own teammates found her personality challenging. Didrikson played with great intensity and thoroughly enjoyed the spotlight, traits that led her to sometimes seek personal accolades at the expense of her own teammates. The press flocked to cover her exploits. Her colorful manner and controversial image made her more visible than any other female athlete had ever been.

Basketball stardom was only a starting point. McCombs nurtured Didrikson's talents, giving her plenty of time to train for the company's basketball and softball teams and encouraging her in other pursuits. In 1932 she turned from basketball to track and field. She set off a firestorm of publicity when she entered the 1932 AAU track and field championships as a one-woman team. Didrikson competed in eight of the ten events that comprised the meet—an unheard-of challenge. Putting on one of the greatest individual sports performances at a national championship, in the course of three hours Didrikson single-handedly overwhelmed the best women track stars from around the country. Jogging from one competition to the next, Didrikson had little time to recover. Amazingly, Didrikson won six of the eight events she entered. She set new world records in the baseball throw, the javelin throw, and the 80-meter hurdles. She bettered the national marks in the shot put, and high jump—an event in which she tied with her rival Jean Shiley, who also shared the new American record. Didrikson also won the long jump. She finished in fourth place in the discus. Her only finish out of point-scoring position in the meet was a disappointing performance in the 100-yard dash in which she failed to make the finals. As a one-woman team Didrikson amassed thirty points, eight more than the entire second-place Illinois Athletic Club team could muster.

The AAU championship also served as the Olympic trials, guaranteeing Didrikson a spot at the 1932 American Olympic team. Olympic rules for women's track and field limited Didrikson to only three events. She chose the javelin throw, the 80-meter hurdles, and the high jump. At the Los Angeles Games, her very first toss of the javelin earned the gold medal and established a new world record. She also won gold and broke the world record in the 80-meter hurdles in a controversial photo-finish. Her third performance also produced controversy. Didrikson and her U.S. teammate Shiley both produced world-record high jumps of 5 feet 5¼ inches. The judges ruled that since Didrikson had jumped with an unorthodox style the victory would go to her teammate, who had used the more conventional style. Didrikson received the silver medal. Didrikson's track and field feats in 1932 won her the Associated Press female athlete of the year award.

Following the Olympics Didrikson sought to cash in on her fame, traveling around the United States putting on shows and exhibitions of her remarkable athletic talents. She pitched for the House of David, a long-bearded, barnstorming baseball team that made national tours for an obscure religious sect. In one exhibition she pitched against the Philadelphia Athletics, a National League power at that time. She also organized a touring basketball squad, Babe Didrikson's All-Americans, which played games all over the United States.

While her basketball and baseball tours earned her money to support her family, they also earned her a reputation as a "mannish" self-promoter in search of a quick buck. Seeking a more "feminine" sport, she migrated to golf where "amateurs" could earn lucrative sums through product endorsements and a variety of other gimmicks. Didrikson pursued golf seriously after the Los Angeles Olympics. In 1935 she won the Texas State amateur championship. Shortly thereafter, the U.S. Golf Association revoked her amateur standing, claiming that the money she earned in baseball, basketball, and billiards tainted her golfing status. The amateur golf powers objected as much to her controversial image and the fact that she was a truck driver's daughter from rural East Texas as they did to her professional earnings in other sports. In response to the snub, Didrikson became an openly professional golfer, signing a lucrative contract to promote golfing equipment.

She continued to try to feminize her image on and off the golf course, switching from slacks to skirts, applying makeup, and in 1938 marrying the famous wrestler and promoter George Zaharias. Still, she pushed at gender lines, becoming the first woman to play in a men's golfing event when she entered the 1938 Los Angeles Open. Though she failed to make the cut, she was paired with Zaharias at the tourney, a match that quickly became a marriage.

Feminine Stereotypes and Sport

While Babe Didrikson reigned as the most famous, and the most controversial, female athlete of the Depression era, other athletes, especially in sports then considered as properly "feminine" such as tennis, swimming, and diving, as well as golf, also enjoyed popular acclaim. Indeed, of the first ten winners of the Associated

The Power of "Sex Appeal" in Women's Sport

Babe Didrikson, born in the United States to Norwegian immigrants, and Sonja Heine, a Norwegian who immigrated to the United States to find her fortune, both rose during the 1930s to the pinnacle of athletic achievement. American society, however, viewed their achievements quite differently. Americans embraced Sonja Heine during the 1930s, even though she was a Norwegian. Heine won figure skating gold medals for Norway at the 1928, 1932, and 1936 Winter Olympics. Her grace and beauty on the ice led the media to make her the biggest star of the Winter Games. Following her Olympic career, Heine toured the United States and Europe, earning a fortune in ice-skating exhibitions.

Heine starred in figure skating during an era in which that sport was perceived as the epitome of female physicality. Figure skating was graceful and elegant, demonstrating the "admirable" qualities in females. While most Americans thought it fine that women competed in sports in growing numbers, many Americans disapproved of competitions in which women showed obvious strain or exertion. Heine's dancing on ice served to highlight her femininity and fit the accepted gender norms quite nicely. When she relocated to the United States in the late 1930s, Heine's sex appeal on the ice made her a headliner in the Ice Capades tours and catapulted her to movie-star status in Hollywood.

Babe Didrikson, by contrast, made her mark in sports that produced copious and visible amounts of sweat and strain. Didrikson dominated basketball and track and field during the early 1930s. Like Heine, she won Olympic medals, earning two golds and a silver in track and field at the Los Angeles Games in 1932. She won her medals for the native land, the United States, rather than for the Norwegian homeland of her parents. The American public, however, did not embrace Didrikson with the ardor it lavished on the Norwegian Olympic star Heine. Didrikson's well-publicized lack of sex appeal, and her participation in sports that did not fit 1930s American gender expectations, made her a much more controversial figure than Heine. Didrikson was frequently forced to defend her femininity.

Both Didrikson and Heine appeared in the movies, but Heine received roles as the heroine of many scripts, while Didrickson was frequently as a sideshow or gimmick. The movie careers of Didrikson and Heine highlight sportswriter Paul Gallico's contention during the 1930s that sex appeal mattered more than any other quality in public acceptance of women's sport.

Press female athlete of the year award, inaugurated in 1931, eight of the winners earned the accolade based on their swimming, diving, golf, or tennis prowess. The only women from other sports to win the honor during the 1930s were selected for their track and field prowess, Didrikson in 1932 and Helen Stephens, the gold medalist in the 100-meter and 200-meter dashes at the Berlin Olympics, in 1936. Tellingly, the press frequently depicted both Didrikson and Stephens as strikingly unfeminine women.

Gender stereotypes were reinforced by the assault of the Women's Division of the NAAF and professional female educators on competitive athletics. They succeeded in scuttling most competitive sports programs in colleges and high schools during the 1930s. Upper-class and middle-class co-eds found fewer opportunities to compete during the era. Women from working-class backgrounds, such as Babe

Didrikson, enjoyed a different set of options. Basketball, volleyball, and softball leagues flourished, attracting working-class women to play at highly competitive levels. Major employers sponsored teams for their workers that played in AAU-sanctioned tournaments around the nation. In an effort to stress the femininity of players, the competitions included not only the games themselves but also beauty contests to stress the attractiveness of players.

Some of the competitive teams transformed themselves into national barnstorming clubs. The most famous example of the Depression era was the All-American Red Heads, a basketball team that got its start in Missouri in 1936. Sporting natural or dyed red hair and sponsored by team founder Connie Mack Olson's chain of Missouri and Kansas beauty parlors, the Red Heads toured small towns throughout the United States, competing mainly against men's teams and displaying the sort of basketball wizardry associated with the great African American men's barnstormers, the Harlem Globetrotters. Playing by the five-on-five version of the men's rules, the Red Heads were reputed to have won 90 percent of their games against male rivals.

Softball joined basketball during the 1930s as an important pastime for women. Though baseball commissioner Kennesaw Mountain Landis had barred women from professional baseball after Didrikson and other women had played exhibition games against men on the grounds that female constitutions were too delicate to withstand the alleged rigors of the national pastime, softball, which had originated in the 1880s, took off during the Great Depression. Requiring lesser expense and lesser expanse than baseball, softball fit the needs of Depression-era American culture. Federal public works projects pushed the game in urban parks and in rural fields. The American Softball Association, organized in 1934, sponsored national championships for both men and women. The women's game became an especially passionate pastime in the small towns and rural areas. Women's softball also proved popular in two major cities, Chicago and Los Angeles, where, as the U.S. economy geared up for a war by the end of the 1930s by employing increasing numbers of women, defense contractors sponsored large numbers of teams in industrial leagues. These leagues would provide a foundation during World War II for the establishment of a professional softball, and then baseball, circuit for women.

Sex Appeal and the Swimming Boom

The Great Depression witnessed a surprising boom in swimming. New Deal agencies dug 770 new swimming pools during the era, expanding opportunities for one of the nation's most popular recreations. A 1933 survey by the National Recreation Association estimated that swimming ranked alongside going to the movies as the most popular American leisure-time activities. Municipal pools became important centers of American life during the 1930s.

In a trend that began after World War I, American pools became increasingly inclusive meeting grounds that cut across social class and gender lines. Reversing earlier trends, swimming pools increasingly mixed men and women, and people from differing economic backgrounds. Indeed, as some historians have observed, women's bathing costumes shrank consistently during this period, making the swimming pool a key space for the development of an eroticized consumer culture that objectified the female body. As the success on the motion-picture screen of the scantily-clad Johnny Weissmuller during the 1930s revealed, swimming also eroticized male bodies.

Weissmuller, who had reigned as the world's greatest swimmer during the 1920s, became a huge star in the Tarzan film series of the 1930s (see chapter 6).

At the same time that class and gender divisions shrank at public swimming pools, racial divisions grew. In the North and West as well as the South, pools became increasingly exclusive in terms of racial interactions. In the South, African American swimmers were kept out of white pools by law, whereas in the North and West residential segregation and social custom made black patronage of pools in white neighborhoods a rare occurrence (Wiltse 2007).

Reinforcing the image of segregation in swimming, at a time when American Olympic track and field witnessed some important signs of integration, American swim teams remained almost exclusively white. In competitive swimming on the world stage the U.S. grip on international dominance slipped markedly during the 1930s. At the 1932 Olympics the U.S. men won fewer medals than the Japanese, the first time the Americans had not dominated the medal standings in the pool in more than a decade. At the 1936 Olympics the Japanese men once again bested the U.S. men.

American women fared a bit better in Olympic pools. American "mermaids," as the press referred to swimmers and divers in the era, thrived at international competitions. At the 1932 Los Angeles Games the United States won six of the seven events contested. The U.S. women did not perform as well at the 1936 Berlin Games, earning just three bronze medals in five events, but they again conquered the diving world, earning five of the six medals in the two diving contests. Olympic swimming medalists Helene Madison and Eleanor Holm, and divers Georgia Coleman, Dorothy Poynton, Marjorie Gestring, and Katherine Rawls became icons of "S.A." (sex appeal), as the sportswriter Paul Gallico dubbed the most prized quality the media identified in female athletes during the Depression.

Female swimmers rivaled Babe Didrikson for celebrity status during the era, and were certainly portrayed in the press as more acceptably feminine than the "Texas Tornado." A scantily clad Eleanor Holm, a 1932 Olympic medalist who was kicked off the 1936 Olympic team for carousing on the voyage to Berlin, attracted enormous attention for her swimming performances at the "Aquacade" show for 1939 World's Fair in New York City. Holm's intricate movements in the pool, choreographed to popular music, introduced Americans to the new sport of synchronized swimming. One of Holm's fellow performers at the Aquacade, Esther Williams, made this particular form of swimming a staple of American movies during the 1940s.

Tennis and Golf in the Great Depression

During the 1930s the number of public tennis facilities and public golf courses, like the number of public swimming pools, expanded as federal public works programs built new recreational facilities for the American public. Those new tennis courts and golf links would eventually help popularize the two games among the middle and working classes as well as the country club set. As with swimming and diving, tennis and golf also provided women with competitive careers that did not challenge the traditional boundaries of femininity.

In women's tennis Helen Wills continued the dominating career that she began in the 1920s. Wills won Wimbledon titles in 1930, 1932, 1933, 1935, and 1938, a U.S. championship in 1931, and a French championship in 1932. A severe back injury in the mid-1930s prevented her from winning even more major tournaments.

During her comeback from the injury the Associated Press in 1935 selected her as their female athlete of the year. Renowned by the media for her girl-next-door attractiveness and for her icy determination on the court, her stoic public demeanor made her a sometimes distant figure for American fans. Like Didrikson, Wills sometimes challenged men in competitive arenas. In 1933 she defeated Phil Neer, then the eighth-ranked U.S. male player, in a San Francisco exhibition match. In matches against other women, Helen Jacobs served as Wills's major challenger in the early 1930s. Jacobs won Wimbledon in 1936 and captured four straight U.S. championships from 1932 to 1935. After Helen Wills retired in 1938, Jacobs briefly reigned as the queen of the women's game until Alice Marble seized the mantle as the nation's greatest player. Marble won Wimbledon in 1939 and earned four U.S. championships, in 1936 and from 1938 to 1940.

In men's tennis, like in the women's game, an aging superstar continued to dominate play well into the 1930s. William "Big Bill" Tilden, who had ruled the tennis world in the 1920s, continued to be a force in the 1930s even though he had turned professional and no longer qualified for the most prestigious tournaments. The major events in tennis such as Wimbledon and the U.S. Championships remained in the hands of organizers who did not want to compensate their laborers for filling the stands and enforced a strict brand of amateurism. Only the greatest stars, such as Tilden, could make money playing public exhibitions. Tilden, who turned forty in 1933, remained the biggest draw in tennis but his declining skills and lack of charismatic challengers meant that professional tennis stagnated during the 1930s.

In the amateur ranks Ellsworth Vines Jr. dominated his fellow Americans and ranked as the top player in the world in 1932 and from 1935 to 1937. Vines turned professional in 1934 and took over from Tilden as the major force in the men's professional game. A splendid all-around craftsman, Vines could not match Tilden's charisma. As Vines moved into the professional ranks Californian Don Budge became the top American amateur. Budge led the United States to a 1932 victory over Germany in the semifinals of the Davis Cup international series, earning the Associated Press tennis player of the year honors and the James Edward Sullivan Award from the AAU as the nation's top amateur athlete for his accomplishments. In 1938 Budge capped his domination of amateur tennis by winning the first "Grand Slam," earning victories in a single calendar year at Wimbledon, the U.S. Championships, the Australian Championships, and the French Championships. After his sweep of the four major amateur tournaments Budge turned professional and toured with Ellsworth Vines and the aging Bill Tilden.

In the Davis Cup, the major international tennis series of the era, Budge and Vines both starred for the United States before they turned professional. The Americans were a major amateur power of the Depression era, generally battling the British, the French, or the Australians for the top spot. The United States won Davis Cup titles in 1937 and 1938 and finished second in 1932, 1934, 1935, and 1939.

The Great Depression had a major impact on golf. During the 1920s the game surged in popularity as middle-class players made golf an essential part of the nation's business culture. Owning golf clubs and a membership at a private links became an important sign of success in American society. During the 1930s, however, nearly one-third of U.S. country clubs went bankrupt, cutting the number of places to play the game substantially. As the economy crumbled, golf's hold on the recreational and business lives of middle-class men declined. In an effort to shore up this particular sector of the economy, the federal government subsidized the building of approximately 200 new courses through New Deal public works programs, boosting the number of public links substantially.

Golf changed in other substantial ways during the Depression. For those who could still afford equipment, new technologies introduced in the 1930s, such as the replacement of wooden club shafts with steel compounds, the introduction of new specialty clubs, and the widespread adoption of high-pressured golf balls, made golf an easier game to learn. The new clubs and balls also markedly improved the scores of the top players. Indeed, the winning scores at U.S. Opens dropped by more than five strokes during the decade. Gene Sarazen, Byron Nelson, and Sam Snead dominated the major tournaments during the era. Fewer fans turned out to witness the higher scores, however. The retirement of Bobby "the Emperor" Jones in 1930 left the golf world without a superstar, in spite of the emergence of the young trio of Sarazen, Snead, and Nelson, to entice crowds to attend major men's tournaments. The men's professional tour faltered during the Depression years as the economic collapse took its toll. Babe Didrikson's adoption of golf as her main sport beginning in 1935 brought more attention to the women's game, and, eventually set the foundation for a professional women's tour.

America at the Races—Horses, Automobiles, and Airplanes

While many sports struggled during the Great Depression, racetracks thrived. More spectators attended horse races than any other sporting events. The introduction of pari-mutuel gambling after World War I led to a resurgence of interest at American horse tracks, a trend that continued in spite of, or perhaps because of, the economic downturn on the 1930s. Gambling represented the central attraction of horse racing, and the chance to earn a lucrative windfall in an era of plummeting fortunes proved irresistible to many. The national passion for horse racing set the stage for the rise of one of the most unlikely sports heroes of the 1930s, a story that has been chronicled in a recent best-selling book (2001) and popular motion picture (2003). Seabiscuit, a puny, gnarly-legged thoroughbred who ran with an odd gait, captured popular imaginations in the 1930s. The horse became a beloved folk hero who encapsulated American hopes in the midst of the Depression.

Seabiscuit served as a symbol of optimism. The public read his story as a testament to the power of perseverance in the face of repeated failures. Seabiscuit rebounded from hard times, eventually triumphing over his many doubters. Though the horse had excellent bloodlines, having descended from some of the greatest horses in the history of American racing, Seabiscuit failed miserably on the race track during his early years. His original owners gave up on him, selling Seabiscuit in 1936 to a California buyer who had no experience in the horse-racing game. Nurtured by a sympathetic trainer, Seabiscuit turned into one of the greatest horses in the history of the American turf. After dominating the West Coast racing circuit, Seabiscuit traveled in 1938 to the traditional home of American thoroughbred racing in the East. Newspaper stories, radio updates, and newsreel footage chronicled every moment of Seabiscuit's journey to challenge the dominant horse of the era, the regal War Admiral. The match race took place on the hallowed turf of Pimlico race track in Baltimore, War Admiral's home course. Experts predicted War Admiral would easily beat the ungainly upstart from California. Thousands of spectators thronged Pimlico on race day, while millions of fans tuned into the radio broadcast of the race. In one of the great upsets in sports history, Seabiscuit sprinted to an easy victory. When chronic leg injuries forced Seabiscuit into retirement in 1940, racing fans lamented the absence the most unexpected and the most engaging racing champion in American history.

While millions of Americans followed horse racing during the 1930s, the American South witnessed the beginnings of organized stock-car racing. Descended from the exploits of "whiskey trippers," drivers who transported bootleg shipments of alcohol during Prohibition and adapted their automobiles to outrun the cars of the federal agents who sought to stop them, stock-car racing found a home at small tracks in the rural Appalachian South during the Depression. Stock-car racers modified the standard mass-production models of automobiles rather than building specialized race cars, an innovation that helped connect the racers to their fan base. During the 1930s the owner of a Daytona Beach, Florida, auto repair shop, William "Big Bill" France, became infatuated with stock-car racing. France organized a local racing circuit that took advantage of the smooth sand spaces of the Florida beach that ran along the Atlantic in his hometown. Understanding the appeal of racing common cars to the nation's common folk, France promoted the new sport as the future of automobile racing. While France's dream of a thriving national circuit of tracks did not fully materialize in the 1930s, in 1948 he would launch the National Association of Stock Car Automobile Racing (NASCAR).

As stock-car racing slowly developed in the American South, the nation remained enchanted by the specialized race cars that sped 500 miles around an Indianapolis oval every Memorial Day. The Indianapolis 500 stood as the most popular automobile race in the American sports calendar. During the 1930s the race witnessed several tragedies, including the death of five drivers and mechanics in the 1933 race. In 1936 Louis Meyer became the first driver to win three Indianapolis 500 titles. Meyer also won the 1928 and 1933 races. During his victory celebration Meyer began an "Indy 500" tradition by taking a swig from a milk bottle. Meyer, unlike current drivers who drink reguar milk, drank buttermilk.

Racing airplanes as well as racing cars captured the public's attention during the 1930s. In an era in which aviation was still a novelty, huge crowds turned out to watch aircraft whip around pylon-marked courses. Beginning in 1926 the National Air Race series, sponsored by the federal government's National Aeronautics Administration, staged races for various classifications of airplanes. During the 1930s Cleveland and Los Angeles became the major sites for these races. In both Ohio and California, tens of thousands of spectators turned out to watch the aircraft duel in time trials and to welcome the winners of a transcontinental air race.

Military aircraft dominated air races in the 1920s but shrinking Depression-era defense budgets opened the door for civilian designers to compete in the 1930s. Aircraft designed by private entrepreneurs including the Seversky SEV and the Gee-Bee won major events. The National Air races awarded two major prizes. The Thompson Trophy was open to aircraft of any engine size or airframe design and was awarded to the fastest plane in a closed-course race. The Bendix Transcontinental Speed Classic Award went to the airplane that traversed a race course that spanned the continental United States the quickest. During the 1930s the Bendix races usually followed a course from Los Angeles to Cleveland, but in several years competitors flew from New York to Los Angeles. James Doolittle, who became a major figure in the U.S. Army Air Corps during World War I, earned the first Bendix title in 1931. Famed aviatrix

Amelia Earhart competed in the race but never won. Two female pilots did earn Bendix championships during the 1930s. Louise Thaden won the 1936 New York to Los Angeles race. Jacqueline Cochran took first place in the 1938 Los Angeles to Cleveland race.

New Markets and New Technologies in Bowling and Cycling

During the 1930s bowling represented one of nation's most popular sports in terms of participation. Americans of all ages, genders, and backgrounds bowled. The game had a particularly strong following among people of British, Dutch, and German descent, European nations where the sport had long and hallowed traditions. Bowling alleys survived the harsh economic climate by offering inexpensive entertainment for the masses. Bowling leagues thrived, particularly among blue-collar workers. Indeed, during the Depression bowling made a return to its working-class roots. During the 1920s the number of bowling alleys sanctioned by the American Bowling Congress had grown from 450 to 2000. Prohibition made these alleys "dry," increasing the number of female patrons and granting bowling a status as a "family" recreation. When Prohibition was repealed in 1933, the newly resurgent beer brewing corporations returned to the bowling alleys in search of customers and advertising opportunities. Budweiser, Blatz, Pabst, Schlitz, and Stroh's beers sponsored local bowling leagues as bowling once again thrived among its traditional core audience, working-class men.

The influence of women in bowling, however, remained strong. One of the few sports that mixed men and women, the gender-blurring dimensions of the sport were expanded in 1939 when the all-male American Bowling Congress (founded in 1895) and the Women's International Bowling Congress (founded in 1916) were joined together in the new International Bowling Association. Underscoring the popularity of the game among women, 1185 five-woman teams entered the 1940 Women's National Bowling Association tournament. While the women's and men's organizations integrated during the 1930s, bowling in the United States remained racially segregated. In 1939 the African American community organized the National Negro Bowling Association after black bowlers were excluded from the new International Bowling Association.

A new technological innovation that would dramatically change the recreational business spawned by the game also appeared during the Great Depression. In 1936, working in his garage, Gottfried Schmidt invented a machine that would in the next few decades revolutionize bowling. After World War II Schmidt's automatic pin-setting device replaced human pinsetters, lowering the costs for bowling alley operators and dramatically expanding the market. The company that purchased Schmidt's patent, American Machine and Foundry (AMF), would make a fortune through his innovation.

During the 1920s, as the automobile became the dominant mode of transportation, bicycle usage declined. Americans increasingly considered bicycles as a children's toy rather than as a tool for the transportation or recreation of adults. Manufacturers concentrated on developing children's models, and one company, Schwinn, became the dominant force in the market. In spite of the Great Depression, Schwinn's Excelsior model, sporting fat tires, a spring fork, and a tough frame—a style that later provided inspiration for the development of the mountain bike—sold extremely well during the 1930s. The Schwinn Excelsior became the standard bicycle for the nation's adolescents.

THE MOST IMPORTANT NEW TECHNOLOGIES IN AMERICAN SPORT—RADIO AND TELEVISION BROADCASTS

New inventions sparked long-term transformations in cycling and bowling during the 1930s. Even more significant were the developments in electronic broadcasting during the decade, changes that would spark an enormous transformation in how Americans consumed sport for the rest of the twentieth century and into the twenty-first century. Regular radio broadcasts became a part of the fabric of American culture during the 1920s and expanded, in spite of the calamity of the Great Depression, in the 1930s. Sports provided a key commodity for radio networks, attracting millions of listeners to broadcasts of major-league baseball, college football, prizefights, auto races, and a host of other events, as noted in previous sections. Among the key developments in the era was the decision by major-league baseball in 1932 to allow franchises to develop their own individual broadcast policies, a development know as "home rule," as well as the adoption of a similar idea of permitting individual institutions to set their own parameters on college football broadcasts by the NCAA. These decisions by the overseers of baseball and college football to refrain from collective bans on broadcasts, in spite of fears that radio coverage would diminish attendance, helped to develop lucrative new markets that eventually generated enormous revenues for the two most popular American spectator sports.

Radio flourished in other sports as well. The 1938 rematch between Max Schmeling and Joe Louis drew the largest audience in the history of the medium. Two of every three American radios were tuned to Louis's smashing victory over his German opponent. By the end of the Great Depression, a new electronic medium that broadcast pictures as well as sound made its debut. Televised sport began at the 1936 Olympics when Germany beamed closed-circuit images of the contests to several German cities.

In April of 1939 at the New York World's Fair, RCA introduced commercial television with President Franklin Roosevelt opening the festivities on the air. Telecasts of sport quickly followed. In May of 1939 the Princeton-Columbia baseball game became the first televised intercollegiate sporting contest in American history. Quickly thereafter New York–based television stations broadcast a six-day bicycle race, a major track and field meet, and a boxing match. In August of 1939 the Cincinnati Reds–Brooklyn Dodgers game from Ebbets Field marked the debut of major-league baseball on television. In September of 1939 a New York City station aired the first televised college football contest when Fordham College and Waynesburg College squared off live from Triborough Stadium. In October of 1939 television cameras returned to Ebbets Field to beam the Philadelphia Eagles–Brooklyn Dodgers NFL tilt. By 1940 the University of Pennsylvania had a television contract for its entire home football schedule. The Rose Bowl aired to a national television audience. RCA demonstrated color television. The Pitt-Fordham college basketball contest was televised in New York City. As World War II loomed, television, arguably the most powerful force in shaping American sport in the second half of the twentieth-century, had established a beachhead in every major athletic spectacle in the nation.

AMERICAN SPORT AND THE GREAT DEPRESSION

As the 1930s drew to a close, the American economy began to revive. A variety of measures of fiscal health, from rising industrial outputs to falling unemployment rates, signaled a recovery from a decade of hard times. The improvements in the American economy were a result of the nation gearing up for the Second World War, rather from any of the New Deal policies that President Franklin Roosevelt and Congress had implemented during the Depression. Indeed, by the end of the 1930s Roosevelt had shifted most of his attention from the sputtering economy to the looming war, a conflagration that the United States would enter at the end of 1941 but that consumed the rest of the world much earlier. The war in the Pacific began in 1937 when Japan invaded the mainland of China. Europe descended into war in 1939 when Germany launched its first major attacks. The war would eventually have dramatic impacts on American society and on American sport, increasing the interconnections between sport and the modern media, fueling the mass fascination with sporting spectacles, and providing a climate that fostered the racial integration of American sport, even major-league baseball.

The war had an immediate effect on American sport, leading to the 1938 cancellation of the 1940 Olympics slated for Tokyo and a brief, unrealized hope in the United States that the games might be moved to Detroit. The American—and the Japanese—national pastime of baseball had been planned as a centerpiece of the 1940 Olympics. The two nations, which many on both sides of the Pacific hoped would be transformed into stalwart allies by baseball, were soon engaged in the bloodiest war in human history.

Sport, Americans learned, could not prevent war. Nor, they came to recognize during the 1930s, could it eradicate the Great Depression. Sport, however, did provide Americans with a temporary escape from their economic misery, and solace during hard times. With smaller discretionary incomes, Americans still chose to use their shrinking number of dollars to buy tickets to the baseball park, or the football stadium, or the basketball arena, or the prize fight, or a myriad of other spectacles.

The Great Depression damaged but did not destroy the vast American sports industry. Some games were canceled due to economic circumstances. Some leagues and franchises folded. Many sports programs at all levels cut back on expenditures. Still, Americans continued to bowl, golf, and ride bicycles. Aging stars such as Babe Ruth and new sluggers such as Hank Greenberg remained national icons. An unlikely Depression-era hero emerged in the form of a horse by the name of Seabiscuit, whom no one expected would ever prosper, lifting the spirits of millions in grim times. An African American unexpectedly earned the title of world heavyweight champion and represented his nation in bouts fraught with international import. Another African American won four gold medals at the Olympic Games in Berlin, defending his nation's honor in a city that was soon to become the capital of what Americans would recognize as the twentieth century's most evil empire. Joe Louis and Jesse Owens were portents of the future, heralding a sea change in race relations on American playing fields and in the larger society that would begin during the coming war and that echoes into the twenty-first century. Throughout the 1930s the Great Depression wracked the nation. It did not, however, extinguish American passions for sport. Indeed, in many ways, the foundations for a huge boom in American sport were laid during one of the nation's most difficult decades.

RECOMMENDED RESOURCES

Print Sources

Alexander, Charles. 2002. *Breaking the slump: Baseball in the Depression era.* New York: Columbia University Press.

Baker, William J. 1986. *Jesse Owens: An American life.* New York: Free Press.

Cahn, Susan K. 1994. *Coming on strong: Gender and sexuality in twentieth-century women's sport.* New York: Free Press.

Carroll, John M. 1992. *Fritz Pollard: Pioneer in racial advancement.* Urbana: University of Illinois Press.

Carroll, John M. 1999. *Red Grange and the rise of modern football.* Urbana: University of Illinois Press.

Cayleff, Susan. 1995. *Babe: The life and legend of Babe Didrikson Zaharias.* Urbana: University of Illinois Press.

Creamer, Robert. 1974. *Babe: The legend comes to life.* New York: Simon and Schuster.

Crepeau, Richard C. 1980. *Baseball: America's diamond mind, 1919–1941.* Orlando: University Presses of Florida.

Deford, Frank. 1975. *Big Bill Tilden: The triumphs and the tragedy.* New York: Simon and Schuster.

Dyreson, Mark. 2008. Mapping an empire of baseball: American visions of national pastimes and global influence, 1919–1941. In *Baseball in America,* ed. Donald Kyle, Robert R. Fairbanks, and Benjamin G. Rader, 143–88. College Station: Texas A&M University Press.

Englemann, Larry. 1988. *The goddess and the American girl.* New York: Oxford University Press.

Fox, Stephen R. 1994. *Big leagues: Professional baseball, football, and basketball in national memory.* New York: William Morrow.

Gallico, Paul. 1938. *Farewell to sport.* New York: Knopf.

Guttmann, Allen. 1992. *The Olympics: A history of the modern games.* Urbana: University of Illinois Press.

Hillebrand, Laura. 2001. *Seabiscuit: An American legend.* New York: Random House.

Keys, Barbara J. 2006. *Globalizing sport: National rivalry and international community in the 1930s.* Cambridge: Harvard University Press.

Lattimer, George M., comp. 1932. *Official Report, III Olympic Winter Games Lake Placid.* New York: Lake Placid Organizing Committee.

Lester, Robin. 1995. *Stagg's university: The rise, decline, and fall of big-time football at Chicago.* Urbana, University of Illinois Press.

Levine, Peter. 1992. *Ellis Island to Ebbets Field: Sport and the American Jewish experience.* New York: Oxford University Press.

Lynd, Robert S., and Helen Merrell Lynd. 1935. *Middletown in transition.* New York: Harcourt Brace.

Margolick, David. 2005. *Beyond glory: Joe Louis vs. Max Schmeling, and a world on the brink.* New York: Knopf.

Mead, Chris. 1985. *Champion—Joe Louis: Black hero in white America.* New York: Scribner's.

Oriard, Michael. 2001. *King football: Sport and spectacle in the golden age of radio and newsreels, movies and magazines, the weekly and the daily press.* Chapel Hill: University of North Carolina Press.

Peterson, Robert W. 1970. *Only the ball was white.* Englewood Cliffs, NJ: Prentice-Hall.

Peterson, Robert W. 1990. *Cages to jump shots: Pro basketball's early years*. New York: Oxford University Press.

Rader, Benjamin G. 1992. *Baseball: A history of America's game*. Urbana: University of Illinois Press.

Ribowsky, Mark. 1995. *A complete history of the Negro Leagues, 1884–1955*. Secaucus, NJ: Carol Publishing Group.

Riess, Steven A., ed. 1998. *Sports and the American Jew*. Syracuse, NY: Syracuse University Press.

Ruck, Rob. 1987. *Sandlot seasons: Sport in black Pittsburgh*. Urbana: University of Illinois Press.

Smith, Ronald A. 2001. *Play-by-play: Radio, television, and big-time college sport*. Baltimore: Johns Hopkins University Press.

Sperber, Murray. 1993. *Shake down the thunder: The creation of Notre Dame football*. New York: Henry Holt and Co.

Tunis, John R. 1934. Changing trends in sports. *Harper's Magazine* (December): 75–86.

Voigt, David Quentin. 1983. *From gentleman's sport to the commissioner system*. Vol. 1 of *American baseball*. University Park: Pennsylvania State University Press.

Watterson, John Sayle. 2000. *College football: History, spectacle, controversy*. Baltimore: Johns Hopkins University Press.

Whitted, P. D. 1936. Scrappy's Sport Scraps. *Dallas Express*, June 27, p. 3.

Will Rogers Remarks. 1932. *Los Angeles Times*, August 4, sec. 1, p. 1.

Wiltse, Jeff. 2007. *Contested Waters: A Social History of Swimming Pools in America*. Chapel Hill: University of North Carolina Press.

Wong, John. 1998. FDR and the New Deal on sport and recreation. *Sport History Review* 29 (November): 173–91.

Films

Baseball: Fifth inning, shadow ball. 1994. Dir. Ken Burns. PBS Video.

The Great Depression: "To be somebody." 1993. Dir. Stephen Stept, Joe Morton, Steve Thayer. PBS Video.

Knute Rockne and his Fighting Irish. 1993. Dir. Lawrence R Hott. WGBH.

People's Century: 1930, Sporting fever. 1998. Dir. David Espar. PBS Video.

Rites of autumn: Seasons of change. 2001. Dir. Don Sperling. Lions Gate Home Entertainment.

Seabiscuit. 2003. Dir. Stephen Ives. Warner Home Video.

Time capsule the Los Angeles Olympic Games of 1932. 1984. Dir. Bud Greeenspan. Family Home Entertainment.